D1417767

CCNA Self-Study: Interconnecting Cisco Network Devices (ICND)
Second Edition

Steve McQuerry, CCIE No. 6108

Cisco Press

800 East 96th Street
Indianapolis, IN 46240 USA

CCNA Self-Study: Interconnecting Cisco Network Devices (ICND)
Second Edition

Steve McQuerry

Copyright© 2004 Cisco Systems, Inc.

Published by:
Cisco Press
800 East 96th Street
Indianapolis, IN 46240 USA

Printed in the United States of America   9 0

Ninth Printing   August 2006

Library of Congress Cataloging-in-Publication Number: 2003104987

ISBN: 1-58705-142-7

Warning and Disclaimer

This book is designed to provide information about Interconnecting Cisco Network Devices. Every effort has been made to make this book as complete and as accurate as possible, but no warranty or fitness is implied.

The information is provided on an "as is" basis. The authors, Cisco Press, and Cisco Systems, Inc., shall have neither liability nor responsibility to any person or entity with respect to any loss or damages arising from the information contained in this book or from the use of the discs or programs that may accompany it.

The opinions expressed in this book belong to the author and are not necessarily those of Cisco Systems, Inc.

The Cisco Press self-study book series is as described, intended for self-study. It has not been designed for use in a classroom environment. Only Cisco Learning Partners displaying the following logos are authorized providers of Cisco curriculum. If you are using this book within the classroom of a training company that does not carry one of these logos, then you are not preparing with a Cisco trained and authorized provider. For information on Cisco Learning Partners please visit:www.cisco.com/go/authorizedtraining. To provide Cisco with any information about what you may believe is unauthorized use of Cisco trademarks or copyrighted training material, please visit: http://www.cisco.com/logo/infringement.html.

Trademark Acknowledgments

All terms mentioned in this book that are known to be trademarks or service marks have been appropriately capitalized. Cisco Press or Cisco Systems, Inc., cannot attest to the accuracy of this information. Use of a term in this book should not be regarded as affecting the validity of any trademark or service mark.

Feedback Information

At Cisco Press, our goal is to create in-depth technical books of the highest quality and value. Each book is crafted with care and precision, undergoing rigorous development that involves the unique expertise of members from the professional technical community.

Readers' feedback is a natural continuation of this process. If you have any comments regarding how we could improve the quality of this book or otherwise alter it to better suit your needs, you can contact us through e-mail at feedback@ciscopress.com. Please make sure to include the book title and ISBN in your message.

We greatly appreciate your assistance.

Corporate and Government Sales

Cisco Press offers excellent discounts on this book when ordered in quantity for bulk purchases or special sales. For more information, please contact:

U.S. Corporate and Government Sales 1-800-382-3419 corpsales@pearsontechgroup.com

For sales outside of the U.S. please contact:

International Sales 1-317-581-3793 international@pearsontechgroup.com

Publisher	John Wait
Editor-In-Chief	John Kane
Cisco Representative	Anthony Wolfenden
Cisco Press Program Manager	Sonia Torres Chavez
Cisco Marketing Communications Manager	Scott Miller
Cisco Marketing Program Manager	Edie Quiroz
Executive Editor	Brett Bartow
Production Manager	Patrick Kanouse
Senior Development Editor	Christopher Cleveland
Project Editor	San Dee Phillips
Copy Editor	Marcia Ellett
Technical Editor(s)	Blair Buchanan, Steve Kalman, Rody McLaughlin
Team Coordinator	Tammi Barnett
Book Designer	Gina Rexrode
Cover Designer	Louisa Adair
Compositor	Mark Shirar
Indexer	Tim Wright

CISCO SYSTEMS

Corporate Headquarters
Cisco Systems, Inc.
170 West Tasman Drive
San Jose, CA 95134-1706
USA
www.cisco.com
Tel: 408 526-4000
　　 800 553-NETS (6387)
Fax: 408 526-4100

European Headquarters
Cisco Systems International BV
Haarlerbergpark
Haarlerbergweg 13-19
1101 CH Amsterdam
The Netherlands
www-europe.cisco.com
Tel: 31 0 20 357 1000
Fax: 31 0 20 357 1100

Americas Headquarters
Cisco Systems, Inc.
170 West Tasman Drive
San Jose, CA 95134-1706
USA
www.cisco.com
Tel: 408 526-7660
Fax: 408 527-0883

Asia Pacific Headquarters
Cisco Systems, Inc.
Capital Tower
168 Robinson Road
#22-01 to #29-01
Singapore 068912
www.cisco.com
Tel: +65 6317 7777
Fax: +65 6317 7799

Cisco Systems has more than 200 offices in the following countries and regions. Addresses, phone numbers, and fax numbers are listed on the **Cisco.com Web site at www.cisco.com/go/offices.**

Argentina • Australia • Austria • Belgium • Brazil • Bulgaria • Canada • Chile • China PRC • Colombia • Costa Rica • Croatia • Czech Republic Denmark • Dubai, UAE • Finland • France • Germany • Greece • Hong Kong SAR • Hungary • India • Indonesia • Ireland • Israel • Italy Japan • Korea • Luxembourg • Malaysia • Mexico • The Netherlands • New Zealand • Norway • Peru • Philippines • Poland • Portugal Puerto Rico • Romania • Russia • Saudi Arabia • Scotland • Singapore • Slovakia • Slovenia • South Africa • Spain • Sweden Switzerland • Taiwan • Thailand • Turkey • Ukraine • United Kingdom • United States • Venezuela • Vietnam • Zimbabwe

About the Author

Steve McQuerry, CCIE No. 6108, is an instructor, technical writer, and internetworking consultant with more than 10 years of networking industry experience. He is a certified Cisco Systems instructor teaching routing and switching concepts to internetworking professionals throughout the world and has been teaching CCNA and CCNP candidates since 1998. Steve is also a consultant with Intrellix, LLC (www.intrellix.com), an internetworking consulting company specializing in post sales consulting services.

About the Technical Reviewers

Blair Buchanan, CCIE No. 1427, has been consulting in telecommunications for 28 years. His experience includes software design and development, internetwork planning and design, and more than 10 years as a Cisco instructor. He is currently developing strategies for Converged IP Networks for the Canadian Federal Government and some of Canada's largest service providers.

Steve Kalman is the principal officer at Esquire Micro Consultants, which offers lecturing, writing, and consulting services. He has more than 30 years of experience in data processing, with strengths in network design and implementation. Kalman is an instructor and author for Learning Tree International. He has written and reviewed many networking-related titles, and, most recently, authored *Web Security Field Guide* with Cisco Press. He holds CCNA, CCDA, ECNE, CEN, and CNI certifications.

Rody McLaughlin is an instructor, technical writer, licensed attorney, and consultant. He has been a Cisco Systems instructor since 1996 and has also been a certified ATM instructor. Rody has also been the Global Knowledge course director for both the original Cisco switching class, CLSC, and the BCMSN course. He has developed and taught routing, switching, and troubleshooting classes and labs for corporations, government agencies, and carriers. Rody has been married 20 years to his wife, Kathy, and they have four children: Tommy, Jimmy, Christian and Patrick. Rody is also a consultant with Intrellix, LLC (www.intrellix.com), an internetworking consulting company specializing in post sales consulting services.

Dedications

I would like to dedicate this work to my loving wife, Becky. As long as I can remember, you have always been there for me; I could not have asked for a more perfect partner in life. I would also like to dedicate this work to my children. Katie, you show a great spirit, work ethic, and determination. I am confident that you will achieve all your goals in life. Logan, your sense of responsibility and fair play will give you the leadership skills to be successful in anything you want to do. Cameron, you have energy and drive that gives you the ability to do great things; I know that you will be able to do anything you desire. It is said that children learn from their parents; I only wish I could take the credit for the roles you are growing into. The truth is, I learn from you, everyday, and it is my wish that you will continue to teach me all the wonder that life holds.

Acknowledgments

If you are reading this, you have probably been involved in some type of publishing process or know someone who has. If you do not fall into one of these categories, let met thank you for taking the time to find out about all the wonderful people behind this book. For anyone who has worked anywhere in the publishing community, it is common knowledge that regardless of whose name is on the cover, dozens of people are behind a successful project, and this one is no exception. As a matter of fact, the people here deserve more credit for this project than I do. So, as insignificant as these acknowledgments seem to be, they are among the most important words I can write in the entire work.

First, I would like to thank the ICND course developers. Most of what is presented in this book is the product of their hard work.

Next, I would like to thank the technical editors: Blair Buchanan, Rody McLaughlin, and Steve Kalman. Without their keen eyesight and insight, my work would be much less polished. With the exception of a few bad Kentucky jokes, all of your input was key in helping mold this work.

I would like to thank all the wonderful people at Cisco Press. This is my fifth writing project in as many years, and I cannot begin to express in this paragraph how great it has been to work with these fine professionals. In particular, I have to thank Chris Cleveland, the true master behind this book. As the development editor, he takes the raw clay that I present and molds and shapes the book into what you have in your hands, like a master sculptor. Thanks to Brett Bartow, the acquisitions editor, who back in 1998 gave me the opportunity to start in the technical writing field. You have been a guiding force in my writing career. Thanks to Tammi Barnett, who puts up with my relentless requests and keeps everything in the proper queues. Also, to John Kane, Patrick Kanouse, and San Dee Phillips, you are the best in the industry!

I would be remiss if I didn't mention all the students and instructors I have had the pleasure of teaching and working with over the past several years. Your questions, comments, and challenges offered many of the tips, cautions, and questions for this book.

I would like to thank my family, for their patience and understanding during this project and all my projects.

Most importantly, I would like to thank God, for giving me the skills, talents, and opportunity to work in such a challenging and exciting profession.

Contents at a Glance

Contents

Icons Used in This Book

Router

Bridge

Hub

DSU/CSU

Catalyst
Switch

Multilayer
Switch

ATM
Switch

ISDN/Frame Relay
Switch

Communication
Server

Gateway

Access
Server

PC

PC with
Software

Sun
Workstation

Macintosh

Terminal

File
Server

Web
Server

Cisco Works
Workstation

Modem

Printer

Laptop

IBM
Mainframe

Front End
Processor

Cluster
Controller

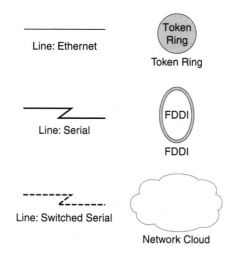

Line: Ethernet

Token Ring

Line: Serial

FDDI

Line: Switched Serial

Network Cloud

Command Syntax Conventions

The conventions used to present command syntax in this book are the same conventions used in the Cisco IOS Command Reference. The Command Reference describes these conventions as follows:

- Vertical bars (|) separate alternative, mutually exclusive elements.

- Square brackets [ ] indicate optional elements.

- Braces { } indicate a required choice.

- Braces within brackets [{ }] indicate a required choice within an optional element.

- **Boldface** indicates commands and keywords that are entered literally as shown. In actual configuration examples and output (not general command syntax), boldface indicates commands that are manually input by the user (such as a **show** command).

- *Italics* indicate arguments for which you supply actual values.

Foreword

CCNA Self-Study: Interconnecting Cisco Network Devices (ICND) is a Cisco authorized, self-paced learning tool that helps you understand foundation concepts covered on the Cisco ICND exam 640-811 or Cisco exam 640-801. This book was developed in cooperation with the Cisco Internet Learning Solutions Group, the team within Cisco responsible for the development of the CCNA exam. As an early-stage exam preparation product, this book presents detailed and comprehensive coverage of the tasks that network engineers need to perform to build and support small- to medium-sized networks. Whether you are studying to become CCNA certified or are simply seeking to gain a better understanding of the products, services, and policies that enable you to build multirouter, multigroup internetworks, you will benefit from the information presented in this book.

Cisco Systems and Cisco Press present this material in text-based format to provide another learning vehicle for our customers and the broader user community in general. Although a publication does not duplicate the instructor-led or e-learning environment, we acknowledge that not everyone responds in the same way to the same delivery mechanism. It is our intent that presenting this material via a Cisco Press publication will enhance the transfer of knowledge to a broad audience of networking professionals.

Cisco Press will present other books in the Certification Self-Study Series on existing and future exams to help achieve Cisco Internet Learning Solutions Group's principle objectives: to educate the Cisco community of networking professionals and to enable that community to build and maintain reliable, scalable networks. The Cisco Career Certifications and classes that support these certifications are directed at meeting these objectives through a disciplined approach to progressive learning.

In order to succeed with Cisco Career Certifications and in your daily job as a Cisco certified professional, we recommend a blended learning solution that combines instructor-led training with hands-on experience, e-learning, and self-study training. Cisco Systems has authorized Cisco Learning Partners worldwide, which can provide you with the most highly qualified instruction and invaluable hands-on experience in lab and simulation environments. To learn more about Cisco Learning Partner programs available in your area, please go to www.cisco.com/go/authorizedtraining.

The books Cisco Press creates in partnership with Cisco Systems will meet the same standards for content quality demanded of our courses and certifications. It is our intent that you will find this and subsequent Cisco Press certification self-study publications of value as you build your networking knowledge base.

Thomas M. Kelly
Vice-President, Internet Learning Solutions Group
Cisco Systems, Inc.
September 2003

Introduction

Since the introduction of the personal computer in the early 1970s, businesses have found more uses and applications for technology in the workplace. With the introduction of local-area networks, file sharing, and print sharing in the 1980s, it became obvious that distributed computing was no longer a passing fad. By the 1990s, computers became less expensive, and innovations such as the Internet allowed everyone to connect to computer services worldwide. Computing services have become large and distributed. The days of punch cards and green-bar paper are behind us, and a new generation of computing experts is being asked to keep this distributed technology operational. These experts are destined to have a new set of issues and problems to deal with, the most complex of them being connectivity and compatibility between differing systems and devices.

The primary challenge with data networking today is to link multiple devices' protocols and sites with maximum effectiveness and ease of use for end users. Of course, this must all be accomplished in a cost-effective way. Cisco Systems offers a variety of products to give network managers and analysts the ability to face and solve the challenges of internetworking.

In an effort to insure that these networking professionals have the knowledge to perform these arduous tasks, Cisco Systems has developed a series of courses and certifications that act as benchmarks for internetworking professionals. These courses help internetworking professionals learn the fundamentals of internetworking technologies along with skills in configuring and installing Cisco products. The certification exams are designed to be a litmus test for the skills required to perform at various levels of internetworking. The Cisco certifications range from the associate level, Cisco Certified Network Associate (CCNA), through the professional level, Cisco Certified Network Professional (CCNP), to the expert level, Cisco Certified Internetwork Expert (CCIE).

The Interconnecting Cisco Network Devices (ICND) course is one of two recommended training classes for CCNA preparation. As a self-study complement to the course, this book helps to ground individuals in the fundamentals of switches and routed internetworks. It presents the concepts, commands, and practices required to configure Cisco switches and routers to operate in corporate internetworks. You will be introduced to all the basic concepts and configuration procedures required to build a multiswitch, multirouter, and multigroup internetwork that uses LAN and WAN interfaces for the most commonly used routing and routed protocols. ICND provides the installation and configuration information that network administrators require to install and configure Cisco products.

CCNA Self-Study: Interconnecting Cisco Network Devices (ICND) is the second part of a two-part, introductory-level series and is recommended for individuals who have one to three years of internetworking experience, are familiar with basic internetworking concepts, and who have basic experience with the TCP/IP protocol. The book assumes a working knowledge of Cisco IOS Software. While the self-study book is designed for those who are pursuing the CCNA certification, it is also useful for network administrators responsible for implementing and managing small and medium-sized business networks. Network support staff who perform a help-desk role in a medium- or enterprise-sized company will find this a valuable resource. Finally, Cisco customers or channel resellers and network technicians entering the internetworking industry who are new to Cisco products can benefit from the contents of this book.

Goals

The goal of this book is twofold. First, it is intended as a self-study book for ICND test 640-811 and the CCNA test 640-801, which are part of the requirements for the CCNA certification. Like the certification itself, the book should help readers become literate in the use of switches, routers, and the associated protocols and technologies. Using these skills, someone who completes the book and the CCNA certification should be able to select, connect, and configure Cisco devices in an internetworking environment. In particular, the book covers the basic steps and processes involved with moving data through the network using routing and Layer 2 switching.

Readers interested in more information about the CCNA certification should consult the Cisco website at http://www.cisco.com/en/US/learning/le3/le2/le0/le9/learning_certification_type_home.html. To schedule a Cisco certification test, contact Pearson Vue on the web at http://www.PearsonVue.com/cisco or Prometric on the web at www.2test.com.

Chapter Organization

This book is divided into four parts and is designed to be read in order because many chapters build on content from a previous chapter.

Part I, "Interconnecting Local Area Networks," includes chapters that contain an overview of basic networking concepts:

- Chapter 1, "Internetworking Concepts Review," reviews some basic internetworking concepts that are used as foundations for the rest of the book.

- Chapter 2, "Configuring Catalyst Switch Operations," explores the operation and configuration of Layer 2 devices within the network. This chapter covers topics such as switch forwarding and the Spanning Tree Protocol.

- Chapter 3, "Extending Switched Network with Virtual LANS," explores the theory and operation of virtual LANs and interswitch VLAN configurations. This chapter includes discussions of frame tagging using IEEE 802.1Q and Cisco's Inter-Switch Link (ISL). The chapter also discusses the maintenance of VLANs and the use of the Virtual Trunking Protocol (VTP).

Part II, "Controlling Traffic Between Local-Area Networks," explores the operation and configuration of routers in the internetwork:

- Chapter 4, "Determining IP Routes," looks at how a router provides connectivity between the different networks in an internetwork. You also learn how routers exchange and maintain routing information.

- Chapter 5, "Configuring IP Routing Protocols," discusses the steps involved in configuring distance vector and link-state routing protocols, such as the Routing Information Protocol (RIP), Cisco's Interior Gateway Routing Protocol (IGRP), Enhanced Interior Gateway Routing Protocol (EIGRP), and the IETF Open Shortest Path First (OSPF) standard. In addition, the chapter discusses the use of variable-length subnet masks (VLSMs) for IP addressing management.

- Chapter 6, "Basic IP Traffic Management and Translation with Access Lists," discusses the control of IP traffic. It discusses the need to effectively manage IP traffic in the internetwork and shows you how access lists provide traffic management on Cisco routers. The chapter includes Network Address Translation (NAT) operation and configuration parameters.

Part III, "Interconnecting Wide-Area Networks," looks beyond the local-area network (LAN) and discusses connecting devices across wide geographic locations.

- Chapter 7, "Establishing Serial Point-to-Point Connections," provides an overview of wide-area networking (WAN) connectivity. This chapter discusses methods of connecting to remote sites using leased lines with protocols such as Point-to-Point Protocol (PPP) and High-Level Data Link Control (HDLC). This chapter also discusses PPP options such as authentication.

- In Chapter 8, "Establishing a Frame Relay PVC Connection," you learn how to connect remote sites through Frame Relay services. This chapter discusses the Frame Relay terminology, concepts, and parameters required to allow connectivity between remote locations.

- Finally, in Chapter 9, "Completing an ISDN BRI Call," you learn how to establish a dial-on-demand circuit to a remote site using Integrated Services Digital Network (ISDN) circuits. This chapter shows you how this digital technology can be used to provide on-demand access to and from remote sites.

Part IV, "Appendixes," is the final part of this book:

- Appendix A, "Password Recovery," covers how to restore administrative control for a router or a switch.

- Appendix B, "Recovering a Lost Switch Image Using Xmodem," explains how to recover a switch that has lost its operating system.

- Appendix C, "Configuring the Catalyst 1900 Series Switch," offers a look at the unique configuration commands used in managing the 1900 Series products.

- Appendix D, "Answers to Section Quizzes and Final Review Questions," provides answers to the review questions at the end of each topical section and at the end of each chapter.

- Appendix E, "Case Study Review," examines a methodology used to provide the connectivity and configuration required by the case study in each chapter.

- The Glossary provides a list of the key terms with their definitions, as discussed throughout the book.

Features

This book features actual router and switch output to aid in the discussion of the configuration of these devices. Many notes, tips, and cautions are also spread throughout the text. In addition, you can find many references to standards, documents, books, and websites to help you understand networking concepts. At the end of each chapter, your comprehension and knowledge are tested by review questions prepared by a certified Cisco Systems instructor.

NOTE	The operating systems used in this book are Cisco IOS Software Release 12.2 for the routers, and Cisco Catalyst 2950 is based on Cisco IOS Software Release 12.1.13.EA1b.

Case Study

This book also features a case study at the end of Chapters 3, and 5 through 9. The case study follows a network administrator through common tasks that might be required of a CCNA-level analyst. Each chapter case study focuses on concepts and technologies learned in the chapter and presents the reader with a group of items that need to be considered for a sample organization. The goal of the case study is to help the reader to identify how to use the topics covered in real-world scenarios.

Interconnecting LANs

After completing this chapter, you will be able to perform the following tasks:

- Describe the process by which data is transmitted by network elements in an internetwork.

- Given a network topology, identify the roles and functions of each network device and determine where each device best fits into the network.

- Describe how different networking devices map to a design hierarchy.

CHAPTER 1

Internetworking Concepts Review

This chapter's purpose is to review basic internetworking concepts. Much of this chapter is a review of materials covered in the *CCNA Self-Study: Introduction to Cisco Networking (INTRO)* title. These concepts are used throughout this book and are fundamental in understanding the functions of Cisco network devices.

Defining Network Components

A data internetwork helps an organization increase productivity by linking all the computers and computer networks so that people have access to the information regardless of differences in time, location, or type of computer equipment.

Data internetworks have changed how we view our companies and employees. Having everyone in the same location is no longer necessary to access the information needed to do the job. Because of this, many companies have changed their business strategy to utilize these internetworks in the way they do business. Companies now typically organize the corporate internetwork in a way that allows it to optimize its resources. Figure 1-1 shows that the network is defined based on grouping employees (users) in the following ways:

- The main office is where everyone is connected to a LAN and where the majority of the corporate information is located. A main office could have hundreds or thousands of users who depend on the network to do their jobs. The main office might be a building with many LANs or might be a campus of such buildings. Because everyone needs access to central resources and information, it is common to see a high-speed backbone LAN as well as a centralized data center with mainframe computers and application servers.

- The other connections are a variety of remote access locations that need to connect to the resources at the main offices and each other, including the following:

    - **Branch offices**—These are remote locations where smaller groups of people work. These users connect to each other via a LAN. To access the main office, these users access WAN services. Although some information might be stored at the branch office, most of the data users access is likely at the main office. How often the main office network is accessed determines whether the WAN connection will be a permanent or dialup connection.

— **Telecommuters**—These employees work out of their homes. These users typically require an on-demand connection to the main office and the branch office to access network resources.

— **Mobile users**—These individuals work from various locations and rely on different services to connect to the network. While at the main or branch offices, these users connect to the LAN. When they are out of the office, they usually rely on dialup services or high-speed Internet access links to connect to the corporate network using virtual private network (VPN) services.

Figure 1-1 *Corporate Networking Strategy*

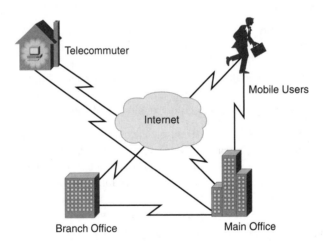

To understand what types of equipment and services to deploy in your network and when, it is important to understand business and user needs. You can then subdivide the network into a hierarchical model that spans from the end user's machine to the core (backbone) of the network. Figure 1-2 shows how the different employee groups interconnect.

Figure 1-2   *Group Interconnection*

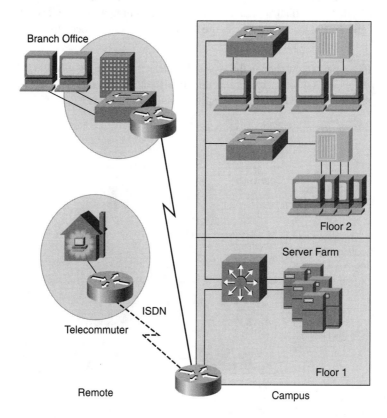

To subdivide an internetwork into smaller components, Cisco uses a three-layer hierarchical model, as described in the following section.

Mapping Business Needs to a Hierarchical Model

To simplify network designs, implementation, and management, Cisco uses a hierarchical model to describe the network. Although using this model is typically associated with designing a network, you should understand the model to know what equipment and features are needed in your network.

Campus networks have traditionally placed basic network-level intelligence and services at the center of the network and shared bandwidth at the user level. As businesses continue to place more emphasis on the network as a productivity tool, distributed network services and switching continue to migrate to the desktop level.

User demands and network applications have forced networking professionals to use the traffic patterns in the network as the criteria for building an internetwork. Internetworks cannot be divided into subnetworks based only on the number of users. The emergence of servers that run global applications also has a direct impact on the load across the network. A higher traffic load across the entire network results in the need for more efficient routing and switching techniques.

Traffic patterns now dictate the type of services that end users need in internetworks. To properly build an internetwork that effectively addresses a user's needs, a three-layer hierarchical model is used to organize traffic flow. (See Figure 1-3.)

Figure 1-3   *Three-Layer Hierarchical Network Model*

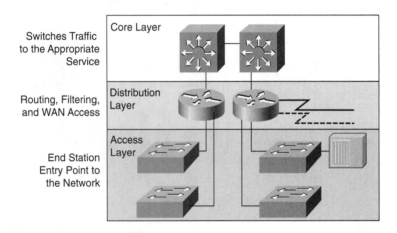

The model consists of three layers:

- Access
- Distribution
- Core

Each of these layers serves a function in delivering network services, as described in the following sections.

Access Layer

The network's access layer is the point at which end users are connected to the network. This is why the access layer is sometimes referred to as the *desktop layer*. Users, and the resources they need to access most, are locally available. Traffic to and from local resources is confined between the resources, switches, and end users. Multiple groups of users and their resources exist at the access layer.

In many networks, providing users with local access to all services, such as database files, centralized storage, or dial-out access to the web, is not possible. In these cases, user traffic for these services is directed to the next layer in the model, the distribution layer.

Distribution Layer

The network's distribution layer marks the point between the access layer and the network's core services. This layer's primary task is to perform functions such as routing, filtering, and WAN access. In a campus environment, the distribution layer represents a multitude of functions, including the following:

- Serving as an aggregation point for access layer devices
- Routing traffic to provide departmental or workgroup access
- Segmenting the network into multiple broadcast/multicast domains
- Translating between different media types, such as Token Ring and Ethernet
- Providing security and filtering services

The distribution layer can be summarized as the layer that provides policy-based connectivity because it determines if and how packets can access the core services of the network. The distribution layer determines the fastest way for a user request (such as file server access) to be forwarded to the server. After the distribution layer chooses the path, it forwards the request to the core layer. The core layer then quickly transports the request to the appropriate service.

Core Layer

The core layer (also called the *backbone layer*) switches traffic as fast as possible to the appropriate service. Typically, the traffic being transported is to and from services common to all users. These services are referred to as *global or enterprise services*. Examples of these services are e-mail, Internet access, and videoconferencing.

When a user needs access to enterprise services, the request is processed at the distribution layer. The distribution layer device then forwards the user's request to the backbone. The backbone provides quick transport to the desired enterprise service. The distribution layer device provides controlled access to the core.

OSI Reference Model Overview

To properly build an internetwork, you must first understand how your internetwork will be used, your business needs, and your user needs. You can then map those needs into a model that can be used to build your internetwork.

One of the best ways to understand how to build an internetwork is to first understand the way in which traffic is passed across the network. This is done through a conceptual network framework, the most popular of which is the OSI reference model.

The OSI reference model serves a couple of functions for the internetworking community:

- Provides a way to understand how an internetwork operates
- Serves as a guideline or framework for creating and implementing network standards, devices, and internetworking schemes

Here are some of the advantages of using a layered model:

- Breaks down the complex operation of networking into simple elements
- Enables engineers to specialize design and development efforts on modular functions
- Provides the capability to define standard interfaces for "plug-and-play" compatibility and multivendor integration

As shown in Figure 1-4, the OSI reference model has seven layers. The four lower layers define ways for end stations to establish connections to each other to exchange data. The three upper layers define how the applications within the end stations communicate with each other and with the users.

Figure 1-4   *OSI Reference Model*

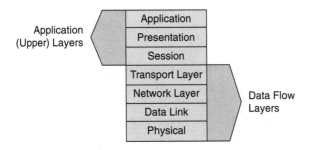

The following sections break down the layers and look at how they function to provide network connectivity.

Upper Layers

The three upper layers of the OSI reference model are often referred to as the *application* layers. These layers deal with the user interface, data formatting, and application access. Figure 1-5 shows the upper layers and provides information on their functionality with some examples.

Figure 1-5   *Upper Layers*

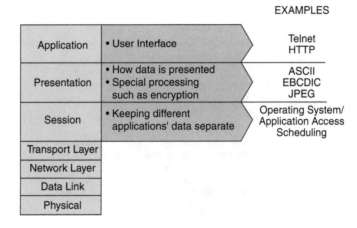

- **Application layer**—The model's highest layer. It is the point where the user or application interfaces with the protocols to gain access to the network. For example, a word processor is serviced by file transfer services at this layer.

- **Presentation layer**—Provides a variety of coding and conversion functions that are applied to application layer data. These functions ensure that data sent from the application layer of one system can be read by the application layer of another system. An example of coding functions is the encryption of data after it leaves an application. Another example is the *.jpg* and *.gif* file formats of images displayed on web pages. This formatting ensures that all web browsers, regardless of operating system, can display the images.

- **Session layer**—Responsible for establishing, managing, and terminating communications sessions between presentation layer entities. Communication at this layer consists of service requests and responses that occur between applications located in different devices. For example, this type of coordination occurs between a database server and a database client.

Lower Layers

The four lower layers of the OSI reference model are responsible for defining how data is transferred across a physical wire, through internetwork devices, to the desired end station, and finally to the application on the other side. This book focuses on Cisco's implementation of these layers. Figure 1-6 summarizes the basic functions of these four layers. Each layer is discussed in greater detail later in this chapter.

Figure 1-6 *Lower Layers*

		Examples
Application		
Presentation		
Session		
Transport	• Reliable or unreliable delivery • Error correction before retransmit	TCP UDP SPX
Network	• Provide logical addressing which routers use for path determination	IP IPX
Data Link	• Combines bits into bytes and bytes into frames • Access to media using MAC address • Error detection not correction	802.3 / 802.2 HDLC
Physical	• Move bits between devices • Specifies voltage, wire speed, and pin-out cables	EIA/TIA-232 V.35

Communicating Between OSI Reference Model Layers

It is the *protocol stack's* responsibility to provide communications between network devices. A protocol stack is the set of rules that define how information travels across the network. An example of this is TCP/IP. The OSI reference model provides the basic framework common to most protocol stacks.

Each layer of the model allows data to pass across the network. These layers exchange information to provide communications between the network devices. The layers communicate with one another using protocol data units (PDUs). These PDUs control information that is added to the user data. The control information resides in fields called *headers* and *trailers*. In Figure 1-7, the Media Access Control (MAC) header and frame check sequence (FCS) at the data link layer represent a header and trailer.

Figure 1-7 *Data Encapsulation*

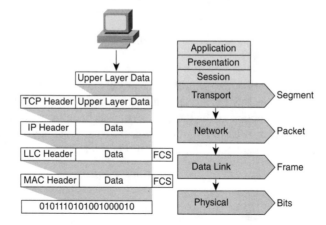

Because a PDU includes different information as it goes up or down the layers, it is given a name according to the information it is carrying. For example, in a TCP/IP stack (see Figure 1-7), after a transport layer TCP header has been added to the upper-layer data, that unit is called a *segment*. The segment is then passed down to the network layer, where an IP header is added, and it becomes a *packet*. The packet is packaged into a Layer 2 header, which becomes a *frame*. Finally, the frame is converted into bits, and transmitted across the network media.

This method of passing data down the stack and adding headers and trailers is called *encapsulation*. After the data is encapsulated and passed across the network, the receiving device removes the information added, using the messages in the header as directions on how to pass the data up the stack to the appropriate application.

Data encapsulation is an important concept to networks. It is the function of like layers on each device, called *peer* layers, to communicate critical parameters such as addressing and control information between devices.

Although encapsulation seems like an abstract concept, it is actually quite simple. Imagine that you want to send a coffee mug to a friend in another city. How will the mug get there? Basically, it will be transported on the road or through the air. You cannot go outside and set the mug on the road or throw it up in the air and expect it to get there. You need a service to pick it up and deliver it. So, you call your favorite parcel carrier and give them the mug. You must also give the carrier some information as to where the mug is going. So, you provide the parcel carrier with an address and send the mug on its way. But first, the mug needs to be packaged. Here is the complete process:

Step 1   Pack the mug in a box.

Step 2   Place an address label on the box.

Step 3   Give the box to a parcel carrier.

Step 4   The carrier drives it down the road toward its final destination.

This process is similar to the encapsulation method that protocol stacks use to send data across networks. After the package arrives, your friend has to reverse the process. He takes the package from the carrier, reads the label to see whom it is from, and finally opens the box and removes the mug. The reverse of the encapsulation process is known as de-encapsulation. Figure 1-8 represents the de-encapsulation process up a protocol stack.

As networking professionals, it is your responsibility to implement networks that support the transport of user data. To implement and configure devices to do this, you must understand the processes of the lower layers of the OSI model. Understanding these processes makes configuring and troubleshooting network devices less troublesome.

Figure 1-8   *De-Encapsulation*

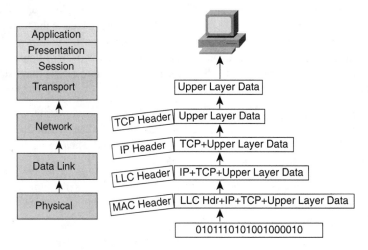

Physical Layer Functions

To fully understand the network process, you must first closely examine each of the lower layers. Start with the physical layer, shown in Figure 1-9, to examine the function of each layer.

Figure 1-9   *Physical Layer*

The physical layer defines the media type, connector type, and signaling type. It specifies the electrical, mechanical, procedural, and functional requirements for activating, maintaining, and deactivating the physical link between end systems. The physical layer also specifies characteristics such as voltage levels, data rates, maximum transmission distances, and physical connectors. In the analogy used earlier, the physical layer is the road on which the mug is carried. The roadway is a physical connection between different cities that allows you to go from one place to another. Different roads have different rules, such as speed limits or weight limits, just as different network media have different bandwidths or maximum transmission units (MTUs).

Physical Media and Connectors

The physical media and the connectors used to connect devices into the media are defined by standards at the physical layer. In this book, the primary focus is on the standards associated with Ethernet implementations.

The Ethernet and IEEE 802.3 (CSMA/CD) standards define a bus topology LAN that operates at a baseband signaling rate of 10 megabits per second (Mbps). Figure 1-10 shows three physical layer wiring standards, defined as follows:

- **10BASE2**—Known as Thinnet. Allows network segments up to 185 meters on coaxial cable by interconnecting or chaining devices together.

- **10BASE5**—Known as Thicknet. Allows network segments up to 500 meters on large coaxial cable with devices tapping into the cable to receive signals.

- **10BASE-T**—Carries Ethernet signals up to 100 meters on inexpensive twisted-pair wiring back to a centralized concentrator called a *hub*.

Figure 1-10   *Defined Physical Layer 10BASE Wiring Standards*

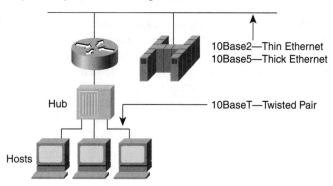

The 10BASE5 and 10BASE2 standards provide access for multiple stations on the same segment by physically connecting each device to a common Ethernet segment. 10BASE5 cables attach to the bus using a cable and an attachment unit interface (AUI). 10BASE2 networks chain devices together using coaxial cable and T connectors to connect the stations to the common bus.

Because the 10BASE-T standard provides access for a single station at a time, each station must attach to a common bus structure to interconnect all the devices. The hub becomes the Ethernet devices' bus and is analogous to the segment.

Collision and Broadcast Domains

Because all stations on an Ethernet segment connect to the same physical media, signals sent out across that wire are received by all devices. This also means that if any two devices send out a signal at the same time, those signals will collide. The Ethernet structure must, therefore, have rules that allow only one station to access the media at a time. There must also be a way to detect and correct errors known as *collisions* (when two or more stations try to transmit at the same time).

When discussing networks, defining two important concepts is critical:

- **Collision domain**—A group of devices that connect to the same physical media so that if two devices access the media at the same time, the result is a collision of the two signals

- **Broadcast domain**—A group of devices in the network that receive one another's broadcast messages

These terms help you understand the basic structure of traffic patterns and help define the needs for devices such as switches and routers.

Most Ethernet segments today are devices interconnected with hubs. Hubs allow the concentration of many Ethernet devices into a centralized device that connects all the devices to the same physical bus structure in the hub. All the devices connected to the hub share the same media and, consequently, share the same collision domain, broadcast domain, and bandwidth. The resulting physical connection is that of a star topology as opposed to a linear topology. Figure 1-11 shows a common connection to the hub.

Figure 1-11 *Ethernet Hub*

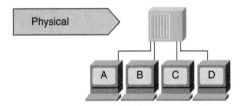

A hub does not manipulate or view the traffic that crosses that bus; it is used only to extend the physical media by repeating the signal it receives in one port out all the other ports. A hub is a physical layer device. It is concerned only with propagation of the physical signaling, without any regard for upper-layer functions. This does not change the rules of Ethernet, however. Stations still share the hub's bus, which means that contention still occurs.

Because all devices are connected to the same physical media, a hub is a single collision domain. If one station sends out a broadcast, the hub propagates it to all other stations, so it is also a single broadcast domain.

The Ethernet technology used in this instance is known as carrier sense multiple access/ collision detection (CSMA/CD). Multiple stations have access to the media, and before one station can access that media, it must first "listen" (carrier sense) to make sure that no other station is using the same media. If the media is in use, the station must wait before sending out any data. If two stations both listen and hear no other traffic, and then they both try to transmit at the same time, the result is a collision.

For example, in Figure 1-12, both cars try to occupy the same road at the same time, and they collide. In a network, as with cars, the resulting collision causes damage. The damaged frames become error frames, which the stations detect as a collision, forcing both stations to retransmit their respective frames. A backoff algorithm determines when the stations retransmit to minimize the chance of another collision. The more stations that exist on an Ethernet segment, the greater the chance that collisions will occur. These excessive colli- sions are the reason that networks are segmented (broken up) into smaller collision domains using switches, bridges, and/or routers.

Figure 1-12   *Ethernet Collisions*

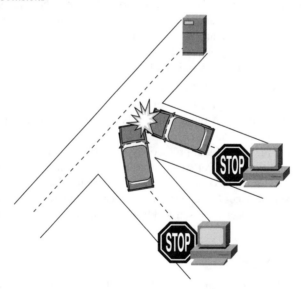

Data Link Layer Functions

Before traffic can be placed on the network, it must be given some details about where to go and what to do when it gets there. The data link layer provides this function. The data link layer is Layer 2 of the OSI reference model, and it differs depending on the topology. Figure 1-13 shows the various physical topologies and some corresponding data link encap- sulation methods.

Figure 1-13   *Data Link Layer*

Physical	Data Link
Ethernet	
802.3	802.2
EIA/TIA-232	HDLC
V.35	Frame Relay

This layer provides communication between workstations at the first logical layer above the bits on the wire. Because of this, many functions are provided by the data link layer. The physical addressing of the end stations is done at the data link layer to help the network devices determine whether they should pass a message up the protocol stack. Fields also exist in this layer to tell the device which upper-layer stack to pass the data to (such as IP, IPX, AppleTalk, and so on). The data link layer provides support for connection-oriented and connectionless services and provides for sequencing and flow control.

To provide these functions, the IEEE data link layer is defined by two sublayers:

- **Media Access Control (MAC) Sublayer (802.3)**—The MAC sublayer is responsible for how the data is transported over the physical wire. This is the part of the data link layer that communicates downward to the physical layer. It defines such functions as physical addressing, network topology, line discipline, error notification, orderly delivery of frames, and optional flow control.

- **Logical Link Control (LLC) Sublayer (802.2)**—The LLC sublayer is responsible for logically identifying protocol types and then encapsulating them to be transmitted across the network. A type code or service access point (SAP) identifier performs the logical identification. The type of LLC frame used by an end station depends on what identifier the upper-layer protocol expects. Additional LLC options include support for connections between applications running on the LAN, flow control to the upper layer, and sequence control bits. For some protocols, LLC defines reliable or unreliable services for data transfer, instead of the transport layer. (Reliable and unreliable services are discussed further in the section, "Transport Layer Functions.")

MAC Sublayer Frames

Figure 1-14 illustrates the frame structure for the MAC sublayer IEEE 802.3 frames.

Figure 1-14   *MAC Sublayer Frame*

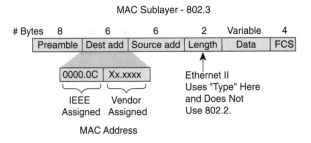

Figure 1-14 shows the standard frame structure to provide an example of how control information is used to transmit data at this layer. The definitions of the MAC sublayer fields are as follows:

- The IEEE 802.3 frame begins with an alternating pattern of 1s and 0s called a *preamble*. The preamble, which is 7 bytes in length, informs receiving stations that a frame is coming.

- After the preamble is a 1-byte field called the start of frame delimiter that indicates to the receiving stations that the address information is next.

- Immediately following the preamble and start of frame are the *Destination* and *Source Physical Address* fields. These addresses are referred to as *MAC layer addresses*. They are unique to each device in the internetwork. On most LAN interface cards, the MAC address is burned into ROM, thus explaining the term *burned-in-address (BIA)*. When the network interface card (NIC) initializes, this address is copied into RAM to identify the device on the network.

  The MAC address is a 48-bit address expressed as 12 hexadecimal digits. The first 24 bits or 6 hexadecimal digits of the MAC address contain a manufacturer identification or vendor code. Another name for this part of the address is the *Organizationally Unique Identifier (OUI)*. To ensure vendor uniqueness, the IEEE administers OUIs. The last 24 bits or 6 hexadecimal digits are administered by each vendor and often represent the interface serial number.

  The source address is always a unicast (single node) address, and the destination address might be unicast, multicast (group of nodes), or broadcast (all nodes).

- In IEEE 802.3 frames, the 2-byte field following the source address is a *Length* field, which indicates the number of bytes of data that follow this field and precede the FCS field.

- Following the Length field is the *Data* field, which includes the LLC control information, other upper-layer control information, and the user data.

- Finally, following the Data field is a 4-byte *FCS* field containing a cyclic redundancy check (CRC) value. The CRC is created by the sending device and recalculated by the receiving device to check for damage that might have occurred to the frame in transit.

LLC Sublayer Frames

The two LLC frame types are Service Access Point (SAP) and Subnetwork Access Protocol (SNAP). Which frame type your system uses depends on the applications that you have running on your system. Some applications define themselves with a SAP ID, and others define themselves using a type code. Figure 1-15 shows the format of the SAP and SNAP frame types.

Figure 1-15   *SAP and SNAP LLC Sublayer Frames*

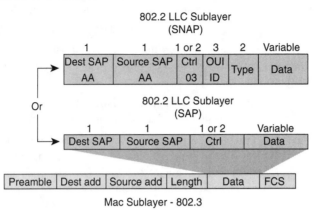

In the LLC header, the destination SAP (DSAP) and source SAP (SSAP) fields are 1 byte each and act as pointers to the upper-layer protocols in a station. For example, a frame with a SAP of 06 hex is destined for IP, and a frame with a SAP of E0 hex is destined for IPX. From the perspective of these lower MAC sublayers, the SAP process provides a convenient interface to the protocol stack's upper layers. These SAP entries allow the physical and data link connections to provide services for many upper-layer protocols.

To specify that the frame uses SNAP, the SSAP and DSAP addresses are both set to AA hex, and the Control field is set to 03 hex. In addition to the SAP fields, a SNAP header has a Type Code field that allows for the inclusion of the EtherType. The EtherType defines which upper-layer protocol receives the data.

In a SNAP frame, the first 3 bytes of the SNAP header after the Control field are the OUI vendor code. Following the OUI vendor code is a 2-byte field containing the EtherType for the frame. The backward-compatibility with Ethernet Version II is implemented here. As with the 802.3 frame, a 4-byte FCS field follows the data field and contains a CRC value.

Data Link Layer Devices

Bridges and Layer 2 switches are devices that function at the protocol stack's data link layer. Figure 1-16 shows the devices typically encountered at Layer 2.

Layer 2 switching is hardware-based bridging. In a switch, frame forwarding is handled by specialized hardware called application-specific integrated circuits (ASICs). The ASIC technology allows a silicon chip to be programmed to perform a specific function as it is built. This technology allows functions to be performed at much higher rates of speed than that of a chip that is programmed by software. Because of ASIC technology, switches provide scalability to gigabit speeds with low latency.

Figure 1-16 *Data Link Devices*

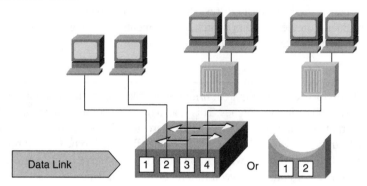

NOTE   Although some Layer 3 and Layer 4 switches perform routing, this book uses the term *switch* to refer to a Layer 2 device.

When a bridge or switch receives a frame, it uses the data link information to process the frame. In a transparent bridge environment, the bridge processes the frame by determining whether it needs to be copied to other connected segments. A transparent bridge receives every frame that crosses a segment and views each frame and source address field to determine on what segment the source station resides. The transparent bridge stores this information in memory in what is known as a *forwarding table*. The forwarding table lists each end station (from which the bridge has received a frame within a particular time period) and the segment on which it resides. When a bridge receives a frame on the network, it compares the destination address to the forwarding table to determine whether to filter, flood, or copy the frame onto another segment.

This decision process occurs as follows:

- If the destination device is on the same segment as the frame, the bridge blocks the frame from going on to other segments. This process is known as *filtering*.

- If the destination device is on a different segment, the bridge forwards the frame to the appropriate segment. This process is known as *forwarding*.

- If the destination address is unknown to the bridge, the bridge forwards the frame to all segments except the one on which it was received. This process is known as *flooding*.

Because a bridge learns all the station destinations by examining to source addresses, it never learns the broadcast address. Therefore, all broadcasts are always flooded to all the segments on the bridge or switch. All segments in a bridged or switched environment are considered to be in the same broadcast domain.

NOTE	This book focuses on transparent bridging because this is the function performed by the Catalyst 1900 series of switches. This is also the most common form of bridging/switching in Ethernet environments. Also note that there are other types of bridges, such as source-route bridging, in which the source determines the route to be taken through the network, and translational bridging, which allows the frame to move from a source route to a transparent environment between Ethernet and Token Ring.

A bridged/switched network provides excellent traffic management. The purpose of the Layer 2 device is to reduce collisions, which waste bandwidth and prevent packets from reaching their destinations. Part A of Figure 1-17 shows how a switch reduces collisions by giving each segment its own collision domain. Part B of Figure 1-17 shows that when two or more packets need to get onto a segment, they are stored in memory until the segment is available for use.

Bridged/switched networks have the following characteristics:

- Each segment is its own collision domain.
- All devices connected to the same bridge or switch are part of the same broadcast domain.
- All segments must use the same data link layer implementation, such as all Ethernet or all Token Ring. If an end station must communicate with another end station on different media, some device, such as a router or translational bridge, must translate between the different media types.

In a switched environment, there can be one device per segment, and each device can send frames at the same time, allowing the primary pathway to be shared.

Figure 1-17 *Bridging Reduces Collisions*

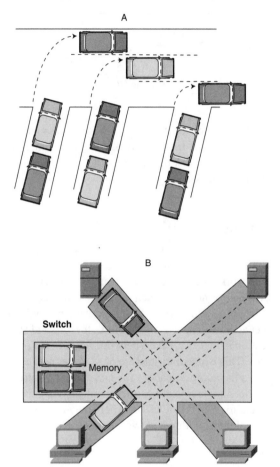

Network Layer Functions

The network layer defines how to transport traffic between devices that are not locally attached in the same broadcast domain. Two pieces of information are required to achieve this:

- A logical address associated with the source and destination stations
- A path through the network to reach the desired destination

Figure 1-18 shows the network layer's location in relation to the data link layer. The network layer is independent of the data link layer and can be used to connect devices residing on different physical media. The logical addressing structure provides this connectivity.

Figure 1-18   *Location of the Network Layer in the Protocol Model*

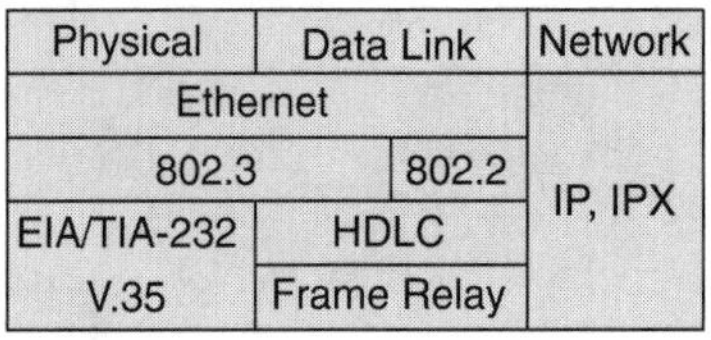

Physical	Data Link	Network
Ethernet		
802.3	802.2	IP, IPX
EIA/TIA-232	HDLC	
V.35	Frame Relay	

Logical addressing schemes identify networks in an internetwork and the location of the devices within the context of those networks. These schemes vary based on the network layer protocol in use. This book discusses the network layer operation for the TCP/IP and IPX (Novell) protocol stacks.

Network Layer Addresses

Network layer addresses (also called *virtual* or *logical addresses*) exist at Layer 3 of the OSI reference model. Unlike data link layer addresses, which usually exist within a flat address space, network layer addresses are usually hierarchical in that they define networks first, and then devices or nodes on each of those networks. In other words, network layer addresses are like postal addresses, which describe a person's location by providing a ZIP code and a street address. The ZIP code defines the city and state, and the street address is a particular location in that city. Like a network address, if a person moves, the address and zip code changes. This is in contrast to the MAC layer address, which is flat in nature. A good example of a flat address space is the U.S. Social Security numbering system; each person has a single, unique Social Security number. When assigned, this number remains with the individual for life, regardless of where they reside. Figure 1-19 shows a sample logical address as defined within a network layer packet.

Figure 1-19   *Network Layer Logical Addressing*

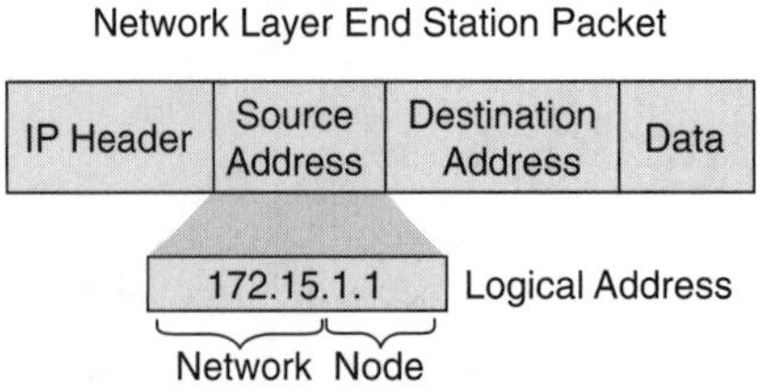

Network Layer End Station Packet

IP Header	Source Address	Destination Address	Data

172.15.1.1   Logical Address

Network Node

The logical network address consists of two portions. One part uniquely identifies each network within the internetwork, and the other part uniquely identifies the hosts on each of those networks. Combining both portions results in a unique network address for each device. This unique network address has two functions:

- The network portion identifies each network in the internetwork structure, allowing the routers to identify paths through the network cloud. The router uses this address to determine where to send network packets, in the same manner that the ZIP code on a letter determines the state and city to which a package should be delivered.

- The host portion identifies a particular device or a device's port on the network in the same manner that a street address on a letter identifies a location within that city.

There are many network layer protocols, and they all share the function of identifying networks and hosts throughout the internetwork structure. Most of these protocols have different schemes for accomplishing this task. TCP/IP is a common protocol used in routed networks. An IP address has the following components to identify networks and hosts:

- A 32-bit address, divided into four 8-bit sections called *octets*. This address identifies a specific network and a specific host on that network by subdividing the bits into network and host portions.

- A 32-bit subnet mask that is also divided into four 8-bit octets. The subnet mask determines which bits represent the network and which represent the host. The bit pattern for a subnet mask is a series of 1s followed by a series of 0s. Figure 1-20 shows that the boundary between the 1s and the 0s marks the boundary for the network and host portions of the address, the two components necessary to define an IP address on an end device.

Figure 1-20   *IP Address Components*

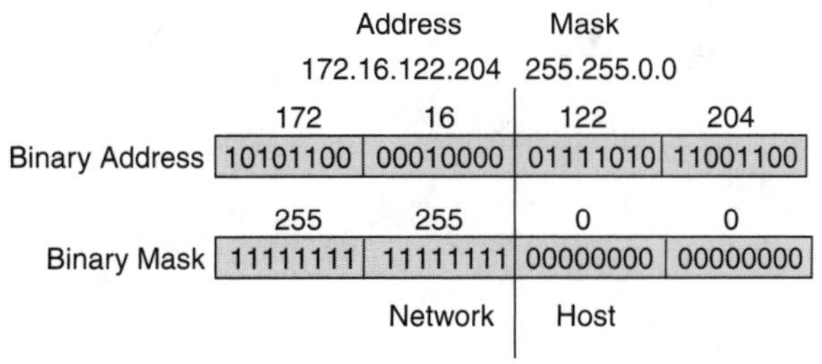

NOTE   IP addresses are represented by taking the 8-bit octets and converting them to decimal, and then separating the octets with dots or periods. This format is known as *dotted decimal* and is done to simplify addressing for those of us who count in Base10.

Router Operation at the Network Layer

Routers operate at the network layer by tracking and recording the different networks and choosing the best path to those networks. The routers place this information in a routing table, which includes the following items (see Figure 1-21):

- **Network addresses**—Represent known networks to the router. A network address is protocol-specific. If a router supports more than one protocol, it has a unique table for each protocol.

- **Interface**—Refers to the interface the router uses to reach a given network. This interface forwards packets destined for the listed network.

- **Metric**—Refers to the cost or distance to the target network. This is a value that helps the router choose the best path to a given network. This metric changes depending on how the router chooses paths. Common metrics include the number of networks that must be crossed to get to a destination (also known as *hops*), the time it takes to cross all the interfaces to a given network (also known as *delay*), or a value associated with the speed of a link (also known as *bandwidth*).

Figure 1-21 *Routing Tables*

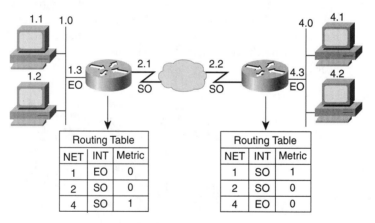

Because routers function at the network layer of the OSI model, they separate segments into unique collision and broadcast domains. Each segment is referred to as a *network* and must be identified by a network address to be reached by end stations. In addition to identifying each segment as a network, each station on that network must also be uniquely identified by the logical address. This addressing structure allows for hierarchical network configuration (that is, a station is not known merely by a host identifier) but is defined by the network it is on as well as a host identifier. For routers to operate on an internetwork, each interface must be configured on the unique network it represents. The router must also have a host address on that network. The router uses the interface's configuration information to determine the network portion of the address to build a routing table.

In addition to identifying networks and providing connectivity, routers also provide other functions:

- Routers do not forward Layer 2 broadcast or multicast frames.

- Routers attempt to determine the next-best destination along a path through a routed network based on routing algorithms.

- Routers strip Layer 2 headers on incoming frames and forward packets based on Layer 3 destination addresses by rebuilding the appropriate Layer 2 information and forwarding to the next hop device.

- Routers map a single Layer 3 logical address to a single network device; therefore, routers can limit or secure network traffic based on identifiable attributes within each packet. These options, controlled by access lists, can be applied to inbound or outbound packets.

- Routers can be configured to perform both bridging and routing functions.

- Routers provide connectivity between different virtual LANs (VLANs) in a switched environment.

- Routers can deploy quality of service (QoS) parameters for specified types of network traffic.

In addition to the benefits in the campus, routers can connect remote locations to the main office using WAN services, as illustrated in Figure 1-22.

Figure 1-22   *Routers Connect Remote Locations to the Main Office*

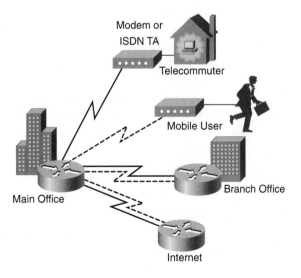

Routers support a variety of physical layer connectivity standards that allow you to build WANs. In addition, they can provide the security and access controls that are needed when interconnecting remote locations.

Transport Layer Functions

To connect two devices in the fabric of the internetwork, a connection must be established. The transport layer defines the end-to-end station establishment guidelines between two end stations. This constitutes a logical connection between the peer transport layers in source and destination end stations. Figure 1-23 shows the relationship of some transport layer protocols to their respective network layer protocols. Different transport layer functions are provided by these protocols.

Figure 1-23   *Transport Layer Protocols*

Network	Transport
IP	TCP
	UDP
IPX	SPX

Specifically, the transport layer defines the following functions:

- Allows end stations to assemble and disassemble multiple upper-layer segments into the same transport layer data stream. This is accomplished by assigning upper-layer application identifiers. Within the TCP/IP protocol suite, these identifiers are known as *port numbers*. The OSI reference model refers to these identifiers as Service Access Points (SAPs). The transport layer uses these port numbers to identify application layer entities such as FTP and Telnet. An example of a port number is 23, which identifies the Telnet application. Data with a transport port number of 23 is destined for the Telnet application.

- Allows applications to request reliable data transport between communicating end systems. Reliable transport uses a connection-oriented relationship between the communicating end systems to accomplish the following:

  — Ensure that segments delivered will be acknowledged back to the sender

  — Provide for retransmission of any segments that are not acknowledged

  — Put segments back into their correct sequence order at the receiving station

  — Provide end-to-end flow control

At the transport layer, data can be transmitted reliably or unreliably. For IP, the TCP protocol is reliable or connection-oriented, and UDP is unreliable or connectionless. A good analogy to connection-oriented versus connectionless is a phone call versus a postcard. With a phone call, you establish a dialogue that lets you know how well you are communicating. A postcard offers no real-time feedback.

For a connection-oriented transport layer protocol to provide these functions reliably, a connection must be established between the end stations, data is then transmitted, and the session is disconnected.

As with a phone call, to communicate with a connection-oriented service, you must first establish the connection. To do this within the TCP/IP protocol suite, the sending and receiving stations perform an operation known as a three-way handshake. (See Figure 1-24.) A three-way handshake is accomplished by the sending and receiving of synchronization and acknowledgment packets. With a phone call, this would be like a phone ringing, being answered, and each party saying "hello" to indicate that they are ready to talk.

Figure 1-24   *Three-Way Handshake*

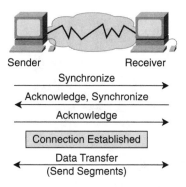

After the synchronization has occurred, the transfer of information begins. During the transfer, the two end stations continue to communicate with their network layer PDUs to verify that the data is received correctly. If the receiving station does not acknowledge a packet within a predefined amount of time, the sender retransmits the package. This ensures reliable delivery of all traffic. After the data transfer is complete, the session is disconnected, like saying "good-bye" to end a telephone conversation.

OSI Lower Layer Review

Now that you have an understanding of the lower four layers of the OSI model and are familiar with the concepts of collision and broadcast domains, review what you learned.

Each device shown in Figure 1-25 operates at a different layer of the OSI model:

- At Layer 1 (the physical layer) is the hub. The hub retransmits packets and acts as a concentration device for other network devices. The hub forms a single segment, providing one collision domain and one broadcast domain.

- The switch and the bridge are Layer 2 devices. These devices divide the network into separate segments, providing fewer users per segment. Each segment is a single collision domain, so in the figure, the bridge and switch each supports four collision domains. Broadcast traffic, however, propagates across all segments, so only one broadcast domain is associated with each device.

- At Layer 3 (the network layer), the router provides paths to all the networks throughout the internetwork. The router segments the network into separate collision domains and broadcast domains. In Figure 1-25, you can see four collision domains and four broadcast domains.

Figure 1-25   *Network Device Functions*

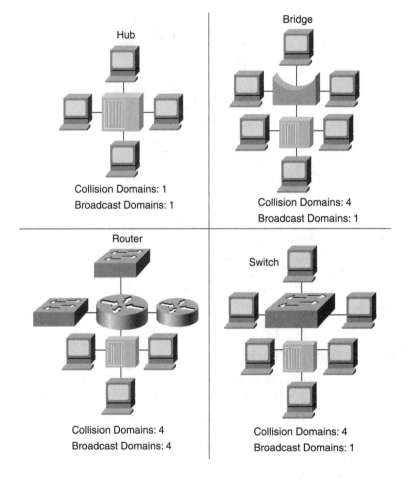

Hub

Collision Domains: 1
Broadcast Domains: 1

Bridge

Collision Domains: 4
Broadcast Domains: 1

Router

Collision Domains: 4
Broadcast Domains: 4

Switch

Collision Domains: 4
Broadcast Domains: 1

Mapping Devices to Layers and the Hierarchical Model

Earlier in this chapter, you learned about the hierarchical model used to design and implement networks. Figure 1-26 reviews the structure of this model (shown earlier in Figure 1-3). Given a particular function of networking and what was discussed about the service performed at each layer, you should be able to match internetworking devices to your internetworking needs.

Figure 1-26   *Three-Layer Hierarchical Network Model*

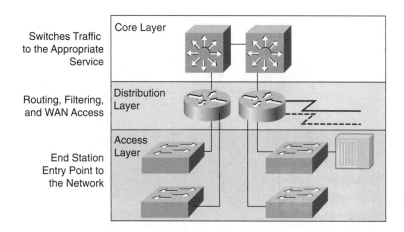

The following list summarizes the factors for selecting networking devices:

- Provides desired functionality and features
- Has required capacity and performance
- Is easy to install and offers centralized management
- Provides network resiliency
- Provides investment protection in existing infrastructure
- Provides migration path for change and growth

The most important task is to understand the needs and then identify the device functions and features that meet those needs. To accomplish this, obtain information about where in the internetworking hierarchy the device needs to operate, and then consider factors such as ease of installation, capacity requirements, and so forth.

Other factors, such as remote access, also play a role in product selection. When supporting remote access requirements, you must first determine the kind of WAN services that meet your needs. Then, you can select the appropriate device.

The type and number of required WAN connections significantly affects your choice of devices. The most important factor in choosing WAN services is the availability of the service. Knowing what your bandwidth requirements are and how much the service costs is also important.

Choosing a service that your product can support is also important.

When determining WAN service bandwidth requirements, you must look at the type of traffic that needs to cross the WAN service. Figure 1-27 gives you an idea of WAN technology as it maps to a given application.

Figure 1-27 *Application Bandwidth Requirements*

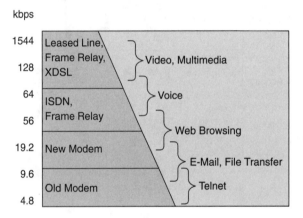

After you choose the type of network device you need, you can select a particular product. Cisco Systems offers a large variety of networking products, including hubs, switches, and routers.

Layer 2 Devices

Layer 2 devices are networking devices that forward traffic based on the data link layer of the OSI model. On a LAN, these are devices that use end stations' physical MAC addresses for forwarding purposes. Both bridges and switches are Layer 2 internetworking devices. Today, the Layer 2 switch is the predominant data link layer device used in internetworking.

Most network designers use Layer 2 switches in the access layer of the design model's hierarchy. These devices use ASICs to provide low-latency traffic forwarding. Layer 2 switches offer the capability of providing each device with dedicated 10 or 100 Mbps access and eliminate collisions. Furthermore, switches can provide separate broadcast domains for a port or group of ports using VLANs.

The downside of using Layer 2 switching is the inability to control broadcasts within a VLAN. This characteristic means that the Spanning Tree Protocol must be employed to prevent bridging loops. If such a loop does occur, it has a serious impact on the network performance.

An example of a Layer 2 device is the Cisco 2950 series switches.

Layer 3 Devices

Layer 3 devices are networking devices that forward traffic based on the network layer of the OSI reference model. Layer 3 devices use the logical network address to learn and exchange information about these networks to provide communication between end stations based on the Layer 3 address, such as an IP address. The most recognizable Layer 3 device is a router; however, a growing number of Layer 3 switches are also popular. Both a router and a Layer 3 switch perform the same basic functions; however, a Layer 3 switch is usually specialized so that it supports only a single LAN protocol (Ethernet) and a few network layer protocols (IP and IPX) at high rates of speed. A router can usually support almost all LAN protocols (Ethernet, Token Ring, and FDDI) and all network layer protocols.

Most network designers use Layer 3 devices in the Distribution and Core layers of the network. The Layer 3 device provides the interVLAN routing capabilities required to communicate between access layer VLANs and provides the broadcast control that is lacking in a Layer 2 device. Another advantage of Layer 3 devices is the capability of maintaining and using multiple paths between devices.

The disadvantage of a device that supports only Layer 3 services is the inability to provide quality Layer 2 support. If a device that supports only Layer 3 services is deployed in a network between two access layer switches, those two switches will be in separate broadcast domains.

An example of a device that supports only Layer 3 is a Cisco 2600 series router or a Cisco 2948G-L3 switch.

Multilayer Devices

Multilayer devices combine the best of both worlds. A multilayer switch has interfaces that can be configured as Layer 2 ports, using MAC address information for forwarding, or configured for Layer 3 ports, using IP address for forwarding. A multilayer switch runs using ASIC technologies so that it has the speed of a Layer 2 or Layer 3 switch and is limited in the amount of protocols and topologies it supports, like that of the Layer 3 switch.

Multilayer devices are typically deployed in place of Layer 3 devices in network designs. These devices are placed in the distribution and core layers. The Layer 3 capabilities of these devices provide interVLAN routin,g and the Layer 2 capabilities allow the switch to provide Layer 2 connectivity between the access devices. Because the switch has the characteristics of both Layer 2 and Layer 3 devices, it allows the appropriate features to be configured when needed.

The disadvantage to the multilayer device is that, like the Layer 3 switch, it supports a limited number of protocols and typically works only on Ethernet media.

Some examples of a multilayer device include the Cisco 3550 series, Cisco 4500 series, and Cisco 6500 series switches.

NOTE   This assumes the Cisco 4500 and Cisco 6500 series switches are running Cisco IOS Software.

Summary

This chapter introduced some basic concepts of internetworking. These concepts include the ability to describe (using the OSI reference model) the process in which data transfers from an application across the network. You learned the roles of each network device discussed in this book and saw how each fits into the hierarchy of network design. You learned at which layer of the OSI model each of these devices functions. Finally, you learned how to use this information to place devices in the hierarchy based on the needs of your network.

Review Questions

1 Which three functions does the Cisco hierarchical model define?

2 What is one advantage of the OSI reference model?

3 Describe the data encapsulation process.

4 Define a collision domain and give an example of a device that combines all devices into a single collision domain.

5 Define a broadcast domain and give an example of a device that separates each segment into different broadcast domains and provides connectivity between the segments.

6 At which layer of the OSI model does a bridge or switch operate?

7 How many broadcast domains are associated with a bridge or switch (assuming no VLANs)?

8 Which OSI layer defines an address that consists of a network portion and a node portion?

9 Which OSI layer defines a flat address space?

10 Which process establishes a connection between two end stations using a reliable TCP/IP transport layer protocol?

After completing this chapter, you will be able to perform the following tasks:

- Understand the reasons for using Layer 2 devices to control network traffic and enhance network performance.

- Describe the components and processes involved in Layer 2 switching (bridging) operations.

- Understand the need for Spanning Tree Protocol in a Layer 2 environment.

- Verify a Catalyst switch's default configuration.

- Build a functional access switch configuration to support the specified network operational parameters, given a network design.

- Execute an add, move, or change on an access layer switch, given a new network requirement.

- Use **show** commands to verify Catalyst switch configuration and operations.

CHAPTER 2

Configuring Catalyst Switch Operations

This chapter introduces the major concepts involved with Layer 2 switching, covers key operational components of a Catalyst switch, and introduces other functional aspects that influence the switch environment.

In addition, this chapter reviews OSI Layer 2 functions as they apply to Ethernet switching (bridging). This chapter also discusses the operations of Layer 2 switching and how a switch forwards frames to segments. You also learn to configure the Catalyst family of Ethernet switches to implement these Layer 2 functions.

Enhancing Ethernet Networks Using Layer 2 Switches

The majority of networks today run on Ethernet technologies. While Ethernet is a popular, simple, and cost-effective way to interconnect computing devices, it lacks the scalability to deal with most large network environments. Ethernet was originally designed to be shared media, which means that all the devices on a particular segment must share the Ethernet segment. Only one device can access the media at any given point in time. As the number of users on the Ethernet media increases, gaining access to the media becomes challenging for a device.

When more than one user is on a shared Ethernet segment, media contention and collisions are an inevitable result. The more devices that are sharing the Ethernet segment, the more likely the collisions are to occur. Collisions occur when two devices attempt to send data on the shared segment at the same time. The result is an unusable frame for either device. When a collision occurs, the devices on the network wait some random time before resending the frame to try and prevent another collision. Media contention occurs when a device is unable to transmit a frame because the Ethernet segment is in use by another device. Media contention creates delay in the network because devices must wait their turn to use the segment.

The best way to eliminate the collision and contention problems in Ethernet networks is to reduce the number of users on a particular segment. A switch or a bridge is a network device that allows the separation of individual Ethernet segments by using a forwarding process based on Layer 2 MAC addresses of the frames. By using a deterministic method of forwarding frames between ports, the switch provides a separate segment on each port. With more segments available, the switch enables the network administrator to reduce the number of users on each segment. If only one user is off a switch port, there is only one user on the segment, and it is possible to eliminate collisions altogether.

Each segment on a switch is called a *collision domain* because collisions on one segment will not be noticed on other segments. Each port on a switch is a separate segment or collision domain, so each device that is connected directly to a switch port has a dedicated segment and does not share the bandwidth of that segment with any other device. These devices are said to have dedicated bandwidth. Using switches to connect to the end devices eliminates the possibility of collisions and contention issues in the network.

Layer 2 Networking Components

The Layer 2 switch gets its name from Layer 2 of the OSI model. This is because a switch and bridge operate by using the protocol data unit (PDU) information added at Layer 2 during frame encapsulation. As data is passed down to the Ethernet card from upper-layer protocols, the information must be encapsulated into an Ethernet frame before it can be transmitted onto the physical media. The frame consists of the following required components:

- Addressing
- Upper Layer Protocol Identification
- Error Checking

NOTE   In addition to the required components, a frame might also have optional components, such as frame tagging and Classification of Services indicators, for enhanced switching services. These options are discussed in greater detail in the 802.1Q section of Chapter 3, "Extending Switched Network with Virtual LANs."

Each device on an Ethernet network has a unique device ID known as the Media Access Control (MAC) address. The MAC address is a 6-byte (48-bit) address that typically consists of a 3-byte Vendor ID and a 3-byte serial number. Figure 2-1 shows a typical MAC address.

Figure 2-1   *MAC Address*

As a frame travels along an Ethernet segment, each device examines the addressing in the frame to determine if it should read the entire frame or ignore the frame completely. Much like a letter you receive in the mail, the address tells the reader to whom the letter is going. This address is called a *destination address* and is the first 6 bytes of an Ethernet frame. Like a return address on a letter, the Ethernet frame also contains a source address to identify the device that sent the frame. This is called a source address and is the 6 bytes following the destination address. A Layer 2 switch uses these addresses to determine which segment to forward frames onto. Figure 2-2 shows the addressing portions of an Ethernet frame.

Figure 2-2   *Ethernet Frame Addressing Fields*

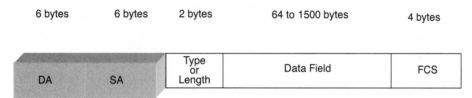

The next two bytes of the Ethernet frame are either a Length field or a Type field, depending on the particular kind of Ethernet frame. Three encapsulation methods exist for Ethernet:

- Ethernet_II (ARPA)
- IEEE 802.2/802.3
- IEEE 802.2/802.3 SNAP

NOTE   ARPA is a Cisco term that references Ethernet type 2 frames.

Each of these frames has the same 6-byte source and destination MAC address fields, but they differ in how they indicate which upper-layer protocol is contained inside the frame. In an Ethernet_II frame, the 2 bytes directly after the source address are known as a Type field. The receiving device uses this field to determine which upper-layer protocol the frame should be given to for further de-encapsulation. An example of a frame type is 0x0800, which is IP.

An IEEE 802.3 and a Sub-Network Access Point (SNAP) frame both have a 2-byte field following the source address, which is known as a Length field. This field tells the device how many bytes of information are located in the frame's Data field. A standard Ethernet frame must have a length between 64 and 1500 bytes or 0x0040 and 0x05DC. Any number greater than 0x05DC would be a Type field and indicate an Ethernet_II Frame. An IEEE 802.3 frame has what is known as a Logical Link Control (LLC) sublayer, which contains a 1-byte field called the destination service access point (DSAP). This field indicates the upper-layer protocol. A DSAP of 0x06 indicates an IP frame. A DSAP of 0xAA indicates that the frame is a SNAP frame.

A SNAP frame uses an Ethertype frame in the SNAP field to indicate the upper-layer protocol. The SNAP Ethertype uses the same values as the Ethernet_II Type field; for example, if the Type field in the Ethernet frame is 0x0800, the frame is an IP frame. Figure 2-3 shows the layout of the three frames, highlighting the way that they communicate with the upper-layer protocols.

Figure 2-3   *Upper-Layer Protocol Fields*

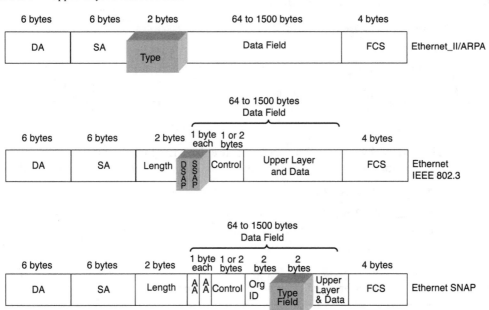

The next portion of the frame after the 2-byte Type or Length field is called the Data field. A standard Ethernet frame can have between 46 and 1500 bytes in the Data field. In an IEEE 802.3 and SNAP frame, the LLC and SNAP fields are located inside the frame Data field. In addition, the Data field transports the entire upper-layer protocol PDU, including the actual data. The final field in the frame is called the frame check sequence (FCS). This 4-byte field is a cyclic redundancy check (CRC) value computed during transmit and receive that verify the frame was transmitted without errors. The receiving device performs a checksum on the frame and compares it to the CRC value in the FCS field. If the values match, the frame is error free; if the values do not match, the frame has errors and is discarded. Figure 2-4 shows the location of the Data and FCS fields in an Ethernet frame.

Figure 2-4   *Data and FCS Fields*

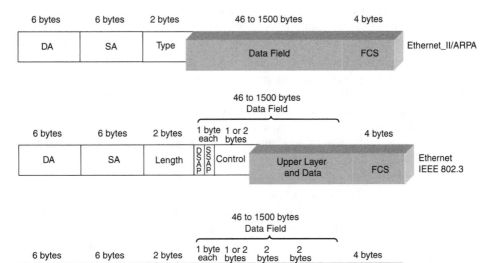

Layer 2 switches learn the identity of a device connected to a particular switch port from the Source MAC Address field and make a forwarding or filtering decision using the Destination MAC Address field. The next section explains how a Layer 2 switch functions.

Basic Layer 2 Switching (Bridging) Technologies

To configure a switch to properly operate in a network environment, you must first understand how it functions. Ethernet switches segment the network into multiple collision domains by forwarding frames between segments only when needed. Layer 2 switches have three major functions:

- Address learning
- Packet forwarding/filtering
- Loop avoidance

The switching functions are similar to those provided by Ethernet bridges:

- An Ethernet switch learns the MAC addresses of devices attached to each of its ports by examining the MAC address incoming frames. The address-to-port mappings are stored in a MAC database. For Catalyst switches, the MAC database is called the MAC address table.

- When an Ethernet switch receives a frame, it consults the MAC database to determine which port can reach the station identified as the destination in the frame. If the address is found, the frame is transmitted on only that port. If the destination address is not found, the frame is transmitted out every port except the incoming port.

- When the switched network includes multiple pathways between networks for redundancy, an Ethernet switch must prevent frames from retransmitting between these multiple pathways forever. The continuous retransmission of packets across redundant Layer 2 links is called a loop (or bridge loop). These loops bring down a network by uselessly retransmitting frames until all the bandwidth in the network is absorbed. Because of the potential for bridge loops, multiple active pathways must be disabled. Spanning Tree Protocol is the correct mechanism here to prevent loops while still allowing backup paths to exist in the event of a link failure.

When the switch receives the frame, the switch must transmit the frame out to the appropriate interfaces using the MAC address table information. The way the switch moves the frame from one interface to another is called the *forwarding mode* or *operation mode*. The three primary operating modes that handle frame switching are as follows:

- **Store-and-forward**—In store-and-forward mode, the switch must receive the complete frame before forwarding takes place. The destination and source addresses are read, the cyclic redundancy check (CRC) is performed, the relevant filters are applied, and the frame is forwarded. If the CRC is bad, the frame is discarded. The latency (or delay) through the switch varies with frame length. This is the only operational mode of the Catalyst 2950, 3550, 4500, and 6500 series switches.

- **Cut-through**—In cut-through mode, the switch checks the destination address (DA) as soon as the header is received and immediately begins forwarding the frame. Depending on the network transport protocol being used (connectionless or connection-oriented), a significant decrease in latency occurs from input port to output port. The delay in cut-through switching remains constant regardless of frame size because this switching mode starts to forward the frame as soon as the switch reads the destination addresses. (In some switches, only the destination addresses are read.) The disadvantage of this process is that a switch would still forward a collision frame or a frame with a bad CRC value. Some switches continue to read the CRC and keep a count of errors. If the error rate is too high, the switch can be set—either manually or automatically—to use store-and-forward.

- **Fragment-free**—In fragment-free mode (also known as modified cut-through), the switch reads into the first 64 bytes before forwarding the frame. Collisions normally occur within the first 64 bytes of a frame. By reading 64 bytes, the switch can filter out collision frames. Fragment-free switching is the default operating mode for the Catalyst 1900.

NOTE   *Latency* is defined as the delay through a network device. When expressed in marketing literature for switches, the latency varies based on switching methods. Of note in the switching methods described here, latency is measured as the first bit in the switch to the first bit out. This measurement gives a true representation of the time involved in switching a packet. When you read latency values for store-and-forward switching modes, however, note that latency is usually measured as last bit in to first bit out because there is no other true way to measure latency due to variable frame sizes. The size of the frame doesn't matter in fragment-free or cut-through because you are always dealing with a fixed amount of information.

The idea behind the forwarding mode is to enhance the services between the network segments without adding latency. In earlier switches with slower hardware, the forwarding modes were beneficial; however, today's Catalyst switches operate in a store-and-forward mode.

Ethernet switching increases a network's available bandwidth, reducing the number of users per segment or even allowing dedicated segments and interconnecting of these segments. Layer 2 switches are functionally equivalent to bridges; however, switches have superior throughput performance, higher port densities, lower per-port costs, and greater flexibility. These factors contributed to the emergence of Layer 2 switches as replacement technology for bridges and as complements to routing technologies.

NOTE   Bridges are typically not available or used in networks today. Bridges are mentioned here because Layer 2 functionality is based on the same principles as that of bridges.

Address Learning Function

An Ethernet switch learns addresses and operates like a transparent bridge. The learning function uses the source address of an Ethernet frame to determine a device's location. The switch maintains a MAC address table used to track the locations of devices connected to the switch. It then uses that table to decide which packets need to be forwarded to other segments. Figure 2-5 shows an initial MAC address table. Notice that upon initialization, the switch does not know on which interface a host resides. If a frame were sent to a switch with an empty MAC address table, the switch would need to send the frame to all ports except the receiving port. This is a process known as *flooding* and is counterproductive to the function of the switch because the frame is sent out all ports. The learning process is critical to the proper operation of the switch.

Figure 2-5 *Address Learning: Initial MAC Address Table*

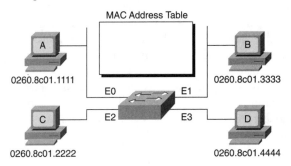

The goal of the switch is to segment the traffic so that packets destined for a host in a given collision domain do not propagate onto another segment, but, instead, are forwarded only to the segment where the destination host resides. This is accomplished by the switch's "learning" where the hosts are located. The following items outline the major learning and forwarding process:

- When a switch is first initialized, the switch's MAC address table is empty, as shown in Figure 2-5.

- With an empty MAC address table, no destination address-based filtering or forwarding decision is possible, so the switch must forward each frame to all connected ports other than that on which it arrived.

- Forwarding a frame to all connected ports is called *flooding* the frame.

- Flooding is the least-efficient way to transmit data across a switch because it wastes bandwidth by transmitting the frame onto a segment where it is not needed.

- Because switches handle traffic for multiple segments at the same time, switches implement buffering memory so that they can receive and transmit frames independently on each port or segment.

To understand the learning process, take a look at Figure 2-6, which illustrates a transaction between two workstations on different segments.

Figure 2-6 *Address Learning: Flooded Packet*

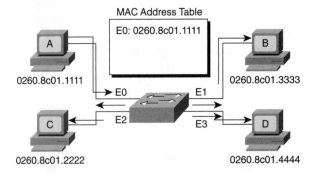

In Figure 2-6, Station A with MAC address 0260.8c01.1111 wants to send traffic to Station C with MAC address 0260.8c01.2222. The switch receives this frame and performs several actions:

1 The frame is initially received from the physical Ethernet and stored in temporary buffer space.

2 Because the switch does not yet know what interface connects it to the destination station, it is obligated to flood the frame through all other ports.

3 While flooding the frame from Station A, the switch learns the source address and associates it with Port E0 in a new MAC address table entry. The switch has now "learned" Station A's location.

4 A MAC table entry for Station A is cached. If the entry is not refreshed by a new frame transiting to the switch within a time limit (300 seconds on most Catalyst switches), the entry is discarded.

Switches and bridges become efficient because of the learning process. As stations continue to send frames to one another, the learning process continues, as illustrated in Figure 2-7.

Figure 2-7   *Address Learning: Continued*

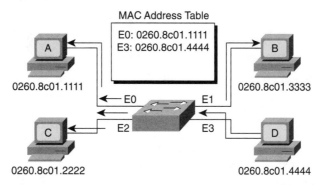

In Figure 2-7, Station D with MAC address 0260.8c01.4444 sends traffic to Station C with MAC address 0260.8c01.2222. The switch takes several actions:

1 The source address, 0260.8c01.4444, is added to the MAC address table.

2 The destination address, 0260.8c01.2222 (Station C), in the transmitted frame is compared to entries in the MAC address table.

3 When the software determines that no port-to-MAC address mapping yet exists for this destination, the frame is flooded to all ports except the one on which it was received.

4 When Station C sends a frame back to Station A, the switch can learn Station C's MAC address at Port E2.

5   As long as all stations send data frames within the MAC address table entry lifetime, a complete MAC address table is built. These entries are then used to make intelligent forwarding and filtering decisions.

Forward/Filter Decision

When a frame arrives with a known destination address, it is forwarded only on the specific port connected to that station, not to all stations.

In Figure 2-8, Station A sends a frame to Station C. When the destination MAC address (Station C's MAC address) exists in the MAC address table, the switch retransmits the frame only on the port listed.

Figure 2-8   *Switch Filtering Decision*

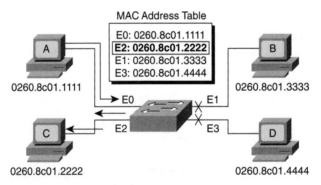

The sequence for Station A sending a frame to Station C is as follows:

1   The destination MAC address from the transmitted frame, 0260.8c01.2222, is compared to entries in the MAC address table.

2   When the switch determines that the destination MAC address can be reached through Port E2, it retransmits the frame to only this port.

3   The switch does not retransmit the frame on Port E1 or Port E3 to preserve bandwidth and eliminate collisions on these links. This action is known as *frame filtering*.

If a hub or switch were attached to a switch port and multiple hosts were connected to that hub, as the switch learned of these devices, frames traveling from one device to another device on that segment would not be forwarded to any port on the connected switch. Figure 2-9 illustrates this behavior.

Figure 2-9 *Multiple Hosts*

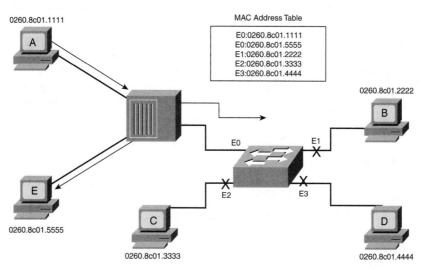

A broadcast address in Ethernet is FFFF.FFFF.FFFF. A frame with this address is destined for all devices. A multicast address usually starts with 01, which means it is destined for multiple hosts. Broadcast and multicast addresses are always destination address and are handled the same way each time by a switch. If Station D in Figure 2-10 sends a broadcast or multicast frame, that frame is forwarded to all ports other than the originating port.

Figure 2-10 *Broadcast Frame*

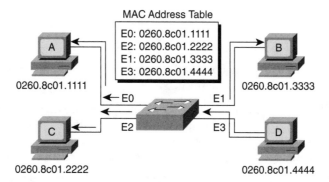

The fact that all stations receive the broadcast frame means that all the segments in the switched network are in the same broadcast domain.

NOTE   Broadcast and multicast frames constitute a special case. Because broadcast and multicast frames might be of interest to all stations, the switch normally floods broadcast and multicast frames to all ports other than the originating port. A switch never learns a broadcast or multicast address because broadcast and multicast addresses never appear as a frame's source address. Reducing the effect of multicast traffic on a switch is possible with techniques such as IGMP snooping. IGMP snooping is covered in greater detail in the *Building Cisco Multilayer Switched Networks Exam Certification Guide* from Cisco Press.

Loop Avoidance

The third function of the switch is loop avoidance. Bridged networks, including switched networks, are commonly designed with redundant links and devices. Such designs eliminate the possibility that a single point of failure results in loss of function for the entire switched network. Figure 2-11 illustrates a switched network designed with redundancy between Segment 1 and Segment 2.

Figure 2-11   *Redundant Topology for a Switched Network*

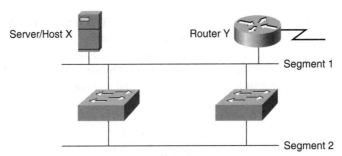

Although redundant designs might eliminate a single point of failure, they introduce several problems that you need to consider:

- Without some loop-avoidance service in operation, each switch will flood broadcasts endlessly. This situation is commonly called a *bridge loop*. The continual propagation of these broadcasts through the loop produces a broadcast storm, which results in wasted bandwidth and severely impacts network and host performance.

- Multiple copies of nonbroadcast frames might be delivered to destination stations. Many protocols expect to receive only a single copy of each transmission. Multiple copies of the same frame might cause unrecoverable errors.

- Instability in the MAC address table contents results from copies of the same frame being received on different ports of the switch. Data forwarding might be impaired when the switch consumes resources in coping with address thrashing in the MAC address table.

Layer 2 LAN protocols, such as Ethernet, lack a mechanism to recognize and eliminate endlessly looping frames. Because of this, when a loop exists, frames retransmit through the network indefinitely or until the network crashes because all the resources have been used up by the loop. The sections that follow address how loop avoidance can solve each problem.

Eliminating Broadcast Storms

Switches flood broadcast frames to all ports except the one on which the frame is received. Figure 2-12 illustrates the problem of broadcast storms, in which switches propagate broadcast traffic continuously.

Figure 2-12 *Broadcast Storms*

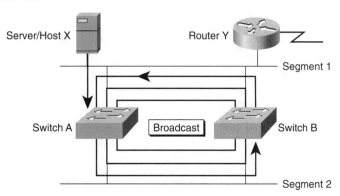

A broadcast storm is a condition of extreme congestion because of too many broadcasts on the network. If you recall from the previous section, all the ports are in the same broadcast domain, so this condition affects all devices attached to the switch. This broadcast storm can be caused by a misbehaving network interface card (NIC), a poorly designed network, or a bridging/switching loop. The broadcast storm illustrated in Figure 2-12 is caused by the following sequence of events:

1 When Host X sends a broadcast frame—for example, an ARP for resolving its default gateway at Router Y—the frame is received by Switch A.

2 Switch A examines the Destination Address field in the frame and determines that the frame must be flooded onto the bottom Ethernet link, Segment 2.

3 When this copy of the frame arrives at Switch B, the process repeats, and a copy of the frame is transmitted onto the top Ethernet, Segment 1.

Because the original copy of the frame arrives at Switch B on Segment 1 some time after the frame is received by Switch A, it would have also been forwarded by Switch B to Segment 2. These frames would travel around the loop in both directions even after the destination station has received a copy of the frame.

A loop-avoidance solution eliminates this problem by preventing one of the four interfaces from transmitting or receiving frames during normal operation.

Eliminating Duplicate Nonbroadcast Frame Transmissions

Most protocols are not designed to recognize or cope with duplicate transmissions. In general, protocols that make use of a sequence-numbering mechanism assume that many transmissions have failed and that the sequence number has recycled. Other protocols attempt to hand the duplicate transmission to the appropriate upper-layer protocol, causing unpredictable results. Figure 2-13 illustrates how multiple transmissions occur within a switched network.

Figure 2-13 *Multiple Frame Copies*

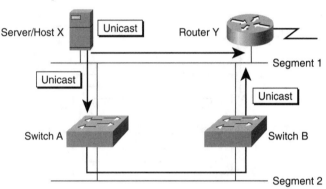

The following list documents how multiple transmissions can occur:

1 When Host X sends a unicast frame to Router Y, one copy is received over the direct Ethernet connection, Segment 1. At more or less the same time, Switch A receives a copy and puts it into its buffers.

2 If Switch A examines the Destination Address field in the frame and finds no entry in the MAC address table for Router Y, Switch A floods the frame out on all ports except for the originating port.

3 When Switch B receives a copy of the frame through Switch A on Segment 2, Switch B also forwards a copy of the frame on to Segment 1 if no entry is in the MAC address table for Router Y.

4 Router Y receives a copy of the same frame for the second time.

A loop-avoidance solution eliminates this problem by preventing one of the four interfaces from transmitting or receiving frames during normal operation. This is another purpose of Spanning Tree Protocol.

Eliminating Database Instability

Database instability results when multiple copies of a frame arrive on different ports of a switch. In Figure 2-14, Switch B learns a mapping between Station X and the port to Segment 1 when the first frame arrives. Some time later, when the copy of the frame transmitted through Switch A arrives, Switch B must remove the first entry and learn one that maps Station X's MAC address to the port on Segment 2.

Figure 2-14 *Database Instability Resulting from Multiple Frames Received on Different Switch Ports*

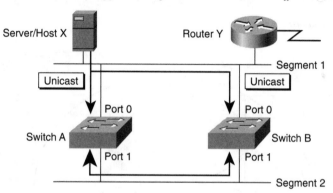

In Figure 2-14, the redundant path without Spanning Tree would create MAC database instability. This is caused when the following steps occur:

1 Host X sends a unicast frame to Router Y.

2 Neither switch has yet learned the Router Y MAC address.

3 Switches A and B learn Host X's MAC address on Port 0.

4 The frame to Router Y is flooded.

5 Switches A and B incorrectly learn Host X's MAC address on Port 1.

Depending on the internal architecture of the switch in question, it might or might not cope well with rapid changes in its MAC database.

Again, in this instance, a loop-avoidance solution eliminates this problem by preventing one of the four interfaces from transmitting or receiving frames during normal operation. Preventing database instability is another function of the Spanning Tree Protocol.

Multiple Loops in a Switched Network

A large, complex switched or bridged network with multiple switches can cause multiple loops to occur in the switched network. As depicted in Figure 2-15, you can run into the following multiple-loop scenarios:

- A loop can exist within another loop.
- A broadcast storm of looping packets can quickly clog the network with unneeded traffic and prevent packet switching.

Figure 2-15 *Multiple Loops*

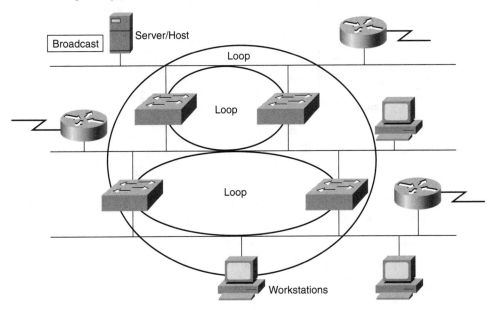

Layer 2 LAN protocols, such as Ethernet, lack a mechanism to recognize and eliminate endlessly looping packets. Some Layer 3 protocols, such as IP, implement a Time-To-Live (TTL) mechanism that limits the number of times a packet can be retransmitted by networking devices. Lacking such a mechanism, Layer 2 devices continue to retransmit looping traffic indefinitely.

Therefore, there must be a mechanism to prevent loops in the bridged (or switched) network. This loop-avoidance mechanism is the main reason for the Spanning Tree Protocol.

How Spanning Tree Protocol Works

Spanning Tree Protocol is a bridge-to-bridge protocol developed by DEC. The DEC Spanning-Tree Algorithm was subsequently revised by the IEEE 802 committee and published in the IEEE 802.1D specification. The DEC and the IEEE 802.1D algorithm are not the same and are not compatible. The Catalyst switches use the IEEE 802.1D Spanning Tree Protocol.

The purpose of Spanning Tree Protocol is to maintain a loop-free network. A loop-free path is accomplished when a device recognizes a loop in the topology and blocks one or more redundant ports. As illustrated in Figure 2-16, there is now only one active path from Segment 1 to Segment 2.

Figure 2-16   *Port Blocking*

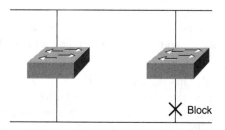

Spanning Tree Protocol runs continually so that a failure or addition of a link, switch, or bridge is discovered quickly. When the network topology changes, Spanning Tree Protocol reconfigures switch or bridge ports to avoid a total loss of connectivity or the creation of new loops.

NOTE   Spanning Tree Protocol is enabled by default on all Layer 2 ports on all Catalyst switches.

Figure 2-17 illustrates a loop-free network, as created by the Spanning Tree Protocol.

Figure 2-17   *Spanning Tree Operation*

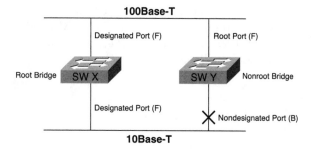

The Spanning Tree Protocol uses two key concepts when creating a loop-free, logical topology—the bridge ID (BID) and the path cost. The Spanning Tree Protocol provides a loop-free network topology by doing the following:

- **Electing a root bridge**—Only one bridge is designated as the root bridge in a given broadcast domain. The root bridge is the device with the lowest overall bridge ID. All ports on the root bridge are in the forwarding state and are called designated ports. When in the forwarding state, a port can send and receive traffic. In Figure 2-17, Switch X is elected as the root bridge.

- **For each nonroot bridge, there will be one root port**—The root port has the lowest-cost path from the nonroot bridge to the root bridge. Root ports are in the forwarding state and provide connectivity back to the root bridge. Spanning Tree path cost is an accumulated cost based on the bandwidth of the receiving ports. In Figure 2-17, from Switch Y, the lowest-cost path to the root bridge is through the 100BASE-T Fast Ethernet link. If the cost is the same, the next factor is the sending bridge ID, and the deciding factor would be the lowest sending-port number.

- **On each segment, there is one designated port**—The designated port is selected on the bridge that has the lowest-cost path to the root bridge. Designated ports are in the forwarding state and are responsible for forwarding traffic for the segment. In Figure 2-17, the designated ports for both segments are on the root bridge because the root bridge is directly connected to both segments. The 10BASE-T Ethernet port on Switch Y is a nondesignated port because there is only one designated port per segment. Nondesignated ports are placed in the blocking state to break the loop topology. When a port is in the blocking state, the port is not sending or receiving traffic. This does not mean that the port is disabled. It means that Spanning Tree is preventing it from sending and receiving user traffic; however, BPDUs are still received by the port.

Bridge IDs

Switches (bridges) running the Spanning-Tree Algorithm exchange configuration messages with other switches (bridges) at regular intervals using a multicast frame called the Bridge Protocol Data Unit (BPDU). By default, on Catalyst switches, the BPDU is sent every two seconds. One of the pieces of information included in the BPDU is the bridge ID.

Spanning Tree calls for each bridge to be assigned a unique identifier (bridge ID). The bridge ID consists of a priority (2 bytes) plus the bridge MAC address (6 bytes). The (IEEE 802.1D) recommended default priority is 32,768, the midrange value. The root bridge is the bridge with the lowest overall bridge ID.

NOTE	Each switch selects one of its MAC addresses for use in the Spanning Tree bridge ID. A switch with multiple VLANs (discussed in the next chapter) uses an increment from this base MAC address for the Spanning Tree bridge ID for each VLAN.

Spanning Tree Port States

For a port to forward frames or to block frames in the network, Spanning Tree must transition to the appropriate port state. There are four Spanning Tree Port states:

- Blocking
- Listening
- Learning
- Forwarding

Spanning Tree transitions through these states to maintain a loop-free topology.

During normal operations, a port is in either the forwarding or blocking state. Forwarding ports provide the lowest-cost path to the root bridge. Two transitional states occur when a device recognizes a change in the forwarding topology. During a topology change where a forwarding port is lost, a blocking port temporarily implements the listening and learning states before transitioning to forwarding.

All ports start in the blocking state to prevent bridge loops. The port stays in a blocked state if the Spanning Tree determines that another path to the root bridge has a better cost. Blocking ports can still receive BPDUs but do not send BPDUs.

Ports transition from the blocked state to the listening state. When the port is in the transitional listening state, it can check for BPDUs. In listening state, a port sends and receives BPDUs to determine the best topology.

When the port is in learning state, it can populate its MAC address table with MAC addresses heard on its ports, but it does not forward frames. This state indicates that the port is getting ready to transmit but wants to learn addresses on the segment to prevent unnecessary flooding in the network

In the forwarding state, the port can send and receive data.

The normal time, based on the default operation of a Catalyst switch, it takes for a port to transition from the blocking state to the forwarding state is 50 seconds. Spanning Tree timers can be tuned to adjust the timing. Normally, you should set these timers to the default value. The default values are put in place to give the network enough time to gather all the correct information about the network topology. The time it takes for a port to transition from the listening state to the learning state, or from the learning state to the forwarding state, is called the forward delay. Spanning Tree timers are consistent throughout the bridge/switch topology, and the root bridge sets their values. Table 2-1 lists the default values for Spanning Tree timers.

Table 2-1   *Spanning Tree Timers*

Timer	Primary Function	Default Setting
Hello Time	Time between sending of configuration BPDUs by the root bridge	2 seconds
Forward Delay	Duration of listening and learning states	15 seconds
Max Age	Time BPDU is stored	20 seconds

NOTE   The forward delay timer is set to 15 seconds by default. This is the timer for the listening state and the learning state. The port transitions to each state for a period of the forward delay, so the total amount of time between these states is 2 times the default of 15 seconds, or 30 seconds.

Using BIDs, path costs, and port states, STP builds a loop-free topology. In Figure 2-18, because both switches use the same default priority, the one with the lower MAC address is the root bridge. In this example, Switch X is the root bridge, with a bridge ID of 8000.0c00.1111.1111. The hexadecimal value 8000 is the bridge priority (decimal 32,768). The 0c00.1111.1111 value is the device's MAC address.

Figure 2-18   *Bridge Communication*

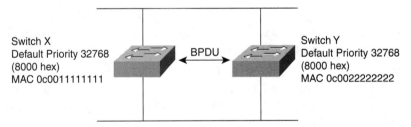

CAUTION   Spanning Tree root selection is automatic. Although this is convenient, it might not be acceptable because it could cause your traffic to flow in a suboptimal path. Setting the priority of the switch or bridge that needs to be designated as the root is always good practice. To have a bridge become the root, you want to lower the priority.

After the BPDUs have been exchanged, the port states on the switches are in the states shown in Figure 2-19:

- The ports on Switch X, the root bridge, are designated ports (forwarding).

- The Fast Ethernet port on Switch Y is the root port (forwarding). It has a lower-cost path to the root bridge than the Ethernet port.

- The Ethernet port on switch Y is the nondesignated port (blocking). There is only one designated port per segment.

Figure 2-19   *Spanning Tree Port States*

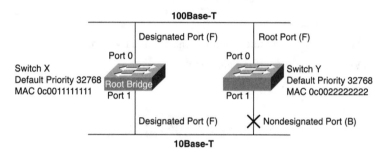

Spanning Tree Path Cost

Spanning Tree path cost is an accumulated total path cost based on the bandwidth of all the links in the path. Table 2-2 shows some of the path costs specified in the IEEE 802.1D specification.

Table 2-2   *Spanning Tree Path Cost*

Link Speed	Cost (Revised IEEE Specification)	Cost (Previous IEEE Specification)
10 Gbps	2	1
1 Gbps	4	1
100 Mbps	19	10
10 Mbps	100	100

The IEEE 802.1D specification was revised in January 2003; in the older specification (1998), the cost is calculated as 1000 Mbps/bandwidth. The new specification adjusted the calculation to accommodate higher-speed interfaces, including 1 Gbps and 10 Gbps.

NOTE   The current version of the Catalyst 1900 Software uses the older calculation for Spanning
Tree costs. All other Catalyst switches incorporate the revised calculations. This could be
problematic, because a 1900 using the old calculation will have a cost of 10 for a Fast
Ethernet port, whereas a newer switch has a cost of 19. This means the 1900 would be
chosen as the designated port for that segment.

Based on the setup of the switched network in Figure 2-20, try to determine the following
(the subsequent list provides the answers):

- What is the root bridge?

- What are the designated, nondesignated, and root ports?

- What are the forwarding and blocking ports?

Figure 2-20   *Spanning Tree Example*

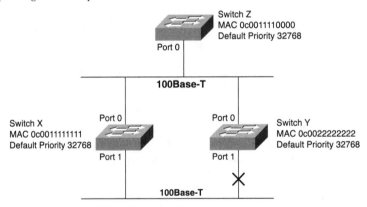

Using the Spanning Tree Protocol, you can determine the following for the switched
network in Figure 2-20:

- **Root bridge**—Switch Z, because it has the lowest bridge ID (priority and MAC
  address).

- **Root port**—Port 0s of Switches X and Y, because they are the least-cost path to the
  root on each switch.

- **Designated port**—The switch Z Port 0. All ports on the root are designated ports. The
  switch X Port 1 is a designated port. Because both Switch X and Switch Y have the
  same path cost to the root bridge, the designated port is selected to be on Switch X
  because it has a lower bridge ID than Switch Y.

- **Blocking**—The switch Y Port 1, the nondesignated port on the segment.

- **Forwarding**—All designated ports and root ports are in the forwarding state.

Spanning Tree Recalculation

When a topology change occurs due to a bridge or link failure for the forwarding ports, the Spanning Tree Protocol readjusts the network topology to ensure connectivity by placing blocked ports to the forwarding states.

In Figure 2-21, if Switch X (the root bridge) fails, Switch Y detects the missing BPDU from the root bridge. One of the Spanning Tree timers is called the Max Age timer. When the Max Age timer expires and a new BPDU has not been received from the neighbor, a new Spanning Tree recalculation is initiated. Port 1 moves to listening and then transitions to learning and, finally, to forwarding.

Figure 2-21 *Spanning Tree Recalculation*

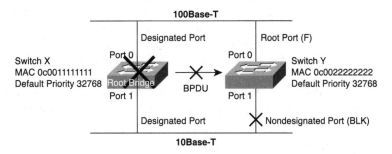

After the network converges, Switch Y becomes the root bridge. It forwards traffic between the two segments when its ports transition to the forwarding state and become the designated ports.

How Devices Stay Informed About the Topology

Convergence is a necessity for normal network operations in a bridged/switched environment. For a switched or bridged network, a key issue is the amount of time required for convergence when network topology changes. Convergence in the Spanning Tree Protocol means a state where all the switches and bridge ports have transitioned to either the forwarding or blocking state.

Fast convergence is a desirable network feature because it reduces the period of time that bridges and switches have ports in transitional states and are not sending traffic. Although the term fast is ambiguous at best, what is being stated here is that a topology change in the bridged/switched network requires time to re-establish full connectivity. Remember this when designing bridged/switched networks.

During a topology change, affected devices cannot fully communicate until Spanning Tree has converged. Because of the timers involved, convergence with 802.1D is slow.

Rapid Spanning Tree Protocol 802.1w

Recently, the IEEE committee has been working to standardize a new version of Spanning Tree. The version is covered in the IEEE 802.1w standard and is called the Rapid Spanning Tree Protocol (RSTP), which significantly speeds up the time it takes for the recalculation and convergence of the Spanning Tree when network topology changes occur. RSTP accomplishes this by slightly altering the BPDUs and using them to act as keepalives between the switch links. RSTP also defines the additional port roles of alternate and backup, and defines port states such as discarding, learning, or forwarding.

RSTP works exactly like 802.1D STP for the selection of a root bridge and the selection of active ports to create a topology. It differs in the way the switches exchange BPDUs and how quickly a port can transition into a forwarding state by defining port roles and exchanging that information between the switches. RSTP chooses an alternate root port for each switch during the STP calculation. Following the failure of a switch, switch port, or a LAN segment, the alternate port becomes the new root port for the affected switch. The new root port and designated port on the other side of the link rapidly transition to forwarding through an explicit handshake using BPDUs. RSTP also allows the configuration of switch ports, called *edge ports*, which transition directly to forwarding when the port or the switch initializes. While 802.1w supersedes 802.1D, it does remain compatible and interoperates with 802.1D STP.

The key to RSTP is the use of the BPDUs to act as communication directly between two switches. Within an 802.1w BPDU, the switches send their current port state and role. The port roles are defined as follows:

- **Root port**—A forwarding port elected for the Spanning Tree topology. This is the port that has the least cost path back to the root. Every nonroot switch has only one root port.

- **Alternate port**—An alternate path to the root. This port becomes the root port if the link or path of the current root port fails. The alternate port does not forward frames and is excluded from the active topology.

- **Designated port**—A forwarding port. Each LAN segment has at least one designated port. The other side of the link is either nondesignated or a root port.

- **Backup port**—A backup for the path provided by a designated port toward the leaves (or devices) of the Spanning Tree. A backup port does not forward frames and is excluded from the active topology. Backup ports can exist only where two ports connect together in a point-to-point connection between the switches.

NOTE   Sometimes, a vendor will describe another port role as *disabled*. A port that is disabled is defined to have no role within the operation of the Spanning Tree, which contradicts that it is, in fact, a port role. Ports that are shutdown, have no connection, or otherwise do not participate in the STP are considered disabled.

Figure 2-22 shows the selection of bridges and ports to be active in the 802.1w topology. It also shows how the port roles work in that topology.

Figure 2-22   *RSTP Topology*

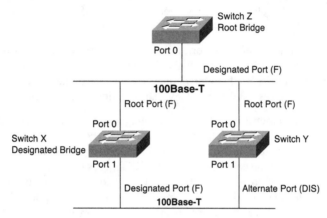

By defining backup and alternate ports, a switch already knows which path will become active if a failure occurs in the active topology. In some instances, the port on a switch that is aware of the topology change might already be forwarding packets for a segment, so it is important for each side of the link to communicate the port state as well as the port role. This communication also allows ports to transition quickly without creating loops. In STP, four distinct port states exist, all of which are controlled by timers. In RSTP, there are only three states, and they are controlled by communications between the switches on the links. Table 2-3 shows the comparison between the STP port states and the RSTP port states.

Table 2-3   *Spanning Tree Port State Comparison*

Operational Status	STP Port State	RSTP Port State	Port Included in the Active Topology
Enabled	Blocking	Discarding	No
Enabled	Listening	Discarding	No
Enabled	Learning	Learning	Yes
Enabled	Forwarding	Forwarding	Yes
Disabled*	Disabled	Discarding	No

*The operational status of Disabled means a port is disabled by the operating system and is not functional. Although disabled is not an actual STP port, the STP port state is shown here because it is important to understand how the STP and RSTP view a nonfunctioning port as the output is displayed.

The focus of all the port states and the port roles is the capability to provide rapid transition. Before the introduction of 802.1w, the Spanning-Tree Algorithm waited passively for the network to converge before transitioning a port to the forwarding state. The new RSTP actively confirms that a port can safely transition to forwarding without relying on a timer configuration. To achieve fast convergence on a port, RSTP relies on two new configuration variables: edge ports and link type.

If a port is defined as an edge port, it is supposed to be connected to an end device such as a server, router, or PC. This means that it cannot create a loop in the network and can, therefore, be moved directly to forwarding, skipping the discarding and learning phase. When an edge port changes state, no topology change notifications are generated to the RSTP.

The key to rapid transition for nonforwarding ports is the capability of each end of a link to communicate directly about the port state and role. For this reason, RSTP achieves only rapid transition to forward on edge ports and point-to-point connections between switches. On a shared link (one connected to a hub) RSTP uses the timers, such as 802.1D, to transition between port states and, consequently, loses the rapid transition function. In modern switched networks, the fact that RSTP works only on point-to-point and edge ports is not a constraint because that is how most networks are designed. RSTP defines link types based on the duplex mode of a connected port. A port operating in full-duplex mode is point-to-point, while a port operating in half-duplex mode is considered shared by default. You can override the automatic link type setting with an explicit configuration. Do this when you have a connection to a switch that is not capable of performing full-duplex. You must also configure edge ports to be defined within the topology. Figure 2-23 shows link types used in 802.1w and when they are relevant.

Figure 2-23 *RSTP Link Types*

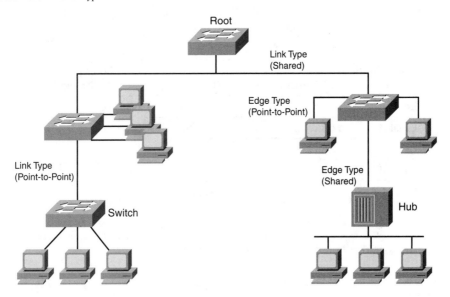

The improvements in 802.1w have been a major factor in the usefulness of Layer 2 devices in recent years. As Layer 2 has become an important part in networks, the principles of operation remain the same as they have been for years.

Section 1 Quiz

1 A Layer 2 switch normally uses which of the following Ethernet Frame fields to decide where to forward a frame?

   A Source Address

   B Destination Address

   C Length field

   D Type field

   E FCS

2 The process of sending out a frame to all ports except the one on which it was received is known as what?

   A Filtering

   B Learning

   C Designated port

   D Forwarding

   E Flooding

3 Which of the following frame types are flooded?

   A Multicast frames

   B Unicast frames

   C Broadcast frames

   D Unknown unicast frames

4 What default priority do Catalyst switches use in the Bridge ID? (Choose all that apply.)

   A The switch MAC Address

   B The switch serial number

   C 0

   D 8000

   E 32,768

   F 0x8000

5 Which of the following are true concerning STP and RSTP?

    A   RSTP chooses a root bridge differently than STP.

    B   RSTP port states are slightly different than STP port states.

    C   For STP, backup and alternate paths are not known until a failure occurs.

    D   RSTP and STP use the same calculations for choosing the best path.

    E   RSTP converges faster than STP on a shared segment.

Configuring a Catalyst Switch

This section contains an overview and concepts of configuring a Cisco IOS Software-based Catalyst switch. Over the past few years, Cisco switches have gone from a variety of operating systems and configuration modes, such as menus and set-based commands, to a common operating system. This operating system is the Cisco Internetwork Operating System. While this text deals primarily with the Cisco 2950 series of switches, these commands and parameters are the same for most IOS-based switches.

A Catalyst switch comes with factory default settings that allow it to operate right out of the box. The default configuration will essentially set up the switch to function as a transparent bridge, with no management IP address, default gateway, port settings, passwords, or VLAN configuration parameters. You might want to change some of these default values to meet your specific goals. This chapter familiarizes you with the default settings and the steps required to configure the switch. This chapter deals with current IOS switches; if you have a Catalyst 1900, refer to Appendix C.

NOTE   This chapter assumes a working knowledge of the Cisco IOS command line and modes. The best reference for IOS is the ABCs of Cisco IOS Software documentation page at Cisco.com (http://www.cisco.com/en/US/products/sw/iosswrel/products_abc_ios_overview.html#abc01). In addition, the Cisco Press title *CCNA Self-Study: Introduction to Cisco Networking Technologies* ia a good source.

Default Configuration Settings for the Catalyst Switch

Although the Catalyst switch factory default settings will suit your needs for many parameters, you might want to change some of the default values to meet your specific network topology. The default values vary depending on the switch features. The following list provides some of the default settings for the Catalyst switch. Not all the defaults are listed:

- IP address: 0.0.0.0
- CDP: Enabled

- 10/100 port: Autonegotiate duplex mode
- Spanning Tree: Enabled
- Console password: None

Default Port Configurations for the Catalyst Switch

The 2950 is one of the switches in the Catalyst switch family. The 2950 is a typical access layer switch found in a wiring closet that connects PCs to the network. The Layer 2 port configuration on the 2950 is representative of the Layer 2 ports throughout the Catalyst product line. A port on a switch is identified by its type and its location. There are three controller types for Ethernet on a Catalyst switch: Ethernet (10 Mbps), FastEthernet (100 Mbps), and GigabitEthernet (1000 Mbps). Port location is indicated in two parts, recorded as *slot/port*, but for fixed configuration switches the slot number is always 0. Table 2-4 documents the ports found on the 2950-12 and 2950-24 switches.

Table 2-4   *Catalyst 2950-12 and 2950-24 Ports*

	Catalyst 2950-12	Catalyst 2950-24
100BASE-T Ports	12 total (Fa0/1 to Fa0/12)	24 total (Fa0/1 to Fa0/24)
1000-Mbps GBIC Ports	None	G 0/1, G 0/2

Ports on the Catalyst switch are referenced as either *port* or *interface*.

For example, for Fa0/1, the following points are true:

- The **show running-config** output (see Example 2-1) refers to Fa0/1 as interface FastEthernet 0/1.
- The **show spanning-tree** output (see Example 2-2) refers to Fa0/1 as interface Fa0/1.
- The **show vlan** output (see Example 2-3) refers to Fa0/1 as port Fa0/1.
- The **show interface status** output (see Example 2-4) refers to Fa0/1 as port Fa0/1.

Example 2-1   **show running-config** *Output Refers to Fa0/1 as Interface FastEthernet 0/1*

```
Switch#show running-config
Current configuration : 2175 bytes
!
version 12.1
no service pad
service timestamps debug uptime
service timestamps log uptime
no service password-encryption
!
interface FastEthernet0/1
!
interface FastEthernet0/2
--More--
```

Example 2-2 **show spanning-tree** *Output Refers to Fa0/1 as Interface Fa 0/1*

```
Switch#show spanning-tree

VLAN0001
  Spanning tree enabled protocol ieee
  Root ID    Priority    32769
             Address     000b.5f2a.5a00
             This bridge is the root
             Hello Time   2 sec  Max Age 20 sec  Forward Delay 15 sec

  Bridge ID  Priority    32769  (priority 32768 sys-id-ext 1)
             Address     000b.5f2a.5a00
             Hello Time   2 sec  Max Age 20 sec  Forward Delay 15 sec
             Aging Time 300

Interface        Port ID                Designated              Port ID
Name             Prio.Nbr   Cost Sts    Cost Bridge ID          Prio.Nbr
---------------- --------  --------- ---  --------- -------------------- --------
Fa0/1            128.1       100 FWD          0 32769 000b.5f2a.5a00 128.1
```

Example 2-3 **show vlan** *Output Refers to Fa 0/1 as Port Fa 0/1*

```
Switch#show vlan
VLAN Name                             Status    Ports
---- -------------------------------- --------- -------------------------------
1    default                          active    Fa0/1, Fa0/2, Fa0/3, Fa0/4
                                                Fa0/5, Fa0/6, Fa0/7, Fa0/8
                                                Fa0/9, Fa0/10, Fa0/11, Fa0/12
                                                Gi0/1, Gi0/2
1002 fddi-default                     active
1003 token-ring-default               active
1004 fddinet-default                  active
1005 trnet-default                    active
```

Example 2-4 **show interfaces status** *Output Refers to Fa0/1 as Port Fa0/1*

```
Switch#show interfaces status
Port      Name            Status       Vlan     Duplex  Speed Type
Fa0/1                     connected    1        a-half  a-10 10/100BASE-TX
Fa0/2                     notconnect   1          auto  auto 10/100BASE-TX
Fa0/3                     notconnect   1          auto  auto 10/100BASE-TX
Fa0/4                     notconnect   1          auto  auto 10/100BASE-TX
Fa0/5                     connected    1        a-full  a-100 10/100BASE-TX
Fa0/6                     notconnect   1          auto  auto 10/100BASE-TX
Fa0/7                     notconnect   1          auto  auto 10/100BASE-TX
Fa0/8                     notconnect   1          auto  auto 10/100BASE-TX
Fa0/9                     notconnect   1          auto  auto 10/100BASE-TX
Fa0/10                    notconnect   1          auto  auto 10/100BASE-TX
Fa0/11                    notconnect   1          auto  auto 10/100BASE-TX
Fa0/12                    notconnect   1          auto  auto 10/100BASE-TX
Gi0/1                     notconnect   1          auto  auto 1000BaseSX
Gi0/2                     notconnect   1          auto  auto 1000BaseSX
```

Configuring the IP Address, Subnet Mask, and Default Gateway on a Layer 2 Catalyst Switch

An IP address is required on a Layer 2 switch for management purposes. For example, using Telnet to configure a switch requires the switch to have an IP address configured on an active link associated with the management interface. You must also assign an IP address if you plan to use SNMP or the Visual Switch Manager/Cluster Management Suite (web-enabled GUI) to manage the switch.

For Layer 2 IOS switches, the IP address is assigned to a VLAN interface. The VLAN interface is associated with a port or group of ports in the same VLAN. This interface can communicate with any port or device connected to a port within this VLAN. The VLAN interface does not have a physical location but is associated with the switch CPU and is the management connection. To configure an IP address and subnet mask for the switch, you must first select to which VLAN the management address will be assigned. VLAN 1 is the common management VLAN, but it can be any VLAN as long as at least one port on the switch is in that VLAN. Use the global configuration command **interface vlan** *vlannumber* to select the management interface for configuration:

```
Switch(config)#interface vlan vlannumber
```

After you access the VLAN interface, use the **ip address** command to assign the IP address and subnet mask:

```
Switch(config-if)#ip address address mask
```

For example, to configure a switch with IP address 10.5.5.11 and subnet mask 255.255.255.0, enter the following command:

```
Switch(config-if)#ip address 10.5.5.30 255.255.255.0
```

Finally, you need to activate the interface with the command **no shutdown**:

```
Switch(config-if)#no shutdown
```

NOTE

A Layer 2 switch, such as a 2950, can have only one active management interface at a time. If you configure multiple VLAN interfaces, only the interface that you last enter the **no shutdown** command on will be active. Do not confuse Interface VLAN 1 with VLAN 1. VLAN 1 defines a broadcast domain that you can put ip hosts in, including your switch. Interface VLAN 1 is a virtual interface on your switch that is assigned an IP address so that the switch can communicate with other IP hosts.

Use the **no ip address** command on an interface to remove the IP address from the switch.

The switch is assigned an IP address for management purposes. If the switch needs to send traffic to a different IP network than the one it is on, the switch sends the traffic to the default gateway, which is typically the router. A router routes traffic between different networks.

The router will be the default gateway for traffic originating from the switch and destined for a subnet that is different than the one for which the VLAN interface is configured. Use the **ip default-gateway** global configuration command to configure the default gateway. The **ip default-gateway** command takes the following form:

```
Switch(config)#ip default-gateway ip address
```

For example, to configure the management port default gateway with IP address 10.5.5.3 for a switch, enter the following command:

```
Switch(config)#ip default-gateway 10.5.5.1
```

Use the **no ip default-gateway** command to remove a configured default gateway, and set the gateway address to the default value of 0.0.0.0.

To verify the IP address and subnet mask settings, use the **show interface vlan** *number* command from the privileged EXEC mode. To view the default gateway, use the command **show ip default**. These commands are demonstrated in Example 2-5.

Example 2-5   **show interface vlan** *and* **show ip default** *Verify IP Settings*

```
Switch#show interfaces vlan 1
Vlan1 is up, line protocol is up
  Hardware is CPU Interface, address is 000b.5f2a.5a00 (bia 000b.5f2a.5a00)
  Internet address is 10.5.5.30/24
  MTU 1500 bytes, BW 1000000 Kbit, DLY 10 usec,
     reliability 255/255, txload 1/255, rxload 1/255Name server 1: 0.0.0.0
<output ommited>

Switch#show ip default
10.5.5.1
```

Duplexing and Speed

A network switch provides connectivity between devices in the network. One of the main reasons switches are used in the network is to improve this connectivity. As an intermediate device between end devices, the switch provides various speeds and modes of communication from the switch to the end device. The modes shown in Figure 2-24 that are used to communicate between the switch and the end device are half-duplex and full-duplex. Both speed and duplex are configurable parameters that can affect how fast the device sends packets to the switch for transmission.

Half-duplex transmission mode implements Ethernet carrier sense multiple access collision detect (CSMA/CD). The traditional shared LAN operates in half-duplex mode and is susceptible to transmission collisions across the wire. Half duplex is basically like a one-lane bridge across a stream–only one car can cross the stream at a time.

Figure 2-24 *Duplex Overview*

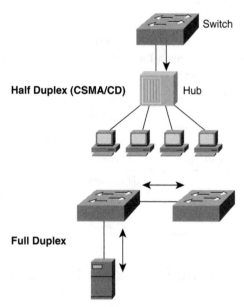

Full-duplex Ethernet significantly improves network performance without the expense of installing new media. You can achieve full-duplex transmission between stations by using point-to-point Ethernet and Fast Ethernet connections. This arrangement is collision-free. Frames sent by the two connected end nodes cannot collide because they use two separate circuits in the twisted-pair cable. This is like a two-lane bridge crossing a stream. A given wire can accommodate twice the initial payload, effectively doubling the medium payload capabilities and eliminated collisions. Each full-duplex connection uses only one port.

NOTE   Performance improvements will be realized only if the device attached to the full-duplex link transmits and receives at the same time. This is unlikely on a PC because of the nature of applications on the end device. Full duplex is most effective when configuring ports attach to switches, routers, and some servers.

Full-duplex port connections can use 10BASE-T, 100BASE-TX, and 100BASE-FX media to provide point-to-point links between switches or end nodes, but not between shared hubs. Nodes directly attached to a dedicated switch port and with network interface cards that support full duplex should be connected to switch ports configured to operate in full-duplex mode. Most Ethernet and Fast Ethernet network interface cards (NICs) sold today offer full-duplex capability.

Nodes attached to hubs, or nodes sharing their connection to a switch port, must operate in half-duplex mode because the end stations must be able to detect collisions.

Standard Ethernet configuration efficiency is typically rated at 50 to 60 percent of the 10-Mbps bandwidth. Full-duplex Ethernet offers 100 percent efficiency in both directions (100 Mbps transmit and 100 Mbps receive). Table 2-5 summarizes the differences between half-duplex and full-duplex connections.

Table 2-5 *Half Duplex Versus Full Duplex*

Half Duplex (CSMA/CD)	Full Duplex
Unidirectional data flow	Point-to-point only
Higher potential for collision	Collision-free
Hubs connectivity	Collision detect circuit disabled
	Attached to dedicated switched port
	Requires full-duplex support on both ends

Configuring the Speed and Duplex Mode for a Catalyst Switch Interface

By default, the FastEthernet ports on a switch are in Autodetect mode for speed and duplex. If you want to control exactly how the port operates, you must first set the speed; then you can control the duplex. Use the **speed** interface configuration command to change the speed for an interface. The syntax for this command (on interface Fa0/1, for example) is as follows:

```
Switch(config)#interface Fa0/1
Switch(config-if)#speed {10 | 100 | auto}
```

Options for the **speed** interface configuration command include the following:

- **10**—Forces the port to operate in 10-Mbps mode.
- **100**—Forces the port to operate in 100-Mbps mode.
- **auto**—Allows the port to use 802.1u autonegotiation to choose the port speed.

Use the **duplex** interface configuration command to change the duplex mode for an interface. The syntax for this command (on interface Fa0/1, for example) is as follows:

```
Switch(config)#interface Fa0/1
Switch(config-if)#duplex {auto | full | half}
```

The options for the **duplex** interface configuration command include the following:

- **auto**—Sets the autonegotiation of duplex mode; **auto** is the default option for 100-Mbps TX ports.
- **full**—Sets full-duplex mode.
- **half**—Sets half-duplex mode.

For example, if you want to set full-duplex mode for interface Fa0/1 on a switch, enter the following:

```
Switch(config)#interface Fa0/1
Switch(config-if)#duplex full
```

To verify the duplex settings on a given interface, use the **show interface** or **show interfaces status** command. To display statistics for and the status of all or specified interfaces, use the **show interfaces** privileged EXEC command, as demonstrated in Example 2-6.

Example 2-6 **show interfaces** *and* **show interfaces status** *Output Displays Interface Status and Statistics*

```
Switch#show interfaces fa 0/1
FastEthernet0/1 is down, line protocol is down
  Hardware is Fast Ethernet, address is 000b.5f2a.5a01 (bia 000b.5f2a.5a01)
  MTU 1500 bytes, BW 10000 Kbit, DLY 1000 usec,
     reliability 255/255, txload 1/255, rxload 1/255
  Encapsulation ARPA, loopback not set
  Keepalive set (10 sec)
  Full-duplex, 100Mb/s
  input flow-control is off, output flow-control is off
  ARP type: ARPA, ARP Timeout 04:00:00
  Last input never, output 00:13:19, output hang never
  Last clearing of "show interface" counters never
  Input queue: 0/75/0/0 (size/max/drops/flushes); Total output drops: 0
  Queueing strategy: fifo
  Output queue :0/40 (size/max)
  5 minute input rate 0 bits/sec, 0 packets/sec
  5 minute output rate 0 bits/sec, 0 packets/sec
     14 packets input, 896 bytes, 0 no buffer
     Received 13 broadcasts, 0 runts, 0 giants, 0 throttles
     0 input errors, 0 CRC, 0 frame, 0 overrun, 0 ignored
     0 watchdog, 0 multicast, 0 pause input
     0 input packets with dribble condition detected
     2376 packets output, 185061 bytes, 0 underruns
     0 output errors, 0 collisions, 2 interface resets
     0 babbles, 0 late collision, 0 deferred
     0 lost carrier, 0 no carrier, 0 PAUSE output
     0 output buffer failures, 0 output buffers swapped out

Switch#show interface status

Port      Name            Status        Vlan     Duplex  Speed Type
Fa0/1                     notconnect    1        full    100   10/100BASE-TX
Fa0/2                     notconnect    1        auto    auto  10/100BASE-TX
Fa0/3                     notconnect    1        auto    auto  10/100BASE-TX
Fa0/4                     notconnect    1        auto    auto  10/100BASE-TX
Fa0/5                     connected     1        a-full  a-100 10/100BASE-TX
Fa0/6                     notconnect    1        auto    auto  10/100BASE-TX
Fa0/7                     notconnect    1        auto    auto  10/100BASE-TX
Fa0/8                     notconnect    1        auto    auto  10/100BASE-TX
Fa0/9                     notconnect    1        auto    auto  10/100BASE-TX
Fa0/10                    notconnect    1        auto    auto  10/100BASE-TX
Fa0/11                    notconnect    1        auto    auto  10/100BASE-TX
Fa0/12                    notconnect    1        auto    auto  10/100BASE-TX
Gi0/1                     notconnect    1        auto    auto  1000BaseSX
Gi0/2                     notconnect    1        auto    auto  1000BaseSX
```

As you can be see by the first and third highlighted portions in Example 2-6, the **show interface** or **show interface status** commands can determine the duplex setting for any given interface.

Autonegotiation can, at times, produce unpredictable results. If an attached device does not support autonegotiation and is operating in full duplex, by default, the Catalyst switch sets the corresponding switch port to half-duplex mode. This configuration—half duplex on one end and full duplex on the other—causes late collision errors at the full-duplex end. To avoid this situation, manually set the switch duplex parameters to match the attached device.

If the switch port is in full-duplex mode and the attached device is in half-duplex mode, check for FCS errors and late collisions on the switch full-duplex port.

Use the **show interfaces** command to check for FCS or late collision errors. A high number of late collisions often indicates a mismatch in duplex configuration. A mismatch results in slow network response for the client. You can see late collision counters in the second highlighted line in Example 2-6.

Configuring spanning-tree portfast

Another port setting that is useful for ports connected to end devices is **spanning-tree portfast**. This command allows a port on a switch 802.1D or 802.1w to move directly into forwarding state. This can prevent problems such as DHCP timeouts for devices attaching to the network. The syntax for this command (on interface Fa0/1, for example) is as follows:

```
Switch(config)#interface Fa0/1
Switch(config-if)#spanning-tree portfast
```

Managing the MAC Address Table

Switches use the MAC address table to forward traffic between ports. The MAC table includes dynamic, permanent, and static addresses. Entering the **show mac-address-table** command displays the MAC address table and helps you determine how many dynamic, permanent, and static addresses are present and which type is used for each interface. (See Example 2-7.)

Example 2-7 **show mac-address-table** *Output Displays the MAC Address Table for the Port Interfaces on a Specified Switch*

```
Switch#show mac-address-table
          Mac Address Table
-------------------------------------------

Vlan    Mac Address      Type        Ports
----    -----------      ----        -----
  1     0050.5611.2f01   DYNAMIC     Fa0/5
Total Mac Addresses for this criterion: 1
```

Dynamic MAC Addresses

Dynamic addresses are source MAC addresses that the switch learns and then drops when they are not refreshed and aged out. The switch provides dynamic address learning by noting the source address of each packet it receives on each port, and adding the address and its associated port number to the address table. As stations are added to or removed from the network, the switch updates the address table, adding new entries and aging out those that are currently not in use. The maximum size of the MAC address table varies with different switches. The Catalyst 2950 switch can store up to 8192 MAC addresses. When the MAC address table is full, no more addresses can be learned until some age out. When this occurs, any frame with a new, unlearned source address will be flooded out all ports.

Static MAC Addresses

A static address allows you to specify an entry in the MAC address table that will not age out. This entry is saved in configuration and will be loaded into the table when the switch is rebooted.

Use the **mac-address-table static** global configuration command to specify a MAC address and associate it with a VLAN and an interface. The syntax for this command is as follows:

```
Switch(config)#mac-address-table static mac-address vlan number interface type slot/
  port
```

Table 2-6 describes the **mac-address-table static** command arguments.

Table 2-6   **mac-address-table static** *Command Arguments*

Command Argument	Meaning
mac-address	A MAC unicast address in dotted hexadecimal format (0000.0c12.3456)
vlan *number*	The VLAN where this MAC address can be reached
interface *type*	The interface type: FastEthernet, GigabitEthernet, or port-channel
slot/port	Module number: 0 for a Catalyst 2950 series Port number: the physical port number

Use the **no mac-address-table static** command to delete a static entry.

The switch sends traffic to the MAC address 0000.0c12.2345 to interface Fa 0/1 if you enter the following command:

```
Switch(config)#mac-address-table static 0000.0c12.2345 vlan 1 interface
  FastEthernet0/1
```

To verify that assigning the static MAC address was successful, enter the **show mac-address-table** command, as demonstrated in Example 2-8.

Example 2-8 **show mac-address-table** *Output Verifies Restricted Static MAC Addresses*

```
Switch#show mac-address-table
          Mac Address Table
-------------------------------------------

Vlan    Mac Address      Type       Ports
----    -----------      ----       -----
   1    0000.0c12.2345   STATIC     Fa0/1
   1    0050.5611.2f01   DYNAMIC    Fa0/5
   1    00c0.b764.f722   DYNAMIC    Fa0/1
```

Configuring Port Security on a Catalyst Switch

Another MAC-based restriction available as an option on the switch is port security. Port security has the following advantages:

- Configures an interface to be a secured port so that only certain devices are permitted to connect to a given switch port

- Defines the maximum number of MAC addresses allowed in the address table for this port (ranging from 1 to 132, where 132 is the default)

Use the **switchport port-security** interface configuration command to enable addressing security. The syntax for this command is as follows:

```
Switch(config-if)#switchport port-security
```

NOTE   You can configure port security only on a port known as an access port. Before you can enter the **switchport port-security** command, you must first configure a port to be an access port, a port connected to a single user device, with the command **switchport mode access**.

Configuring the **switchport port-security** command enables the switch to learn the address of the first device that is attached to the port and secure that address. If you want the switch to secure multiple addresses for this interface, you must increase the maximum number of addresses that can be learned. The **switchport port-security maximum** *value* command allows you to assign a value from 1 to 132. This stipulates the maximum number of addresses allowed to be secured on the port. For example, to set 4 as the maximum number of addresses allowed to connect to interface Fa0/4, enter the following command:

```
Switch(config)#interface Fa0/4
Switch(config-if)#switchport port-security maximum 4
```

Use the **no switchport port-security** command to disable addressing security.

Secured ports restrict the use of a port to a user-defined group of stations. The number of devices on a secured port can range from 1 to 132. The MAC addresses for the devices on a secure port are statically assigned by an administrator, or are *sticky-learned*. Sticky learning takes place when the address table for a secured port does not contain a full complement of static addresses. The port sticky-learns the source address of incoming frames and automatically assigns them as permanent addresses.

Use the **show port-security** privileged EXEC command to display and verify the port security configurations. Use the **show port-security addresses** command to see the addresses that have been secured for a port. Example 2-9 shows some sample output from the **show port-security** command.

Example 2-9   **show port-security** *Output Verifies Port Security Configurations*

```
Switch#show port-security
Secure Port      MaxSecureAddr  CurrentAddr  SecurityViolation  Security Action
                 (Count)        (Count)      (Count)
-----------------------------------------------------------------------------
    Fa0/1            1              1            0               Shutdown
-----------------------------------------------------------------------------
Total Addresses in System : 1
Max Addresses limit in System : 1024
```

An address violation occurs when a secured port receives a source address that has been assigned to another secured port, or when an unknown MAC address appears on a secure port after the maximum number of addresses has been reached. When a security violation occurs, the options for action to be taken on a port include protecting, securing, or shutting down the port. When a port is protected, it stops learning addresses when it reaches its maximum number, and does not send any frame with a source address that is not added to the port security address list. When a port is in secure mode, it behaves the same way as a prohibited port, but it also generates a console message and an SNMP trap. When a port is in shutdown mode, the port shuts down when a security violation occurs and must be re-enabled by the administrator.

Use the **switchport port-security violation** interface configuration command to specify the action for a port address violation. The syntax for this command is as follows:

```
Switch(config)#switchport port-security violation {protect | restrict | shutdown}
```

Use the **no switchport port-security violation** command to set the switch to its default value (**shutdown**).

Executing Adds, Moves, and Changes for Port Security

As your network topology changes by adding new devices or interfaces or moving and changing existing ones, you might need to modify the switch configuration if you enabled port security. To add a new MAC address for port security, complete the following tasks:

Step 1   Configure port security.

Step 2   Configure the MAC address to the port allocated for the new interface using the command **switchport port-security mac-address** *mac-address* so that only this MAC address will be permitted to use the port.

To delete a MAC address on a secured port, remove the port restrictions by issuing the command **no switchport port-security**.

To move a MAC address from one secured port to another, you must delete the MAC address restriction from one port and assign it to a new port. To move a MAC address for port security, use the following tasks:

Step 1   Configure port security on the new port.

Step 2   Configure the MAC address to the port allocated for the new interface using the **switchport port-security mac-address** *mac-address* command so that only this MAC address will be permitted to use the port.

Step 3   Plug the device into the newly configured port.

Step 4   Remove port security and the MAC address assignment from the original port.

If an Ethernet NIC fails, that MAC address is no longer valid. Installing a new Ethernet NIC on a device that is plugged into a secure port will violate that port's security. You must make a change to the MAC address secured on that port if the hardware on the PC is changed.

The options listed in this chapter provide basic port configuration and control. You can set these options to provide more robust features than the default configuration for the switch.

Section 2 Quiz

1   Which of the following is not a default on a Catalyst Switch running IOS? (Choose all that apply.)

   A   IP address is 0.0.0.0.

   B   All ports are set to full duplex.

   C   The system password is cisco.

   D   CDP is enabled.

   E   Spanning Tree is enabled.

2 If 10/100Mbps port 0/1 is configured to run at 10 Mbps, which of the following port names will be used to identify the port in the **show spanning-tree** command?

A Interface Ethernet 0/1

B Interface FastEthernet 0/1

C Fa0/1

D Interface Fa0/1

E E0/1

F Interface E0/1

3 Which of the following command sequences will set the IP address for the switch in VLAN 1 to 10.1.1.1 with a mask of 255.255.255.0 and activate the port?

A
```
Switch(config)# ip address 10.1.1.1 255.255.255.0
Switch(config)# management-vlan 1
```

B
```
Switch(config)# interface vlan 1
Switch(config-if)# ip address 10.1.1.1 255.255.255.0
```

C
```
Switch(config)# interface vlan 1
Switch(config-if)# ip address 10.1.1.1/24
Switch(config-if)# no shutdown
```

D
```
Switch(config)# interface vlan 1
Switch(config-if)# ip address 10.1.1.1 255.255.255.0
Switch(config-if)# no shutdown
```

4 Which commands display the duplex settings for a port? (Choose all that apply.)

A show interface

B show port

C show interface summary

D show duplex

E show interface status

F show interface duplex

5 What is the maximum number of MAC address that can be learned by a Catalyst 2950?

A 1024

B 16,384

C 32,768

D 2048

E 8192

F There is no limit

Case Study

Ann E. Won has been hired by International Widgets, Ltd. to help upgrade and maintain the company network. International Widgets, Ltd. has multiple offices in various locations, and each office is currently using shared networks (hubs) operating at 10 Mbps to connect to all the PCs and servers in the organization. Because of the number of users on each segment, the company is experiencing delay and sluggishness in the network.

The corporate location has 90 users on 2 floors, and 2 wiring closets on each floor, each with a 24-port hub. These 4 closet hubs connect to a hub in the computer room that connects to 4 servers and a router, which is used to connect to branch offices and the Internet. Figure 2-25 shows the layout of the current network.

Figure 2-25 *International Widgets, Ltd. Network Diagram*

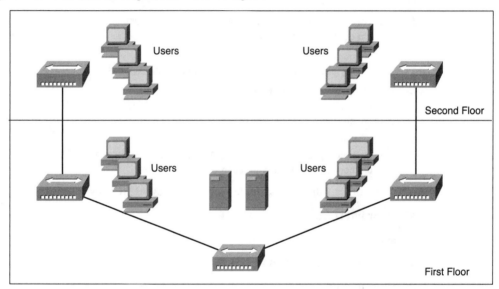

Ann's first task is to devise a plan for installing switches in the network to replace the hubs. The PCs will remain at 10 Mbps. Ann must first answer the following questions:

1 How should the links between the switches be configured to insure maximum throughput?

2 Are any special cables needed to interconnect the switches?

3 Do the NICs in the servers need to be upgraded and, if so, why?

4 After installing the switches, Ann has encountered problems with PCs not getting their DHCP address when they are booted. What could be causing this problem, and how can it be corrected?

5 One application server that is connected to the network rarely sends out frames; because of this, when devices send data to the device, the switches flood the traffic everywhere in the network. How can Ann configure the switch so that this flooding will not occur?

6 There have been some problems with people plugging into the network using the conference room port. Only the training laptops should access the port. What option can Ann configure to prevent anyone from using this port?

Catalyst Switch Command Summary

Table 2-7 lists some useful commands discussed in this chapter.

Table 2-7   *Commands for Catalyst Switch Configuration*

Command	Description
interface vlan *number*	Selects the VLAN interface to be used for management purposes.
ip address *address mask*	Sets the IP address for the management interface.
ip default-gateway	Sets the default gateway so that the management interface can be reached from a remote network.
show interface vlan *number*	Displays IP address configuration.
show ip default	Displays the default gateway for the switch.
speed {auto I 10 I 100}	Sets the speed of the port.
duplex {auto I half I full}	Sets the duplex for the port. (Speed cannot be auto to set the port duplex.)
spanning-tree portfast	Sets Spanning Tree on a port to move directly into forwarding mode.
show interfaces	Displays interface information.
show interface status	Displays information about the ports in a table format.
mac-address-table static *mac-address* **vlan** *number* **interface** *type slot/port*	Sets a static MAC address in the MAC address table and associates it with a port and VLAN.
show mac-address-table	Displays the dynamic and static MAC addresses learned by the switch.
switchport port-security	Enables port security for a port (requires the switch be configured with the command **switchport mode access**).
switchport port-security maximum 4	Sets the maximum number of MAC addresses that can be secured on a port.

Table 2-7   *Commands for Catalyst Switch Configuration*

switchport port-security mac-address *mac-address*	Secures a specified MAC address for a port.
switchport port-security violation {**protect** I **restrict** I **shutdown**}	Specifies how a port will react if a security violation occurs.
show port-security [addresses]	Displays the port security configuration on a switch. The **addresses** option displays a list of addresses that have been configured for use in port security.

Summary

This chapter discussed the three functions of a switch (bridge):

- Address learning
- Data forwarding/filtering
- Loop avoidance

You learned about the operation of the Spanning Tree Protocol and how it maintains loop-free network connections. You examined several switching technologies implemented in Catalyst switches, including switching modes and duplex modes. Finally, you learned how to use the IOS command-line interface (CLI) to configure the Catalyst switch.

Review Questions

1   What function does the Spanning Tree Protocol provide?

2   Which version of Spanning Tree Protocol do the Catalyst switches support?

3   What are the different Spanning Tree port states for IEEE 802.1D?

4   Describe the difference between full-duplex and half-duplex operations.

5   What is the default duplex setting on the Catalyst switch ports?

6   What is the switching mode used by the 2950?

7   What are the commands to assign the IP address to the default VLAN 192.168.1.5 with a mask of 255.255.255.0 and activate that interface?

8   What is the IP address used for on the Catalyst switch?

9   Which type of MAC address entry does not age out of the MAC address table?

10   What is the command to display the dynamic contents of the MAC address table?

After completing this chapter, you will be able to perform the following tasks:

- Identify what a VLAN is and how it operates.
- Configure a VLAN to improve network performance.
- Identify what role the switch plays in the creation of VLANs.
- Identify how network devices communicate about VLANs.
- Describe the need and operation of the VLAN Trunking Protocol.
- Configure the Catalyst Switch for VLAN operation.

CHAPTER 3

Extending Switched Networks with Virtual LANs

The design and function of a bridged/switched network is to provide enhanced network services by segmenting the network into multiple collision domains. The fact remains, however, that without any other mechanism, the bridged/switched network is still a single broadcast domain. A broadcast domain is a group of devices that can receive one another's broadcast frames. For example, if device A sends a broadcast frame and that frame is received by devices B and C, all three devices are said to be in a common broadcast domain. Because broadcast frames are flooded out all ports on a bridge/switch (by default), the devices connected to the bridge/switch are in a common broadcast domain.

Controlling broadcast propagation throughout the network is important to reduce the amount of overhead associated with these frames. Routers, which operate at Layer 3 of the OSI model, provide broadcast domain segmentation for each interface. Switches can also provide broadcast domain segmentation using virtual LANs (VLANs). A VLAN is a group of switch ports, within a single or multiple switches, that is defined by the switch hardware and/or software as a single broadcast domain. A VLAN's goal is to group devices connected to a switch into logical broadcast domains to control the effect that broadcasts have on other connected devices. A VLAN can be characterized as a logical network.

The benefits of VLANs include the following:

- Security
- Segmentation
- Flexibility

VLANs enable you to group users into a common broadcast domain regardless of their physical location in the internetwork. Creating VLANs improves performance and security in the switched network by controlling broadcast propagation and requiring that communications between these broadcast be carried out by a Layer 3 device that is capable of implementing security features such as access control lists (ACLs).

In a broadcast environment, a broadcast sent out by a host on a single segment would propagate to all segments. In normal network operation, hosts frequently generate broadcast/multicast traffic. If hundreds or thousands of hosts each sent this type of traffic, it would saturate the bandwidth of the entire network, as shown in Figure 3-1. Also, without forcing some method of checking at an upper layer, all devices in the broadcast domain would be able to communicate via Layer 2. This severely limits the amount of security you can enforce on the network.

Figure 3-1 *Broadcast Propagation*

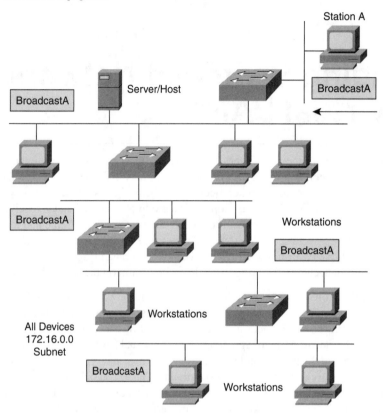

Before the introduction of switches and VLANs, internetworks were divided into multiple broadcast domains by connectivity through a router. Because routers do not forward broadcasts, each interface is in a different broadcast domain. Figure 3-2 shows an internetwork broken into multiple broadcast domains using routers. Notice that each segment is an individual IP subnet and that regardless of a workstation's function, its subnet is defined by its physical location.

A VLAN is a logical broadcast domain that can span multiple physical LAN segments. A VLAN can be designed to provide independent broadcast domains for stations logically segmented by functions, project teams, or applications, without regard to the users' physical location. Each switch port can be assigned to only one VLAN. Ports in a VLAN share broadcasts. Ports that do not belong to the same VLAN do not share broadcasts. This control of broadcast improves the internetwork's overall performance.

VLANs enable switches to create multiple broadcast domains within a switched environment, as illustrated in Figure 3-3.

Figure 3-2   *Multiple Broadcast Domains Using Routers*

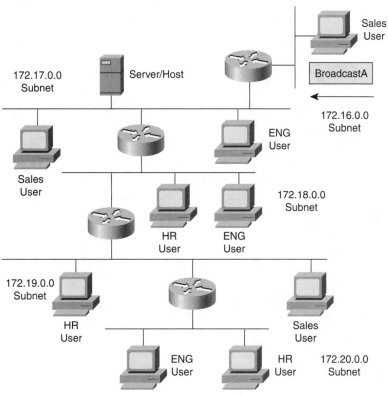

Notice that now all users in a given group (department in this example) are defined to be in the same VLAN. Any user in this VLAN receives a broadcast from any other member of the VLAN, while users of other VLANs do not receive these broadcasts. Each of the users in a given VLAN is also in the same IP subnet. This is different from the broadcast domains of Figure 3-2, in which the physical location of the device determines the broadcast domain. However, there is a similarity with a legacy, non-VLAN internetwork because a router is still needed to get from one broadcast domain to another, even if a VLAN is used to define the broadcast domain instead of a physical location. Therefore, the creation of VLANs does not eliminate the need for routers.

Within the switched internetwork, VLANs provide segmentation and organizational flexibility. Using VLAN technology, you can group switch ports and their connected users into logically defined communities of interest, such as coworkers in the same department, a cross-functional product team, or diverse user groups sharing the same network application.

A VLAN can exist on a single switch or span multiple switches. VLANs can include stations in a single building or multiple-building infrastructures. In rare and special cases, they can even connect across wide-area networks (WANs).

Figure 3-3   *VLAN Overview*

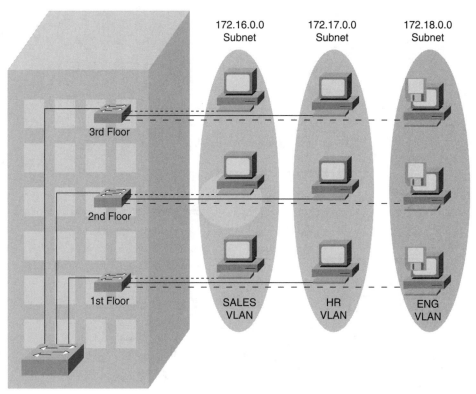

VLAN Concepts

As mentioned previously, prior to the VLAN, the only way to control broadcast traffic was through segmentation using routers. VLANs are an extension of a switched and routed internetwork. By having the ability to place segments (ports) in individual broadcast domains, you can control where a given broadcast is forwarded. The sections that follow expand on these concepts. Basically, each switch acts independently of other switches in the network. With the concept of VLANs, a level of interdependence is built into the switches themselves. The characteristics of a typical VLAN setup are as follows:

- Each logical VLAN is like a separate physical bridge.
- VLANs can span multiple switches.
- Trunk links carry traffic for multiple VLANs.

With VLANs, each switch can distinguish traffic from different broadcast domains. Each forwarding decision is based on which VLAN the packet came from; therefore, each VLAN acts like an individual bridge within a switch. To bridge/switch between switches, you must either connect each VLAN independently (that is, dedicate a port per VLAN) or have some method of maintaining and forwarding the VLAN information with the packets. A process called *trunking* allows this single connection. Figure 3-4 illustrates a typical VLAN setup in which multiple VLANs span two switches interconnected by a Fast Ethernet trunk.

Figure 3-4   *Multiple VLANs Can Span Multiple Switches*

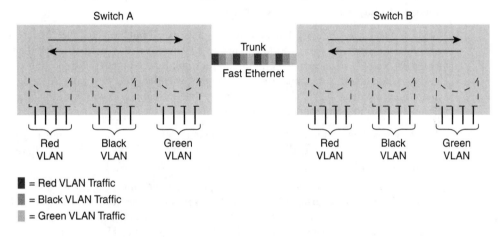

How VLANs Operate

A Catalyst switch operates in your network like a traditional bridge. Each VLAN configured on the switch implements address learning, forwarding/filtering decisions, and loop avoidance mechanisms as if it were a separate physical bridge. This VLAN might include several ports, possibly on multiple switches.

Internally, the Catalyst switch implements VLANs by restricting data forwarding to destination ports in the same VLAN as originating ports. In other words, when a frame arrives on a switch port, the Catalyst must retransmit the frame only to a port that belongs to the same VLAN as that of the incoming port. The implication is that a VLAN operating on a Catalyst switch limits transmission of unicast, multicast, and broadcast traffic. Flooded traffic originating from a particular VLAN floods out only other ports belonging to that VLAN. Each VLAN is an individual broadcast domain because a broadcast in a given VLAN will never reach any ports in other VLANs.

Normally, a port carries traffic only for the single VLAN to which it belongs. For a VLAN to span multiple switches on a single connection, a trunk is required to connect two switches. A trunk carries traffic for all VLANs by identifying the originating VLAN as the frame is carried between the switches. Figure 3-4 shows a Fast Ethernet trunk carrying multiple VLANs between the two switches. Most ports on Catalyst switches are capable of being trunk ports. Any port on a Catalyst 2950 can be a trunk port.

VLAN Membership Modes

VLANs are a Layer 2 implementation in your network's switching topology. Because they are implemented at the data link layer, they are protocol-independent. To put a given port (segment) into a VLAN, you must create a VLAN on the switch and then assign that port membership on the switch. After you define a port to a given VLAN, broadcast, multicast, and unicast traffic from that segment will be forwarded by the switches only to ports in the same VLAN. If you need to communicate between VLANs, you must add a router (or Layer 3 switch) and a Layer 3 protocol to your network.

The ports on a Layer 2 Catalyst switch, such as a 2950, all function as Layer 2 ports. In Cisco IOS Software, a Layer 2 port is known as a *switchport*. A switchport can either be a member of a single VLAN or be configured as a trunk link to carry traffic for multiple VLANs. When a port is in a single VLAN, the port is called an *access port*. Access ports are configured with a VLAN membership mode that determines to which VLAN they can belong. The membership modes follow:

- **Static**—When an administrator assigns a single VLAN to a port, it is called *static assignment*. By default, all Layer 2 switchports are statically assigned to VLAN 1 until an administrator changes this default configuration.

- **Dynamic**—The IOS Catalyst switch supports the dynamic assignment of a single VLAN to a port by using a VLAN Membership Policy Server (VMPS). The VMPS must be a Catalyst Operating System switch, such as a Catalyst 5500 or 6500, running the set-based operating system. An IOS-based Catalyst switch cannot operate as the VMPS. The VMPS contains a database that maps MAC addresses to VLAN assignment. When a frame arrives on a dynamic port, the switch queries the VMPS for the VLAN assignment based on the arriving frame's source MAC address.

A dynamic port can belong to only one VLAN at a time. Multiple hosts can be active on a dynamic port only if they all belong to the same VLAN. Figure 3-5 demonstrates the static and dynamic VLAN membership modes.

Figure 3-5   *VLAN Membership Modes*

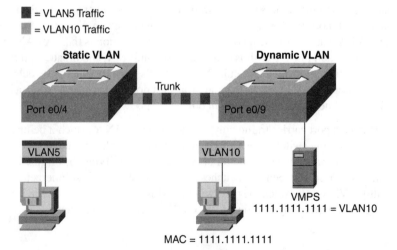

For an access port, the VLAN identity is not known by the sender or receiver attached to the access port. Frames going into and out of access ports are standard Ethernet frames, as discussed in Chapter 2, "Configuring Catalyst Switch Operations." The VLAN identity is used only within the switch to provide broadcast domain boundaries.

Trunk Links

A broadcast domain must sometimes exist on more than one switch in the network. To accomplish this, one switch must send frames to another switch and indicate which VLAN a particular frame belongs to. On Cisco switches, a *trunk link* is created to accomplish this VLAN identification. ISL and IEEE 802.1Q are different methods of putting a VLAN identifier in a Layer 2 frame.

A trunk link is the other type of Layer 2 port supported on Cisco switches. When a trunk port is configured, it begins marking frames as they exit the port to indicate which VLAN each frame is associated with. The trunk port can also read the markings, called tags, as they enter the trunk port. This enables the switch to send a frame only to the ports for the given VLAN associated with the incoming frame.

The main purpose of trunking is to carry traffic between switches and maintain the VLAN information. Unlike an access link, the trunk link does not belong to a single VLAN but instead can carry traffic from several VLANs over a point-to-point link between two devices that understand the protocol. Because a trunk is typically a point-to-point connection between two switches, it is very efficient and highly recommended that it runs in full-duplex mode. Figure 3-6 shows trunk links between switches carrying traffic for multiple VLANS.

Figure 3-6   *Trunking*

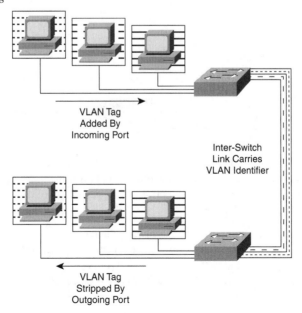

VLAN Tag
Added By
Incoming Port

Inter-Switch
Link Carries
VLAN Identifier

VLAN Tag
Stripped By
Outgoing Port

Two forms of trunking are used for Cisco switches on Ethernet networks:

- An IEEE industry standard called IEEE 802.1Q. This is a frame-tagging mechanism that adds a VLAN identifier to the frame by inserting a tag at Layer 2.

- Another form of trunking on Cisco switches is called Inter-Switch Link (ISL), which is a Cisco proprietary trunking mechanism. ISL uses a frame encapsulation method that adds a header to identify the VLAN.

802.1Q Trunking

The IEEE 802.1Q protocol interconnects VLANs between multiple switches, routers, and servers. With 802.1Q, a network administrator can define a VLAN topology to span multiple physical devices. If you examine Figure 3-6, you can see that VLANs 1, 2, and 3 are physically attached to different switches; however, because the trunk link carries traffic for all of these VLANs, all the users in a given VLAN are in the same broadcast domain.

Cisco switches support IEEE 802.1Q for FastEthernet and GigabitEthernet interfaces. An 802.1Q trunk link provides VLAN identification by adding a 4-byte tag to an Ethernet Frame as it leaves a trunk port. Because the frame has been changed, a new frame check sequence (FCS) must also be computed and added to the frame. Figure 3-7 shows a frame entering an access port and leaving a trunk port with a tag.

NOTE   On Cisco switches, 802.1Q is usually referred to as *dot1Q* after the IEEE standard number.

Figure 3-7   *802.1Q Frame Tagging*

The 4-byte tag is inserted into the frame immediately following the source address field and is composed of two separate 2-byte sections—the Tag Protocol ID (TPID) field and the Tag Control Information (TCI) field.

The TPID field, for Ethernet frames, is always the hexadecimal value 8100 (0x8100). You might recall from Chapter 2 that any value over 05DC following the source address is an Ethertype field. The value 0x8100 tells an 802.1Q-compliant device that this is a tagged frame and to use the next 2 bytes for 802.1Q information.

In the next 2-byte TCI field, the first 3 bits of the TCI are referred to as the Priority bits. These bits indicate the priority of the frame for quality of service (QoS) reasons. For example, an IP telephone will mark any voice traffic with a priority of 5, indicating to a switch running QoS that the frame should be sent through the network as fast as possible. In some implementations, the priority bits are the information in the TCI that are most important to the user. For this reason, 802.1Q is sometimes referred to as 802.1p. These are the same frames with an emphasis on different part of the TCI.

The next bit in the TCI field is called a Canonical Format Identifier (CFI). This is a 1-bit field that, when off, indicates that the device should read the information in a field canonically (right-to-left or low-order bits first). The reason for this bit is that 802.1Q can be used for Token Ring or Ethernet frames. An Ethernet device reads canonically, but Token Ring devices read in a noncanonical form. For an Ethernet frame, this value will always be 0, but if the tag is in a Token Ring frame, it will be 1. For this reason, the CFI is sometimes referred to as the *Token Ring Encapsulation Flag*.

The last 12 bits in the CFI are the VLAN ID. This allows for the identification of 4096 unique VLANs. Figure 3-8 shows the components of the 802.1Q tag.

Figure 3-8   *802.1Q Tag Components*

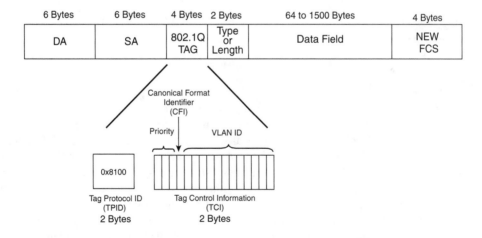

With 802.1Q, a trunk link can tag frames between devices that understand the protocol. This allows for multiple VLANs to exist on a single topology. Because 802.1Q is defined as a type of Ethernet frame, it does not require that every device on a link speaks the 802.1Q protocol. Because Ethernet is a shared media and more than two device could be connected on this media, all devices on the link must still be capable of communicating even if they do not speak the 802.1Q protocol. For this reason, 802.1Q also defines a Native VLAN. A trunk port on a switch is defined to be in a Native VLAN, and the 802.1Q trunk will not tag frames that are going out the port that came in on any port that belongs to the same VLAN

that is the Native VLAN on the switch. Any Ethernet device would be capable of reading frames for the Native VLANs. The Native VLAN is important on an 802.1Q trunk link. If both sides of the link do not agree on the Native VLAN, the trunk will not operate properly. Figure 3-9 shows how frames on the Native VLAN are not tagged out trunk links.

Figure 3-9   *Native VLAN*

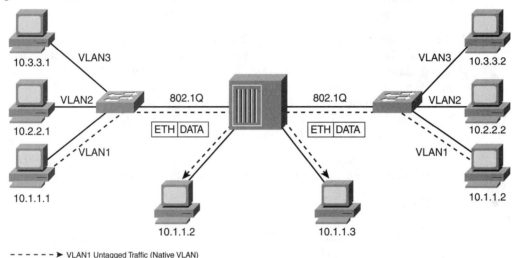

- - - - - - ▶ VLAN1 Untagged Traffic (Native VLAN)

Inter-Switch Links

Inter-Switch Link (ISL) tagging accomplishes the same task as 802.1Q trunking but uses a different frame format. ISL trunks are Cisco proprietary and define only a point-to-point connection between two devices, typically switches. The name *Inter-Switch Link* hints at this design. ISL frame tagging uses a low-latency mechanism for multiplexing traffic from multiple VLANs on a single physical path. ISL has been implemented for connections among switches, routers, and network interface cards (NICs) used on nodes such as servers. To support the ISL feature, each connecting device must be ISL-configured. A router that is ISL-configured can allow inter-VLAN communications. A non-ISL device that receives ISL-encapsulated Ethernet frames will most likely consider them protocol errors because of the format and size of the frames.

ISL functions at Layer 2 of the OSI model like 802.1Q, but it differs by encapsulating the entire Layer 2 Ethernet frame inside an ISL header and trailer. Because ISL encapsulates the entire frame, it is protocol-independent and can carry any type of Layer 2 frame or upper-layer protocol between the switches. ISL has the following characteristics:

- Performed with application-specific integrated circuits (ASIC)
- Not intrusive to client stations; client does not see the ISL header
- Effective between switches, routers and switches, and switches and servers with ISL NICs

The following section addresses ISL tagging and ISL encapsulation.

ISL Encapsulation

ISL functions at OSI Layer 2 by encapsulating a data frame with a new (ISL) header and an additional (ISL) cyclic redundancy check (CRC). ISL-encapsulated frames are passed over trunk lines. ISL is protocol-independent because the data frame might carry any data-link protocol.

Ports configured as ISL trunks encapsulate each frame with a 26-byte ISL header and a 4-byte CRC before sending it out the trunk port. Because ISL technology is implemented in ASICs, frames are tagged with low latency. The ISL header supports 10 bits for ISL identification. Each bit can be one of two values, 2^{10}, allowing for the 1024 unique VLANs. The number of actual VLANs supported by a switch depends on the switch hardware. Figure 3-10 illustrates a typical ISL-encapsulated data frame.

Figure 3-10   *ISL Encapsulation*

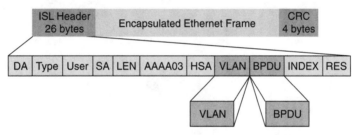

As illustrated in Figure 3-10, the ISL frame header contains the following information fields:

- **DA**—40-bit multicast destination address.
- **Type**—4-bit descriptor of the encapsulated frame types—Ethernet (0000), Token Ring (0001), FDDI (0010), and ATM (0011).
- **User**—4-bit descriptor used as the type field extension or to define Ethernet priorities. This is a binary value from 0, the lowest priority, to 3, the highest priority.
- **SA**—48-bit source MAC address of the transmitting Catalyst switch.
- **LEN**—16-bit frame-length descriptor minus DA type, user, SA, LEN, and CRC.
- **AAAA03**—Standard SNAP 802.2 LLC header.
- **HSA**—First 3 bytes of SA (manufacturer's ID or organizational unique ID).
- **VLAN**—15-bit VLAN ID. Only the lower 10 bits are used for 1024 VLANs.
- **BPDU**—1-bit descriptor identifying whether the frame is a Spanning Tree bridge protocol data unit (BPDU). Also set if the encapsulated frame is a Cisco Discovery Protocol (CDP) frame.

- **INDEX** — 16-bit descriptor that identifies the transmitting port ID. Used for diagnostics.

- **RES** — 16-bit reserved field used for additional information, such as Token Ring and Fiber Distributed Data Interface (FDDI) frame Frame Check (FC) field.

VLAN Trunking Protocol

To provide VLAN connectivity throughout the switched network, VLANs must be configured on each switch. If you are going to trunk VLAN10 from Switch A to Switch C through Switch B, as shown in Figure 3-11, VLAN10 must exist on Switch B even though none of the access ports on that switch are in VLAN10.

Figure 3-11 *Purpose for VTP*

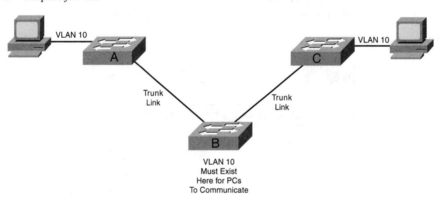

To ensure that a VLAN exists between every pair of Trunked switches, an administrator must manually create all the needed VLANs on each of the switches individually. Cisco's VLAN Trunking Protocol (VTP) provides an easier method for maintaining consistent VLAN configuration throughout the switched network.

VTP is a protocol used to distribute and synchronize identifying information about VLANs configured throughout a switched network. Configurations made to a single VTP server are propagated across trunk links to all connected switches in the network. VTP enables switched network solutions to scale to large sizes by reducing the network's manual configuration needs.

VTP is a Layer 2 messaging protocol that maintains VLAN configuration consistency throughout a common administrative domain by managing the additions, deletions, and name changes of VLANs across networks. VTP minimizes misconfigurations and configuration inconsistencies that can cause problems, such as duplicate VLAN names or incorrect VLAN-type specifications.

A VTP domain is one switch or several interconnected switches sharing the same VTP environment. A switch can be configured only in one VTP domain.

By default, a Catalyst switch is in the no-management-domain (or null domain) state until it is configured with a domain or receives an advertisement for a domain over a trunk link. Configuration changes made to the VLANs on a single VTP server switch are propagated across Trunk links to all trunk-connected switches in the network.

Figure 3-12 illustrates how VLAN configuration information is propagated from switch to switch.

Figure 3-12   *VTP Operation*

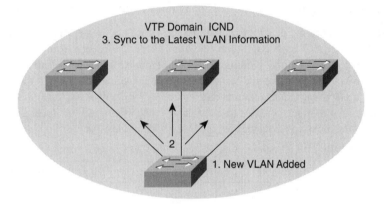

Figure 3-12 shows a VLAN added to the switched network. The steps illustrated in the figure are as follows:

1 A new VLAN is added. At this point, VTP makes your job easier.

2 The VTP advertisement is sent to the other switches in the VTP domain.

3 The new VLAN is added to the other switch configurations. The result is consistent VLAN configuration.

VTP Modes

VTP operates in one of three modes:

- Server mode
- Client mode
- Transparent mode

The default VTP mode is server mode, but VLANs are not propagated over the network until a management domain name is specified or learned and trunking has been established.

A Catalyst switch operating in the VTP server mode can create, modify, and delete VLANs and other configuration parameters for the entire VTP domain. In server mode, VLAN configurations are saved in the Catalyst nonvolatile random-access memory (NVRAM). When you make a change to the VLAN configuration on a VTP server, the change is propagated to all switches in the VTP domain. VTP messages are transmitted out all trunk connections, such as ISL.

A device operating as a VTP client cannot create, change, or delete VLANs. A switch in client mode does send VTP messages, however. A VTP client does not save VLAN configurations in nonvolatile memory.

In both client and server mode, the switches synchronize their VLAN configuration to that of the switch with the highest revision number in the VTP domain.

A switch operating in VTP transparent mode does not create VTP advertisements or synchronize its VLAN configuration with information received from other switches in the management domain. A switch in transparent mode forwards VTP advertisements received from other switches that are part of the same management domain. A switch configured in VTP transparent mode can create, delete, and modify VLANs, but the changes are not transmitted to other switches in the domain; they affect only the local switch. Table 3-1 offers a comparative overview of the three VTP modes.

Table 3-1   *VTP Modes*

Server Mode	Client Mode	Transparent Mode
Sends/forwards VTP advertisements.	Sends/forwards VTP advertisements.	Forwards VTP advertisements.
Synchronizes VLAN configuration information with other switches.	Synchronizes VLAN configuration information with other switches.	*Does not* synchronize VLAN configuration information with other switches.
VLAN configurations are saved in NVRAM.	VLAN configurations *are not* saved in NVRAM.	VLAN configurations are saved in NVRAM.
Catalyst switch can create VLANs.	Catalyst switch *cannot* create VLANs.	Catalyst switch can create VLANs.
Catalyst switch can modify VLANs.	Catalyst switch *cannot* modify VLANs.	Catalyst switch can modify VLANs.
Catalyst switch can delete VLANs.	Catalyst switch *cannot* delete VLANs.	Catalyst switch can delete VLANs.

When setting up VTP on a switch, choosing the appropriate mode is important. Because VTP is a simple and dangerous tool, it can overwrite VLAN configurations on some switches and create network problems. The next section further explains this phenomenon. Nevertheless, you must be aware that the mode you choose can eliminate the chance of these problems:

- Choose server mode for the switch that you will use to create, change, or delete VLANs. The server will propagate this information to other switches that are configured as servers or clients.

- Set client mode on any switch where you do not want to create, change, or delete VLANS.

- Use transparent mode on a switch that needs to pass VTP advertisements to other switches but also needs the capability to have its VLANs independently administered.

How VTP Works

VTP advertisements are flooded throughout the management domain every five minutes or whenever a change occurs in VLAN configurations. VTP advertisements are sent over a factory default VLAN (VLAN 1) using multicast frames. Included in a VTP advertisement is a configuration revision number. A higher configuration revision number indicates that the VLAN information being advertised is more current than the stored information.

A device that receives VTP advertisements must check various parameters before incorporating the received VLAN information.

First, the management domain name and the password, which can be configured to prevent unauthorized switches from altering the VTP domain, must match those configured in the local switch before information can be used.

Next, if the configuration revision number indicates that the message was created after the configuration currently in use, the switch overwrites its VLAN database with the advertised VLAN information. To reset the configuration revision number on a Catalyst switch, you must either change the switch mode to transparent then back to server or client with the command **vtp mode** [**server** I **client** I **transparent**] in global configuration mode, or change the VTP domain name and then set it back using the command **vtp domain** *name* in global configuration mode. Example 3-1 demonstrates changing the mode and then setting it back to reset the configuration revision number. The command **show vtp status** is executed before and after the change to show the configuration number being reset.

Example 3-1   *Resetting a Switches VTP Configuration Revision Number*

```
Switch#show vtp status
VTP Version                      : 2
Configuration Revision           : 5
Maximum VLANs supported locally  : 250
Number of existing VLANs         : 10
VTP Operating Mode               : Server
VTP Domain Name                  : switch_domain_1
VTP Pruning Mode                 : Disabled
```

continues

Example 3-1   *Resetting a Switches VTP Configuration Revision Number (Continued)*

```
VTP V2 Mode                        : Disabled
VTP Traps Generation               : Disabled
MD5 digest                         : 0x1E 0xED 0x19 0x49 0x0F 0x37 0x65 0x64
Configuration last modified by 192.168.255.21 at 3-1-93 00:02:39
Local updater ID is 192.168.255.21 on interface Vl1 (lowest numbered VLAN interface
found)
Switch#config t
P2_2950(config)#vtp mode transparent
Setting device to VTP TRANSPARENT mode.
Switch(config)#vtp mode server
Setting device to VTP SERVER mode
Switch(config)#end

Switch#show vtp status
VTP Version                        : 2
Configuration Revision             : 0
Maximum VLANs supported locally    : 250
Number of existing VLANs           : 10
VTP Operating Mode                 : Server
VTP Domain Name                    : switch_domain_1
VTP Pruning Mode                   : Disabled
VTP V2 Mode                        : Disabled
VTP Traps Generation               : Disabled
MD5 digest                         : 0x1E 0xED 0x19 0x49 0x0F 0x37 0x65 0x64
Configuration last modified by 192.168.255.21 at 3-1-93 00:02:39
Local updater ID is 192.168.255.21 on interface Vl1 (lowest numbered VLAN interface
found)
```

NOTE   Underscores are used in the VTP domain name because a domain name cannot contain spaces.

One of the most critical components of VTP is the configuration revision number. Each time a VTP server modifies its VLAN information, it increments the configuration revision number by one. The VTP server then sends out a VTP advertisement with the new configuration revision number. If the configuration revision number being advertised is higher than the number stored on the other switches in the VTP domain, the other switches will overwrite their VLAN configurations with the new information being advertised. The configuration revision number in VTP transparent mode is always 0. Figure 3-13 illustrates how VTP operates in a switched network.

CAUTION   The overwrite process would mean that the VTP server with the highest revision number determines the overall VLAN configuration for the domain. For example, if you deleted all VLANs on a VTP server and that server had the higher revision number, the other devices in the VTP domain would also delete their VLANs. This could create a loss of connectivity.

Figure 3-13 *VTP Operation*

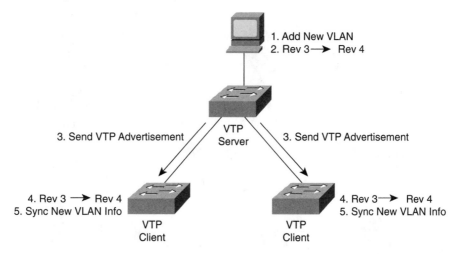

VTP Pruning

Because ISL trunk lines carry VLAN traffic for all VLANs by default, some traffic might be needlessly flooded across links that do not need to carry that traffic. VTP pruning uses VLAN advertisements to determine when a trunk connection is flooding traffic needlessly.

By default, a trunk connection carries traffic for all VLANs in the VTP management domain. Often, some switches in an enterprise network do not have local ports configured in each VLAN. In Figure 3-14, Switches 1 and 4 support ports statically configured in VLAN10. As illustrated, with VTP pruning enabled, when Station A sends a broadcast, the broadcast is flooded only toward any switch with ports assigned to VLAN10. As a result, broadcast traffic from Station A is not forwarded to Switches 3, 5, and 6 because traffic for VLAN10 has been pruned on the links indicated on Switches 2 and 4. Pruning must be enabled on one VTP server, and it will be propagated to all other switches in the VTP domain.

VTP pruning increases available bandwidth by restricting flooded traffic to those trunk links that the traffic must use to access the appropriate network devices.

NOTE   Because VLAN1 is the management VLAN and is used for administrative functions such as VTP advertisements, it will not be pruned from a trunk line by VTP pruning.

Figure 3-14 *VTP Pruning*

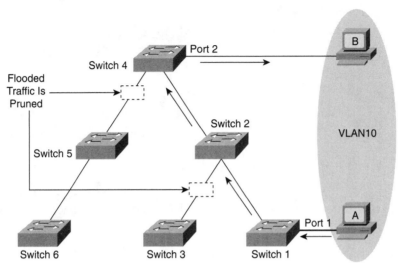

Per-VLAN Spanning Tree

One of the things that must be considered with VLANs is the function of the Spanning Tree Protocol (STP). STP is designed to prevent loops in a switch/bridged topology to eliminate the endless propagation of broadcast around the loop. With VLANs, there are multiple broadcast domains to be considered. Because each broadcast domain is like a unique bridged internetwork, you must consider how STP will operate.

The 802.1Q standard defines one unique Spanning Tree instance to be used by all VLANs in the network. STP runs on the Native VLAN so that it can communicate with both 802.1Q and non-802.1Q compatible switches. This single instance of STP is often referred to as 802.1Q Mono Spanning Tree or Common Spanning Tree (CST). A single spanning tree lacks flexibility in how the links are used in the network topology. Cisco implements a protocol known as Per-VLAN Spanning Tree Plus (PVST+) that is compatible with 802.1Q CST but allows a separate spanning tree to be constructed for each VLAN. There is only one active path for each spanning tree; however, in a Cisco network, the active path can be different for each VLAN.

NOTE The term Mono Spanning Tree is typically not used anymore because the IEEE 802.1s standard has now defined a Multiple Spanning Tree (MST) protocol that uses the same acronym.

Because a trunk link carries traffic for more than one broadcast domain and switches are typically connected together via trunk links, it is possible to define multiple Spanning Tree topologies for a given network. With PVST+, a root bridge and STP topology can be defined for each VLAN. This is accomplished by exchanging BPDUs for each VLAN operating on the switches. By configuring a different root or port cost based on VLANs, switches could utilize all the links to pass traffic without creating a bridge loop. Using PVST+, administrators can use ISL or 802.1Q to maintain redundant links and load balance traffic between parallel links using the Spanning Tree Protocol. Figure 3-15 shows an example of load balancing using PVST+.

Figure 3-15 *PVST Load Balancing*

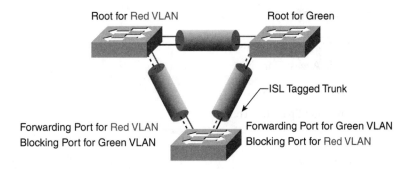

Cisco developed PVST+ to allow running several STP instances, even over an 802.1Q network by using a tunneling mechanism. PVST+ utilizes Cisco devices to connect to a Mono Spanning Tree zone, typically another vendor's 802.1Q-based network, to a PVST+ zone, typically a Cisco ISL-based network. No specific configuration is needed to achieve this. PVST+ provides support for 802.1Q trunks and the mapping of multiple spanning trees to the single spanning tree of standard 802.1Q switches running Mono Spanning Tree.

The PVST+ architecture distinguishes three types of regions:

- A PVST region (PVST switches using ISL only)
- A PVST+ region (PVST+ using ISL and/or 802.1Q between Cisco switches)
- A Mono Spanning Tree region (Common or Mono Spanning Tree using 802.1Q and exchanging BPDUs on the Native VLAN only between a Cisco and Non-Cisco switches using 802.1Q)

Each region consists of a homogenous type of switch. You can connect a PVST region to a PVST+ region using ISL ports. You can also connect a PVST+ region to a Mono Spanning Tree region using 802.1Q ports.

At the boundary between a PVST region and a PVST+ region, the mapping of Spanning Tree is one-to-one. At the boundary between a Mono Spanning Tree region and a PVST+ region, the Spanning Tree in the Mono Spanning Tree region maps to one PVST in the PVST+ region. The one it maps to is the CST. The CST is the PVST of the Native VLAN (VLAN 1 by default).

On a 802.1Q trunk, BPDUs can be sent or received only by the Native VLAN. Using PVST+, Cisco can send its PVST BPDUs as tagged frames using a Cisco multicast address as the destination. When a non-Cisco switch receives the multicast, it is flooded (but not interpreted as a BPDU, thus maintaining the integrity of CST). Because it is flooded, it will eventually reach Cisco switches on the other side of the CST domain. This allows the PVST fames to be tunneled through the MST region. Tunneling means that the BPDUs are flooded through the Mono Spanning Tree region along the single spanning tree present in the Mono Spanning Tree region.

PVST+ networks must be in a tree-like structure for proper STP operation.

Section 1 Quiz

1 Which of the following are valid Layer 2 (switchport) types?

   A Static Access Port

   B Trunk Port

   C Common Spanning Tree Port

   D Root Port

   E Dynamic Access Port

2 True or False: A Catalyst 2950 cannot act as a VMPS server and it cannot have ports with dynamically assigned VLANs.

3 VLANs provide which of the following? (Choose all that apply.)

   A Security

   B Redundancy

   C Segmentation

   D Loop prevention

   E Collision domains

   F Flexibility

   G All of the above

4 How many bytes of overhead are added to a frame for 802.1Q frame tagging and ISL frame tagging?

   A 4 bytes ISL & 30 bytes 802.1Q

   B 8 bytes ISL & 26 bytes 802.1Q

   C 26 bytes ISL & 4 bytes 802.1Q

D   30 bytes ISL & 8 bytes 802.1Q

E   30 bytes ISL & 4 bytes 802.1Q

F   None. The frame tagging is performed in Hardware ASICs.

5   Which of the following is true for VTP? (Choose the best answers.)

A   VTP is required for proper VLAN operation.

B   VTP eases VLAN creation for a switched network.

C   Changes need to be made to only one VTP server in a domain.

D   A switch in VTP transparent mode will increment its configuration revision number but will not synchronize with other switches.

E   VTP will run only across trunk links.

F   VTP requires a domain name to operate.

G   The default VTP domain name for all Catalyst switches is Cisco.

H   VTP is completely safe and will never cause problems in your network.

VLAN Configuration

This section discusses the guidelines for configuring VLANs on the Catalyst switch. You will learn the steps to configure VLANs, how to enable VTP domains, how to define a trunk, how to create a VLAN, and how to verify proper VLAN operation.

You should remember several facts before you begin VLAN configuration:

* The maximum number of VLANs that can operate on a switch is switch-dependent.
* VLAN1 is one of the factory default VLANs.
* Cisco Discovery Protocol (CDP) and VTP advertisements are sent on VLAN1.
* The switch must be in VTP server mode or transparent mode to create, add, or delete VLANs.

VLAN Configuration Guidelines

The Catalyst switches have a factory default configuration in which various default VLANs are preconfigured. One of the default VLANs is VLAN1, which is used for CDP and VTP advertisements. The VLAN1 interface on a switch is also in the default VLAN1. As you'll recall, the switch requires an IP address for management purposes—for example, to allow Telnet connections into the switch, or to use the Visual Switch Manager (VSM) via an HTTP browser to configure the switch.

Before you can create a VLAN, the switch must be in VTP server mode or VTP transparent mode. If you want to propagate the VLAN to other switches in the domain, use server mode.

VLAN Configuration Steps

Before you create VLANs, you must decide whether to use VTP to maintain global VLAN configuration information for your network.

To allow VLANs to span multiple Catalyst switches on a single link, you must configure trunks to interconnect the switches.

By default, a switch is in VTP server mode so that VLANs can be added, changed, or deleted. If the switch is set to VTP client mode, VLANs cannot be added, changed, or deleted from that switch.

VLAN membership on the switch ports is assigned manually on a port-by-port basis. When you assign switch ports to VLANs using this method, it is known as port-based, or static, VLAN membership.

The following sections elaborate on the details of the steps to configure VLANs.

VTP Configuration Guidelines

The default VTP configuration parameters for the Catalyst switch are as follows:

- VTP domain name: None
- VTP mode: Server
- VTP password: None
- VTP pruning: Disabled
- VTP trap: Disabled

The VTP domain name can be specified by the administrator or learned across a configured trunk line from a server with a domain name configured. By default, the domain name is not set.

By default, the switch is set to the VTP server mode.

A password can be set for the VTP management domain. The password entered must be the same for all switches in the domain. If you configure a VTP password, VTP does not function properly unless you assign the same password to each switch in the domain.

VTP pruning eligibility is one VLAN parameter advertised by the VTP protocol. Enabling or disabling VTP pruning on a VTP server propagates the change throughout the management domain. Enabling or disabling VTP pruning on a VTP server affects the entire management domain.

VTP trap is disabled by default. If you enable this feature, it causes an SNMP message to be generated every time a new VTP message is sent.

CAUTION   When adding a new switch to an existing domain, you should verify that the configuration revision number for the switch is 0 to prevent the new switch from propagating incorrect VLAN information. Example 3-1, in the "How VTP Works" section, demonstrated one method for resetting the VTP configuration revision number on the new switch.

Configuring VTP

Use the **vtp** global configuration command to specify the operating mode, domain name, password, generation of traps, and pruning capabilities of VTP. The syntax for this command is as follows:

```
switch(config)# vtp { [mode {server | transparent | client}] [domain domain-name]
    [password password] [pruning {enable | disable}]}
```

To verify a recent configuration change, or to just view the VTP configuration information, use the **show vtp status** privileged EXEC command, as demonstrated in Example 3-2. Also displayed is the IP address of the device that last modified the configuration and a time stamp showing when the modification was made. VTP has two versions:

- VTP version 1 only supports Ethernet.
- VTP version 2 supports Ethernet and Token Ring.

Example 3-2   **show vtp status** *Output*

```
Switch#show vtp status
VTP Version                   : 2
Configuration Revision        : 5
Maximum VLANs supported locally : 250
Number of existing VLANs      : 10
VTP Operating Mode            : Server
VTP Domain Name               : switch_domain_1
VTP Pruning Mode              : Disabled
VTP V2 Mode                   : Disabled
VTP Traps Generation          : Disabled
MD5 digest                    : 0x1E 0xED 0x19 0x49 0x0F 0x37 0x65 0x64
Configuration last modified by 192.168.255.21 at 3-1-93 00:02:39
Local updater ID is 192.168.255.21 on interface Vl1 (lowest numbered
  VLAN interface found)
```

Trunk Line Configuration

Use the command **switchport mode trunk** at the interface configuration mode to set a port to trunk. On the Catalyst 2950, this enables 802.1Q trunking. On other Cisco IOS Software-based switches, such as the 3550, 4500, or 6500, you will need to choose an encapsulation method before you can enable trunking. The command **switchport trunk encapsulation** [**isl** | **dot1q**] chooses an encapsulation mode.

The Catalyst IOS switches also support Dynamic Trunking Protocol (DTP), which manages automatic trunk negotiation. The **switchport mode** command specifies a Layer 2 ports operation:

```
switch(config-if)# switchport mode [trunk | access | dynamic
  [desirable | auto | nonegotiate]]
```

The options for the **switchport mode** command are as follows:

- **trunk**—Configures the port to permanent trunk mode and negotiates with the connected device on the other side to convert the link to trunk mode. If multiple trunk encapsulations are available, the encapsulation must be chosen before this command will work.

- **access**—Disables port trunk mode and negotiates with the connected device to convert the link to nontrunk. This port will belong to only the configured access VLAN.

- **dynamic desirable**—Triggers the port to negotiate the link from nontrunk to trunk mode. The port negotiates to a trunk port if the connected device is in the **trunk, dynamic desirable**, or **dynamic auto** state. Otherwise, the port becomes a nontrunk port. This is the default for IOS switch ports

- **dynamic auto**—Enables the port to become a trunk only if the connected device has the state set to **trunk** or **dynamic desirable**.

- **nonnegotiate**—Configures the port to permanent trunk mode. No negotiation takes place with the partner. The other side must be **trunk** or **nonegotiate** for the trunk to work. You must also specify the encapsulation before choosing this mode.

Verifying Trunk Line Configuration

To verify a trunk configuration, use the command **show interface switchport** or **show interface trunk** privileged EXEC command. The syntax for the **show interface switchport** and privileged EXEC command is as follows:

```
switch(config)# show interface [type module/port] switchport
```

The syntax for the **show interface trunk** and privileged EXEC command is as follows:

```
switch(config)# show interface [type module/port] trunk
```

These commands display the trunk parameters, as demonstrated in Example 3-3.

Example 3-3 **show interface trunk** *and* **show interface switchport** *Output*

```
Switch#show interface trunk

Port      Mode        Encapsulation  Status     Native vlan
Fa0/1     on          802.1q         trunking   1
Gi0/1     on          802.1q         trunking   1


Port      Vlans allowed on trunk
```

Example 3-3   show interface trunk *and* show interface switchport *Output (Continued)*

```
Fa0/1      1-4094
Gi0/1      1-4094

Port       Vlans allowed and active in management domain
Fa0/1      1,101,202,303,404,505
Gi0/1      1,101,202,303,404,505

Port       Vlans in spanning tree forwarding state and not pruned
Fa0/1      1,101,202,303,404,505
Gi0/1      1,101,202,303,404,505

Switch#show interfaces fastEthernet 0/1 switchport
Name: Fa0/1
Switchport: Enabled
Administrative Mode: trunk
Operational Mode: trunk
Administrative Trunking Encapsulation: dot1q
Operational Trunking Encapsulation: dot1q
Negotiation of Trunking: On
Access Mode VLAN: 1 (default)
Trunking Native Mode VLAN: 1 (default)
Administrative private-vlan host-association: none
Administrative private-vlan mapping: none
Operational private-vlan: none
Trunking VLANs Enabled: ALL
Pruning VLANs Enabled: 2-1001

Protected: false

Voice VLAN: none (Inactive)
Appliance trust: none
```

Adding a VLAN

Use the **vlan** global configuration command to configure a VLAN. The syntax for the **vlan** global configuration command is as follows:

```
Switch(config)#vlan number
Switch(config-vlan)#[name | mtu | shutdown | exit]
```

Each VLAN has a unique four-digit ID that can be a number from 0001 to 4096. To add a VLAN to the VLAN database, assign a number and name to the VLAN. After creating the VLAN, you will be in VLAN configuration mode. In this mode, use the **name** command to give the VLAN a name. VLAN1, VLAN1002, VLAN1003, VLAN1004, and VLAN1005 are the factory default VLANs. These VLANs exist on all Catalyst switches and are used as default VLANs for other topologies, such as Token Ring and FDDI. None of the default VLANs can be modified or deleted.

To add an Ethernet VLAN, you must specify at least a VLAN number. If no VLAN name is entered for the VLAN, the default is to append the VLAN number to the word *VLAN*. For example, *VLAN0404* could be a default name for *VLAN404* if no name is assigned.

Remember that to add, change, or delete VLANs, the switch must be in VTP server or transparent mode.

Verifying a VLAN/Modifying VLAN Parameters

When the VLAN is configured, the parameters for that VLAN should be confirmed to ensure validity. To verify the VLAN's parameters, use the **show vlan id** *vlan#* privileged EXEC command to display information about a particular VLAN. Use **show vlan** to show all configured VLANs.

The **show vlan** command output in Example 3-4 also shows which switch ports are assigned to the VLAN.

Example 3-4 **show vlan** *Output*

```
Switch#show vlan

VLAN Name                             Status    Ports
---- -------------------------------- --------- -------------------------------
1    default                          active    Fa0/2, Fa0/3, Fa0/4, Fa0/6
                                                Fa0/7, Fa0/8, Fa0/9, Fa0/10
                                                Fa0/11, Fa0/12, Gi0/2
101  VLAN0101                         active
202  VLAN0202                         active
303  VLAN0303                         active
404  VLAN0404                         active
505  VLAN0505                         active
986  VLAN0986                         active
1002 fddi-default                     active
1003 token-ring-default               active
1004 fddinet-default                  active
1005 trnet-default                    active

VLAN Type  SAID       MTU   Parent RingNo BridgeNo Stp  BrdgMode Trans1 Trans2
---- ----- ---------- ----- ------ ------ -------- ---- -------- ------ ------
1    enet  100001     1500  -      -      -        -    -        0      0
101  enet  100101     1500  -      -      -        -    -        0      0
202  enet  100202     1500  -      -      -        -    -        0      0
303  enet  100303     1500  -      -      -        -    -        0      0

VLAN Type  SAID       MTU   Parent RingNo BridgeNo Stp  BrdgMode Trans1 Trans2
---- ----- ---------- ----- ------ ------ -------- ---- -------- ------ ------
404  enet  100404     1500  -      -      -        -    -        0      0
505  enet  100505     1500  -      -      -        -    -        0      0
986  enet  100986     1500  -      -      -        -    -        0      0
1002 fddi  101002     1500  -      -      -        -    -        0      0
1003 tr    101003     1500  -      -      -        -    -        0      0
```

Example 3-4   **show vlan** *Output (Continued)*

```
1004 fdnet 101004     1500  -      -      -       ieee -     0    0
1005 trnet 101005     1500  -      -      -       ibm  -     0    0

Remote SPAN VLANs
..............................................................................


Primary Secondary Type          Ports
........ ......... ................ ...........................................
```

Other VLAN parameters shown in Example 3-4 include the following:

- Type (default is Ethernet)
- Security Association ID (SAID), which is used for the FDDI trunk
- Maximum transmission unit (MTU, where the default is 1500 for Ethernet VLAN)
- Other parameters used for Token Ring or FDDI VLANs

To modify an existing VLAN parameter (such as the VLAN name), use the same command syntax used to add a VLAN.

In Example 3-5, the VLAN name for VLAN986 is changed to CSR_VLAN.

Example 3-5   *Change VLAN Name*

```
Switch# config t
Enter configuration commands, one per line. End with CNTL/Z
Switch(config)#vlan 986
Switch(config-vlan)#name CSR_VLAN
```

Use the **show vlan id 986** command, as demonstrated in Example 3-6, to verify the change.

Example 3-6   *Verify VLAN Change*

```
Switch# show vlan id 986

VLAN Name                         Status   Ports
---- -------------------------------- -------- ------------------------------
986  CSR_VLAN                     active   Fa0/1, Gi0/1

VLAN Type  SAID       MTU   Parent RingNo BridgeNo Stp  BrdgMode Trans1 Trans2
---- ----- ---------- ----- ------ ------ -------- ---- -------- ------ ------
986  enet  100986     1500  -      -      -        -    -        0      0

Remote SPAN VLAN
----------------
Disabled

Primary Secondary Type          Ports
------- --------- ---------------- ---------------------------------------
```

Assigning Ports to a VLAN

After creating a VLAN, you can statically assign a port or a number of ports to that VLAN. A port can belong to only one VLAN at a time.

Configure the VLAN port assignment from the interface configuration mode using the interface command **switchport access vlan** number, as shown in the following syntax:

```
Switch(config-if)#switchport access vlan [1-4096 | dynamic]
```

dynamic means that the Catalyst switch queries a VMPS for VLAN information based on a MAC address. A number in the range of 1 to 4096 would represent the VLAN assignment for the port.

By default, all ports are members of the default VLAN—VLAN1.

Use the **show vlan brief** privileged EXEC command to display the VLAN assignment for all switch ports, as demonstrated in Example 3-7.

Example 3-7   *Displaying VLAN Assignments and Membership for All Switch Ports*

```
Switch#show vlan brief

VLAN Name                             Status    Ports
---- -------------------------------- --------- -------------------------------
1    default                          active    Fa0/2, Fa0/3, Fa0/4, Fa0/6
                                                Fa0/7, Fa0/8, Fa0/9, Fa0/10
                                                Fa0/11, Fa0/12, Gi0/2
101  VLAN0101                         active
202  VLAN0202                         active
303  VLAN0303                         active
404  VLAN0404                         active
505  VLAN0505                         active
986  CSR_VLAN                         active
1002 fddi-default                     active
1003 token-ring-default               active
1004 fddinet-default                  active
1005 trnet-default                    active
```

Displaying Spanning Tree Protocol Configuration Status

Use the **show spanning-tree** privileged EXEC command to display the switch's Spanning Tree Protocol configuration status, as demonstrated in Example 3-8. The basic syntax for the **show spanning-tree** privileged EXEC command is as follows:

```
Switch# show spanning-tree [vlan number]
```

Example 3-8   **show spanning-tree** *Output*

```
Switch# show spanning-tree vlan 1
VLAN0001
  Spanning tree enabled protocol ieee
  Root ID    Priority    0
             Address     0005.00a9.2401
```

Example 3-8   **show spanning-tree** *Output (Continued)*

```
                 Cost      8
                 Port      13 (GigabitEthernet0/1)
                 Hello Time  2 sec  Max Age 20 sec  Forward Delay 15 sec

   Bridge ID  Priority    32769  (priority 32768 sys-id-ext 1)
              Address     000b.5f2a.5a40
              Hello Time  2 sec  Max Age 20 sec  Forward Delay 15 sec
              Aging Time 300

Interface       Port ID                    Designated            Port ID
Name            Prio.Nbr    Cost Sts        Cost Bridge ID        Prio.Nbr
--------------- --------- ---------  ---  --------- ------------------- --------
Fa0/1           128.1        100 FWD        8 32769 000b.5f2a.5a40 128.1
Gi0/1           128.13         4 FWD        4 32768 0005.3104.c000  32.65
```

Example 3-8 displays various spanning tree information for VLAN1, including the following:

- Port Fa0/1 and G0/1 are in the forwarding state for VLAN1.
- The root bridge for VLAN1 has a bridge priority of 0 with a MAC address of 0005.00a9.2401.
- The switch is running the IEEE 802.1D Spanning Tree Protocol.

Recall that a Catalyst switch can support a separate Spanning Tree instance per VLAN. This allows for load balancing between switches. For example, one switch can be the root for VLAN1, and another switch can be the root for VLAN2.

VLAN Command Summary

Table 3-2 lists the commands covered in this chapter and briefly describes each command's function.

Table 3-2   *VLAN Command Summary*

Command	Description
vtp mode [**server** ׀ **client** ׀ **transparent**]	In global configuration mode, this command sets the operational VTP mode for the switch. The default is **server**.
vtp domain *name*	In global configuration mode, this command assigns a VTP domain name, which allows the switch to send VTP advertisements out trunk links. The default is NULL, which would allow a switch to join the first domain it received an update from.
show vtp status	Displays VTP status information including configuration revision number, domain name, and switch mode.

continues

Table 3-2   *VLAN Command Summary (Continued)*

switchport mode [trunk ǀ access ǀ dynamic [desirable ǀ auto ǀ nonegotiate]]	In interface configuration mode, this configures the behavior of the interface. **Trunk** mode will force frame tagging. **Dynamic** mode can become a trunk if it negotiates with the other side of the link. **Access** mode is a nontrunk port.
switchport trunk encapsulation [isl ǀ dot1q]	Used in interface configuration mode to specify a trunking protocol. For some switches, before you can set an interface to **trunk** mode, you must first specify the encapsulation.
show interface [*type module/port*] **trunk**	Displays trunking information about the active or specified trunk links on the switch.
show interface [*type module/port*] **switchport**	Displays Layer 2 configuration and operational parameters of the switch. This includes VLAN membership and trunking status.
vlan *number*	In global configuration mode, this command defines a VLAN and puts the switch into VLAN configuration mode. In VLAN configuration mode, commands such as **name** can be used to further define the VLAN.
show vlan [id *vlan#*]	Displays VLAN information. The **id** option allows you to specify a particular VLAN.
switchport access vlan [*1-4096* ǀ **dynamic]**	In interface configuration mode, this command assigns an **access** port to a VLAN or makes it a dynamic port.
show vlan brief	Displays a brief table of the VLANs, including the port membership for each VLAN.
show spanning-tree [vlan *number*]	Displays Spanning Tree information for the switch or a VLAN if the **vlan** option is used.

Section 2 Quiz

1   A VLAN can be created or modified on a switch in which of the following VTP modes? (Choose all that apply.)

   A   Server

   B   Access

   C   Client

   D   Transparent

   E   Root

2 Regarding VTP configuration revision numbers, which of the following statements are true? (Choose all that apply.)

A A transparent switch will always have a higher configuration revision number than any other switch on the network.

B VTP configuration revision numbers are changed on a switch when a VLAN is created, deleted, or modified.

C If a switch with a higher configuration revision number is added to an existing network with the same VTP domain name, it will have no effect on the VLANs on all the functioning switches.

D VTP configuration revision numbers can be reset to 0 by changing the VTP to transparent mode and then back to server or client.

E You can view a switch's current VTP configuration revision number by issuing the command **show vtp status**.

3 Choose the commands that force an IOS switch to perform trunking on a FastEthernet interface 0/12. (Choose the best answer.)

A **set trunk on**

B **interface Fa0/12 trunk on**

C **switchport mode trunk**

D **interface Fa0/12 mode trunk**

E **interface Fa0/12 then switchport mode trunk**

4 Which of the following is the default mode for a Layer 2 port on an IOS switch?

A **switchport mode access**

B **switchport mode dynamic auto**

C **switchport mode nonegotiate**

D **switchport mode dynamic desirable**

E **switchport mode trunk**

5 Which of the following commands you can use to see which VLAN a port is assigned to? (Choose all that apply.)

A **show interface trunk**

B **show interface** *type slot/port*

C **show vtp status**

D **show interface status**

E **show vlan brief**

F **show interface** *type slot/port* **switchport**

Summary

This chapter discussed how VLANs operate to provide more effective networks by controlling broadcasts in your network. To configure VLANs on a Catalyst switch, you must first configure VTP to administer VLANs. Therefore, you learned how VTP operates and how it is configured. You also learned how to create a trunk link to carry all VLAN traffic, and how to configure a VLAN. Finally, this chapter discussed the verification of Spanning Tree operations, including the following:

- How VLANs operate
- How to configure VTP
- How to configure a trunk
- How to configure a VLAN
- How to verify Spanning Tree operations

Case Study

Now that Ann has used switches to segment the network using switches, the network performance has noticeably improved. However, some of the servers are having some CPU utilization issues. After some research by the vendor who installed the servers, it has been determined that the problem is the amount of broadcast traffic. It seems that one of the servers runs an application that uses broadcasts to locate and poll all of its clients on the network. These broadcasts are affecting both servers and clients throughout the network, but it is more noticeable on the servers. Because of this, Ann has decided to implement VLANs. Based on the following requirements, what steps should Ann take in creating her VLANs? Figure 3-16 shows the layout of the switched network and location of the servers.

Figure 3-16   *International Widgets Ltd. Switched Network Diagram*

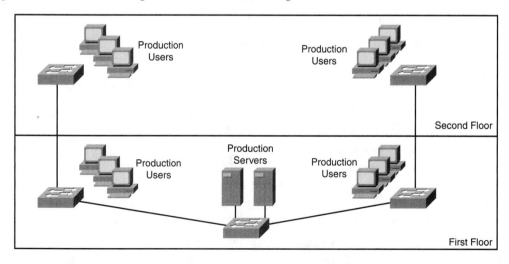

Ann has five servers. One server for production uses an all network broadcast to communicate with its clients. Those clients are located on both floors of the building, as shown in Figure 3-16. Of the other four servers, all use TCP/IP to communicate with various departments all over the company. It has been decided that for clients not using the production server, PCs and servers will be placed in a VLAN base at the location:

1 How many VLANs will Ann need and where will they need to be located in relation to the switches?

2 Do any of the switches have multiple VLANs on them? If so, what will Ann need to configure to ensure that multiple VLANs can pass between the switches?

3 In the future, Ann might need to create VLANs that will need to be used on some or all of the switches. To ensure that all VLANs exist on all trunked switches, what should Ann do?

Review Questions

1 VLANs allow for the creation of what in switched networks?

2 What are the two types of VLAN port assignments?

3 What type of port is capable of carrying all VLAN traffic?

4 What mechanism is used by switches to provide inter-switch communication between devices about which VLAN a packet originated from?

5 What is the purpose of VTP?

6 What is the default VTP mode for a Catalyst Switch?

7 Assume that a Catalyst switch is being added to your network. The switch needs to learn VLANs from the other switches in the network. You are not sure of the current VTP configuration and are fearful that it might overwrite your current VLAN information. How could you prevent the switch from accidentally overwriting the VLANs in your VTP domain?

8 What is unique about the Native VLAN on an IEEE 802.1Q trunk link?

9 List all the steps required to configure a VLAN on a Catalyst switch port.

10 Which command would you use to view the Spanning Tree configuration for VLAN9 on a Catalyst switch?

PART II

Controlling Traffic Between LANs

After completing this chapter, you will be able to perform the following tasks:

- Identify the information a router needs to make routing decisions.
- Identify the mechanisms for routers to obtain both dynamic and static routing information.
- Understand the process of how dynamic routing protocols, such as RIP, IGRP, OSPF and EIGRP, learn routes.

CHAPTER 4

Determining IP Routes

For a router to send packets to a network, it must determine which path the packet is to take. This chapter discusses path determination. Paths are determined with static routes and dynamic routing protocols such as Routing Information Protocol (RIP), Interior Gateway Routing Protocol (IGRP), Open Shortest Path First (OSPF), Intermediate System-to-Intermediate System (IS-IS), and Enhanced Interior Gateway Routing Protocol (EIGRP). The IP routing process and dynamic routing protocols are discussed in volumes of books in the networking industry. This chapter's purpose is to provide you with an overview of IP routing, focusing on interior routing protocols.

NOTE   The IS-IS routing protocol is beyond the scope of this book, but is mentioned occasionally for comparison purposes.

Routing Overview

For information to travel from one network to another, some device must know how to transport that information. Routing is the process by which an item gets from one location to another. Many items get routed, such as mail, telephone calls, and trains. In networking, a router is the device used to route traffic. Figure 4-1 illustrates an example of connected routers. For a host on the 10.120.2.0 subnet to communicate with a host on the 172.16.1.0 subnet, the routers between them must maintain and choose the paths to be used.

Figure 4-1   *Routing Overview*

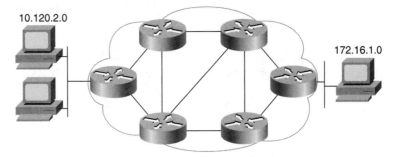

10.120.2.0

172.16.1.0

To route packets of information, a router (or any other entity that performs routing, such as a UNIX workstation running the route daemon, or a Layer 3 switch) needs to know how to perform the following key functions:

- **Know destination address** — What is the destination (or address) of the item that needs to be routed? This is the host's responsibility.

- **Identify information sources** — From which source is the router learning the paths to a given destination, dynamically from other routers or statically from an administrator?

- **Discover possible routes** — What are the initial possible routes, or paths, to the intended destinations?

- **Select best routes** — What is the best path to the intended destination, and should the router load balance the data between this path and other equal or less optimal paths?

- **Verify and maintain the routing information** — Are the known paths to destinations valid and the most current?

The routing information that a router learns from its routing sources is placed in its routing table. The router relies on this table to determine which outgoing port to use when forwarding a packet toward its destination. The routing table is how a router knows about the networks. Figure 4-2 illustrates how a router builds a routing table.

Figure 4-2   *Connected Routes*

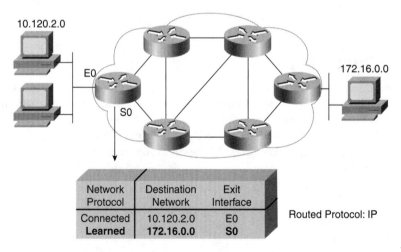

If the destination network is directly connected, the router already knows which port to use when forwarding packets.

If destination networks are not directly attached, the router must learn about and compute the best route to use when forwarding packets to these networks. The routing table is populated through one of the following methods:

- Manually by the network administrator
- Collected through dynamic processes running in the network

Here are two ways to tell the router where to forward packets that are not directly connected:

- **Static routes**—Routes learned by the router when an administrator manually establishes the route. The administrator must manually update this static route entry whenever an internetwork topology requires an update, such as during a link failure.
- **Dynamic routes**—Routes learned by the router from another router or routers after an administrator configures a routing protocol. Unlike static routes, as soon as the network administrator enables dynamic routing, route knowledge is both propagated from that router and learned automatically from other routers. A routine process updates this routing information whenever new topology information is received from other routers within the internetwork.

Enabling Static Routes

For a router to route packets, it needs only to know a route to the given network.

Static routes are administratively defined routes that specify the address or interface of the next hop in the path that packets must take while moving between a source station and a destination station. These administrator-defined routes allow precise control over the IP internetwork's routing behavior.

Static routes can be important if Cisco IOS Software cannot build a route to a particular destination. Static routes are also useful for specifying a "gateway of last resort." The gateway of last resort is the address that a router would send a packet destined for a network not listed in the routing table.

Static routes are commonly used when routing from a network to a *stub network*. A stub network (sometimes called a leaf node) is a network accessed by a single route. Often, static routes are used because only one way exists on to or off of a stub network. Figure 4-3 illustrates a stub network. Because there is only one path to and from this network, static routes can be configured on each router to provide information about this path without the overhead traffic of a routing protocol.

Figure 4-3   *Static Routes*

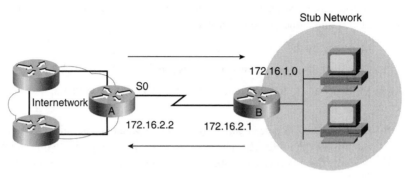

To configure a static route, enter the **ip route** command in global configuration mode. The parameters for the **ip route** command further define the static route. A static route allows manual configuration of the routing table. This table entry remains in the routing table as long as the path is active. The only exception to this rule is the **permanent** option shown in the following example. With the **permanent** option, the route remains in the table even if the path is not active. The syntax for the **ip route** command is as follows:

```
ip route network [mask] {address ? interface} [distance] [permanent]
```

Where:

- *network* is the destination network or subnet.
- *mask* is the subnet mask.
- *address* is the IP address of the next-hop router.
- *interface* is the name of the interface to use to get to the destination network.
- *distance* is an optional parameter that defines the administrative distance. Administrative distance is covered later in this chapter.
- **permanent** is an optional parameter that specifies that the route will not be removed, even if the interface shuts down.

Consider the example shown in Figure 4-4.

Figure 4-4   *Static Route Example*

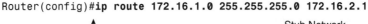

```
Router(config)#ip route 172.16.1.0 255.255.255.0 172.16.2.1
```

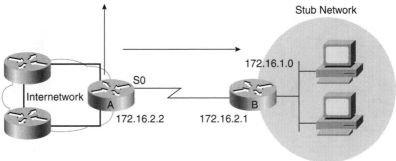

In Figure 4-4, the static route from Router A to the stub network is configured as follows:

```
Router(config)#ip route 172.16.1.0 255.255.255.0 172.16.2.1
```

Where:

- **ip route** identifies the static route command.
- **172.16.1.0** specifies a static route to the destination subnetwork.
- **255.255.255.0** indicates the subnet mask (8 bits of subnetting are in effect).
- **172.16.2.1** specifies the IP address of the next-hop router in the path to the destination.

The assignment of a static route to reach the stub network 172.16.1.0 is proper for Router A because there is only one way to reach that network. You must have a route configured in the opposite direction for bidirectional communication.

A default route is a special type of static route used for situations in which the route from a source to a destination is not known or when it is unfeasible for the routing table to store sufficient information about all the possible routes. The default route is also known as the *gateway of last resort*.

In Figure 4-5, you would need to configure Router B to forward all frames for which the destination network is not explicitly listed in its routing table to Router A. This route allows the stub network to reach all known networks beyond Router A. If a default route was not used in this situation, you would need to configure many individual static routing entries on the router connected to the stub network.

Figure 4-5 *Default Route*

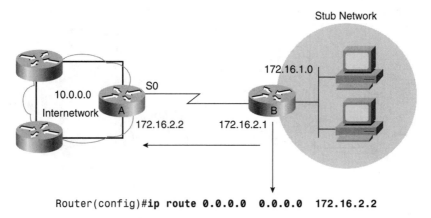

```
Router(config)#ip route 0.0.0.0  0.0.0.0  172.16.2.2
```

To configure the default route, enter the following command:

```
Router(config)#ip route 0.0.0.0 0.0.0.0 172.16.2.2
```

Where:

- **ip route** identifies the static route command.

- **0.0.0.0** routes to a nonexistent subnet. (With a special mask, it denotes the default network.)

- **0.0.0.0** specifies the mask for the default route.

- **172.16.2.2** specifies the IP address of the next-hop router to be used as the default for packet forwarding.

To see the connected networks for a Layer 3 device, or to verify that a static route has been properly configured for the router, use the command **show ip route**. Example 4-1 shows the output for a Router B from Figure 4-5.

Example 4-1 **show ip route** *Output for Router B*

```
Router#show ip route
Codes: C - connected, S - static, I - IGRP, R - RIP, M - mobile, B - BGP
       D - EIGRP, EX - EIGRP external, O - OSPF, IA - OSPF inter area
       E1 - OSPF external type 1, E2 - OSPF external type 2, E - EGP
       i - IS-IS, L1 - IS-IS level-1, L2 - IS-IS level-2, * - candidate default
       U - per-user static route
Gateway of last resort is 0.0.0.0 to network 0.0.0.0
       172.16.0.0/16 is subnetted, 2 subnets
C        172.16.2.0 is directly connected, Serial0
C        172.16.1.0 is directly connected, Ethernet0
S*    0.0.0.0/0 is directly connected, Serial0
```

The output here shows the connected route with a **C** to the left of the route, and the static route with an **S** to the left of the route. The asterisk (*) located next to the **S** indicates that this path will be chosen as a default if no other route is found for a packet.

InterVLAN Routing

In a virtual LAN (VLAN) environment, frames are Layer 2 switched only between ports within the same *broadcast domain* or VLAN. The VLANs perform network partitioning and traffic separation at Layer 2 just as if two separate physical segments existed. InterVLAN communication cannot occur without a Layer 3 device such as a router. A router must be able to physically connect to each broadcast domain to route between them. In a situation where the router connects to separate segments, this is done with each individual interface connecting to the segment. Each interface is then assigned an IP address, becomes connected to the network, and can route between connected networks, as discussed previously. Because the switch is capable of identifying each VLAN or *broadcast domain* by tagging the frames, it becomes possible to have a single physical point of connection to the router, yet still provide communications between the connected VLANs.

Figure 4-6 illustrates a router attached to a core switch with a single physical connection. This configuration is sometimes referred to as a "router on a stick." The router can receive packets on one VLAN and forward them to another VLAN. To perform interVLAN routing functions, the router must know how to reach all VLANs being interconnected. A separate logical connection must exist on the router for each VLAN. You can accomplish this connectivity by enabling Inter Switch Link (ISL) or 802.1Q trunking on a single physical connection between the switch and router. After the IP addresses have been configured on subinterfaces, the router will be aware of the network associated with every VLAN as a directly connected network.

Figure 4-6   *InterVLAN Routing*

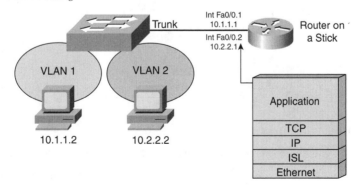

To support ISL or 802.1Q trunking, you must subdivide the router's physical Fast Ethernet interface into multiple, logical, addressable interfaces, one per VLAN. The resulting logical interfaces are called *subinterfaces* and appear to the router as connected networks. Without this subdivision, a separate physical interface would need to be dedicated to each VLAN.

In Figure 4-7, the FastEthernet0/0 interface is divided into multiple subinterfaces:

- FastEthernet0/0.1
- FastEthernet0/0.2
- FastEthernet0/0.3

Figure 4-7 *Using Subinterfaces*

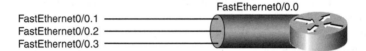

Use the **encapsulation isl** *vlan identifier* subinterface configuration command to enable ISL on a router's subinterface (where *vlan identifier* is the VLAN number).

Figure 4-8 shows a router connected to a switch with the FastEthernet 0/0 interface connected to a trunk port on a switch. The FastEthernet interface will be divided into logical interfaces for each of the two VLANs and assigned an IP address to act as a gateway for each broadcast domain.

Figure 4-8 *Configuring InterVLAN Routing*

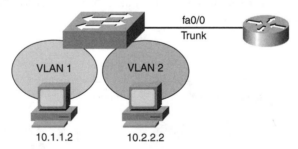

To configure the router on a stick for interVLAN routing, complete the following tasks:

Step 1 Configure ISL trunking on the switch port connecting to the router.

Step 2 Enable ISL encapsulation on the router's Fast Ethernet subinterface.

Step 3 Assign a network layer address to each subinterface.

Example 4-2 shows the configuration required for the router in Figure 4-8 if you are using ISL frame tagging.

Example 4-2 *Router on a Stick Configuration*

```
Router(config)#interface Fastethernet 0/0
Router(config-if)#no ip address
Router(config-if)#exit
Router(config)#interface Fastethernet 0/0.1
Router(config-if)#encapsulation ISL 1
Router(config-if)#ip address 10.1.1.1 255.255.255.0
Router(config-if)#exit
Router(config)#interface Fastethernet 0/0.2
Router(config-if)#encapsulation ISL 2
Router(config-if)#ip address 10.2.2.1 255.255.255.0
```

This router on a stick could also route between VLANs if the switch it was connected to was using 802.1Q trunking instead. For this configuration, you use the **switchport trunk encapsulation dot1q** subinterface configuration command to enable 802.1Q encapsulation trunking on a router's subinterface.

802.1Q is slightly different from ISL. The native VLAN frames in 802.1Q do not carry a tag. Therefore, a trunk's major interface has an address, or you can identify a particular interface as belonging to the native VLAN with the keyword **native** when issuing the **encapsulation** command. Any other configuration information for the VLAN subinterfaces is configured with the dot1Q encapsulation, IP address, and so on. The subinterface number does not need to be the same as the dot1Q VLAN number. However, management is easier when the two numbers are the same.

The Catalyst 2950 switches support only 802.1Q encapsulation, which is configured automatically when trunking is enabled on the interface by using the **switchport mode trunk** command. Other IOS switches require the command **switchport trunk encapsulation dot1Q**.

Example 4-3 shows the configuration required for the router in Figure 4-8 if you are using 802.1Q frame tagging and the native VLAN is VLAN 1.

Example 4-3 *802.1Q Router on a Stick Configuration*

```
Router(config)#interface Fastethernet 0/0
Router(config-if)#ip address 10.1.1.1 255.255.255.0
Router(config-if)#exit
Router(config)#interface Fastethernet 0/0.2
Router(config-if)#encapsulation dot1Q 2
Router(config-if)#ip address 10.2.2.1 255.255.255.0
```

An alternative configuration for this would be to use the **native** keyword with the **encapsulation** command to identify the Native VLAN, as shown in Example 4-4.

Example 4-4   *Using the **native** Keyword with 802.1Q Encapsulation*

```
Router(config)#interface Fastethernet 0/0.1
Router(config-if)#encapsulation dot1Q 1 native
Router(config-if)#ip address 10.1.1.1 255.255.255.0
Router(config-if)#exit
Router(config)#interface Fastethernet 0/0.2
Router(config-if)#encapsulation dot1Q 2
Router(config-if)#ip address 10.2.2.1 255.255.255.0
```

In these examples, the VLANs are directly connected, so the router can pass traffic. Routing between networks not directly connected requires that the router learn the routes either statically or dynamically (through a routing protocol).

Section 1 Quiz

1   By default, which of the following networks are known by a router that has configured interfaces?

   A   All routes in the network

   B   Only the statically configured routes

   C   The default route

   D   Connected Networks

   E   All of the above

2   In the routing table displayed with the **show ip route** command, which of the following symbols indicates a route to be used for networks not found in the routing table?

   A   S

   B   C

   C   D

   D   E

   E   O

   F   *

3   True or False: A static route dynamically adjusts to changes in the routing topology without any user intervention?

4 A router connected only to a trunk link on a switch is called which of the following?

   A A bad design

   B A router on a stick

   C A jalapeño on a stick

   D Impossible

   E InterVLAN router

   F Trunk router

5 For the 802.1Q native VLAN, which of the following methods satisfy the requirement of not tagging the native VLAN frames?

   A Configure the major interface with an IP address.

   B Use ISL as the encapsulation type.

   C Configure Frame Relay for the subinterface.

   D Configure the subinterface of the Native VLAN with the encapsulation option **native.**

   E Use the global command **dot1q native vlan 1**.

Learning Routes Dynamically Using Routing Protocols

Although static routes might be useful in some situations, when the network experiences a change, the administrator must reconfigure all the routers to accommodate that change. Another method of learning about available routes and accommodating the changes is through the use of a dynamic routing protocol. Figure 4-9 illustrates that a router can populate the routing table by learning and choosing routes through dynamic routing protocols.

Figure 4-9   *Routing Protocols Build Routing Tables*

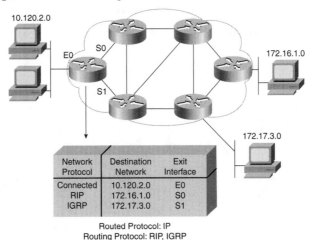

Routed Protocol: IP
Routing Protocol: RIP, IGRP

Dynamic routing relies on a routing protocol to disseminate and gather knowledge. A routing protocol defines the set of rules used by a router when it communicates with neighboring routers; that is, a routing protocol determines routing paths and maintains routing tables.

A routing protocol is a network layer protocol that uses packets from other participants to learn and maintain a routing table. Do not confuse *routing* protocols with a *routed* protocol, also known as a *routable* protocol. A *routed* protocol means that the network layer address has two components, a network portion and a host or node portion. The network portion of the address is used to route the packet, making it a *routed*, or *routable*, protocol. This would be impossible without a network identifier. A *routing* protocol is then used to pick the best path from the packet's source network to the packet's destination network. As soon as the routing protocol determines a valid path between routers, the router can route a routed protocol. Routing protocols also describe the following information:

- How updates are conveyed
- What knowledge is conveyed
- When to convey knowledge
- How to locate recipients of the updates

Two examples of routing protocols discussed later in this chapter are Routing Information Protocol (RIP) and Interior Gateway Routing Protocol (IGRP).

Interior Gateway Protocols Versus Exterior Gateway Protocols

The two major types of routing protocols are as follows:

- **Interior Gateway Protocols (IGP)**—Used to exchange routing information within an autonomous system. RIP and IGRP are examples of IGPs.
- **Exterior Gateway Protocols (EGP)**—Used to exchange routing information between autonomous systems. Border Gateway Protocol (BGP) is an example of an EGP.

Figure 4-10 helps distinguish the difference between IGPs and EGPs.

Figure 4-10   *IGPs Versus EGPs*

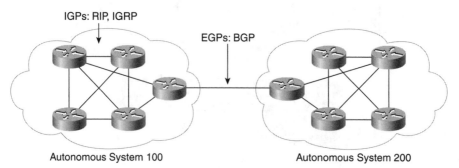

An autonomous system (AS) is a collection of networks under a common administrative domain. The Internet Assigned Numbers Authority (IANA) is the umbrella organization responsible for allocating autonomous system numbers. Specifically, the American Registry for Internet Numbers (ARIN) has the jurisdiction for assigning numbers for the Americas, Caribbean, and Africa. Réseaux IP Européens-Network Information Center (RIPE-NIC) administers the numbers for Europe, and the Asia Pacific-NIC (AP-NIC) administers the AS numbers for the Asia-Pacific region. This autonomous system designator is a 16-bit number.

NOTE   Using the IANA-assigned AS number rather than some other number is necessary only if your organization plans to use an EGP, such as BGP, on a public network, such as the Internet.

Administrative Distance

Multiple routing protocols and static routes can be used at the same time. If several routing sources are providing common routing information, an administrative distance value is used to rate the trustworthiness or believability of each routing source. Specifying administrative distance values enables Cisco IOS Software to discriminate between sources of routing information. For each network learned, IOS selects the route from the routing source with the lowest administrative distance. An administrative distance is an integer from 0 to 255. In general, if a routing protocol with a lower administrative distance has a path to a network, it will be used over a routing protocol with a path to the same network that has a higher administrative distance. Figure 4-11 demonstrates an example of where administrative distance comes into play.

Figure 4-11   *Administrative Distance*

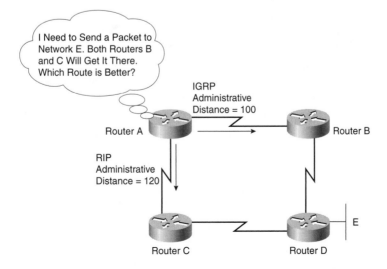

In this figure, Router A has learned a RIP path to Network E from Router C, but it has also learned an IGRP path to Network E from Router B. In this case, IGRP has the lower administrative distance, so the router will choose that route.

Table 4-1 shows the default administrative distance for some routing information sources.

Table 4-1   *Default Administrative Distance Values*

Route Source	Default Distance
Connected interface	0
Static route address	1
Internal EIGRP	90
IGRP	100
OSPF	110
IS-IS	115
RIP	120
External EIGRP	170
Unknown/Unbelievable	255 (Will not be used to pass traffic)

NOTE   The default administrative distances are assigned by Cisco IOS Software. This is a subjective evaluation determined by Cisco.

If the default values are not desired, such as when you are redistributing routes, a network administrator can use IOS to configure administrative distance values on a per-router, per-protocol, or per-route basis.

Overview of Routing Protocol Classes

Although all routing protocols perform the functions highlighted in the previous sections, there are different ways to arrive at the end result. Essentially, you have three classes of routing protocols. Figure 4-12 shows routers exchanging information. They do this through a protocol that falls into one of these categories.

Figure 4-12   *Classes of Routing Protocols*

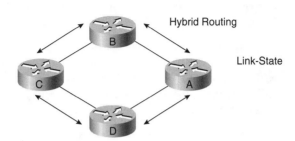

Within an autonomous system, most IGP routing algorithms can be classified as conforming to one of the following algorithms:

- **Distance vector**—The distance vector routing approach determines the direction (vector) and distance to any link in the internetwork. Examples include RIP and IGRP.

- **Link-state**—The link-state (also called shortest path first) approach re-creates the exact topology of the entire internetwork for route computation (or at least the partition in which the router is situated). Examples include OSPF and IS-IS.

- **Balanced hybrid**—A balanced hybrid approach combines aspects of the link-state and distance vector algorithms. Cisco's proprietary EIGRP is an example of a balanced hybrid routing protocol.

NOTE   The Cisco term *hybrid routing protocol* describes the nature of EIGRP, which uses a database to keep alternate routes. It is similar to OSPF, but it uses distance vector metrics, such as RIP or IGRP, so it has qualities of both distance vector and link-state protocols. EIGRP is more of a distance vector routing protocol, but the best way to describe EIGRP would be as a Diffusing Update protocol because it is based on a Diffusing Update Algorithm.

Another way of classifying routing protocols is based on how they deal with subnets for IP network addresses. Originally, IP network addresses were designed based on class. Each class had a certain number of bits used for network identification and bits used for host addresses. This number of bits was based completely on the address; therefore, a routing protocol could determine the class of network and know what portion of the address was to be used to identify the network in the routing table. Later, when subnets were added to IP addresses, the routers maintained information about subnets locally and did not pass subnet information about routes between each other. This is called *classful routing* because the router keys only on the IP addressing class for routing information.

When using a classful routing protocol, all subnets of the same major class (A, B, or C) network must use the same subnet mask throughout the network. This means that the address space would be the same on every network in the enterprise. Furthermore, routers running a classful routing protocol send only an update about the major class network when an update is sent across a network boundary (a different major network number).

When a router receives an update from another router across a network that contains the same major network number as the receiving interface, the router applies the subnet mask that is configured for that interface for all updates. If the routing update contains a different major network than the one on the receiving network, the router applies the default classful mask (based on the address class), as follows:

- For Class A addresses, the default classful mask is 255.0.0.0.
- For Class B addresses, the default classful mask is 255.255.0.0.
- For Class C addresses, the default classful mask is 255.255.255.0.

Examples of classful routing protocols are as follows:

- RIP Version 1 (RIP-1)
- IGRP

Classful routing protocols present major challenges in addressing and subnetting a network based on actual needs. As IP variable-length subnet masking (different length mask based on addressing needs) became available, routing protocols became more sophisticated so that they could handle IP subnet masks with routing updates. These protocols are called *classless routing protocols*.

Classless routing protocols can be considered second-generation protocols because they are designed to address the limitations of the classful routing protocol. Classless routing protocols, however, do not key on an address's major class and actually pass subnet information. This allows for better management of IP addresses. Another benefit is the ability to control routing updates by manually summarizing routes between networks. This is very useful in maintaining the size of routing tables between devices. Examples of classless routing protocols are as follows:

- RIP Version 2 (RIP-2)
- EIGRP
- OSPF
- IS-IS

Another issue that occurs with classful routing protocols concerns the default route of 0.0.0.0. A router running a classful routing protocol uses a default route only if it has no knowledge of the major network. In Figure 4-13, Router B is directly connected to subnetwork 172.16.1.0 and has a default route to send all other frames to Router A.

Figure 4-13   *Default Routes with Classful Routing Protocols*

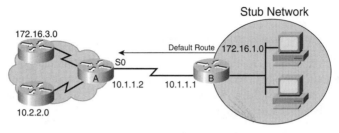

A router running a classful routing protocol assumes that all subnets of a directly attached network are presented in the IP routing table. If a packet is received with a destination address within an unknown subnet of a directly attached network, the router assumes that the subnet does not exist and drops the packet. This behavior holds true even if the IP routing table contains a default route. In Figure 4-13, if a device on the 172.16.1.0 subnet were to send a frame to the 172.16.3.0 subnet, Router B would drop the frame because it would not know about the subnet, which is a part of the attached 172.16.0.0 major network.

For a Cisco IOS device, a network administrator can change this behavior with the global **ip classless** command, which is enabled by default:

```
Router(config)#ip classless
```

With **ip classless** configured, if a packet is received with a destination address within an unknown subnet of a directly attached network, the router uses the default route and forwards the frame to the next-hop router, as specified in the static route.

NOTE   The command **ip classless** is on by default for most Layer 3 devices.

There is no single best routing algorithm for all internetworks. All routing protocols provide the information differently. Table 4-2 compares the characteristics of the routing protocols.

Table 4-2   *Routing Protocol Characteristics*

Characteristics	RIP-1	IGRP	EIGRP	IS-IS	OSPF
Distance vector	√	√	√		
Link-state				√	√
Automatic route summarization	√	√	√	√	
Manual route summarization	√	√	√	√	√
VLSM support			√	√	√
Proprietary		√	√		
Convergence time	Slow	Slow	Very fast	Very fast	Very fast

EIGRP is best classified as an advanced distance vector protocol with some link-state features.

The following sections cover the different routing protocol classes in greater detail.

Distance Vector Routing Protocols

Distance vector-based routing algorithms (also known as Bellman-Ford-Moore algorithms) pass periodic copies of a routing table from router to router and accumulate distance vectors (distance means how far, and vector means in which direction). Regular updates between routers communicate topology changes.

Each router receives a routing table from its direct neighbor. For example, in Figure 4-14, Router B receives information from Router A. Router B adds a distance vector metric (such as the number of hops), increasing the distance vector. It then passes the routing table to its other neighbor, Router C. This same step-by-step process occurs in all directions between direct-neighbor routers. (This is also known as "routing by rumor.")

Figure 4-14 *Distance Vector Protocols*

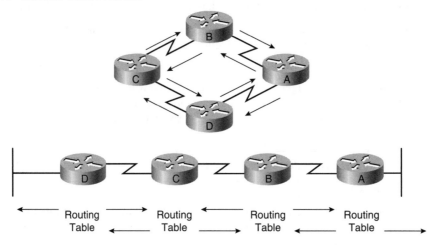

In this way, the algorithm accumulates network distances so that it can maintain a database of internetwork topology information. Distance vector algorithms do not allow a router to know an internetwork's exact topology.

The following section explains how distance vector routing protocols perform the following:

- Identify sources of information.
- Discover routes.
- Select the best route.
- Maintain routing information.

Route Discovery, Selection, and Maintenance

In Figure 4-15, the interface to each directly connected network is shown as having a distance of 0.

Figure 4-15   *Routing Information Sources*

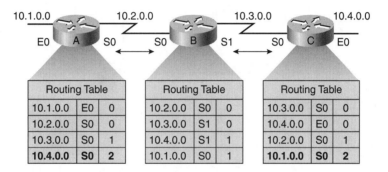

As the distance vector network discovery process proceeds, routers discover the best path to nondirectly connected destination networks based on accumulated metrics from each neighbor.

For example, Router A learns about other networks based on information it receives from Router B. Each of these other network entries in the routing table has an accumulated distance vector to show how far away that network is in the given direction.

Multiple paths might exist to any given destination network. When a routing protocol's algorithm updates the routing table, its primary objective is to determine the best possible route to each network. Each distance vector routing protocol uses a different routing algorithm to determine the best route. The algorithm generates a number called the *metric value* for each path through the network. The smaller the metric, the better the path. Figure 4-16 shows a network with multiple paths between Host A and Host B. Each routing protocol would choose the best path between these hosts by looking at the metrics. Each routing protocol uses a different value to calculate metrics.

Figure 4-16   *Routing Metrics*

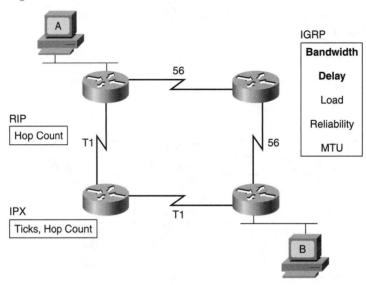

Metrics can be calculated based on either a single characteristic of a path or multiple path characteristics. Figure 4-16 lists some of the metrics that protocols could use. The metrics that routers most commonly use are as follows:

- **Hop count**—Number of routers through which a packet will pass.
- **Cost**—Arbitrary value, usually based on bandwidth, dollar expense, or another measurement, that can be assigned by a network administrator.
- **Bandwidth**—Data capacity of a link. For example, normally, a 10-Mbps Ethernet link is preferable to a 64-Kbps leased line.
- **Delay**—Length of time required to move a packet from source to destination.
- **Load**—Amount of activity on a network resource, such as a router or link.
- **Reliability**—Usually refers to the bit-error rate of each network link.
- **Maximum transmission unit (MTU)**—The maximum frame length in octets that is acceptable to all links on the path.

Table 4-3 shows the metrics used by various routing protocols.

Table 4-3   *Routing Protocol Metrics*

Routing Protocol	Metric
RIP-1	Hop count
RIP-2	Hop count
IGRP	Calculated based on constraining bandwidth and cumulative delay; can include reliability, load, and MTU

Table 4-3   *Routing Protocol Metrics (Continued)*

Routing Protocol	Metric
EIGRP	Same as IGRP, except multiplied by 256
OSPF	Cost, as derived from bandwidth by default
Integrated IS-IS	Cost, as derived from bandwidth by default

In Figure 4-16, each protocol would have chosen a route based on metrics. IGRP would have based the decision on combined characteristics, including bandwidth, delay, reliability, and MTU. Because bandwidth and delay are the most heavily weighed parts of the metric, IGRP would have chosen the route with the T1 lines. RIP, which looks only at hop counts, would say the links were equal and would have load-balanced between the paths.

When the topology in a distance vector protocol internetwork changes, routing table updates must occur. As with the network discovery process, topology change updates proceed step-by-step from router to router.

Distance vector algorithms call for each router to send its entire routing table to each of its adjacent or directly connected neighbors. Distance vector routing tables include information about the total path cost (defined by its metric) and the logical address of the first router on the path to each network it knows about.

When a router receives an update from a neighboring router, it compares the update to its own routing table. The router adds the cost of reaching the neighboring router to the path cost reported by the neighbor to establish the new metric. If the router learns about a better route (smaller total metric) to a network from its neighbor, the router updates its own routing table.

For example, if Router B in Figure 4-17 is one unit of cost from Router A, Router B would add 1 to all costs reported by Router A when Router B runs the distance vector processes to update its routing table.

Figure 4-17   *Maintaining Routes*

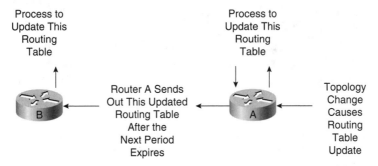

Routing Loops

When maintaining the routing information, routing loops can occur if the internetwork's slow convergence after a topology change causes inconsistent routing entries. The example presented in the next few pages uses a simple network design to convey the concepts. Later in this chapter, you look at how routing loops occur and are corrected in more complex network designs. Figure 4-18 illustrates how each node maintains the distance from itself to each possible destination network.

Figure 4-18   *Routing Loops*

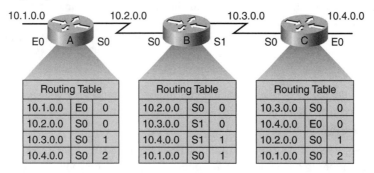

Just before the failure of network 10.4.0.0, shown in Figure 4-19, all routers have consistent knowledge and correct routing tables. The network is said to have *converged*. For this example, the cost function is hop count, so the cost of each link is 1. Router C is directly connected to network 10.4.0.0 with a distance of 0. Router A's path to network 10.4.0.0 is through Router B, with a hop count of 2.

Figure 4-19   *Slow Convergence Produces Inconsistent Routing*

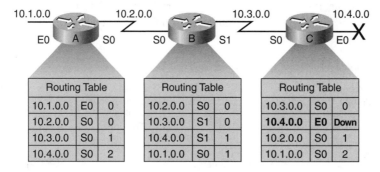

When network 10.4.0.0 fails, Router C detects the failure and stops routing packets out its E0 interface. However, Routers A and B have not yet received notification of the failure.

Router A still believes it can access 10.4.0.0 through Router B. Router A's routing table still reflects a path to network 10.4.0.0 with a distance of 2.

Because Router B's routing table indicates a path to network 10.4.0.0, Router C believes it has a viable path to network 10.4.0.0 through Router B. Router C updates its routing table to reflect a path to network 10.4.0.0 with a hop count of 2, as illustrated in Figure 4-20.

Figure 4-20   *Inconsistent Path Information Between Routers*

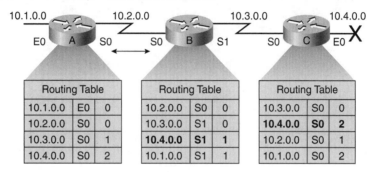

Router B receives a new update from Router C (3 hops). Router A receives the new routing table from Router B, detects the modified distance vector to network 10.4.0.0, and recalculates its own distance vector to 10.4.0.0 as 4.

Because Routers A, B, and C conclude that the best path to network 10.4.0.0 is through each other, packets destined to network 10.4.0.0 continue to bounce between the three routers, as illustrated in Figure 4-21.

Figure 4-21   *Routing Loop Exists Because of Erroneous Hop Count*

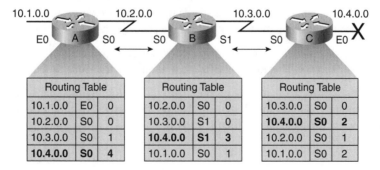

Continuing the example in Figure 4-22, the invalid updates about network 10.4.0.0 continue to loop. Until some other process can stop the looping, the routers update each other inappropriately, considering that network 10.4.0.0 is down.

This condition, called *count-to-infinity*, causes the routing protocol to continually increase its metric and route packets back and forth between the devices, despite the fundamental fact that the destination network, 10.4.0.0, is down. While the routing protocol counts to infinity, the invalid information allows a routing loop to exist, as illustrated in Figure 4-22.

Figure 4-22 *Count-to-Infinity Condition*

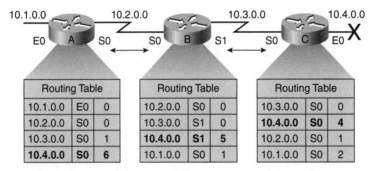

Without countermeasures to stop this process, the distance vector of hop count increments each time the routing update is broadcast to another router. This causes data packets to be sent through the network because of wrong information in the routing tables. The following sections cover the countermeasures that distance vector routing protocols use to prevent routing loops from running indefinitely.

Troubleshooting Routing Loops with Maximum Metric Settings

IP packets have inherent limits via the Time-To-Live (TTL) value in the IP header. In other words, a router must reduce the TTL field by at least 1 each time it gets the packet. If the TTL value becomes 0, the router discards that packet. However, this would not stop the router from continuing to attempt to send the packet to a network that is down.

To avoid this prolonged problem, distance vector protocols define infinity as some maximum number. This number refers to a routing metric, such as a hop count.

With this approach, the routing protocol permits the routing loop until the metric exceeds its maximum allowed value. Figure 4-23 shows this defined maximum as 16 hops. After the metric value exceeds the maximum, network 10.4.0.0 is considered unreachable.

Figure 4-23   *Maximum Metric*

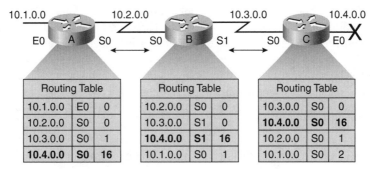

Preventing Routing Loops with Split Horizon

One way to eliminate routing loops and speed up convergence is through the technique called *split horizon*. The split horizon rule is that sending information about a route back in the direction from which the original update came is never useful. For example, Figure 4-24 illustrates the following:

- Router B has access to network 10.4.0.0 through Router C. It makes no sense for Router B to announce to Router C that Router B has access to network 10.4.0.0 through Router C.

- Given that Router B passed the announcement of its route to network 10.4.0.0 to Router A, it makes no sense for Router A to announce its distance from network 10.4.0.0 to Router B.

- Having no alternative path to network 10.4.0.0, Router B concludes that network 10.4.0.0 is inaccessible.

Figure 4-24   *Split Horizon*

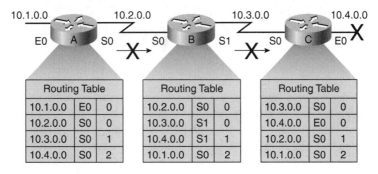

Preventing Routing Loops with Route Poisoning

Another operation complementary to split horizon is a technique called *route poisoning*. Route poisoning attempts to improve convergence time and eliminate routing loops caused by inconsistent updates. With this technique, when a router loses a link, the router advertises the loss of a route to its neighbor device. Route poisoning allows the receiving router to advertise a route back toward the source with a metric higher than the maximum. The advertisement back seems to violate split horizon, but it lets the router know that the update about the down network was received. The router that received the update also sets a table entry that keeps the network state consistent while other routers gradually converge correctly on the topology change. This mechanism allows the router to learn quickly of the down route and to ignore other updates that might be wrong for the holddown period. This prevents routing loops.

Figure 4-25 illustrates the following example. When network 10.4.0.0 goes down, Router C poisons its link to network 10.4.0.0 by entering a table entry for that link as having infinite cost (that is, being unreachable). Poisoning its route to network 10.4.0.0 makes Router C not susceptible to other incorrect updates about network 10.4.0.0 coming from neighboring routers that might claim to have a valid alternative path.

Figure 4-25 *Route Poisoning*

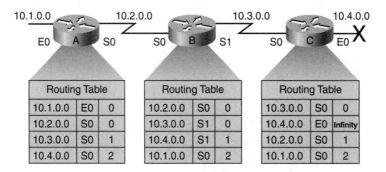

When Router B sees the metric to 10.4.0.0 jump to infinity, it sends an update called a *poison reverse* back to Router C, stating that network 10.4.0.0 is inaccessible, as illustrated in Figure 4-26. This is a specific circumstance overriding split horizon, which occurs to make sure that all routers on that segment have received information about the poisoned route.

Figure 4-26 *Poison Reverse*

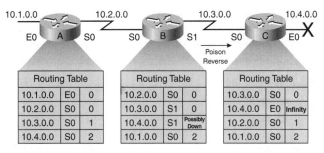

Route Maintenance Using Holddown Timers

Holddown timers prevent regular update messages from inappropriately reinstating a route that might have gone bad. Holddowns tell routers to hold any changes that might affect routes for some period of time. The holddown period is usually calculated to be just greater than the period of time necessary to update the entire network with a routing change.

Holddown timers work as follows:

1 When a router receives an update from a neighbor indicating that a previously accessible network is now inaccessible, the router marks the route as inaccessible and starts a holddown timer.

2 If an update arrives from a neighboring router with a better metric than originally recorded for the network, the router marks the network as accessible and removes the holddown timer.

3 If at any time before the holddown timer expires, an update is received from a different neighboring router with a poorer metric, the update is ignored. Ignoring an update with a higher metric when a holddown is in effect allows more time for the knowledge of the change to propagate through the entire network.

4 During the holddown period, routes appear in the routing table as "possibly down."

Figure 4-27 illustrates the holddown timer process.

Figure 4-27 *Holddown Timers*

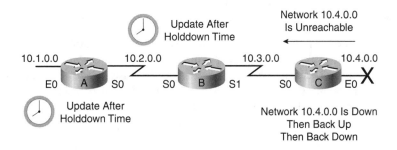

Route Maintenance Using Triggered Updates

In the previous examples, routing loops were caused by erroneous information calculated as a result of inconsistent updates, slow convergence, and timing. If routers wait for their regularly scheduled updates before notifying neighboring routers of network catastrophes, serious problems can occur, such as loops or traffic being dropped.

Normally, new routing tables are sent to neighboring routers on a regular basis. A *triggered update* is a new routing table that is sent immediately, in response to a change. The detecting router immediately sends an update message to adjacent routers, which, in turn, generate triggered updates notifying their adjacent neighbors of the change. This wave propagates throughout the portion of the network that was using the affected link. Figure 4-28 illustrates what takes place when using triggered updates.

Figure 4-28 *Triggered Updates*

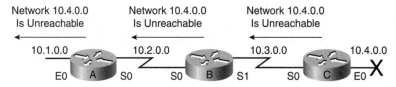

Triggered updates would be sufficient with a guarantee that the wave of updates reached every appropriate router immediately. However, two problems exist:

- Packets containing the update message can be dropped or corrupted by some link in the network.

- The triggered updates do not happen instantaneously. A router that has not yet received the triggered update can issue a regular update at just the wrong time, causing the bad route to be reinserted in a neighbor that had already received the triggered update.

Coupling triggered updates with holddowns is designed to get around these problems.

Route Maintenance Using Holddown Timers with Triggered Updates

Because the holddown rule says that when a route is invalid, no new route with the same or a higher metric will be accepted for the same destination for some period of time, the triggered update has time to propagate throughout the network.

The troubleshooting solutions presented in the previous sections work together to prevent routing loops in a more complex network design. As depicted in Figure 4-29, the routers have multiple routes to each other. As soon as Router B detects the failure of network 10.4.0.0, Router B removes its route to that network. Router B sends a trigger update to A and D, poisoning the route to network 10.4.0.0 by indicating an infinite metric to that network.

Figure 4-29   *Implementing Multiple Solutions*

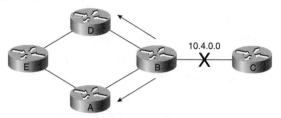

Routers D and A receive the triggered update and set their own holddown timers, noting that the 10.4.0.0 network is "possibly down." Routers D and A, in turn, send a triggered update to Router E, indicating the possible inaccessibility of network 10.4.0.0. Router E also sets the route to 10.4.0.0 in holddown. Figure 4-30 depicts how Routers A, D, and E implement holddown timers.

Figure 4-30   *Route Fails*

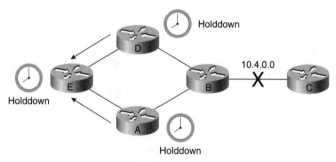

Router A and Router D send a poison reverse to Router B, stating that network 10.4.0.0 is inaccessible. Because Router E received a triggered update from A and D, it sends a poison reverse to A and D. Figure 4-31 illustrates the sending of poison reverse updates.

Figure 4-31   *Route Holddown*

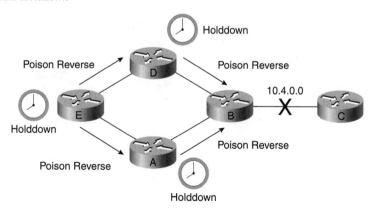

Routers A, D, and E will remain in holddown until one of the following events occurs:

- The holddown timer expires
- Another update is received, indicating a new route with a better metric
- A flush timer, which is the time a route would be held before being removed, removes the route from the routing table

During the holddown period, Routers A, D, and E assume that the network status is unchanged from its original state and attempt to route packets to network 10.4.0.0. Figure 4-32 illustrates Router E attempting to forward a packet to network 10.4.0.0. This packet will reach Router B. However, because Router B has no route to network 10.4.0.0, Router B will drop the packet and send back an ICMP network unreachable message.

Figure 4-32   *Packets During Holddown*

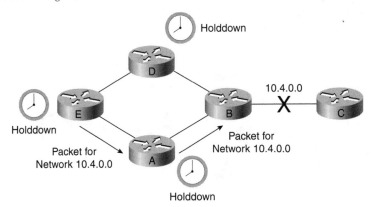

When the 10.4.0.0 network comes back up, Router B sends a trigger update to Routers A and D, notifying them that the link is active. After the holddown timer expires, Routers A and D add route 10.4.0.0 back to the routing table as accessible, as illustrated in Figure 4-33.

Figure 4-33   *Network Up*

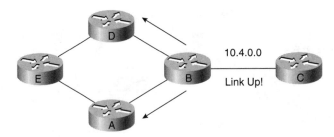

Routers A and D send Router E a routing update stating that network 10.4.0.0 is up, and Router E updates its routing table after the holddown timer expires, as illustrated in Figure 4-34.

Figure 4-34   *Network Converges*

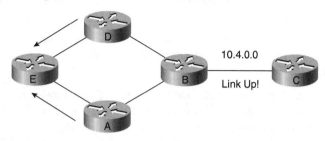

Link-State and Hybrid Routing Protocols

In addition to distance vector-based routing, the second basic algorithm used for routing is the link-state algorithm. Link-state protocols build routing tables based on a topology database. This database is built from link-state packets that are passed between all the routers to describe the state of a network. The shortest path first algorithm uses the database to build the routing table. Figure 4-35 shows the components of a link-state protocol.

Figure 4-35   *Link-State Protocols*

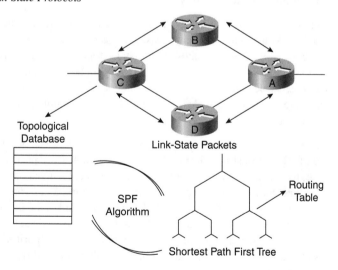

Understanding the operation of link-state routing protocols is critical to being able to enable, verify, and troubleshoot their operation.

Link-state-based routing algorithms—also known as shortest path first (SPF) algorithms—maintain a complex database of topology information. Whereas the distance vector algorithm has nonspecific information about distant networks and no knowledge of distant routers, a link-state routing algorithm maintains full knowledge of distant routers and how they interconnect.

Link-state routing uses link-state advertisements (LSAs), a topological database, the SPF algorithm, the resulting SPF tree, and, finally, a routing table of paths and ports to each network.

Open Shortest Path First (OSPF) and Intermediate System-to-Intermediate System (IS-IS) are classified as link-state routing protocols. RFC 2328 describes OSPF link-state concepts and operations. Link-state routing protocols collect routing information from all other routers in the network or within a defined area of the internetwork. After all of the information is collected, each router, independently of the other routers, calculates its best paths to all destinations in the network. Because each router maintains its own view of the network, it is less likely to propagate incorrect information provided by any one particular neighboring router.

Link-state routing protocols were designed to overcome the limitations of distance vector routing protocols. Link-state routing protocols respond quickly to network changes, send triggered updates only when a network change has occurred, and send periodic updates (known as link-state refreshes) at long time intervals, such as every 30 minutes. A hello mechanism determines the reachability of neighbors.

When a failure occurs in the network, such as a neighbor becomes unreachable, link-state protocols flood LSAs using a special multicast address throughout an area. Each link-state router takes a copy of the LSA, updates its link-state (topological) database, and forwards the LSA to all neighboring devices. LSAs cause every router within the area to recalculate routes. Because LSAs need to be flooded throughout an area and all routers within that area need to recalculate their routing tables, you should limit the number of link-state routers that can be in an area.

A link is similar to an interface on a router. The state of the link is a description of that interface and of its relationship to its neighboring routers. A description of the interface would include, for example, the IP address of the interface, the mask, the type of network to which it is connected, the routers connected to that network, and so on. The collection of link states forms a link-state, or topological, database. The link-state database is used to calculate the best paths through the network. Link-state routers find the best paths to a destination by applying Dr. Edsger Dijkstra's shortest path first (SPF) algorithm against the link-state database to build the SPF tree. The best paths are then selected from the SPF tree and placed in the routing table.

As networks become larger in scale, link-state routing protocols become more attractive for the following reasons:

- Link-state protocols always send updates in the event of a topology change.
- Periodic refresh updates are more infrequent than for distance vector protocols.

- Networks running link-state routing protocols can be segmented into area hierarchies, limiting the scope of route changes.

- Networks running link-state routing protocols support classless addressing.

- Networks running link-state routing protocols support route summarization.

Link-state protocols use a two-layer network hierarchy, as shown in Figure 4-36.

Figure 4-36   *Link-State Network Hierarchy*

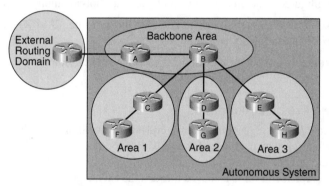

The two-layer network hierarchy contains two primary elements:

- **Area**—An area is a grouping of networks. Areas are logical subdivisions of the autonomous system (AS).

- **Autonomous system**—An AS consists of a collection of networks under a common administration that share a common routing strategy. An AS, sometimes called a domain, can be logically subdivided into multiple areas.

Within each AS, a contiguous backbone area must be defined. All other nonbackbone areas are connected off the backbone area. The backbone area is the transition area because all other areas communicate through it. For OSPF, the nonbackbone areas can be additionally configured as a stub area, a totally stubby area, a not-so-stubby area (NSSA), or a totally not-so-stubby area to help reduce the link-state database and routing table size.

Routers operating within the two-layer network hierarchy have different routing entities. The terms used to refer to these entities are different for OSPF than IS-IS. Refer to the following example:

- Router B is called the backbone router in OSPF and the L2 router in IS-IS. The backbone, or L2, router provides connectivity between different areas.

- Routers C, D, and E are called area border routers (ABRs) in OSPF, and L1/L2 routers in IS-IS. ABR, or L1/L2, routers attach to multiple areas, maintain separate link-state databases for each area to which they are connected, and route traffic destined for or arriving from other areas.

- Routers F, G, and H are called nonbackbone internal routers in OSPF, or L1 routers in IS-IS. Nonbackbone internal, or L1, routers are aware of the topology within their respective areas and maintain identical link-state databases about the areas.

- The ABR, or L1/L2, router will advertise a default route to the nonbackbone internal, or L1, router. The nonbackbone internal, or L1, router will use the default route to forward all interarea or interdomain traffic to the ABR, or L1/L2, router. This behavior can be different for OSPF, depending on how the OSPF nonbackbone area is configured (stub area, totally stubby area, or not-so-stubby area).

- Router A is the autonomous system boundary router (ASBR) that connects to an external routing domain or an AS.

- Router I is a router that belongs to another routing domain (AS).

Link-State Routing Protocol Algorithms

Link-state routing algorithms, known collectively as Shortest Path First (SPF) protocols, maintain a complex database of the network's topology. Unlike distance vector protocols, link-state protocols develop and maintain full knowledge of the network's routers and how they interconnect. This is achieved through the exchange of link-state packets (LSPs) with other routers in a network.

Each router that has exchanged LSPs constructs a topological database using all received LSPs. An SPF algorithm is then used to compute reachability to networked destinations. This information is used to update the routing table. This process can discover changes in the network topology caused by component failure or network growth.

In fact, the LSP exchange is triggered by an event in the network, instead of running periodically. This can greatly speed up the convergence process because there is no need to wait for a series of timers to expire before the networked routers can begin to converge.

If the network shown in Figure 4-37 uses a link-state routing protocol, there would be no concern about connectivity between New York City and San Francisco. Depending on the actual protocol employed and the metrics selected, it is highly likely that the routing protocol could discriminate between the two paths to the same destination and try to use the best one.

Figure 4-37   *Link-State Algorithms*

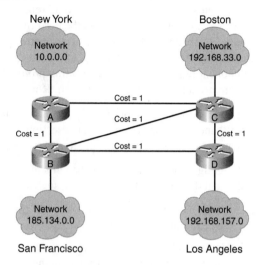

Table 4-4 summarizes the contents of the routing database of each router in the figure.

Table 4-4   *Link-State Routing Database*

Router	Destination	Next Hop	Cost
A	185.134.0.0	B	1
	192.168.33.0	C	1
	192.168.157.0	B	2
	192.168.157.0	C	2
B	10.0.0.0	A	1
	192.168.33.0	C	1
	192.168.157.0	D	1
C	10.0.0.0	A	1
	185.134.0.0	B	1
	192.168.157.0	D	1
D	10.0.0.0	B	2
	10.0.0.0	C	2
	185.134.0.0	B	1
	192.168.33.0	C	1

As shown in the table's link-state database entries for the New York (Router A) to Los Angeles (Router D) routes, a link-state protocol would remember both routes. Some link-state protocols can even provide a way to assess the performance capabilities of these two routes and bias toward the better-performing one. If the better-performing path, such as the route through Boston (Router C), experienced operational difficulties of any kind, including congestion or component failure, the link-state routing protocol would detect this change and begin forwarding packets through San Francisco (Router B).

Link-state routing might flood the network with LSPs during initial topology discovery and can be both memory- and processor-intensive. This section describes the benefits of link-state routing, the caveats to consider when using it, and the potential problems.

The following list highlights some of the many benefits that link-state routing protocols have over the traditional distance vector algorithms, such as RIP-1 or IGRP:

- Link-state protocols use cost metrics to choose paths through the network. For Cisco IOS devices, the cost metric reflects the capacity of the links on those paths.

- By using triggered, flooded updates, link-state protocols can immediately report changes in the network topology to all routers in the network. This immediate reporting generally leads to fast convergence times.

- Because each router has a complete and synchronized picture of the network, it is difficult for routing loops to occur.

- Because LSPs are sequenced and aged, routers always base their routing decisions on the latest set of information.

- With careful network design, the link-state database sizes can be minimized, leading to smaller SPF calculations and faster convergence.

The link-state approach to dynamic routing can be quite useful in networks of any size. In a well-designed network, a link-state routing protocol enables your network to gracefully adapt to unexpected topology changes. Using events, such as changes, to drive updates, rather than fixed-interval timers, enables convergence to begin that much more quickly after a topological change.

The overhead of the frequent, time-driven updates of a distance-vector routing protocol is also avoided. This allows more bandwidth to be available for routing traffic rather than for network maintenance, provided you design your network properly.

A side benefit of the bandwidth efficiency of link-state routing protocols is that they facilitate network scalability better than either static routes or distance vector protocols. When compared with the limitations of static routes or distance vector protocols, you can easily see that link-state routing is best in larger, more complex networks, or in networks that must be highly scalable. Initially configuring a link-state protocol in a large network can be challenging, but it is well worth the effort in the long run.

Link-state protocols do, however, have the following limitations:

- Link-state protocols require a topology database, an adjacency database, and a forwarding database, in addition to the routing table. This can require a significant amount of memory in large or complex networks.

- Dijkstra's algorithm requires CPU cycles to calculate the best paths through the network. If the network is large or complex (that is, the SPF calculation is complex), or if the network is unstable (that is, the SPF calculation is running on a regular basis), link-state protocols can use a significant amount of CPU power.

- To avoid an excessive use of memory or CPU power, a strict hierarchical network design is required, dividing the network into smaller areas to reduce the size of the topology tables and the length of the SPF calculation. However, this dividing can cause problems because areas must remain contiguous at all times. The routers in an area must always be capable of contacting and receiving LSPs from all other routers in their area. In a multi-area design, an area router must always have a path to the backbone, or it will have no connectivity to the rest of the network. Additionally, the backbone area must remain contiguous at all times to avoid some areas becoming isolated (partitioned).

- The configuration of link-state networks is usually simple, provided that the underlying network architecture has been soundly designed. If the network design is complex, the operation of the link-state protocol might have to be tuned to accommodate it.

- Troubleshooting is usually easier in link-state networks because every router has a complete copy of the network topology, or at least of its own area of the network. However, interpreting the information stored in the topology, neighbor databases, and routing table requires a good understanding of the concepts of link-state routing.

- Link-state protocols usually scale to larger networks than distance vector protocols, particularly the traditional distance vector protocols such as RIPv1 and IGRP.

Despite all its features and flexibility, link-state routing raises two potential concerns:

- During the initial discovery process, link-state routing protocols can flood the network with LSPs and significantly decrease the network's capability to transport data because no traffic would be passed until after the initial network convergence. This performance compromise is temporary but can be very noticeable. Whether this flooding process will noticeably degrade a network's performance depends on two things: the amount of available bandwidth, and the number of routers that must exchange routing information. Flooding in large networks with relatively small links, such as low-bandwidth links, is much more noticeable than a similar exercise on a small network with large-sized links, such as T3s, Ethernet, and so on.

- Link-state routing is both memory- and processor-intensive. Consequently, more fully configured routers are required to support link-state routing than distance vector routing. This increases the cost of the routers that are configured for link-state routing.

You can address and resolve the potential performance impacts of both drawbacks through foresight, planning, and engineering.

Hybrid Routing Protocol Algorithm

An emerging third type of routing protocol combines aspects of both distance vector and link-state. This third type is called *balanced hybrid* in this book.

The balanced hybrid routing protocol uses distance vectors with more accurate metrics to determine the best paths to destination networks. However, it differs from most distance vector protocols by using topology changes to trigger routing database updates, as opposed to periodic updates.

The balanced hybrid routing type converges more rapidly, like the link-state protocols. However, it differs from these protocols by emphasizing economy in the use of required resources, such as bandwidth, memory, and processor overhead.

An example of a balanced hybrid protocol is Cisco's Enhanced Interior Gateway Routing Protocol (EIGRP).

Section 2 Quiz

1 Which of the following describe classes of Cisco routing protocols?

   A Distance vector

   B Classless

   C Classful

   D Open systems

   E SPF

   F Link-state

   G Hybrid

2 Classful routing protocols provide which of the following features?

   A Use of variable length subnet masks

   B Auto summarization across networks

   C Fixed-length subnet masks

   D Manual summarization

   E Link-state databases

3 True or False: The Bellman-Ford-Moore algorithm is used for distance vector routing protocols?

4 OSPF uses a hierarchy that consists of which of the following elements?

  A Topology database

  B Areas

  C Core

  D Access

  E Hybrid

  F Autonomous system

5 EIGRP is considered which of the following types of routing protocols?

  A Link-state

  B Distance vector

  C Classful

  D Classless

  E Hybrid

  F Proprietary

  G Interior Gateway Protocol

  H Exterior Gateway Protocol

  I Advanced distance vector

Routing Protocol Command Summary

Table 4-5 briefly describes the commands covered in this chapter.

Table 4-5 *Routing Command Summary*

Command	Description
ip route *network mask* {*address* | *interface*} [*distance*] [**permanent**]	Defines a static route
show ip route	Displays the IP routing table
ip classless	Allows a routing protocol to send traffic to a less-specific route if one is available

Summary

In this chapter, you learned the components that a router needs to perform routing: information sources, available routes, best routes, and maintaining of routes. You learned about the different types of protocols: distance vector, link-state, and hybrid. You also learned the shortcomings and workarounds for distance vector routing protocols. You learned how connected routes are used and how to configure a "router on a stick" for interVLAN communication of connected networks. Finally, you learned how to configure static routes on a Cisco router.

Review Questions

1 Which four things does a router need to route?

2 What are the three types of routes?

3 Which type of route do an administrators enter based on their knowledge of the network environment?

4 When does a router use a default route?

5 Give two examples of an Interior Gateway Protocol.

6 When faced with two routes from different protocols for the same network, what does a Cisco router employ to determine which route to use?

7 Which metric is used by RIP? IGRP? OSPF?

8 Name one method used to eliminate routing loops.

9 What happens to traffic destined for a network that is currently in a holddown state?

10 What command displays the routing table?

After completing this chapter, you will be able to perform the following tasks:

- Enable and configure interior routing protocols RIP, IGRP, OSPF, and EIGRP for operation on Cisco routers.

- Use the **debug** commands to see how the router exchanges routing information.

CHAPTER 5

Configuring IP Routing Protocols

A router or Layer 3 switch is designed to carry traffic between devices in different broadcast domains. These devices accomplish this by identifying and switching traffic between the logical Layer 3 networks associated with the different broadcast domains in the inter-network. For a connected network, it is easy for the router or Layer 3 switch to know the location of the networks; however, if the device does not know the location of the end network, the frame is dropped and does not reach its destination. Chapter 4, "Determining IP Routes," discussed the process of manually configuring static and default routes to provide connectivity between these networks, how dynamic routing protocols operated, and how you can use these routing protocols to allow a Layer 3 switch or router to dynam-ically learn the best path to a remote network.

For routers to dynamically learn the available and best routes in a network, they must be configured with a common routing protocol. This common routing protocol is then used to advertise information about both directly connected and learned routes to other routers. This chapter provides you with the basic information required to configure and verify the operation of RIP Version 1 (RIP-1), IGRP, EIGRP, and OSPF.

NOTE   The routing protocols discussed in this book are interior routing protocols, which are typically used in enterprise networks. Border Gateway Protocol (BGP) and all relevant commands have been purposely omitted.

Configuring Dynamic Routing Protocols

Several different types of routing protocols exist, and although they all perform the same basic function, their operation and configuration differ slightly. Ultimately, to enable a dynamic routing protocol, you must perform the following tasks:

- Select a routing protocol, such as RIP, IGRP, EIGRP, or OSPF.
- Select IP networks to be advertised and the interfaces on which to run the protocol.

You must also assign network and subnet addresses and the appropriate subnet mask to interfaces.

Dynamic routing uses broadcasts and multicasts to communicate with other routers. As
soon as a router receives information from other routers, it uses the routing metric to find
the best path to each network or subnet. Figure 5-1 shows that after you select a protocol
and set the networks to be advertised, the process begins.

Figure 5-1   *IP Routing Configuration Tasks*

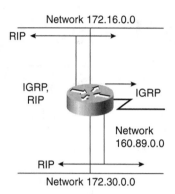

The **router** command starts the routing process. The syntax for this command is as follows:

```
router(config)#router protocol [keyword]
```

Where:

- *protocol* is RIP, IGRP, OSPF, or EIGRP.

- *keyword* refers to an autonomous system (AS) or process-id, which is used with
  protocols that require this information, such as IGRP, EIGRP, and OSPF.

The **network** command is required because it allows the routing process to determine
which interfaces will participate in sending and receiving routing updates. The **network**
command starts the routing protocol on all of a router's interfaces that have IP addresses
within the specified network scope. The **network** command also allows the router to
advertise that network to other routers. The syntax for this command is as follows:

```
router(config-router)#network network-number
```

The *network-number* parameter specifies a directly connected network.

The *network-number* parameter for RIP and IGRP must be based on the major-class
network numbers, not subnet numbers or individual addresses because, as discussed in
Chapter 4, these are classful networks. The network number also must identify a network
to which the router is physically connected.

After you enable the protocol and choose which networks to advertise, the router begins to
dynamically learn the networks and paths available in the internetwork.

Enabling RIP

In this section, you learn about the operation of the Routing Information Protocol (RIP) and how to configure it on a Cisco router. Figure 5-2 shows how RIP would choose a route based on the single metric of hop count.

Figure 5-2   *RIP Overview*

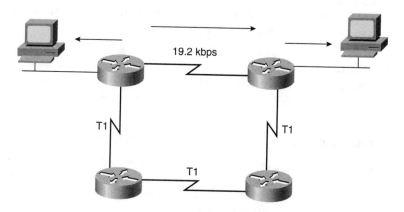

RFC 1058 describes RIP Version 1 (RIP-1). An enhanced version, RIP Version 2 (RIP-2), a classless routing protocol, is defined in RFC 1721 and 1722.

NOTE   You can find all RFCs online at http://www.isi.edu/in-notes/rfcxxxx.txt, where xxxx is the number of the RFC. If you do not know the number of the RFC, you can try searching by topic at http://www.rfc-editor.org/cgi-bin/rfcsearch.pl.

Key characteristics of RIP include the following:

- It is a distance vector routing protocol.
- Hop count is used as the metric for path selection.
- The maximum allowable hop count is 15.
- Routing updates in the form of the routing table are broadcast every 30 seconds, by default.
- For Cisco routers, RIP can load balance over as many as six equal-cost paths. (Four paths is the default.)

- RIP-1 requires that for each major classful network number being advertised, only one network mask can be used per network number. The mask is a fixed-length subnet mask. Standard RIP-1 does not offer triggered updates.

- RIP-2 permits variable-length subnet masks (VLSMs) on the internetwork. (Standard RIP-2 supports triggered updates.)

Defining the maximum number of parallel paths allowed in a routing table enables RIP load balancing. With either version of RIP, the path costs must be equal. If the **maximum-paths** command is set to 1, load balancing is disabled.

NOTE   Cisco routers support RIP-1 and RIP-2. In this book, you learn how to enable only RIP-1.

The **router rip** command selects RIP as the routing protocol.

The **network** command assigns a major network number to which the router is directly connected. The routing process associates interface addresses with the advertised network number and begins packet processing on the specified interfaces. Figure 5-3 demonstrates how you would configure RIP on a network.

Figure 5-3   *RIP Configuration Example*

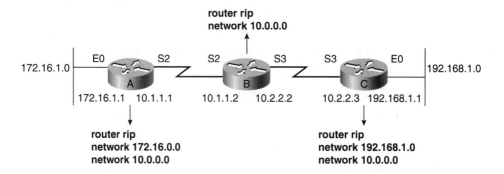

The following points are true for Router A in Figure 5-3:

- **router rip** selects RIP as the routing protocol.

- **network 172.16.0.0** specifies a directly connected network.

- **network 10.0.0.0** specifies a directly connected network.

The Router A interfaces connected to networks 172.16.0.0 and 10.0.0.0 will send and receive RIP updates. These interfaces, or any interfaces with subnets of these network addresses, will also be advertised to neighboring routers. These routing updates allow the router to learn the network topology.

Verifying RIP Routing Information

The **show ip protocols** command displays values associated with routing timers and network information associated with the entire router. Use this information to identify a router that is suspected of delivering bad routing information. For example, running **show ip protocols** on Router A in Figure 5-3 results in the output shown in Example 5-1.

Example 5-1   **show ip protocols** *Displays Routing Timer Values and Router Network Information*

```
RouterA#show ip protocols
Routing Protocol is "rip"
  Sending updates every 30 seconds, next due in 0 seconds
  Invalid after 180 seconds, hold down 180, flushed after 240
  Outgoing update filter list for all interfaces is
  Incoming update filter list for all interfaces is
  Redistributing: rip
  Default version control: send version 1, receive any version
    Interface       Send  Recv   Key-chain
    Ethernet0        1     1 2
    Serial2          1     1 2
  Routing for Networks:
    10.0.0.0
    172.16.0.0
  Routing Information Sources:
    Gateway         Distance      Last Update
    10.1.1.2             120      00:00:10
  Distance: (default is 120)
```

From the output in Example 5-1, you can see that Router A sends updated routing table information every 30 seconds. (This interval can be configured, but it must be the same on the sending and receiving routers.) If a router running RIP does not receive an update from another router for 180 seconds, it marks the routes served by the nonupdating router as being invalid. As shown in Example 5-1, the holddown timer is set to 180 seconds, so an update to a route that was down and is now up will not be made until 180 seconds have passed.

If still no update materializes after 240 seconds, the router removes all routing table entries from Router B. As shown in the highlighted line of Example 5-1, it has been 10 seconds since Router A received an update from Router B.

The router is advertising routes for the networks listed after the **Routing for Networks:** line.

The distance default of 120 refers to the administrative distance for a RIP route.

Displaying IP Routing Table Information in RIP Networks

The **show ip route** command displays the contents of the IP routing table for Router A in Figure 5-3, as demonstrated in Example 5-2.

Example 5-2 **show ip route** *Displays IP Routing Table Contents*

```
RouterA#show ip route
Codes: C - connected, S - static, I - IGRP, R - RIP, M - mobile, B - BGP
       D - EIGRP, EX - EIGRP external, O - OSPF, IA - OSPF inter area
       N1 - OSPF NSSA external type 1, N2 - OSPF NSSA external type 2
       E1 - OSPF external type 1, E2 - OSPF external type 2, E - EGP
       i - IS-IS, L1 - IS-IS level-1, L2 - IS-IS level-2, * - candidate default
       U - per-user static route, o - ODR
       T - traffic engineered route

Gateway of last resort is not set

       172.16.0.0/24 is subnetted, 1 subnets
C         172.16.1.0 is directly connected, Ethernet0
       10.0.0.0/24 is subnetted, 2 subnets
R         10.2.2.0 [120/1] via 10.1.1.2, 00:00:07, Serial2
C         10.1.1.0 is directly connected, Serial2
R      192.168.1.0/24 [120/2] via 10.1.1.2, 00:00:07, Serial2
```

The routing table contains entries for all known networks and subnetworks. It also contains a code that indicates how that information was learned. Table 5-1 explains the output of key fields and their functions from the **show ip route** command.

Table 5-1 **show ip route** *Output Fields*

Output	Description
R or C	Identifies the source of the route. For example, a C indicates that the route was learned from a directly connected interface on the router. R indicates that RIP is the routing protocol that learned of the route.
192.168.1.0	Indicates the route's address of the destination network.
[120/1]	The first number in brackets is the administrative distance of the information source; the second number is the metric for the route (for example, 1 hop).
via 10.1.1.2	Specifies the address of the next-hop router to reach the remote network.
00:00:07	Specifies the time since the route was updated in hours:minutes:seconds.
Serial2	Specifies the interface through which the specified network can be reached.

Examine the output to see if the routing table is populated with routing information.

If routing information is not being exchanged (that is, if the output of the **show ip route** command shows no entries that were learned from a routing protocol), use the **show running-config** or **show ip protocols** privileged EXEC commands on the router to check for a possible misconfigured routing protocol.

Displaying RIP Routing Updates

The **debug ip rip** command displays RIP routing updates as they are sent and received. Example 5-3 displays the output that results when you run **debug ip rip** on Router A in Figure 5-3.

Example 5-3   **debug ip rip** *Displays RIP Routing Update Information*

```
RouterA#debug ip rip
RIP protocol debugging is on
RouterA#
00:06:24: RIP: received v1 update from 10.1.1.2 on Serial2
00:06:24:       10.2.2.0 in 1 hops
00:06:24:       192.168.1.0 in 2 hops
00:06:33: RIP: sending v1 update to 255.255.255.255 via Ethernet0 (172.16.1.1)
00:06:34:       network 10.0.0.0, metric 1
00:06:34:       network 192.168.1.0, metric 3
00:06:34: RIP: sending v1 update to 255.255.255.255 via Serial2 (10.1.1.1)
```

The **no debug all** command turns off all debugging. Because debugging output can be overwhelming, turning off all debugging is often useful.

Section 1 Quiz

1 Which of the following are true of RIPv1. (Choose all that apply.)

   A It is a distance vector protocol.

   B It uses bandwidth for a metric.

   C It stores information about all routes in the network in a database.

   D It sends broadcast updates.

   E It sends updates every 30 seconds.

2 True or False: When a router has a route to a network in holddown state, it will not attempt to forward packets to that network.

3 RIP will advertise for which networks?

   A All connected networks

   B All connected networks identified with a network statement

   C Networks learned via the RIP protocol

   D All networks identified with a network statement

4 Which of the following is the administrative distance for RIP?

   A 110

   B 100

   C 155

   D 90

   E 120

5 Which **show** command will display the local networks being advertised by the RIP process?

   A **show ip route**

   B **show ip protocol**

   C **show rip networks**

   D **show rip protocol**

   E **show ip route rip**

Enabling IGRP

This section provides an overview of Interior Gateway Routing Protocol (IGRP) and describes how to configure it on a Cisco router.

IGRP is an advanced distance vector routing protocol developed by Cisco in the mid-1980s. IGRP has several features that differentiate it from other distance vector routing protocols, such as RIP:

- **Increased scalability**—Improved for routing in larger networks compared to networks that use RIP. You can use IGRP to overcome RIP's 15-hop limit. IGRP has a default maximum hop count of 100 hops, which can be configured to a maximum of 255 hops.

- **Sophisticated metric**—IGRP uses a composite metric that provides significant route selection flexibility. By default, internetwork delay and bandwidth are used to arrive at a composite metric. Optionally, reliability, load, and MTU can also be included in the metric computation.

- **Multiple path support**—IGRP can maintain up to six unequal cost paths between a network source and destination; unlike RIP, the paths do not mandate equal costs. You can use multiple paths to increase available bandwidth or for route redundancy.

Use IGRP in IP networks that require a simple, robust, and more scalable routing protocol than RIP. IGRP also performs triggered updates, which gives it another advantage over RIP-1.

IGRP Metrics

IGRP uses a composite routing metric. This combination metric provides greater accuracy than RIP's hop count metric when choosing a path to a destination. The path that has the smallest metric value is the best route. By default, the IGRP metrics are weighted with the constants K1 through K5. These constants convert an IGRP metric vector into a scalar quantity.

NOTE   The constants listed are used to compute values for path selection. You can control the weight of the different metric items by changing the constants (k).

The IGRP metric formula is as follows:

metric = [k1 * *bandwidth* + (k2 * *bandwidth*)/(256 - load) + k3 * *delay*]

If k5 does not equal zero, an additional operation is performed:

metric = *metric* * [k5/(*reliability* + k4)]

IGRP's metric includes the following components:

- **Bandwidth**—The lowest bandwidth value in the path
- **Delay**—The cumulative interface delay along the path
- **Reliability**—The reliability between source and destination, determined by the exchange of keepalives
- **Load**—The load on a link between source and destination, based on bits per second
- **MTU**—The maximum transfer unit value of the path

By default, only bandwidth and delay are used by the IGRP metric. Nonetheless, IGRP permits a wide range of components for its metrics. Reliability and load are expressed only as a percentage of a number divided by 255 and can take on any value between 0 percent and 100 percent. Bandwidth can take on values reflecting speeds from 1200 bps to 10 Gbps. Delay can take on any value from 1 to $2 * 10^{23}$. Based on the composite metric, IGRP would choose the lower path in Figure 5-4 because of the high-bandwidth links.

Wide metric ranges allow satisfactory metric settings in internetworks with widely varying performance characteristics. Most importantly, the metric components are combined in a user-definable algorithm.

As a result, network administrators can influence route selection in an intuitive fashion. Adjusting IGRP metric values can dramatically affect network performance. Make all metric adjustment decisions carefully.

Figure 5-4 *Composite Metric*

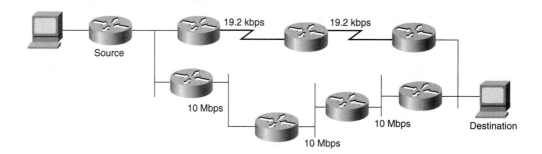

IGRP Unequal-Cost Load Balancing

Using the IGRP composite routing metric, IGRP supports multiple paths between source and destination. For example, dual, equal-bandwidth lines can run a single stream of traffic in a round-robin fashion, with automatic switchover to the second line if one line goes down.

Also, multiple paths can be used even if the metrics for the paths are different. If, for example, one path is three times better than another because its metric is three times lower, the better path will be used three times as often. Only routes with metrics that are within a certain range of the best route are used as multiple paths. Figure 5-5 illustrates that IGRP can use multiple paths between source and destination.

Figure 5-5 *IGRP Unequal Multiple Paths*

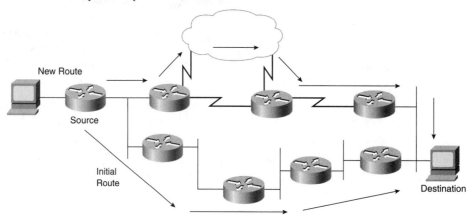

Unequal-cost load balancing allows traffic to be distributed among up to six unequal-cost paths to provide greater overall throughput and reliability.

The following general rules apply to IGRP unequal-cost load balancing:

- IGRP accepts up to six paths for a given destination network (four is the default).
- The next-hop router in any of the paths must be closer to the destination than the local router is by its best path. This ensures that a routing loop will not begin.
- The alternative path metric must be within the specified variance of the best local metric. Variance is discussed in the next section.

IGRP Routing Process

Use the **router igrp** and **network** commands to create an IGRP routing process. Note that IGRP requires an AS number. The AS number does not have to be registered. All routers within an AS, however, must use the same AS number, or they will not exchange routing information. The **network** command identifies a major network number to which the router is directly connected. The routing process associates interface addresses with the advertised network number and begins packet processing on the specified interfaces. The syntax for the **router igrp** and **network** commands is as follows:

```
router(config)#router igrp autonomous-system
router(config-router)#network network-number
```

Figure 5-6 presents a sample IGRP configuration.

Figure 5-6   *IGRP Configuration Example*

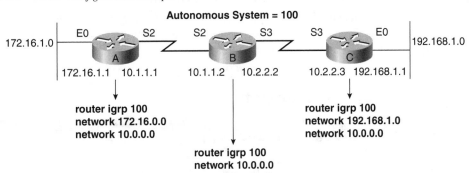

The following points are true for Router A in Figure 5-6:

- **router igrp 100** enables the IGRP routing process for AS 100.
- **network 172.16.0.0** associates network 172.16.0.0 and its interfaces with the IGRP routing process.
- **network 10.0.0.0** associates network 10.0.0.0 and its interfaces with the IGRP routing process.

IGRP sends updates out interfaces in networks 10.0.0.0 and 172.16.0.0. It also advertises directly connected networks 10.0.0.0 and 172.16.0.0, as well as other networks that it learns about through IGRP. (Therefore, it also sends information about 192.168.1.0.)

IGRP Load Balancing and Sharing

IGRP supports load balancing and load sharing. The **variance** router configuration command controls load balancing in an IGRP environment. Use the **variance** command to configure unequal-cost load balancing by defining the difference between the best metric and the worst acceptable metric. The syntax for the **variance** command is as follows:

```
router(config-router)#variance multiplier
```

The *multiplier* parameter specifies the range of metric values that will be accepted for load balancing. This range is from the lowest (or best) metric value to the lowest metric value multiplied by the variance *multiplier* value. Acceptable values are nonzero, positive integers. The default value is 1, which means equal-cost load balancing.

Setting the difference between the best metric and the worst acceptable metric allows the router to determine the feasibility of a potential route. A route is feasible if the next router in the path is closer to the destination than the current router, and if the metric for the entire path is within the variance. Only paths that are feasible can be used for load balancing and are included in the routing table.

You can use the **traffic-share {balanced | min}** command to control how traffic is distributed among IGRP load-sharing routes. The syntax for this command is as follows:

```
router(config-router)#traffic-share {balanced | min}
```

Using the **balanced** option with the **traffic-share** command distributes traffic proportionally to the metrics' ratios. Using the **min** option with the **traffic-share** command specifies to use routes that have minimum costs.

Verifying IGRP Routing Information

The **show ip protocols** command displays parameters, filters, and network information about the entire router. Running the **show ip protocols** command on Router A in Figure 5-6 results in the output shown in Example 5-4.

Example 5-4   **show ip protocols** *Displays Router Parameters, Filters, and Network Information*

```
RouterA#show ip protocols
Routing Protocol is "igrp 100"
  Sending updates every 90 seconds, next due in 21 seconds
  Invalid after 270 seconds, hold down 280, flushed after 630
  Outgoing update filter list for all interfaces is
  Incoming update filter list for all interfaces is
  Default networks flagged in outgoing updates
  Default networks accepted from incoming updates
```

Example 5-4   **show ip protocols** *Displays Router Parameters, Filters, and Network Information (Continued)*

```
IGRP metric weight K1=1, K2=0, K3=1, K4=0, K5=0
IGRP maximum hopcount 100
IGRP maximum metric variance 1
Redistributing: igrp 100
Routing for Networks:
  10.0.0.0
  172.16.0.0
Routing Information Sources:
  Gateway         Distance      Last Update
  10.1.1.2             100      00:01:01
Distance: (default is 100)
```

The information from the **show ip protocols** command output includes the AS, routing timers, networks, and administrative distance. Table 5-2 documents the key fields in the **show ip protocols** output in Example 5-4.

Table 5-2   **show ip protocols** *Output Fields*

Output	Description
Routing Protocol	Routing protocol and AS.
Update	Rate at which updates are sent.
Invalid	Number of seconds after which a route is declared invalid. The default value of **invalid** should be three times the update value.
Hold down	Number of seconds during which routing information regarding the worst path is suppressed. The value of **hold down** should be at least three times the value of **update**.
Flushed	Number of seconds that must pass before the route is removed from the routing table. The value of **flushed** should be equal to or greater than the sum of the values of **invalid** and **hold down**.

The constants used to weigh the metrics in the IGRP routing algorithm are also displayed with the **show ip protocols** command. Only the bandwidth (K1) and delay (K3) are used in the algorithm by default, because they are set to 1, as highlighted in Example 5-4.

Displaying IP Routing Table Information in IGRP Networks

The **show ip route** command displays the contents of the IP routing table. The table contains a list of all known networks and subnets associated with each entry. Running the **show ip route** command on Router A in Figure 5-6 results in the output shown in Example 5-5.

Example 5-5 **show ip route** *Displays IP Routing Table Contents*

```
RouterA#show ip route
Codes: C - connected, S - static, I - IGRP, R - RIP, M - mobile, B - BGP
       D - EIGRP, EX - EIGRP external, O - OSPF, IA - OSPF inter area
       N1 - OSPF NSSA external type 1, N2 - OSPF NSSA external type 2
       E1 - OSPF external type 1, E2 - OSPF external type 2, E - EGP
       i - IS-IS, L1 - IS-IS level-1, L2 - IS-IS level-2, * - candidate default
       U - per-user static route, o - ODR
       T - traffic engineered route

Gateway of last resort is not set

     172.16.0.0/24 is subnetted, 1 subnets
C       172.16.1.0 is directly connected, Ethernet0
     10.0.0.0/24 is subnetted, 2 subnets
I       10.2.2.0 [100/90956] via 10.1.1.2, 00:00:23, Serial2
C       10.1.1.0 is directly connected, Serial2
I    192.168.1.0/24 [100/91056] via 10.1.1.2, 00:00:23, Serial2
```

Note that in Example 5-5, the information was learned from IGRP (I) or from directly connected interfaces (C). In the routing table, the highlighted **[100/90956]** output is the IGRP administrative distance and the metric.

Displaying IGRP Routing Transaction Information

The **debug ip igrp transactions** command displays transaction information between IGRP routers.

The optional parameter for the **debug ip igrp transactions** command, *ip-address*, specifies an IGRP neighbor's IP address. Using this parameter, the resulting output includes only messages describing updates from that neighbor and updates that the router broadcasts toward that neighbor. Running the **debug ip igrp transactions** command on Router A in Figure 5-6 results in the output shown in Example 5-6.

Example 5-6 **debug ip igrp transactions** *Displays IGRP Routing Transaction Information*

```
RouterA#debug ip igrp transactions
IGRP protocol debugging is on
RouterA#
00:21:06: IGRP: sending update to 255.255.255.255 via Ethernet0 (172.16.1.1)
00:21:06:      network 10.0.0.0, metric=88956
00:21:06:      network 192.168.1.0, metric=91056
00:21:07: IGRP: sending update to 255.255.255.255 via Serial2 (10.1.1.1)
00:21:07:      network 172.16.0.0, metric=1100
```

Example 5-6   **debug ip igrp transactions** *Displays IGRP Routing Transaction Information (Continued)*

```
00:21:16: IGRP: received update from 10.1.1.2 on Serial2
00:21:16:       subnet 10.2.2.0, metric 90956 (neighbor 88956)
00:21:16:       network 192.168.1.0, metric 91056 (neighbor 89056)
```

As Example 5-6 illustrates, Router A exchanges update IGRP messages with its neighbors. Use the **no debug ip igrp transactions** or **no debug all** commands to disable the debugging output.

Displaying IGRP Routing Information Summaries

When you have many networks in your routing table, displaying every update for every route can flood the console and make the router unusable. In this case, the **debug ip igrp events** command displays a summary of the IGRP routing information. This command indicates the source and destination of each update, as well as the number of routes in each update. Messages are not generated for each route. Running the **debug ip igrp events** command on Router A in Figure 5-6 results in the output shown in Example 5-7.

Example 5-7   **debug ip igrp events** *Displays IGRP Routing Information Summaries*

```
RouterA#debug ip igrp events
IGRP event debugging is on
RouterA#
00:23:44: IGRP: sending update to 255.255.255.255 via Ethernet0 (172.16.1.1)
00:23:44: IGRP: Update contains 0 interior, 2 system, and 0 exterior routes.
00:23:44: IGRP: Total routes in update: 2
00:23:44: IGRP: sending update to 255.255.255.255 via Serial2 (10.1.1.1)
00:23:45: IGRP: Update contains 0 interior, 1 system, and 0 exterior routes.
00:23:45: IGRP: Total routes in update: 1
00:23:48: IGRP: received update from 10.1.1.2 on Serial2
00:23:48: IGRP: Update contains 1 interior, 1 system, and 0 exterior routes.
00:23:48: IGRP: Total routes in update: 2
```

If an IGRP neighbor's IP address is specified when issuing the **debug ip igrp events** command, the resulting output includes only messages describing updates from that neighbor and updates that the router broadcasts toward that neighbor. Example 5-7 illustrates updates between Router A and its neighbors.

As with the **debug ip igrp transactions** command, the optional parameter for the **debug ip igrp events** command, *ip-address*, specifies an IGRP neighbor's IP address.

Use the **no debug ip igrp events** or **no debug all** commands to disable the debugging output.

IGRP Routing Update Example

This section runs through a routing update scenario using IGRP when an Ethernet connection fails, as illustrated in Figure 5-7.

Figure 5-7 *IGRP Routing Update with Failed Ethernet Connection*

Example 5-8 shows normal IGRP routing updates being sent and received on the router.

Example 5-8 *IGRP Debugging Example*

```
RouterA#debug ip igrp events
IGRP event debugging is on
RouterA#
00:23:44: IGRP: sending update to 255.255.255.255 via Ethernet0 (172.16.1.1)
00:23:44: IGRP: Update contains 0 interior, 2 system, and 0 exterior routes.
00:23:44: IGRP: Total routes in update: 2
00:23:44: IGRP: sending update to 255.255.255.255 via Serial2 (10.1.1.1)
00:23:45: IGRP: Update contains 0 interior, 1 system, and 0 exterior routes.
00:23:45: IGRP: Total routes in update: 1
00:23:48: IGRP: received update from 10.1.1.2 on Serial2
00:23:48: IGRP: Update contains 1 interior, 1 system, and 0 exterior routes.
00:23:48: IGRP: Total routes in update: 2
```

Next, as demonstrated by Example 5-9, assume the Ethernet network attached to Router A fails. Router A sends a triggered update to Router B, indicating that network 172.16.0.0 is inaccessible (with a metric of 4,294,967,295). Router B sends back a poison reverse update.

Example 5-9 *IGRP Transaction Output*

```
RouterA# debug ip igrp trans
00:31:15: %LINEPROTO-5-UPDOWN: Line protocol on Interface Ethernet0,
  changed state to down
00:31:15: IGRP: edition is now 3
00:31:15: IGRP: sending update to 255.255.255.255 via Serial2 (10.1.1.1)
00:31:15:        network 172.16.0.0, metric=4294967295
00:31:16: IGRP: Update contains 0 interior, 1 system, and 0 exterior routes.
00:31:16: IGRP: Total routes in update: 1
00:31:16: IGRP: broadcasting request on Serial2
00:31:16: IGRP: received update from 10.1.1.2 on Serial2
00:31:16:        subnet 10.2.2.0, metric 90956 (neighbor 88956)
00:31:16:        network 172.16.0.0, metric 4294967295 (inaccessible)
00:31:16:        network 192.168.1.0, metric 91056 (neighbor 89056)
00:31:16: IGRP: Update contains 1 interior, 2 system, and 0 exterior routes.
00:31:16: IGRP: Total routes in update: 3
```

The output in Example 5-10 reveals that Router B receives the triggered update from Router A, sends a poison reverse to Router A, and then sends a triggered update to Router C, notifying both routers that network 172.16.0.0 is "possibly down."

Example 5-10 *IGRP Updates with Network Going into Holddown*

```
RouterB#debug ip igrp trans
IGRP protocol debugging is on
RouterB#
1d19h: IGRP: sending update to 255.255.255.255 via Serial2 (10.1.1.2)
1d19h:        subnet 10.2.2.0, metric=88956
1d19h:        network 192.168.1.0, metric=89056
1d19h: IGRP: sending update to 255.255.255.255 via Serial3 (10.2.2.2)
1d19h:        subnet 10.1.1.0, metric=88956
1d19h:        network 172.16.0.0, metric=89056
1d19h: IGRP: received update from 10.1.1.1 on Serial2
1d19h:        network 172.16.0.0, metric 4294967295 (inaccessible)
1d19h: IGRP: edition is now 10
1d19h: IGRP: sending update to 255.255.255.255 via Serial2 (10.1.1.2)
1d19h:        subnet 10.2.2.0, metric=88956
1d19h:        network 172.16.0.0, metric=4294967295
1d19h:        network 192.168.1.0, metric=89056
1d19h: IGRP: sending update to 255.255.255.255 via Serial3 (10.2.2.2)
1d19h:        subnet 10.1.1.0, metric=88956
1d19h:        network 172.16.0.0, metric=4294967295
```

As demonstrated by Example 5-10, Router B also places the route to network 172.16.0.0 in the holddown state for 280 seconds. During holddown state, the route to network 172.16.0.0 is marked as "possibly down" in the routing table. Router B tries to send traffic to network 172.16.0.0 until the holddown timer expires.

In Example 5-11, an administrator attempts to ping network 172.16.0.0 without success.

Example 5-11 *Routing Table Shows Network in Holddown State*

```
RouterB#show ip route
Codes: C - connected, S - static, I - IGRP, R - RIP, M - mobile, B - BGP
       D - EIGRP, EX - EIGRP external, O - OSPF, IA - OSPF inter area
       N1 - OSPF NSSA external type 1, N2 - OSPF NSSA external type 2
       E1 - OSPF external type 1, E2 - OSPF external type 2, E - EGP
       i - IS-IS, L1 - IS-IS level-1, L2 - IS-IS level-2, * - candidate default
       U - per-user static route, o - ODR
       T - traffic engineered route

Gateway of last resort is not set

I    172.16.0.0/16 is possibly down, routing via 10.1.1.1, Serial2
     10.0.0.0/24 is subnetted, 2 subnets
C       10.1.1.0 is directly connected, Serial2
C       10.2.2.0 is directly connected, Serial3
I    192.168.1.0/24 [100/89056] via 10.2.2.3, 00:00:14, Serial3
RouterB#ping 172.16.1.1
```

continues

Example 5-11 *Routing Table Shows Network in Holddown State (Continued)*

```
Type escape sequence to abort.
Sending 5, 100-byte ICMP Echos to 172.16.1.1, timeout is 2 seconds:
.....
Success rate is 0 percent (0/5)
RouterB#
```

If the link comes back up, Router A sends another triggered update to Router B, stating that network 172.16.0.0 is now accessible (with metric 89,056). In Figure 5-8, Router B would receive the triggered update.

Figure 5-8   *Routing Update*

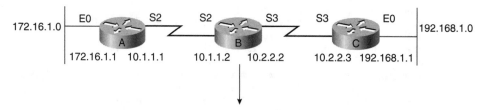

Even though Router B receives the update, Router B keeps the route in holddown state. Router B will not remove the route from holddown state and update its routing table until the holddown timer expires.

In Example 5-11, the holddown timer has not yet expired, so the route is still "possibly down." However, the administrator at Router B can now successfully ping network 172.16.0.0.

Section 2 Quiz

1 Which of the following are true of IGRP. (Choose all that apply.)

   A It is a distance vector protocol.

   B It uses bandwidth when computing the metric.

   C It stores information about all routes in the network in a database.

   D It sends broadcast updates.

   E It sends updates every 45 seconds.

2 True or False: IGRP can be configured to route packets using routes with unequal paths.

3 If a router had three interfaces with the addresses 172.16.1.1/24, 172.16.2.1/24, and 172.61.3.1/24, which of the following **network** statements would need to be added to advertise all these networks?

A   network 172.16.0.0

B   network 172.16.1.0

C   network 172.16.2.0

D   network 172.16.3.0

E   network 172.61.3.0

F   network 172.61.0.0

4 Which of the following is the administrative distance for IGRP?

A   110

B   100

C   155

D   90

E   120

5 Which **debug** command displays a summary of the IGRP routing updates being sent?

A   debug ip route

B   debug ip igrp events

C   debug igrp events

D   debug igrp transactions

E   debug igrp summary

Enabling EIGRP

Enhanced Interior Gateway Routing Protocol (EIGRP) is an enhanced version of the IGRP developed by Cisco. EIGRP is a proprietary interior gateway protocol suited for many different topologies and media. In an internetwork, EIGRP scales well and provides extremely quick convergence times with minimal overhead. EIGRP is a popular choice for routing protocol on Cisco devices, and it is important to know how to configure EIGRP.

Some of the many advantages of EIGRP are as follows:

- Rapid convergence times for changes in the network topology. In some situations, convergence can be almost instantaneous. EIGRP uses the Diffusing Update Algorithm (DUAL) to achieve rapid convergence. A router running EIGRP stores backup routes for destinations, when available, so it can quickly adapt to alternate routes. If no appropriate route or backup route exists in the local routing table, EIGRP queries its neighbors to discover an alternate route. These queries are propagated until an alternate route is found.

- Very low usage of network resources during normal operation; only hello packets are transmitted on a stable network. Like other link-state routing protocols, EIGRP uses EIGRP hello packets to establish neighbor relationships with other EIGRP neighboring routers. Each router builds a neighbor table from hello packets that it receives from adjacent EIGRP routers. EIGRP does not send periodic routing updates like IGRP. When a change occurs, only routing table changes are propagated, not the entire routing table; this reduces the load that the routing protocol itself places on the network by minimizing the bandwidth required for EIGRP packets.

- EIGRP supports automatic (classful) route summarization at major network boundaries as the default. However, unlike other classful routing protocols, such as IGRP and RIP, manual route summarization can be configured on arbitrary network boundaries to reduce the size of the routing table.

- EIGRP supports multiple protocols. The EIGRP routing protocol can be configured to exchange routes for IP, IPX, and AppleTalk networks.

With any new technology, there are several terms that you must become familiar with before learning how it works. Table 5-3 summarizes several terms related to EIGRP.

Table 5-3   *EIGRP Terms*

Term	Definition
Neighbor table (AppleTalk, IPX, IP)	Each EIGRP router maintains a neighbor table that lists adjacent routers. This table is comparable to the adjacencies database used by Open Shortest Path First (OSPF). It serves the same purpose: to ensure bidirectional communication between each of the directly connected neighbors. A neighbor table exists for each protocol that EIGRP supports.
Topology table (AppleTalk, IPX, IP)	Each EIGRP router maintains a topology table for each configured routing protocol. This table includes route entries for all destinations that the router has learned. All learned routes to a destination are maintained in the topology table.
Routing table (AppleTalk, IPX, IP)	EIGRP chooses the best (successor) routes to a destination from the topology table and places these routes in the routing table. The router maintains one routing table for each network protocol.
Term	**Definition**

Table 5-3   *EIGRP Terms (Continued)*

Successor	A route selected as the primary route used to reach a destination. Successors are the entries kept in the routing table.
Feasible successor	A backup route. These routes are selected at the same time the successors are identified, but they are kept in a topology table. Multiple feasible successors for a destination can be retained.

Comparing EIGRP and IGRP

EIGRP is an enhanced proprietary version of the IGRP routing protocol developed by Cisco. EIGRP is sometimes called a hybrid routing protocol because it uses characteristics of both distance vector and link-state routing protocols.

EIGRP uses similar metric calculations and supports unequal-cost path load balancing like IGRP. However, EIGRP's convergence properties and operating efficiency have improved substantially over IGRP. While the metric (bandwidth and delay, by default) is the same for both IGRP and EIGRP, the weight assigned to the metric is 256 times greater for EIGRP.

The convergence technology is based on research conducted at SRI International and employs DUAL. This algorithm guarantees loop-free operation at every instant throughout a route computation, and allows all devices involved in a topology change to synchronize at the same time. Routers that are not affected by topology changes are not involved in recomputations. The convergence time with DUAL rivals that of any other existing routing protocol.

Configuring EIGRP

Use the **router eigrp** and **network** commands to create an EIGRP routing process. Note that EIGRP requires an AS number. The AS number does not need to be registered. However, all routers within an AS must use the same AS number or they will not exchange routing information.

The **network** command assigns a major network number to which the router is directly connected. The EIGRP routing process will associate interface addresses with the advertised network number and will begin EIGRP packet processing on the specified interfaces. The syntax for the **router eigrp** and **network** commands is as follows:

```
router(config)#router eigrp autonomous-system
router(config-router)#network network-number
```

Figure 5-9 presents a sample EIGRP configuration.

Figure 5-9 *EIGRP Configuration Example*

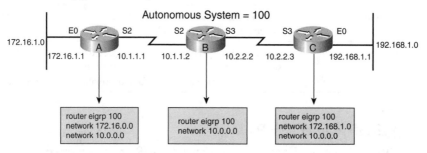

The following points apply to the EIGRP configurations on Router A for Figure 5-9:

- **router eigrp 100** enables the EIGRP routing process for AS 100.

- **network 172.16.0.0** associates network 172.16.0.0 and its interfaces with the IGRP routing process.

- **network 10.0.0.0** associates network 10.0.0.0 and its interfaces with the IGRP routing process.

EIGRP sends updates out interfaces in networks 10.0.0.0 and 172.16.0.0 and includes information about networks 10.0.0.0 and 172.16.0.0, as well as other networks about which it learns.

Verifying the EIGRP Configuration

Use the **show ip eigrp** commands to display information about your EIGRP configuration. This section describes how to verify the EIGRP configuration.

Table 5-4 describes the operation of commands used to verify EIGRP operation:

Table 5-4 *EIGRP* **show** *Commands*

Command	Description
show ip eigrp neighbors	Displays neighbors discovered by EIGRP.
show ip eigrp topology	Displays the EIGRP topology table. This command shows the topology table, the active or passive state of routes, the number of successors, and the feasible distance to the destination.
show ip route eigrp	Displays the current EIGRP entries in the routing table.
show ip protocols	Displays the parameters and current state of the active routing protocol process. This command shows the EIGRP AS number. It also displays filtering and redistribution numbers, as well as neighbors and distance information.
show ip eigrp traffic	Displays the number of EIGRP packets sent and received. This command displays statistics on hello, updates, queries, replies, and acknowledgments.

Troubleshooting the EIGRP Configuration

To display information on EIGRP packets, use the **debug ip eigrp** privileged EXEC command. This section describes the **debug** command to troubleshoot an EIGRP configuration.

This command helps you analyze the packets that are sent and received on an interface. Because the **debug ip eigrp** command generates a substantial amount of output, use it only when traffic on the network is light. Example 5-12 shows some sample **debug ip eigrp** output.

Example 5-12 **debug ip eigrp** *Sample Output*

```
Router#debug ip eigrp
IP-EIGRP: Processing incoming UPDATE packet
IP-EIGRP: Ext 192.168.3.0 255.255.255.0 M 386560 - 256000 130560
  SM 360960 - 256000 104960IP-EIGRP: Ext 192.168.0.0 255.255.255.0
  M 386560 - 256000 130560 SM 360960 - 256000 104960IP-EIGRP:
  Ext 192.168.3.0 255.255.255.0 M 386560 - 256000 130560
  SM 360960 - 256000 104960
IP-EIGRP: 172.69.43.0 255.255.255.0, - do advertise out Ethernet0/1
IP-EIGRP: Ext 172.69.43.0 255.255.255.0 metric 371200 - 256000 115200
IP-EIGRP: 192.135.246.0 255.255.255.0, - do advertise out Ethernet0/1
IP-EIGRP: Ext 192.135.246.0 255.255.255.0 metric 46310656 - 45714176 596480
IP-EIGRP: 172.69.40.0 255.255.255.0, - do advertise out Ethernet0/1
IP-EIGRP: Ext 172.69.40.0 255.255.255.0 metric 2272256 - 1657856 614400
IP-EIGRP: 192.135.245.0 255.255.255.0, - do advertise out Ethernet0/1
IP-EIGRP: Ext 192.135.245.0 255.255.255.0 metric 40622080 - 40000000 622080
IP-EIGRP: 192.135.244.0 255.255.255.0, - do advertise out Ethernet0/1
```

Table 5-5 describes the fields in the sample output from the **debug ip eigrp** command.

Table 5-5   **debug** *Output Descriptions*

Field	Description
IP-EIGRP:	Indicates that this is an IP EIGRP packet.
Ext	Indicates that the following address is an external destination rather than an internal destination, which would be labeled as Int.
M	Displays the computed metric, which includes SM and the cost between this router and the neighbor. The first number is the composite metric. The next two numbers are the inverse bandwidth and the delay, respectively.
SM	Displays the stated metric as reported by the neighbor.

Section 3 Quiz

1 What is the name of the routing algorithm used by EIGRP?

   A   Link-State

   B   Bellman-Ford

   C   Dijkstra

   D   DUAL

   ~~**E**~~   Hybrid

2 True or False: EIGRP maintains a topology table of available routes in the network.

3 EIGRP can route for which of the following protocols?

   A   IP

   B   IPX

   C   VINES

   D   AppleTalk

   E   NetBEUI

4 Which of the following does EIGRP choose as the route to be displayed in the routing table?

   A   Default route

   B   Static route

   C   Feasible successor

   D   Defacto

   E   Successor

5 Which of the following is a shortcoming of EIGRP?

   A   Slow convergence

   B   Multiprotocol support

   C   Advanced distance vector protocol

   D   Proprietary

Enabling OSPF

Open Shortest Path First (OSPF) is an interior gateway protocol. Unlike IGRP, OSPF is a classless link-state routing protocol rather than a classful distance vector protocol. This section describes the function of OSPF and how to configure a single area OSPF network on a Cisco router.

OSPF is standardized and is widely deployed in public and private networks. Knowledge of the configuration and maintenance of OSPF is essential for an internetworking professional.

OSPF Features

OSPF is an interior gateway protocol that provides the same functions as RIP, IGRP, and EIGRP, but based on link states rather than distance vectors. OSPF is a routing protocol developed for Internet Protocol (IP) networks by the Interior Gateway Protocol (IGP) working group of the Internet Engineering Task Force (IETF). The working group was formed in 1988 to design an IGP based on the Shortest Path First (SPF) algorithm.

Similar to IGRP, OSPF was created because in the mid-1980s, RIP was increasingly incapable of serving large, heterogeneous internetworks. OSPF routes packets within a single AS. The OSPF protocol is based on link-state technology, as opposed to distance vector-based algorithms used by traditional Internet intradomain routing protocols, such as RIP.

OSPF has two primary characteristics:

* The protocol is an open standard, which means that its specification is in the public domain. The OSPF specification is published as RFC 1131. The IETF developed OSPF in 1988. The most recent version, known as OSPF version 2, is described in RFC 2328.

* OSPF is based on the SPF algorithm, which sometimes is referred to as the Dijkstra algorithm, named for the person credited with its creation.

Comparing OSPF with Distance Vector Routing Protocols

OSPF advertises information about each of its links rather than sending periodic routing table updates like a distance vector protocol. This is why OSPF is called a link-state protocol. You can think of a *link* as being an interface on a router. The state of the link is a description of that interface and of its relationship to its neighboring routers. A description of the interface would include, for example, the interface's IP address, the mask, the type of network to which it is connected, the routers connected to that network, and so on. The collection of all these link states forms a *link-state database*.

OSPF calls for the sending of link-state advertisements (LSAs) to all other routers within the same hierarchical area. A router sends link-state advertisement packets to advertise its state periodically (at long intervals, such as every 30 minutes) and when the router's state changes. Information on attached interfaces, metrics used, and other variables are included in OSPF LSAs. As OSPF routers accumulate link-state information, they use the SPF algorithm to calculate the shortest path to each node.

As a link-state routing protocol, OSPF contrasts with RIP and IGRP, which are distance vector routing protocols. Routers running the distance vector algorithm send all or a portion of their routing tables in routing-update messages to their neighbors.

Unlike RIP, IGRP, and EIGRP, OSPF can operate within a controlled hierarchy. The largest entity within the hierarchy is the routing domain, which is a collection of networks under common administration that share a common routing strategy. A routing domain can be divided into a number of areas, which are groups of contiguous networks and attached hosts.

A topological (link-state) database is essentially an overall picture of networks in relationship to routers. The topological database contains the collection of LSAs received from all routers in the same area. Because routers within the same area share the same information, they have identical topological databases.

OSPF's capability to separate a large internetwork into multiple areas is also referred to as *hierarchical routing*. Hierarchical routing enables you to separate a large internetwork (autonomous system) into smaller internetworks that are called *areas*. Figure 5-10 shows hierarchical areas within an OSPF AS.

Figure 5-10 *OSPF Areas*

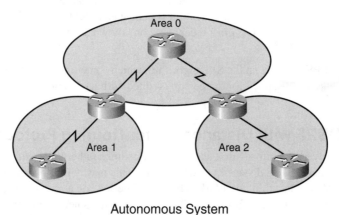

Autonomous System

With this technique, routing still occurs between the areas (called interarea routing), but many of the minute internal routing operations, such as recalculating the database, are kept within an area.

For example, in Figure 5-10, if Area 1 is having problems with a link going up and down, routers in other areas need not continually run their SPF calculation because they are isolated from the Area 1 problem.

The hierarchical topology possibilities of OSPF have some important advantages:

- Reduced frequency of SPF calculations
- Smaller routing tables
- Reduced link-state update overhead

Shortest Path First (SPF) Algorithm

The SPF algorithm places each router at the root of a tree and calculates the shortest path to each node based on the cumulative cost required to reach that destination. Link-state advertisements are flooded throughout the area using a reliable algorithm, which ensures that all routers in an area have exactly the same topological database. Each router uses the information in its topological database to calculate a shortest-path tree, with itself as the root. The router then uses this tree to route network traffic. In Figure 5-11, Router A is the root.

Figure 5-11   *OSPF Areas*

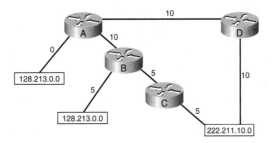

The shortest path is calculated using Dijkstra's algorithm. The algorithm places each router at the root of a tree and calculates the shortest path to each destination based on the cumulative cost required to reach that destination. Each router will have its own view of the topology, even though all the routers will build a shortest-path tree using the same link-state database.

Cisco routers determine a metric for OSPF links called cost. The cost of an interface is an indication of the overhead required to send packets across a certain interface. The cost of an interface is inversely proportional to the bandwidth of that interface, so a higher bandwidth indicates a lower cost. There is more overhead, higher cost, and more time delays involved in crossing a 56-kbps serial line than crossing a 10-Mbps Ethernet line.

The default Cisco formula used to calculate OSPF cost is as follows:

cost = 100000000 / bandwidth in bps

For example, it will cost $10^8/10^7 = 10$ to cross a 10-Mbps Ethernet line, and it will cost $10^8/1544000 = 64$ to cross a T1 line.

NOTE   The bandwidth of 10^8 used by Cisco routers and switches has a fundamental problem. If a link is 100 Mbps, 1 Gbps, or 10 Gbps, Cisco's formula calculates a cost of 1 for each of these links. This would mean that higher-bandwidth links would not be preferred over lower-bandwidth links. To correct this problem, you need to set a higher reference bandwidth for routers or switches that have links of 100 Mbps or greater. You can accomplish this by using the **auto-cost reference-bandwidth** command in router ospf configuration mode.

Configuring Single Area OSPF

Use the **router ospf** command to start an OSPF routing process and the **network** command to associate addresses to an OSPF area. This section describes how to configure OSPF with a single area:

```
router(config)#router ospf process-id
router(config-router)#network address wildcard-mask area area-id
```

The **router ospf** command takes a process identifier as an argument. This is a unique, arbitrary number that you select to identify the routing process. The process ID does not need to match the OSPF process ID on other OSPF routers.

The **network** command identifies which IP networks on the router are part of the OSPF network. For each network, you must also identify the OSPF area to which the networks belong. The **network** command takes three arguments, as described in Table 5-6.

Table 5-6   *OSPF Network Command Arguments*

router ospf Command Parameters	Description
address	Can be the network, subnet, or the interface address.
wildcard-mask	Wildcard mask. This mask identifies the part of the IP address to be matched, where 0 is a match and a 1 is "don't care." For example, a wildcard mask of 0.0.0.0 indicates a match of all 32 bits in the address.
area-id	Area that is to be associated with the OSPF address range. It can be specified as either a decimal value or in dotted-decimal notation.

Figure 5-12 presents a sample OSPF configuration.

Figure 5-12   *OSPF Configuration Example*

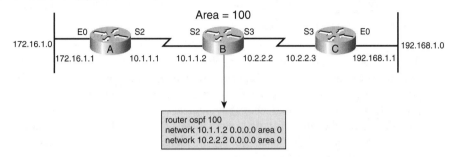

The following points apply to OSPF configurations on Router B for Figure 5-12:

- **router ospf 100** enables the OSPF routing process with a process ID of 100.

- **network 10.1.1.2 0.0.0.0 area 0** enables the OSPF process on interface serial 2, places the interface in Area 0, and advertises the network or subnetwork and mask associated with interface serial 2 using the OSPF process with id 100.

- **network 10.2.2.2 0.0.0.0 area 0** enables the OSPF process on interface serial 3, places the interface in Area 0, and advertises the network or subnetwork and mask associated with interface serial 3 using the OSPF process with id 100.

In this configuration, Router B has specified 100 as the local process ID for the OSPF routing process. Addresses that begin with 10 as the first octet are assigned to Area 0 (the backbone area). In this case, both the S2 and S3 interface on Router B will be in OSPF Area 0. Both Routers A and C will have similar configurations specifying addresses in Area 0.

Routers that share a common segment become neighbors on that segment. In the diagram, Routers A and C are neighbors of Router B, but not of each other.

A router uses the OSPF Hello protocol to establish neighbor relationships. Hello packets also act as keepalives to let routers know that other routers are still functional.

On multiaccess networks (networks supporting more than two routers), such as Ethernet networks, the Hello protocol elects a Designated Router (DR) and a Backup Designated Router (BDR). Among other things, the DR is responsible for generating LSAs for the entire multiaccess network. Designated routers allow a reduction in routing update traffic and manage link-state synchronization. The DR and BDR are elected based on the OSPF priority and OSPF router ID. The priority can be set on an interface-by-interface basis. The default priority is 1, so the router ID would be used to determine the DR and BDR. If you don't want the router to become a DR or BDR on a particular multiaccess network, you can set the priority to 0 for that interface. In nonmultiaccess networks, such as a point-to-point serial link, no DR or BDR will be elected.

Calculating wildcard masks on non-8-bit boundaries can be error-prone. One method to overcome this is to have a **network** statement that matches the IP address on each interface.

To modify the OSPF router ID to a loopback address, first define a loopback interface:

```
Router(config)#interface loopback number
```

The highest IP address used as the router ID can be overridden by configuring an IP address on a loopback interface. OSPF is more reliable if a loopback interface is configured because the interface is always active and cannot go down like a real interface. If you plan to publish your loopback address with the **network area** command, you might consider using a private IP address to save on your registered IP address space. Note that a loopback address requires a different subnet for each router, unless the host address itself is advertised. Another more reliable method for setting the router ID is to use the **router-id** command in the router OSPF configuration mode:

```
Router(config)#router ospf 101
Router(config-if)#router-id routerid
```

The router ID is entered in dotted decimal format like the address used in a loopback or network interface address.

Pros and cons exist to using an address that will not be advertised versus using an address that will be advertised. Using an unadvertised address saves on real IP address space, but the address does not appear in the OSPF table and cannot be pinged. This choice represents a tradeoff between the ease of debugging the network and conservation of address space.

Verifying the OSPF Configuration

You can use any one of a number of **show** commands to display information about an OSPF configuration. This section describes how to verify an OSPF configuration using a few of the **show** commands.

The **show ip protocols** command displays parameters about timers, filters, metrics, networks, and other information for the entire router.

The **show ip route** command displays the routes known to the router and how they were learned. This command is one of the best ways to determine connectivity between the local router and the rest of the internetwork.

The **show ip ospf interface** command verifies that interfaces have been configured in the intended areas. If no loopback address is specified, the interface with the highest address is chosen as the router ID. This command also displays the timer intervals, including the Hello interval, and shows the neighbor adjacencies.

The **show ip ospf neighbor** command displays OSPF neighbor information on a per-interface basis.

Troubleshooting the OSPF Configuration

To display information on OSPF-related events, such as adjacencies, flooding information, designated router selection, and SPF calculation, use the **debug ip ospf events** privileged EXEC command. Example 5-13 shows some sample **debug ip ospf events** output.

Example 5-13 **debug ip ospf events** *Output*

```
Router#debug ip ospf events

OSPF:hello with invalid timers on interface Ethernet0
hello interval received 10 configured 10
net mask received 255.255.255.0 configured 255.255.255.0
dead interval received 40 configured 30
```

The **debug ip ospf events** output shown might appear if any of the following situations occur:

- The IP subnet masks for routers on the same network do not match.
- The OSPF Hello interval for the router does not match that configured for a neighbor.
- The OSPF dead interval for the router does not match that configured for a neighbor.

If a router configured for OSPF routing is not seeing an OSPF neighbor on an attached network, perform the following tasks:

- Make sure that both routers have been configured with the same IP mask, OSPF Hello interval, and OSPF dead interval.
- Make sure that both neighbors are part of the same area type.

The following line from the **debug ospf events** output in Example 5-13 shows that the neighbor and this router are not both part of a stub area (that is, one is a part of a transit area and the other is a part of a stub area, as explained in RFC 1247):

```
OSPF: hello packet with mismatched E bit
```

To display information about each OSPF packet received, use the **debug ip ospf packet** privileged EXEC command. The **no** form of this command disables debugging output.

The **debug ip ospf packet** command produces one set of information for each packet received. The output varies slightly depending on which authentication is used. The following is sample output from the **debug ip ospf packet** command when Message Digest 5 (MD5) authentication is used. Example 5-14 shows some sample output for the **debug ip ospf packet** command.

Example 5-14 **depug ip ospf** *Output*

```
Router# debug ip ospf packet

OSPF: rcv. v:2 t:1 l:48 rid:200.0.0.117
      aid:0.0.0.0 chk:6AB2 aut:0 auk:
```

continues

Example 5-14 depug ip ospf *Output (Continued)*

```
Router#debug ip ospf packet

OSPF: rcv. v:2 t:1 l:48 rid:200.0.0.116
      aid:0.0.0.0 chk:0 aut:2 keyid:1 seq:0x0
```

Table 5-7 describes the fields shown in the **debug ip ospf packet** display.

Table 5-7 **debug ip ospf packet** *Field Descriptions*

Field	Description
v:	OSPF version
t:	OSPF packet type. Possible packet types are: 1: Hello 2: Data description 3: Link state request 4: Link state update 5: Link state acknowledgment
l:	OSPF packet length in bytes
rid:	OSPF router ID
aid:	OSPF area ID
chk:	OSPF checksum
aut:	OSPF authentication type. Possible authentication types are: 0: No authentication 1: Simple password 2: MD5
auk:	OSPF authentication key
keyid:	MD5 key ID
seq:	Sequence number

Section 4 Quiz

1 Which of the following are true of OSPF? (Choose all that apply.)

A It is a distance vector protocol.

B It is a hierarchical protocol.

C It uses multicast updates.

D It only sends advertisements when a link change occurs.

    E It sends broadcast updates.

    F It is a classful routing protocol.

2 True or False: OSPF process IDs must match on every router in the network.

3 What **network** statement would you use to run OSPF only on an interface with the address 192.168.255.1/27 and place it in Area 0?

    A **network 192.168.255.0 0.0.0.0 area 0**

    B **network 192.168.255.1 0.0.0.255 area 1**

    C **network 192.168.255.1 255.255.255.224 area 0**

    D **network 192.168.255.1 0.0.0.0 area 0**

4 Which of the following is the administrative distance for OSPF?

    A 110

    B 100

    C 155

    D 90

    E 155

    F 120

5 Which command can you use to troubleshoot problems with OSPF adjacencies?

    A **show ip ospf adjacencies**

    B **debug ip ospf events**

    C **debug ospf adjacencies**

    D **debug ospf events**

    E **debug ospf neighbors**

Variable-Length Subnet Masks

Variable-length subnet masks (VLSMs) were developed to allow multiple levels of subnetworked IP addresses within a single network. This strategy can be used only when it is supported by a classless routing protocol, such as OSPF and EIGRP. VLSM is a key technology on large, routed networks. Understanding its capabilities is important when planning large networks.

VLSM Features

When an IP network is assigned more than one subnet mask for a given major network, it is considered a network with VLSMs, overcoming the limitation of a fixed number of fixed-size subnetworks imposed by a single subnet mask. Figure 5-13 shows the 172.16.0.0 network with four separate subnet masks.

Figure 5-13   *VLSM Network*

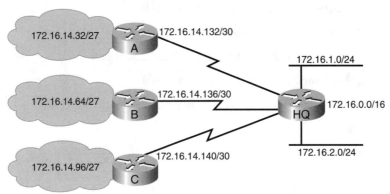

VLSMs provide the capability to include more than one subnet mask within a network and the capability to subnet an already subnetted network address. In addition, VLSM offers the following benefits:

- **Even more efficient use of IP addresses**—Without the use of VLSMs, companies must implement a single subnet mask within an entire Class A, B, or C network number.

  For example, consider the 172.16.0.0/16 network address divided into subnets using /24 masking, and one of the subnetworks in this range, 172.16.14.0/24, further divided into smaller subnets with the /27 masking, as shown in Figure 5-13. These smaller subnets range from 172.16.14.0/27 to 172.16.14.224/27. In the figure, one of these smaller subnets, 172.16.14.128/27, is further divided with the /30 prefix, creating subnets with only two hosts to be used on the WAN links. The /30 subnets range from 172.16.14.128/30 to 172.16.14.156/30. In Figure 5-13, the WAN links used the 172.16.14.132/30, 172.16.14.136/30, and 172.16.14.140/30 subnets out of the range.

- **Greater capability to use route summarization**—VLSM allows more hierarchical levels within an addressing plan, allowing better route summarization within routing tables. For example, in Figure 5-13, subnet 172.16.14.0/24 summarizes all the addresses that are further subnets of 172.16.14.0, including those from subnet 172.16.14.0/27 and from 172.16.14.128/30.

As already discussed, with VLSMs you can subnet an already subnetted address. Consider, for example, that you have a subnet address 172.16.32.0/20, and you need to assign addresses to a network that has ten hosts. With this subnet address, however, you have over

4000 ($2^{12} - 2 = 4094$) host addresses, most of which will be wasted. With VLSMs, you can further subnet the address 172.16.32.0/20 to give you more network addresses and fewer hosts per network. If, for example, you subnet 172.16.32.0/20 to 172.16.32.0/26, you gain 64 (2^6) subnets, each of which could support 62 ($2^6 - 2$) hosts.

Figure 5-14 shows how subnet 172.16.32.0/20 can be divided into smaller subnets.

Figure 5-14   *Calculating VLSM Networks*

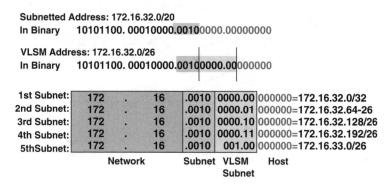

The following procedure shows how to further subnet 172.16.32.0/20 to 172.16.32.0/26:

Step 1   Write 172.16.32.0 in binary form.

Step 2   Draw a vertical line between the 20th and 21st bits, as shown in Figure 5-14. (/20 was the original subnet boundary.)

Step 3   Draw a vertical line between the 26th and 27th bits, as shown in the figure. (The original /20 subnet boundary is extended six bits to the right, becoming /26.)

Step 4   Calculate the 64 subnet addresses using the bits between the two vertical lines, from lowest to highest in value. Figure 5-14 shows the first five subnets available.

VLSMs are commonly used to maximize the number of possible addresses available for a network. For example, because point-to-point serial lines require only two host addresses, using a /30 subnet will not waste scarce IP addresses.

In Figure 5-15, the subnet addresses used on the Ethernets are those generated from subdividing the 172.16.32.0/20 subnet into multiple /26 subnets. The figure illustrates where the subnet addresses can be applied, depending on the number of host requirements. For example, the WAN links use subnet addresses with a prefix of /30. This prefix allows for only two hosts: just enough hosts for a point-to-point connection between a pair of routers.

Figure 5-15 *VLSM Example*

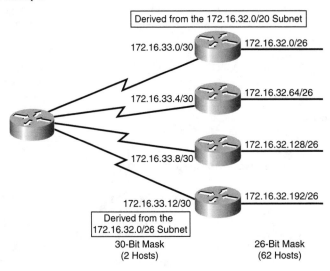

To calculate the subnet addresses used on the WAN links, further subnet one of the unused /26 subnets. In this example, 172.16.33.0/26 is further subnetted with a prefix of /30. This provides four more subnet bits, and therefore 16 (2^4) subnets for the WANs.

NOTE   Remember that only subnets that are unused can be further subnetted. In other words, if you use any addresses from a subnet, that subnet cannot be further subnetted. In the example, four subnet numbers are used on the LANs. Another unused subnet, 172.16.33.0/26, is further subnetted for use on the WANs.

Route Summarization with VLSM

In large internetworks, hundreds or even thousands of network addresses can exist. In these environments, it is often not desirable for routers to maintain many routes in their routing table. Route summarization, also called route aggregation or supernetting, can reduce the number of routes that a router must maintain by representing a series of network numbers in a single summary address. This section describes and provides examples of route summarization, including implementation considerations.

Figure 5-16 shows that Router A can either send three routing update entries or summarize the addresses into a single network number.

Figure 5-16 *VLSM Route Summarization*

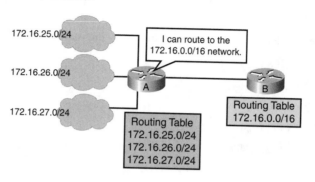

The figure illustrates a summary route based on a full octet: 172.16.25.0/24, 172.16.26.0/24, and 172.16.27.0/24 could be summarized into 172.16.0.0/16.

NOTE

Router A can route to network 172.16.0.0/16, including all subnets of that network. However, if there were other subnets of 172.16.0.0 elsewhere in the network (for example, if 172.16.0.0 were discontiguous), summarizing in this way might not be valid. Discontiguous networks and summarization are discussed later in this chapter.

Another advantage to using route summarization in a large, complex network is that it can isolate topology changes from other routers. That is, if a specific link in the 172.16.27.0/24 domain were "flapping," or going up and down rapidly, the summary route would not change. Therefore, no router external to the domain would need to keep modifying its routing table due to this flapping activity.

Route summarization is most effective within a subnetted environment when the network addresses are in contiguous blocks in powers of two. For example, 4, 16, or 512 addresses can be represented by a single routing entry because summary masks are binary masks—just like subnet masks—so summarization must take place on binary boundaries (powers of two).

Routing protocols summarize or aggregate routes based on shared network numbers within the network. Classless routing protocols, such as RIP-2, OSPF, Intermediate System-to-Intermediate System (IS-IS), and EIGRP, support route summarization based on subnet addresses, including VLSM addressing. Classful routing protocols, such as RIP-1 and IGRP, automatically summarize routes on the classful network boundary and do not support summarization on any other boundaries.

RFC 1518, *An Architecture for IP Address Allocation with CIDR*, describes summarization in full detail.

Suppose a router receives updates for the following routes:

- 172.16.168.0/24
- 172.16.169.0/24
- 172.16.170.0/24
- 172.16.171.0/24
- 172.16.172.0/24
- 172.16.173.0/24
- 172.16.174.0/24
- 172.16.175.0/24

To determine the summary route, the router determines the number of highest-order bits that match in all the addresses. By converting the IP addresses to the binary format, as shown in Figure 5-17, you can determine the number of common bits shared among the IP addresses.

Figure 5-17 *Summarizing Within an Octet*

172.16.168.0/24 =	10101100	. 00010000	. 10101	000 .	00000000
172.16.169.0/24 =	172	. 16	. 10101	001 .	0
172.16.170.0/24 =	172	. 16	. 10101	010 .	0
172.16.171.0/24 =	172	. 16	. 10101	011 .	0
172.16.172.0/24 =	172	. 16	. 10101	100 .	0
172.16.173.0/24 =	172	. 16	. 10101	101 .	0
172.16.174.0/24 =	172	. 16	. 10101	110 .	0
172.16.175.0/24 =	172	. 16	. 10101	111 .	0

Number of Common Bits = 21   Noncommon
Summary: 172.16.168.0/21   Bits = 11

In Figure 5-17, the first 21 bits are in common among the IP addresses. Therefore, the best summary route is 172.16.168.0/21. You can summarize addresses when the number of addresses is a power of two. If the number of addresses is not a power of two, you can divide the addresses into groups and summarize the groups separately.

To allow the router to aggregate the most number of IP addresses into a single route summary, your IP addressing plan should be hierarchical in nature. This approach is particularly important when using VLSMs.

A VLSM design allows for maximum use of IP addresses, as well as more efficient routing update communication when using hierarchical IP addressing. In Figure 5-18, for example, route summarization occurs at two levels.

Figure 5-18   *Summarizing Addresses in a VLSM-Designed Network*

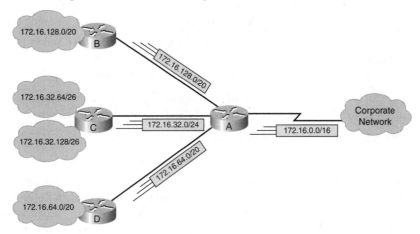

- Router C summarizes two routing updates from networks 172.16.32.64/26 and 172.16.32.128/26 into a single update, 172.16.32.0/24.

- Router A receives three different routing updates but summarizes them into a single routing update before propagating it to the corporate network.

Route summarization reduces memory use on routers and routing protocol network traffic. Requirements for summarization to work correctly are as follows:

- Multiple IP addresses must share the same highest-order bits.

- Routing protocols must base their routing decisions on a 32-bit IP address and a prefix length that can be up to 32 bits.

- Routing protocols must carry the prefix length (subnet mask) with the 32-bit IP address.

Cisco routers manage route summarization in two ways:

- **Sending route summaries**—Routing protocols, such as RIP, IGRP, and EIGRP, perform automatic route summarization across network boundaries. Specifically, this automatic summarization occurs for those routes whose classful network address differs from the major network address of the interface to which the advertisement is being sent. For OSPF and IS-IS, you must configure manual summarization. For EIGRP and RIP-2, you can disable automatic route summarization and configure manual summarization. Whether routing summarization is automatic or not is dependent on the routing protocol. You are recommended to review the documentation for your specific routing protocols. Route summarization is not always a solution. You would not use route summarization if you needed to advertise all networks across a boundary, such as when you have discontiguous networks.

- **Selecting routes from route summaries**—If more than one entry in the routing table matches a particular destination, the longest prefix match in the routing table is used. Several routes might match one destination, but the longest matching prefix is used.

For example, if a routing table has different paths to 192.16.0.0/16 and to 192.16.5.0/24, packets addressed to 192.16.5.99 would be routed through the 192.16.5.0/24 path because that address has the longest match with the destination address.

Classful routing protocols summarize automatically at network boundaries. This behavior, which cannot be changed with RIP-1 and IGRP, has important results, as follows:

- Subnets are not advertised to a different major network.
- Discontiguous subnets are not visible to each other.

In Figure 5-19, RIP-1 does not advertise the 172.16.5.0 255.255.255.0 and 172.16.6.0 255.255.255.0 subnets because RIPv1 cannot advertise subnets; both Router A and Router B advertise 172.16.0.0. This leads to confusion when routing across network 192.168.14.0. In this example, Router C receives routes about 172.16.0.0 from two different directions, so it cannot make a correct routing decision.

Figure 5-19 *Classful Summarization in Discontiguous Networks*

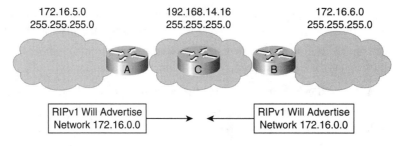

You can resolve this situation by using RIP-2, OSPF, IS-IS, or EIGRP and not using summarization because the subnet routes would be advertised with their actual subnet masks.

Cisco IOS Software also provides an IP unnumbered feature that permits discontiguous subnets to be separated by an unnumbered link.

Section 5 Quiz

1 VLSM helps with which of the following problems in network design?

   A IP addressing waste

   B Illegal IP addresses

   C Route summarization

   D Network Address Translation

2 True or False: VLSMs allow you to further divide a subnetted network.

3 What would be the best summary address for the following networks: 172.16.16.0, 172.16.17.0, 172.16.18.0, 172.16.19.0, and 172.16.24.0?

   A 172.16.0.0 255.255.0.0

   B 172.16.16.0 0.0.15.255

   C 172.0.0.0 255.0.0.0

   D 172.16.16.0 255.255.240.0

   E 172.16.16.0 255.255.248.0

4 Which of the following routing protocols support VLSMs?

   A IGRP

   B OSPF

   C RIPv1

   D EIGRP

   E RTMP

5 True or False: RIP-1 provides route summarization.

Routing Command Summary

Table 5-5 briefly describes the commands covered in this chapter.

Table 5-8   *Routing Command Summary*

Command	Description
ip route *network mask {address | interface}* *[distance]* **[permanent]**	Defines a static route.
router *protocol [keyword]*	Enables a dynamic routing protocol.
network *network-number [wildcard mask | area_ID]*	A router subcommand. Enables a dynamic routing protocol to advertise a route, and enables the protocol on the interfaces on that network.

continues

Table 5-8   *Routing Command Summary (Continued)*

Command	Description
show ip protocols	Displays information about the dynamic routing protocols configured on the router.
show ip route	Displays the IP routing table.
debug ip rip	Enables the router to display the RIP routing updates as they occur.
variance *multiplier*	Enables IGRP to do unequal-path load sharing.
traffic-share {balanced | min}	Tells the router how to load-balance the traffic on the load-sharing links.
debug ip igrp transactions	Displays IGRP transaction information as transactions occur.
debug ip igrp events	Displays IGRP events as they occur.
no debug all	Turns off all debugging displays.
ip classless	Allows a routing protocol to send traffic to a less-specific route if one is available.
show ip eigrp neighbors	Displays neighbors discovered by EIGRP.
show ip eigrp topology	Displays the EIGRP topology table. This command shows the topology table, the active or passive state of routes, the number of successors, and the feasible distance to the destination.
show ip route eigrp	Displays the current EIGRP entries in the routing table.
show ip eigrp traffic	Displays the number of EIGRP packets sent and received. This command displays statistics on hello updates, queries, replies, and acknowledgments.
router-id *routerid*	Sets the router ID for an OSPF router.
show ip ospf interface	Verifies that interfaces have been configured in the intended areas. If no loopback address is specified, the interface with the highest address is chosen as the router ID. This command also displays the timer intervals, including the hello interval, and shows the neighbor adjacencies.
show ip ospf neighbor	Displays OSPF neighbor information on a per-interface basis.

Summary

In this chapter, you learned the components that a router needs to perform routing: information sources, available routes, best routes, and maintaining of routes. You learned about the different types of protocols: distance vector, link-state, and hybrid. You also learned the shortcomings and workarounds for distance vector routing protocols. Finally, you learned how to configure static and dynamic routes on a Cisco router.

Case Study

1   Now that Ann has subdivided the networks using VLANs, she needs to enable packets to be routed between the five TCP/IP VLANs. What will Ann need to configure and how will she need to configure this?

2   Ann also needs to plan the networks needed for communication across the routed WAN links. For each VLAN that supports users, Ann will have an IP address range that supports 255 device addresses. For the WAN links, the address space will need to support only 2 addresses, and for the remote offices, the address space will need to support between 50 and 100 users. Ann needs to choose a routing protocol that will work across multiple vendor platforms and support summarization between the sites. What is Ann's best choice and why?

Review Questions

1   Why are dynamic routing protocols important?

2   RIP uses what as a metric?

3   What are the five composite metrics used by IGRP and EIGRP?

4   What command do you use to choose a routing protocol?

5   Which command do you use to show the routing protocols and the networks they are advertising?

6   What does DUAL stand for?

7   All OSPF networks must have which area?

8   What are the advantages of a hierarchical routing protocol?

9   What type of routing protocol supports VLSMs?

10   What command do you use to stop all debugging?

After completing this chapter, you will be able to perform the following tasks:

- Understand the fundamentals of access lists.
- Understand access list functions and operations.
- Understand TCP/IP access lists.
- Configure standard IP access lists.
- Control vty access with access class entries.
- Understand the fundamentals of extended IP access lists.
- Verify and monitor access lists.
- Use access lists to scale your network address space with Network Address Translation (NAT) and Port Address Translation (PAT).

Basic IP Traffic Management and Translation with Access Lists

This chapter presents coverage of standard and extended IP access lists as a means to classify network traffic. When you complete this chapter, you should be able to describe the functions and processes by which access lists identify traffic and how they can be applied to features such as access control (security), encryption, policy-based routing, quality of service (QoS), and Network Address Translation/Port Address Translation (NAT/PAT). You learn how to configure a standard and extended access list. You also learn to limit Telnet access to and from the router using a standard access list. Finally, you learn how to verify access list configurations.

Understanding Access Lists

Networks are designed to carry user traffic from one location to another, much like roads carry vehicular traffic from one location to another. Routers are the junction points for traffic on data networks. Controlling the flow of traffic on both roads and networks is sometime necessary. There are many ways to do this on a highway, but on a network, you need a way to identify and filter traffic to and from the many different data networks. Access control lists (ACLs) are used in routers to identify traffic and then filter, encrypt, classify, or translate the traffic to better manage and control the network's functions.

The earliest routed networks connected a modest number of LANs and hosts. As router connections increased to legacy and outside networks, and with the increased use of the Internet, new challenges to control access became apparent, as demonstrated by the sample network shown in Figure 6-1.

With the increase in various types of connections to the network, network administrators must decide how to deny unwanted connections while allowing appropriate access. Although tools such as passwords, callback equipment, and physical security devices are helpful, they often lack the flexible and specific controls most administrators prefer.

Access lists offer another powerful tool for network control. Access lists add the flexibility to filter the packet flow in or out of router interfaces. Such control can help limit network traffic and restrict network use by certain users or devices.

The most common use for an access list is as a packet filter. Without packet filters, all packets could be transmitted onto all parts of the internetwork.

Figure 6-1 *Justification for Access Lists*

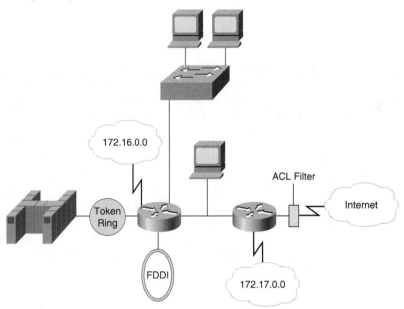

Packet filtering helps control packet movement through the network. Such control can help limit network traffic and restrict network use by certain users or devices. To permit or deny packets from crossing specified router interfaces, Cisco provides access lists. An *IP access list* is a sequential list of permit and deny conditions that apply to IP addresses or upper-layer IP protocols. Access lists identify traffic to be filtered in transit through the router, but they do not filter traffic originating from the router. Because a router can't block a packet originating from a router, you can't block Telnet access from the router. Because of this, access lists can also be applied to the router's virtual terminal line (vty) ports to permit or deny Telnet traffic in or out of the router's vty ports. As shown in Figure 6-2, packets might be traveling through an interface, or they might be accessing a vty port for Telnet connectivity to the router itself. Access lists allow control of this traffic.

Figure 6-2 *Access List as Packet Filter*

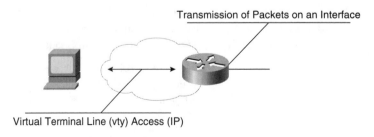

Although access lists are usually associated with packet filters, they have many other uses, as illustrated in Figure 6-3. You can use IP access lists to establish a finer granularity of control when separating traffic into priority and custom queues. An access list can also be used to identify packets of interest that serve to trigger dialing in dial-on-demand routing (DDR). Access lists are also a fundamental component of route maps, which filter and, in some cases, alter the information contained in a routing protocol update.

Figure 6-3   *Other Access List Uses*

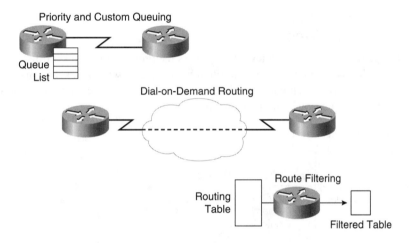

Chapter 9, "Completing an ISDN BRI Call," discusses DDR in greater detail.

Access List Functions and Operations

Access lists are optional mechanisms in Cisco IOS Software that can be configured to filter or test packets to determine whether to forward them toward their destination or to discard them. This section describes what access lists are and how they operate.

There are two general types of access lists:

- **Standard access lists**—Standard IP access lists check the source address of packets that could be routed. The result permits or denies the packet output for the entire protocol suite, based on the source network/subnet/host IP address.

- **Extended access lists**—Extended IP access lists check for both source and destination packet addresses. They can also check for specific protocols, port numbers, and other parameters, giving administrators more flexibility in describing the packets being referenced.

Access lists can be applied as the following:

- **Inbound access lists**—Incoming packets are processed before being routed to an outbound interface. An input access list is more efficient than an output list because it saves the overhead of routing table lookups if the packet is to be discarded by the filtering tests. If the tests permit the packet, it is then processed for routing.

- **Outbound access lists**—Incoming packets are routed to the outbound interface and processed through the outbound access list before transmission.

Access List Operations

Figure 6-4 shows an overview of the access list process for a packet traveling through a router. This process is the same for an inbound packet with the exception of the routing table check. You can think of the list as a traffic cop or traffic regulation that prevents certain traffic from entering certain areas of the network.

Figure 6-4   *Access List Filter Overview*

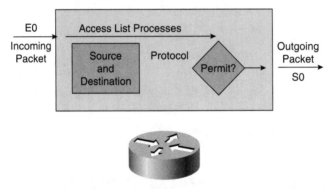

Access lists express the set of rules that give added control for packets that enter inbound interfaces, packets that relay through the router, and packets that exit the router's outbound interfaces. Access lists *do not* act on packets that originate from the router itself, such as routing updates or outgoing Telnet sessions. Instead, access lists are statements that specify conditions for how the router will handle the traffic flow through specified interfaces. Access lists give added control for processing the specific packets.

Figure 6-5 expands the example of an outbound access list.

Figure 6-5   *Outbound Access List Operation*

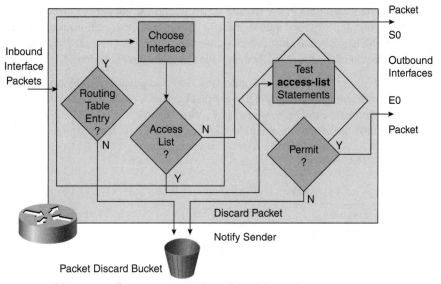

If No **access-list** statement matches, discard the packet.

The beginning of the process is the same regardless of whether outbound access lists are used. As a packet enters an interface, the router checks to see if the packet can be routed checking the routing table. If no route exists to the destination address, the packet is dropped.

Next, the router checks to see whether the destination interface is grouped to an access list. If not, the packet can be sent to the output buffer, for example:

- If the outbound packet is destined for Serial 0, which has not been grouped to an outbound access list, the packet is sent directly to Serial 0.

- If the outbound packet is destined for Ethernet 0, which has been grouped to an outbound access list, before the packet can be sent out on Ethernet 0, it is tested by a combination of access list statements associated with that interface. Based on the access list tests, the packet can be permitted or denied.

For outbound lists, *permit* means send it to the output buffer, and *deny* means discard the packet. For inbound lists, *permit* means continue to process the packet after receiving it on an inbound interface, and *deny* means discard the packet. When an IP packet is discarded, ICMP returns a special packet to notify the sender that the destination is unreachable.

Access List Condition Testing

Access list statements operate in sequential, logical order. They evaluate packets from the top down, one statement at a time. If a packet header and an access list statement match, the rest of the statements in the list are skipped, and the packet is permitted or denied as specified in the matched statement. If a packet header does not match an access list statement, it is tested against the next statement in the list. This matching process continues until the end of the list is reached, at which time the packet is denied by an implicit deny.

Figure 6-6 shows the access list packet test flow; the **permit** or **deny** option is applied, and any subsequent tests are terminated for that packet. A condition that denies a packet in an earlier statement can't be overturned by a later statement. The implication of this behavior is that the order of the statements within any given access list is significant.

Figure 6-6   *Access List Condition Tests*

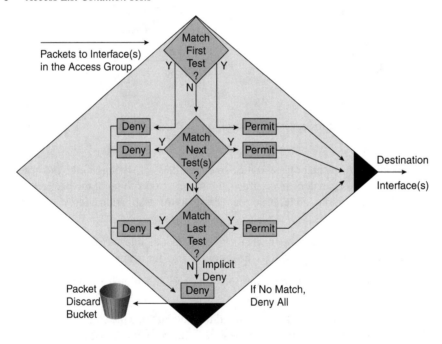

A final implied statement covers all packets for which conditions did not test true. This final test condition matches all other packets and results in a deny condition, thereby denying the packet. Instead of proceeding out an interface, all packets not matched by earlier access list statements are dropped. This final statement is often referred to as the *implicit deny any* at the end of every access list. Although this statement is not displayed in the router configuration, it is always active. Because of the implicit deny any, an access list must contain at least one **permit** statement; otherwise, the access list will block all traffic.

Guidelines for Access List Implementation

An access list can be applied to multiple interfaces; however, only one access list can exist per protocol, per direction, per interface.

Following these general principles helps ensure that the access lists you create have the intended results:

- Use only the access list numbers from the Cisco-defined range for the protocol and type of list you are creating. (See Table 6-1 in the next section, "Access List Command Basics.")

- Only one access list per protocol, per direction, per interface is allowed. Multiple access lists are permitted per interface, but each must be for a different protocol.

- Top-down processing:
  - Organize your access list so that more specific references in a network or subnet appear before more general ones. Place more frequently occurring conditions before less frequently occurring conditions.
  - Subsequent additions are always added to the end of the access list, but before the implicit deny.
  - You cannot selectively add or remove access list statements when using numbered access lists, but you can do so when using named IP access lists (a Cisco IOS Release 11.2 feature).

TIP

Because making changes to active access lists on a router or switch is difficult, it is common practice to copy the text of the access list into a text file and edit it using a text editor. When edited, the access list can be removed completely and the contents of the file can be pasted back into the device's configuration.

- Implicit deny all:
  - Unless you end your access list with an explicit permit any, it will deny by default all traffic that fails to match any of the access list conditions.
  - Every access list must have at least one **permit** statement; otherwise, all traffic will be denied.

- Create the access list before applying it to an interface. An interface with a nonexistent or undefined access list applied to it allows (permits) all traffic.

- Access lists filter only traffic going through the router. They do not filter traffic originating from the router.

Access List Command Basics

In practice, commands to configure access lists can be lengthy character strings. Access lists can be complicated to enter or interpret. However, you can better understand general access list configuration commands by reducing them to two general elements:

- The access list contains global statements to be applied for use in identifying packets. These lists are created with the global **access-list** command.

- The **ip access-group** interface configuration command activates an IP access list on an interface.

The following syntax shows the **access-list** command's general form, which contains global statements:

```
Router(config)# access-list access-list-number {permit · deny} {test conditions}
```

This global statement identifies the access list by an access list number. This number indicates what type of access list this will be. In Cisco IOS Software Release 11.2 and later, access lists for IP can also use an access list name rather than a number. Named IP access lists are covered later in this chapter.

The **permit** or **deny** term in the global **access-list** statement indicates how packets that meet the test conditions will be handled by Cisco IOS Software. The **permit** option means that the packet will be allowed to pass through the interfaces to which you apply the list. The **deny** option means that the router will discard the packet.

The final parameters of the **access-list** statement specifies the test conditions the statement uses. The test can be as simple as checking for a single source address. However, the access list can be expanded to include several test conditions, as you will see in the discussion of extended access lists. You will use several global **access-list** statements with the same access list number or name to stack several test conditions into a logical sequence or list of tests.

The following syntax shows the general form of the *{protocol}* **access-group** command, which is how an access list is applied to an interface:

```
Router(config-if)#{protocol} access-group access-list-number {in · out}
```

For example, applying the **ip access-group** interface configuration command activates an IP access list on an interface.

CAUTION   If you apply an access list with the **ip access-group** command to an interface before any access list lines have been created, the result will be permit any. The list is "live," so if you enter only one permit line, it goes from a permit any to a deny most (because of the implicit deny any at the end) as soon as you press **Enter**. For this reason, create your access list before you apply it to an interface.

Access lists can control most protocols on a Cisco router. Table 6-1 shows the protocols and number ranges of the access list types for IP.

Table 6-1   *Access List Numbers*

IP Access List	Number Range/Identifier
Standard	1 to 99, 1300 to 1999
Extended	100 to 199, 2000 to 2699
Named	Name

An administrator enters a number in the protocol number range as the first argument of the global **access-list** statement. The router identifies which access list software to use based on this numbered entry. Access list test conditions follow as arguments. These arguments specify tests according to the rules of the given protocol suite. The test conditions for an access list vary by protocol.

Many access lists are possible for a protocol. Select a different number from the protocol number range for each new access list. The administrator can specify only one access list per protocol, per direction, per interface.

Specifying an access list number from 1 to 99 or 1300 to 1999 instructs the router to accept standard IP **access-list** statements. Specifying an access list number from 100 to 199 or 2000 to 2699 instructs the router to accept extended IP **access-list** statements.

TCP/IP Access Lists

An access list applied to an interface causes the router to look in the Layer 3 (IP) header and, possibly, the Layer 4 (TCP/UDP) header of a network traffic packet to match test conditions. Standard IP access lists check only the source address in the packet (Layer 3) header. Extended IP access lists can check many options, including segment (Layer 4) header options such as port numbers. Figure 6-7 shows the breakdown of a common IP packet for access list testing.

Figure 6-7   *TCP/IP Packet Testing*

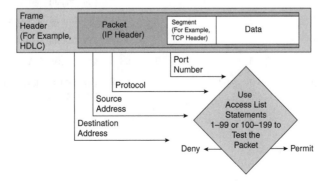

For TCP/IP packet filtering, Cisco IOS IP access lists check the packet and upper-layer headers for the following:

- Source IP addresses using standard access lists. Standard access lists are identified with a number in the range 1 to 99 and 1300 to 1399.

- Destination and source IP address, specific protocols, and TCP or UDP port numbers using extended access lists. Extended access lists are identified with a number in the range 100 to 199 and 2000 to 2699.

For all these IP access lists, as soon as a packet is checked for a match with the **access-list** statement, it can be denied from using, or permitted to use, the interface for which an **access-group** statement is defined.

It might be necessary to test conditions for a group or range of IP addresses or just a single IP address. For this reason, you need a method to identify which bits of a given IP address need to be checked for a match.

Address matching occurs using access list address wildcard masking to identify which bits of an IP address require an explicit match and which bits can be ignored.

Wildcard masking for IP address bits uses the numbers 1 and 0 to indicate how to treat the corresponding IP address bits:

- A wildcard mask bit 0 means "Check the corresponding bit value."

- A wildcard mask bit 1 means "Do not check (ignore) the corresponding bit value."

By carefully setting wildcard masks, an administrator can select a single IP address or several IP addresses for permit or deny tests. Figure 6-8 shows how bits are matched against a wildcard mask.

Figure 6-8 *Wildcard Bits*

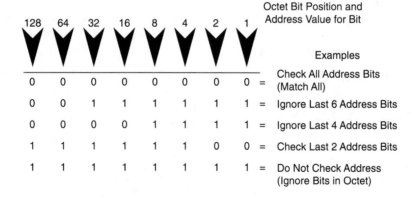

Wildcard masking for access lists operates differently from an IP subnet mask. A 0 in a bit position of the access list mask indicates that the corresponding bit in the address must be checked; a 1 in a bit position of the access list mask indicates that the corresponding bit in the address is not "interesting" and can be ignored.

You have seen how the 0 and 1 bits in an access list wildcard mask cause the access list to either check or ignore the corresponding bit in the IP address. In Figure 6-9, this wildcard masking process is applied in an example.

Figure 6-9   *Matching a Specific IP Host*

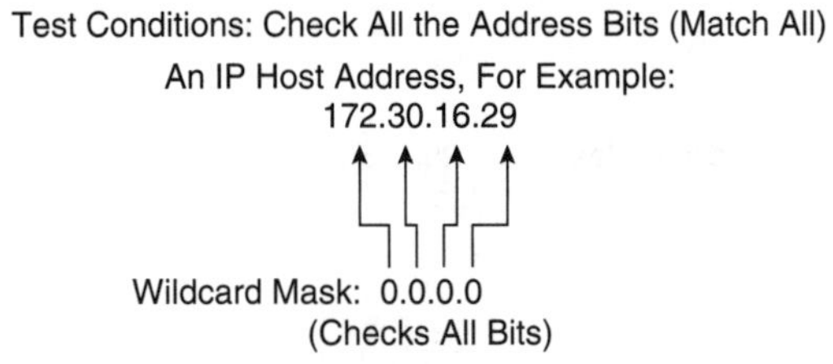

Test Conditions: Check All the Address Bits (Match All)
An IP Host Address, For Example:
172.30.16.29

Wildcard Mask: 0.0.0.0
(Checks All Bits)

Consider a network administrator who wants to specify that a certain IP host address will be denied in an access list test. To indicate a host IP address, the administrator enters the full address—for example, 172.30.16.29. Then, to indicate that the access list should check all the bits in the address, the corresponding wildcard mask bits for this address would be all 0s—that is, 0.0.0.0.

Working with decimal representations of binary wildcard mask bits can be tedious. For the most common uses of wildcard masking, you can use abbreviations. These abbreviations reduce how many numbers an administrator is required to enter while configuring address test conditions. For example, you can use an abbreviation instead of a long wildcard mask string when you want to match a specific host address.

The administrator can use the abbreviation **host** before the IP address to communicate this same test condition to Cisco IOS access list software. So, for example, instead of typing **172.30.16.29 0.0.0.0**, the administrator can use the string **host 172.30.16.29**.

NOTE   For standard access lists, if you do not use a keyword or assign a wildcard mask, the device will assume a wildcard mask of 0.0.0.0 or host.

A second common condition in which Cisco IOS Software permits an abbreviation term in the access list wildcard mask is when the administrator wants to match any IP address. This is commonly done as the last statement in an access list, just before the implicit **deny any**, because the list will have already specifically denied or permitted all other traffic the administrator intended to identify with the ACL.

Consider a network administrator who wants to specify that any destination address will be permitted in an access list test. To indicate any IP address, the administrator enters **0.0.0.0** as the IP address. Then, to indicate that the access list should ignore (allow without checking) any value, the corresponding wildcard mask bits for this address would be all 1s (255.255.255.255), as illustrated in Figure 6-10.

Figure 6-10 *Matching Any IP Address*

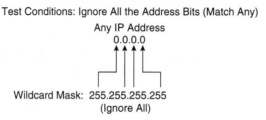

Test Conditions: Ignore All the Address Bits (Match Any)

Any IP Address
0.0.0.0

Wildcard Mask: 255.255.255.255
(Ignore All)

The administrator can use the abbreviation **any** to communicate this same test condition to Cisco IOS access list software. Instead of typing **0.0.0.0 255.255.255.255**, the administrator can use the word **any** by itself as the keyword.

Assume that an administrator wants to test a range of IP subnets that will be permitted or denied. If given a Class B IP address (the first two octets are the network number) with 8 bits of subnetting (the third octet is for subnets), the administrator might want to use the IP wildcard masking bits to match subnets 172.30.16.0/24 to 172.30.31.0/24.

Figure 6-11 shows the wildcard mask that would be used to accomplish this.

Figure 6-11 *Blocking a Range of Subnets*

Check for IP Subnets 172.30.**16**.0/24 to 172.30.**31**.0/24
Address and Wildcard Mask:
172.30.16.0 0.0.15.255

Network .Host
172.30.16.0

Wildcard Mask:	**0**	**0**	**0**	**1**	**0**	**0**	**0**	**0**	
	0	**0**	**0**	**0**	**1**	**1**	**1**	**1**	

|<-------- **Match** ------->|<----- Don't Care ----->|

0	**0**	**0**	**1**	**0**	**0**	**0**	**0**	=	16
0	**0**	**0**	**1**	**0**	**0**	**0**	**1**	=	17
0	**0**	**0**	**1**	**0**	**0**	**1**	**0**	=	18
			:						:
0	**0**	**0**	**1**	**1**	**1**	**1**	**1**	=	31

First, the wildcard mask checks the first two octets (172.30) using corresponding 0 bits in the wildcard mask.

Because there is no interest in an individual host, you want to set the wildcard mask to ignore all bits in the final octet. By setting all the bits in the final octet to 1s, you ignore the host portion of the address. All 1s in an octet is a decimal value of 255.

In the third octet, where the subnet address occurs, the wildcard mask checks that the bit position for the binary 16 is on and that all the higher bits are off using corresponding 0 bits in the wildcard mask. For the final (low-end) 4 bits in this octet, the wildcard mask indicates that these bits can be ignored. In these positions, the address value can be binary 0 or binary 1, but the convention is to assign 0 to the address value being masked by an ignore wildcard mask. Thus, the wildcard mask matches subnets 16, 17, 18, and so on, up to subnet 31. The wildcard mask does not match any other subnets.

In Figure 6-11, the address 172.30.16.0 with the wildcard mask 0.0.15.255 matches subnets 172.30.16.0/24 to 172.30.31.0/24.

NOTE   Although the wildcard mask is sometimes called an *inverted subnet mask*, this is not always the case. The subnet mask in Figure 6-11 is 255.255.255.0. An inverted mask for that would be 0.0.0.255. Because we chose to match only some of the addresses in the range of subnets, our wildcard mask was 0.0.15.255. Also note that you might choose to match only the last octet and ignore the first three octets using a wildcard mask of 255.255.255.0.

Section 1 Quiz

1   True or False: Access lists are used only for security purposes to deny traffic through a device.

2   Which of the following are valid types of access lists? (Choose all that apply.)

   A   Standard access lists

   B   Global access lists

   C   Extended access lists

   D   Named access lists

   E   Interface access lists

   F   Routing access lists

3 Choose the valid number ranges for IP extended access lists. (Choose all that apply.)

A 1 to 99

B 199 to 2699

C 100 to 199

D 1300 to 1399

E 2000 to 2699

F 2000 to 2999

4 Which of the following are true statements? (Choose all that apply.)

A If a packet does not match any explicit condition in the list, an implicit **permit** allows the packet to be forwarded.

B After a packet matches an entry, it is acted upon by that statement and no other entries are checked.

C When an interface receives a packet, all entries in the access list are checked before any decision is made.

D A condition can test only against source and destination addresses.

E If no entry is matched, the packet is denied by an implicit **deny all**.

F All access lists acting as packet filters should have at least one **permit** statement.

5 Given the address 192.168.255.3 and the wildcard mask 0.0.0.252, which of the following addresses would be a match? (Choose all that apply.)

A 192.168.255.3

B 192.166.255.7

C 192.168.255.19

D 192.168.255.255

E 192.168.252.51

Standard IP Access List Configuration

The first access list you learn to configure is a standard access list. Adding an access list to a router as a packet filter is a two-step process. First, you must create the list. Then, you apply that list to any interface for which you want to filter the selected traffic. The steps and commands are as follows:

Step 1   The **access-list** command creates an entry in a standard IP traffic filter list:

```
Router(config)#access-list access-list-number {permit · deny}
    source-address [wildcard mask]
```

Where:

— *access-list-number* identifies the list to which the entry belongs. It's a number from 1 to 99 or 1300 to 1399.

— **permit | deny** indicates whether this entry allows or blocks traffic from the specified address.

— *source-address* identifies the source IP address.

— *wildcard mask* identifies which bits in the address field are matched. The default mask is 0.0.0.0 (match all bits).

Step 2 The **ip access-group** command applies an existing access list to an interface. Only one access list per protocol, per direction, per interface is allowed:

```
Router(config)#interface serial 0
Router(config-if)#ip access-group access-list-number {in ¦ out}
```

Where:

— *access-list-number* indicates the number of the access list to be applied to this interface.

— **in | out** selects whether the access list is applied as an incoming or outgoing filter. If **in** or **out** is not specified, **out** is the default.

NOTE

To remove an IP access list from an interface, first enter the **no ip access-group** *access-list-number* command on the interface. Then, enter the global **no access-list** *access-list-number* command to remove the access list.

The number of the access list indicates which list you are creating. As you add statements to this list, they are added to the end of the list. All entries in access list 1 would start with the command **access-list 1**. The next few pages provide some examples of standard access lists.

Example 1: Access List Blocking Traffic from an External Network

Figure 6-12 and Example 6-1 show an access list applied to the interfaces Ethernet 0 and Ethernet 1 to prevent traffic that did not originate from the 172.16.0.0 network from being passed out those interfaces.

Figure 6-12 *Standard Access List Blocks Non-172.16.0.0 Traffic*

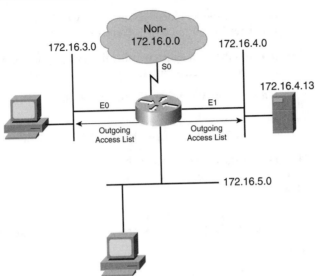

Example 6-1 *Standard Access List to Block Non-172.16.0.0 Traffic*

```
Router(config)#access-list 1 permit 172.16.0.0 0.0.255.255
Router(config)#interface ethernet 0
Router(config-if)#ip access-group 1 out
Router(config)interface ethernet 1
Router(config-if)#ip access-group 1 out
```

All access lists end with an implicit **deny any** statement. Traffic that does not match the first two octets of the network address 172.16.0.0, as shown in Example 6-1, moves to an unseen implicit **deny any** statement.

NOTE   The direction in Example 6-1 is explicitly applied as an outbound list. Depending on the version of IOS you are using, you might or might not be required to specify the direction. For versions that do not require you specify a direction, the default is always **out**.

The following list highlights key parameters from the access list presented in Example 6-1:

- **1** is the access list number that indicates that this is a standard list.
- **permit** indicates that traffic that matches selected parameters will be forwarded.

- **172.16.0.0** is the IP address that will be used with the wildcard mask to identify the source network.

- **0.0.255.255** is the wildcard mask. 0s indicate positions that must match; 1s indicate "don't care" positions.

- **ip access-group 1 out** links the access list to the interface as an outbound filter.

Example 2: Access List Blocking Traffic from a Single Host

Using the network shown in Figure 6-12, Example 6-2 demonstrates a multiple-statement access list denying a single host. Remember that when you start an access list with a **deny** statement, you must have at least one **permit** statement somewhere in the list. If you do not have a **permit** statement, the implicit **deny any** blocks all traffic.

Example 6-2 *Standard Access List to Block Traffic from a Single Host*

```
Router(config)#access-list 1 deny 172.16.4.13 0.0.0.0
Router(config)#access-list 1 permit 0.0.0.0 255.255.255.255
Router(config)#interface ethernet 0
Router(config-if)#ip access-group 1 out
```

The access list in Example 6-2 is designed to block traffic from a specific address, 172.16.4.13, and to allow all other traffic to be forwarded on interface Ethernet 0. Because the first statement of this list uses the mask 0.0.0.0, the entry is for a specific address. The **host** keyword could have been used in this configuration. The **0.0.0.0 255.255.255.255** IP address and wildcard mask combination permits traffic from any source. This combination can also be written using the keyword **any**.

The following list highlights key parameters from the access list shown in Example 6-2:

- **1** is the access list number that indicates that this is a standard list.

- **deny** indicates that traffic that matches selected parameters will not be forwarded.

- **172.16.4.13** is the IP address of the source host to be denied.

- **0.0.0.0** is the mask that requires the test to match all bits. (This is the default mask for a standard IP access list.)

- **1** is the access list number that indicates that this is a standard list.

- **permit** indicates that traffic that matches selected parameters will be forwarded.

- **0.0.0.0** is the IP address of the source host. All 0s indicate a placeholder because an address is required, and the mask will ignore all of this address.

- **255.255.255.255** is the wildcard mask. 0s indicate positions that must match; 1s indicate "don't care" positions. All 1s in the mask indicate that all 32 bits will not be checked in the source address.

- **ip access-group 1 out** links the access list to the interface as an outbound filter.

Example 3: Access List Blocking Traffic from a Single Subnet

Using the network shown in Figure 6-12, Example 6-3 shows a multiple-statement access list denying a single subnet. This list blocks the 172.16.4.0 subnet but allows all other subnets out Ethernet 0. Notice that because the list is not applied to Ethernet 1 or Serial 0, it does not affect traffic traveling on those interfaces.

Example 6-3 *Standard Access List to Block Traffic from a Single Subnet*

```
Router(config)#access-list 1 deny 172.16.4.0 0.0.0.255
Router(config)#access-list 1 permit any
Router(config)#interface ethernet 0
Router(config-if)#ip access-group 1 out
```

The following list highlights key parameters from the access list presented in Example 6-3:

- **1** is the access list number that indicates that this is a standard list.
- **deny** indicates that traffic that matches selected parameters will not be forwarded.
- **172.16.4.0** is the IP address of the source subnet to be denied.
- **0.0.0.255** is the wildcard mask. 0s indicate positions that must match; 1s indicate "don't care" positions. The mask with 0s in the first three octets indicates that those positions must match; the 255 in the last octet indicates a "don't care" condition.
- **1** is the access list number that indicates that this is a standard list.
- **permit** indicates that traffic that matches selected parameters will be forwarded.
- **any** is the abbreviation for the source's IP address. The keyword **any** implies an IP address of all 0s (a placeholder) and a wildcard mask of 255.255.255.255. All 1s in the mask indicate that all 32 bits will not be checked in the source address.
- **ip access-group 1 out** links the access list to the interface as an outbound filter.

Controlling vty Access with Access Class Entries

Just as there are physical interfaces such as E0 and E1, there are also virtual interfaces. These virtual interfaces are called *virtual terminal lines* (*vtys*). By default, there are five such vty lines, numbered vty 0 through vty 4, that are used to Telnet to the router's command-line interface. These are illustrated in Figure 6-13.

Figure 6-13 *Router Connections*

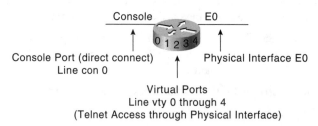

Standard and extended access lists block packets from going through the router. They are not designed to block packets originating from the router. An outbound Telnet extended access list does not prevent router-initiated Telnet sessions.

For security purposes, users can be denied vty access to the router, or users can be permitted vty access to the router but denied access to destinations from that router. Restricting virtual terminal access is less a traffic-control mechanism than one technique for increasing network security.

When users Telnets to a router, they connect on one of the vty lines, as shown in Figure 6-14.

Figure 6-14   *Telnetting to a Router*

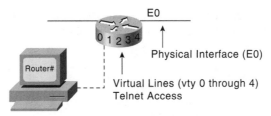

Telnet filtering is normally considered an extended IP access list function because it is filtering a higher-level protocol. However, because you know that anyone Telnetting to a router will be attaching to a virtual line (that is, vty 0 through 4), you can create a standard access list identifying the source address and apply it to the vty lines using the **access-class** command.

The **access-class** command also applies standard IP access list filtering to vty lines for outgoing Telnet sessions originating from within the router.

Normally, you set identical restrictions on all vtyl lines because you cannot control which vty will receive a user's Telnet connection.

Some administrators configure one of the vty lines differently from the others. This way, the administrator has a "back door" into the router, in the event every other vty line is in use.

The following commands show how to apply a standard access list to the Telnet ports.

Use the **line** command to place the router in line configuration mode:

```
Router(config)#line vty {# · vty-range}
```

Where:

- # indicates a specific vty line to be configured.

- *vty-range* indicates a range of vty lines to which the configuration will apply.

Use the **access-class** command to link an existing access list to a terminal line or range of lines:

```
Router(config-line)#access-class access-list-number {in · out}
```

Where:

- *access-list-number* indicates the number of the access list to be linked to a terminal line. This is a decimal number from 1 to 99.

- **in** prevents the router from receiving incoming Telnet connections from the source addresses in the access list.

- **out** prevents the router vty ports from initiating Telnet connections to addresses defined in the standard access list. Note that the source address specified in the standard access list is treated like a destination address when you use **access-class out**.

Example 6-4 permits any device on network 192.89.55.0 to establish a virtual terminal (Telnet) session with the router. Of course, the user must know the appropriate passwords to enter user mode and privileged mode.

Example 6-4   *Access List to Permit a Specified Network to Establish a Telnet Session*

```
Router(config)#access list 2 permit 192.168.55.0 0.0.0.255
Router(config)#line vty 0 4
Router(config-line)#access-class 2 in
```

Notice that identical restrictions have been set on all vty lines (0 to 4) because you cannot control on which vty a user will connect.

The implicit **deny any** still applies to the access list when used as an access class entry.

Extended IP Access Lists

The standard access list (numbered 1 to 99) might not provide the traffic filtering control you need. Standard access lists filter based on a source address and mask. Standard access lists permit or deny the entire TCP/IP protocol suite. You might need a more precise way to filter your network traffic.

For more precise traffic-filtering control, use extended IP access lists. Extended IP access list statements test source and destination addresses. Table 6-2 compares standard and extended access lists.

Table 6-2   *Standard Versus Extended Access Lists*

Standard	Extended
Filters based on source address only.	Filters based on source and destination address and source and destination port number.
Permits or denies entire TCP/IP protocol suite.	Specifies a certain IP protocol and port number.
Range is 1 to 99.	Range is 100 to 199.

In addition, at the end of the extended **access-list** statement, you gain additional precision filtering by specifying the protocol and optional TCP or UDP port number. These port numbers can be the well-known port numbers for TCP/IP. Table 6-3 lists a few of the most common port numbers.

Table 6-3   *Well-Known Port Numbers*

Well-Known Port Number (Decimal)	IP Protocol
20	File Transfer Protocol (FTP) data
21	FTP program
23	Telnet
25	Simple Mail Transport Protocol (SMTP)
69	Trivial File Transfer Protocol (TFTP)
53	Domain Name System (DNS)
80	HyperText Markup Language (WWW)

Table 6-3 is a brief listing of some well-known port numbers. For a more complete and comprehensive listing, check www.iana.com.

NOTE   RFC 1700 was an Internet standard that defined well-known port numbers. RFC 3232, which created a database for port numbers to be maintained at IANA, made RFC 1700 obsolete in January 2002.

By using the protocol and optional TCP or UDP port number, you can specify the logical operation that the extended access list will perform on specific protocols. IP extended access lists use a number from the range 100 to 199.

Configuring an Extended Access List

Configuring an extended access list is similar to the process for configuring a standard access list, except for the options available in the list. Adding an extended access list to a router as a packet filter is a two-step process. First, you must create the access list. Then, you apply that access list to an interface. The steps and commands are as follows:

Step 1   Use the **access-list** command to create an entry to express a condition statement in a complex filter:

```
Router(config)#access-list access-list-number {permit · deny}
    protocol source-address source-wildcard [operator port]
    destination-address destination-wildcard [operator port]
    [established] [log]
```

Where:

— *access-list-number* identifies the list using a number in the range 100 to 199 or 2000 to 2699.

— **permit | deny** indicates whether this entry allows or blocks the specified address.

— *protocol* can be either IP, TCP, UDP, ICMP, GRE, or IGRP.

— *source* and *destination* identify source and destination IP addresses.

— *source-wildcard* and *destination-wildcard* indicate the wildcard mask. 0s indicate positions that must match; 1s indicate "don't care" positions.

— *operator port* can be lt (less than), gt (greater than), eq (equal to), or neq (not equal to) and a protocol port number.

— **established** is used for inbound TCP only. This allows TCP traffic to pass if the packet uses an established connection (for example, if it has ACK bits set).

— **log** sends a logging message to the console.

NOTE   The syntax of the **access-list** command presented here is representative of the TCP protocol form. Not all parameters and options are given. For the complete syntax of all forms of this command, refer to the appropriate Cisco IOS documentation available on CD-ROM or at Cisco.com.

Step 2   Use the **ip access-group** command to apply an existing extended access list to an interface. Only one access list per protocol, per direction, per interface is allowed:

```
Router(config-if)#ip access-group access-list-number {in · out}
```

Where:

— *access-list-number* indicates the number of the access list to be applied to an interface.

— **in | out** specifies whether the access list is applied as an input or output filter. If **in** or **out** is not specified, **out** is the default.

Example 1: Extended Access List Blocking FTP Traffic from a Specified Subnet

Consider the network shown in Figure 6-15.

Figure 6-15   *Extended Access List to Block FTP Traffic*

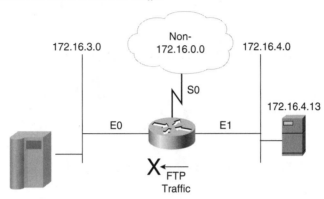

To block FTP traffic from subnet 172.16.4.0 to 172.16.3.0 and permit all other traffic in interface Ethernet 1, you could create a list like that shown in Example 6-5 and apply it as an outbound filter on Ethernet 0.

Example 6-5   *Extended Access List to Deny FTP Traffic from a Specified Subnet Out a Specified Interface*

```
Router(config)#access-list 101 deny tcp 172.16.4.0 0.0.0.255 172.16.3.0
   0.0.0.255 eq 21
Router(config)#access-list 101 deny tcp 172.16.4.0 0.0.0.255 172.16.3.0
   0.0.0.255 eq 20
Router(config)#access-list 101 permit ip any any
Router(config)#interface ethernet 1
Router(config-if)#ip access-group 101 in
```

The following list highlights key parameters from the extended access list presented in Example 6-5:

- **101** is the access list number that indicates that this is an extended IP access list.

- **deny** indicates that traffic that matches selected parameters will be blocked.

- **tcp** indicates the TCP protocol in the protocol number of the IP packet header. This is the transport protocol for FTP.

- **172.16.4.0 0.0.0.255** is the source IP address and mask. The first three octets must match, but do not care about the last octet.

- **172.16.3.0 0.0.0.255** is the destination IP address and mask. The first three octets must match, but do not care about the last octet.

- **eq 21** specifies the well-known port number for FTP control.

- **eq 20** specifies the well-known port number for FTP data.

- **ip access-group 101 in** links access list 101 to interface E1 as an input filter.

The **deny** statements deny FTP traffic from subnet 172.16.4.0 to subnet 172.16.3.0. The **permit** statement allows all other IP traffic out interface E0.

Example 2: Extended Access List Blocking Telnet Traffic from a Specified Subnet

Consider the network in Figure 6-15 again. This time, your goal is to deny any Telnet traffic from the 172.16.4.0 subnet to the 172.16.3.0 subnet. You can accomplish this with the access list shown in Example 6-6.

Example 6-6   *Extended Access List to Deny Telnet Traffic from a Specified Subnet Out a Specified Interface*

```
Router(config)#access-list 101 deny tcp 172.16.4.0 0.0.0.255 172.16.3.0
   0.0.0.255 eq 23
Router(config)#access-list 101 permit ip any any
Router(config)#interface ethernet 0
Router(config-if)#ip access-group 101 out
```

The following list highlights key parameters from the extended access list presented in Example 6-6:

- **101** is the access list number. It indicates that this is an extended IP access list.

- **deny** indicates that traffic that matches selected parameters will not be forwarded.

- **tcp** indicates the TCP protocol in the protocol number of the IP packet header. This is the transport protocol for Telnet.

- **172.16.4.0 0.0.0.255** indicates the source IP address and mask. The first three octets must match, but do not care about the last octet.

- **any** specifies to match any destination IP address. This keyword provides the same effect as, and can be used in place of, 0.0.0.0 255.255.255.255.

- **eq 23** specifies the well-known port number for Telnet.

- **permit** indicates that traffic that matches selected parameters will be forwarded.

- **ip** indicates any IP protocol. Because IP has a protocol field in the header that could be specifically chosen in an extended access list, you must indicate all IP packets to be permitted, or they will be denied by the implicit deny any. The parameter here specifies all IP traffic.

- **any** is the keyword that matches traffic from any source. This keyword provides the same effect as, and can be used in place of, 0.0.0.0 255.255.255.255.

- **any** is the keyword that matches traffic to any destination. This keyword provides the same effect as, and can be used in place of, 0.0.0.0 255.255.255.255.
- **ip access-group 101 out** links access list 101 to interface E0 as an output filter.

Example 6-6 denies Telnet traffic from 172.16.4.0 being sent out interface E0 to hosts in subnet 172.16.3.0. All other IP traffic from any other source to any destination is permitted out E0.

Named IP Access Lists

Announced in Cisco IOS Software Release 11.2, the named IP access list feature allows IP standard and extended access lists to be identified with an alphanumeric string (name) instead of the current numeric (1 to 199) representations.

With a numbered IP access list, an administrator who wants to alter an access list would first be required to delete the entire numbered access list and then re-enter it with corrections. Individual statements within a numbered access list cannot be deleted.

Named IP access lists allow you to delete individual entries from a specific access list. Deleting individual entries allows you to modify your access lists without deleting and then reconfiguring them. Items cannot be selectively inserted into the list, however. If an item is added to the list, it is placed at the end of the list. Use named IP access lists if you want to intuitively identify access lists using an alphanumeric name.

Consider the following before implementing named IP access lists:

- Named IP access lists are not compatible with Cisco IOS Software releases prior to Release 11.2.
- You cannot use the same name for multiple access lists. In addition, access lists of different types cannot have the same name. For example, it is illegal to specify a standard access control list named "Filter-Junk" and an extended access control list with the same name.

Here are the steps to create and activate a named IP access list:

Step 1   Enter named access list configuration mode:

```
Router(config)#ip access-list {standard · extended} name
```

Step 2   In named access list configuration mode, type in the test conditions:

```
Router(config {std- · ext-}nacl)#{permit · deny} {test conditions}
Router(config {std- · ext-}nacl)#no {permit · deny} {test conditions}
```

Step 3   Apply the access list to an interface:

```
Router(config-if)#ip access-group name {in · out}
```

In Step 1, the name must be unique to the router; that is, no other named access list can have the name you choose. The test conditions applied in Step 2 are the same conditions applied in a numbered list. (See Example 6-6 for details.) To remove a single statement, precede the test condition with **no**. Example 6-7 shows a named extended access list that blocks Telnet traffic from the 172.16.4.0 subnet to the 172.16.3.0 subnet out Ethernet 0.

Example 6-7   *Named Extended Access List to Deny Telnet Traffic from a Specified Subnet Out a Specified Interface*

```
Router(config)#ip access-list extended screen
Router(config ext-nacl)# deny tcp 172.16.4.0 0.0.0.255 172.16.3.0 0.0.0.255 eq 23
Router(config ext-nacl)# permit ip any any
Router(config ext-nacl)#interface ethernet 0
Router(config-if)#ip access-group screen out
```

Example 6-7 is the same filter as the one in Example 6-6; however, this time it is accomplished using a named extended access list.

Guidelines for Standard, Extended, and Named Access List Implementation

The basic guidelines of access list configuration are as follows:

- The order of access list statements is crucial to proper filtering. Recommended practice is to create your access list on a TFTP server using a text editor and download it to the router via TFTP. Alternatively, you can use a terminal emulator or Telnet session on a PC to cut and paste the access list into the router while in configuration mode.

- Access lists are processed from the top down. If you place more specific tests and tests that will test true frequently in the beginning of the access list, you can reduce processing overhead.

- While only named lists allow removal, none allow reordering of individual statements within a list. If you want to reorder access list statements, you must remove the entire list and recreate it in the desired order or with the desired statements.

- All access lists end with an implicit **deny any** statement.

You can use access lists to control traffic by filtering and eliminating unwanted packets. Proper placement of an access list statement can reduce unnecessary traffic. Traffic that will be denied at a remote destination should not be allowed to use network resources along the route to that destination only to be denied upon arrival.

Consider the network shown in Figure 6-16. Suppose an enterprise's policy aims to deny Token Ring traffic on Router A to the Ethernet LAN on Router D's E1 port. At the same time, other traffic must be permitted.

Figure 6-16   *Access List Placement*

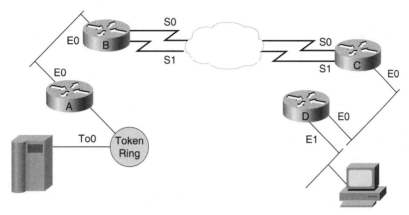

Several approaches can accomplish this policy. The recommended approach uses an extended access list because it specifies both source and destination addresses. Place this extended access list in Router A. Then, packets that will be denied do not cross Router A's Ethernet, do not cross the serial interfaces of Routers B and C, and do not enter Router D. Traffic with other source and destination addresses can still be permitted.

You should normally place extended access lists as close as possible to the source of the traffic to be denied.

Standard access lists do not specify destination addresses. The administrator would have to put the standard access list as close to the destination as possible. For example, you would place a standard access list on E0 of Router D to block Token Ring traffic from entering Router A.

Verifying and Monitoring Access Lists

This section introduces commands that verify and monitor access lists.

The **show ip interface** command displays IP interface information and indicates whether any access lists are set for a specific interface. The syntax for this command is as follows:

```
Router#show ip interface interface-type interface-number
```

Example 6-8 shows the output from the **show ip interface** command. The highlighted lines indicate the status of access lists on interface Ethernet 0.

Example 6-8   **show ip interface** *Displays IP Interface Information and Access List Status*

```
Router#show ip int e0
Ethernet0 is up, line protocol is up
  Internet address is 10.1.1.11/24
  Broadcast address is 255.255.255.255
  Address determined by setup command
  MTU is 1500 bytes
```

continues

Example 6-8 show ip interface *Displays IP Interface Information and Access List Status*

```
Helper address is not set
Directed broadcast forwarding is disabled
Outgoing access list is not set
Inbound  access list is 1
Proxy ARP is enabled
Security level is default
Split horizon is enabled ·
ICMP redirects are always sent
ICMP unreachables are always sent
ICMP mask replies are never sent
IP fast switching is enabled
IP fast switching on the same interface is disabled
IP Feature Fast switching turbo vector
IP multicast fast switching is enabled
IP multicast distributed fast switching is disabled
<text omitted>
```

The **show access-lists** command displays the contents of all access lists. The syntax for this command is as follows:

```
Router#show {protocol} access-lists {access-list-number · name}
```

By entering the access list name or number as an option for this command, you can display a specific access list. To display only the contents of all IP access lists, use the **show ip access-lists** command. To display the contents of all access lists, use the **show access-list** command.

Example 6-9 shows the output from the **show access-lists** command. The highlighted lines indicate the type of access lists that have been applied.

Example 6-9 show access-lists *Displays All Configured Access Lists*

```
Router#show access-lists
Standard IP access list 1
    permit 10.2.2.1
    permit 10.3.3.1
    permit 10.4.4.1
    permit 10.5.5.1
Extended IP access list 101
    permit tcp host 10.22.22.1 any eq telnet
    permit tcp host 10.33.33.1 any eq ftp
    permit tcp host 10.44.44.1 any eq ftp-data
```

Section 2 Quiz

1 Which command creates a standard access list? (Choose all that apply.)

A access-list 101

B access-list 1 standard

C access-list 1

D access-list standard mylist

E standard-access-list 1

2 Which of the following commands would you use to allow traffic from the 192.168.255.0 subnet to be allowed in on interface Ethernet 0? (Choose all that apply.)

A access-list 1 permit 192.168.255.0

B ip access-group 1 in

C access-group 101 permit 192.168.255.0 0.0.0.255

D interface Ethernet 0

E access-list standard OK-Traffic

F permit 192.168.255.0 0.0.0.255

3 Which of the following statements are true? (Choose all that apply.)

A Access lists can be applied only to an interface.

B An interface can only have one access list, per protocol, per direction.

C If you delete an access list, the mapping will be automatically deleted.

D All access lists have an implicit deny any at the bottom.

E Standard access lists should be placed close to the source.

F Extended access lists should be placed close to the source.

G Access list placement does not matter.

4 Which of the following commands would you use to check the mapping of an access list on Ethernet 0? (Choose all that apply.)

A show interface Ethernet 0

B show ip interface Ethernet 0

C show access-lists

D show running-config

E show security

F show ip interface brief

5 True or False: You can delete an individual entry in a numbered access list by using the command **no access-list** *number*.

Scaling the Network with NAT and PAT

Two scalability challenges facing the Internet are the depletion of registered IP address space and scaling in routing. Cisco IOS Network Address Translation (NAT) is a mechanism for conserving registered IP addresses in large networks and simplifying IP addressing management tasks. Cisco IOS NAT translates IP addresses within private internal networks to legal IP addresses for transport over public external networks, such as the Internet. Incoming traffic is then translated back for delivery within the inside network.

NAT provides a mechanism for a privately addressed network to access registered networks, such as the Internet, without requiring a registered subnet address. This eliminates the need for host renumbering and allows the same IP address range to be used in multiple intranets. By using a private addressing scheme inside the network and using an address or pool of addresses to translate traffic to the Internet, NAT eliminates these scalability problems.

Introducing NAT and PAT

Cisco IOS NAT allows an organization that does not have a public addressing scheme to connect to the Internet by translating the private addresses into globally registered IP addresses. Cisco IOS NAT also increases network privacy by hiding internal IP addresses from external networks. Static NAT is designed to allow one-to-one mapping between local and global addresses. Dynamic NAT is designed to map an unregistered IP address to a registered IP address from a group of registered IP addresses. Overloading is a form of dynamic NAT that maps multiple unregistered IP addresses to a single registered IP address (many-to-one) by using different ports, known also as Port Address Translation (PAT). Figure 6-17 shows how private addresses are mapped to global or external addresses to allow communication across a public network, such as the Internet.

Figure 6-17 *Network Address Translation*

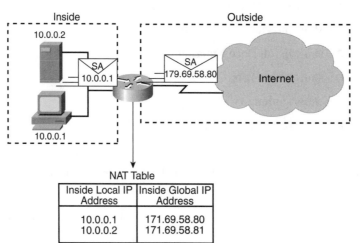

Cisco NAT is designed for IP address simplification and conservation, as it enables private IP internetworks that use nonregistered IP addresses to connect to the Internet. NAT operates on a Cisco router, usually connecting two networks together, and translates the private (inside local) addresses in the internal network to public addresses (inside global) before packets are forwarded to another network. As part of this functionality, you can configure NAT to advertise only one address for the entire network to the outside world. This effectively hides the internal network from the world, providing additional security.

A device that sits between an internal network and the public network, such as a firewall, router, or computer, uses NAT, which is defined in RFC 1631.

In NAT terminology, the *inside network* is the set of networks that are subject to translation. The *outside network* refers to all other addresses. Usually, these are valid addresses located on the Internet.

Cisco defines the following NAT terms:

- **Inside local address**—The IP address assigned to a host on the inside network. The address is likely not an IP address assigned by the IANA, ARIN, APNIC, LACNIC, and RIPE NCC, or service provider. See http://www.iana.org/ipaddress/ip-addresses.htm for more information about address assignments.

- **Inside global address**—A legitimate IP address assigned by the NIC or service provider that represents one or more inside local IP addresses to the outside world.

- **Outside local address**—The IP address of an outside host as it appears to the inside network. Not necessarily a legitimate address, it's allocated from an address space routable on the inside.

- **Outside global address**—The IP address assigned to a host on the outside network by the host's owner. The address is allocated from a globally routable address or network space.

NAT offers the following benefits:

- **Eliminates readdressing overhead.** NAT eliminates the need to re-address all hosts that require external access, saving time and money.

- **Conserves addresses through application port-level multiplexing.** With NAT, internal hosts can share a single registered IP address for all external communications. In this type of configuration, relatively few external addresses are required to support many internal hosts, thus conserving IP addresses.

- **Protects network security.** Because private networks do not advertise their addresses or internal topology, they remain reasonably secure when used in conjunction with NAT to gain controlled external access.

NAT has many forms and can work in the following ways to provide flexibility in controlling your network traffic:

- **Static NAT**—Maps an unregistered IP address to a registered IP address on a one-to-one basis. Static NAT is particularly useful when a device needs to be accessible from outside the network.

- **Dynamic NAT**—Maps an unregistered IP address to a registered IP address from a group of registered IP addresses.

- **Overloading**—A form of dynamic NAT that maps multiple unregistered IP addresses to a single registered IP address (many-to-one) by using different ports (port address translation).

One of the main features of NAT is static PAT, also referred to as "TCP overload" in Cisco IOS configuration. Several internal addresses can be translated using NAT to only one or a few external addresses by using PAT.

PAT uses unique source port numbers on the inside global IP address to distinguish between translations. Figure 6-18 shows an example of PAT. In this figure, both devices in the 10.6.1.0 subnet use the global address of 171.69.68.10 to reach the Internet; however, the source port on the global address is different, making each translation unique.

Figure 6-18   *Port Address Translation*

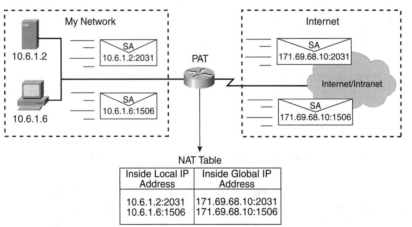

Because the port number is encoded in 16 bits, the total number of internal addresses that can be translated using NAT to one external address could theoretically be as high as 65,536 per IP address. PAT attempts to preserve the original source port. If this source port is already allocated, PAT attempts to find the first available port number starting from the beginning of the appropriate port group 0-511, 512-1023, or 1024-65535. If still no port is available from the appropriate port group and more than one external IP address is configured, PAT will move to the next IP address and try to allocate the original source port again. This continues until it runs out of available ports and external IP addresses.

Translating Inside Source Addresses

To configure NAT, you must translate your own IP addresses into globally unique IP addresses when communicating outside of your network. You can configure static or dynamic inside source translation. After you have configured NAT, a translation occurs on the source addresses as packets travel to the outside network. Figure 6-19 shows the router translating a source address inside a network to a source address outside the network.

Figure 6-19   *Translating an Inside Source Address*

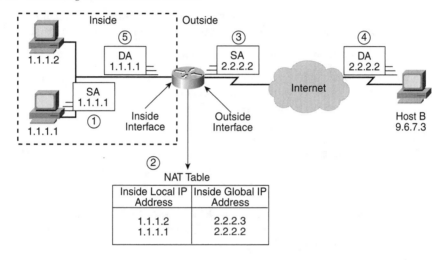

The following process describes inside source address translation, as shown in Figure 6-19:

1 The user at Host 1.1.1.1 opens a connection to Host B.

2 The first packet that the router receives from Host 1.1.1.1 causes the router to check its NAT table:

— If a static translation entry was configured, the router goes to Step 3.

— If no static translation entry exists, the router determines that source address (SA) 1.1.1.1 must be translated dynamically, selects a legal, global address from the dynamic address pool, and creates a translation entry. This type of entry is called a *simple entry.*

3 The router replaces the inside local source address of Host 1.1.1.1 with the translation entry's global address, and forwards the packet.

4 Host B receives the packet and responds to Host 1.1.1.1 using the inside global IP destination address (DA) 2.2.2.2.

5 When the router receives the packet with the inside global IP address, it performs a NAT table lookup by using the inside global address as a key. It then translates the address to the inside local address of Host 1.1.1.1 and forwards the packet to Host 1.1.1.1.

6 Host 1.1.1.1 receives the packet and continues the conversation. The router performs Steps 2 through 5 for each packet.

To configure static inside source address translation, perform the following tasks:

Step 1 Use the global command **ip nat inside source static** to establish static translation between an inside local address and an inside global address:

```
Router(config)#ip nat inside source static local-ip global-ip
```

Step 2 In global configuration mode, choose the interface that will be on the inside of the network with the **interface** command to move to configuration mode for that interface:

```
Router(config)#interface type number
```

Step 3 In interface configuration mode, mark this interface as being connected to the inside network for NAT with the command **ip nat inside**:

```
Router(config-if)#ip nat inside
```

Step 4 Exit to global configuration mode; then, specify the interface that will be on the outside of the private network with the command **interface** to move to configuration mode for that interface:

```
Router(config-if)#exit
Router(config)#interface type number
```

Step 5 In interface configuration mode, mark this interface as being connected to the outside network for NAT with the command **ip nat outside**:

```
Router(config-if)#ip nat outside
```

When static mappings are enabled, you will specify exactly what device and what addresses are to be translated. In Figure 6-20, device 10.1.1.2 needs to be translated to the address 192.168.1.2.

Figure 6-20 *Discrete Static Mappings*

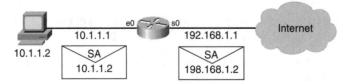

Example 6-10 shows the configuration for this translation.

Example 6-10 *Configuring a Static Translation*

```
Router(config)#ip nat inside source static 10.1.1.2 192.168.1.2
Router(config)#interface Ethernet 0
Router(config-if)#ip address 10.1.1.1 255.255.255.0
Router(config-if)#ip nat inside
Router(config-if)#exit
Router(config)#interface serial 0
Router(config-if)#ip address 192.168.1.1 255.255.255.0
Router(config-if)#ip nat outside
```

While static addressing might eliminate the need to re-address an internal networking schema, it still requires a large amount of configuration to insert a static command for every address to be translated. Using access lists and NAT pools, you can configure a router for NAT using dynamic addressing. With dynamic addressing, the router identifies an address to be translated using an access control list and then dynamically allocates an outside address using a NAT address pool.

To configure dynamic inside source address translation, perform the following tasks:

Step 1   Use the global command **ip nat pool** to define a pool of global addresses that are to be allocated, as needed:

```
Router(config)#ip nat pool name start-ip end-ip {netmask netmask |
prefix-length prefix-length}
```

Step 2   Define a standard access list permitting those addresses that need to be translated from the inside of the network:

```
Router(config)#access-list access-list-number permit source [source-
wildcard]
```

Step 3   Enable dynamic source translation for the inside addresses by specifying the access lists and pool name from the previous steps in the global command **ip nat inside source list**:

```
Router(config)#ip nat inside source list access-list-number pool name
```

Step 4   In global configuration mode, choose the interface that will be on the inside of the network with the command **interface** to move to configuration mode for that interface:

```
Router(config)#interface type number
```

Step 5   In interface configuration mode, mark this interface as being connected to the inside network for NAT with the command **ip nat inside**:

```
Router(config-if)#ip nat inside
```

Step 6 Exit to global configuration mode; then, specify the interface that will be on the outside of the private network with the command **interface** to move to configuration mode for that interface:

```
Router(config-if)#exit
Router(config)#interface type number
```

Step 7 In interface configuration mode, mark this interface as being connected to the outside network for NAT with the command **ip nat outside**.

```
Router(config-if)#ip nat outside
```

CAUTION The access list must permit only those addresses that are to be translated. Remember that an implicit **deny all** appears at the end of each access list. An access list that is too permissive can lead to unpredictable results. Cisco highly recommends that you do not configure access lists referenced by NAT commands with **permit any**. Using **permit any** can result in NAT consuming too many router resources, which can cause network problems.

With dynamic mappings, you do not specify exactly how the translations take place. Instead, you specify the addresses to be translated with an access list and point them to a defined pool of external addresses that can be selected from and returned to the pool, as needed. Figure 6-21 shows the 192.168.1.0 subnet being dynamically translated to the 171.69.233.208 subnet.

Figure 6-21 *Dynamic Mappings*

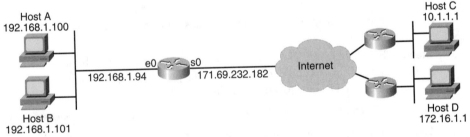

Example 6-11 shows the configuration for this translation. This example translates all source addresses passing access list 1 (having a source address from 192.168.1.0/24) to an address from the pool named net-208. The pool contains addresses from 171.69.233.209/ 28 to 171.69.233.222/28.

Example 6-11 *Configuring Dynamic Translations*

```
Router(config)#ip nat pool net-208 171.69.233.209 171.69.233.222
Router(config)#access-list 1 permit 192.168.1.0 0.0.0.255
Router(config)#ip nat inside source list 1 pool net-208
```

Example 6-11 *Configuring Dynamic Translations (Continued)*

```
Router(config)#interface ethernet 0
Router(config-if)#ip address 192.168.1.94 255.255.255.0
Router(config-if)#ip nat inside
Router(config-if)#exit
Router(config)#interface serial 0
Router(config-if)#ip address 171.69.232.182 255.255.255.240
Router(config-if)#ip nat outside
```

Overloading an Inside Global Address

Dynamic network address translation offers a great improvement over static translations; however, it is still limited by the size of the pool. If only 12 addresses are in the pool, as in Example 6-11, only 12 devices at a time can access the global network. One of the main features of NAT is static PAT ("overload" in Cisco IOS configuration). PAT offers a solution to the address limitation problem of static and dynamic NAT

You can conserve addresses in the inside global address pool by allowing the router to use one inside global address for many inside local addresses. When this overloading is configured, the router maintains enough information from higher-level protocols (for example, TCP or UDP port numbers) to translate the inside global address back to the correct inside local address. When multiple inside local addresses map to one inside global address, the TCP or UDP port numbers of each inside host distinguish between the local addresses.

Figure 6-22 illustrates NAT operation when one inside global address represents multiple inside local addresses.

Figure 6-22 *Overloading a Global Address*

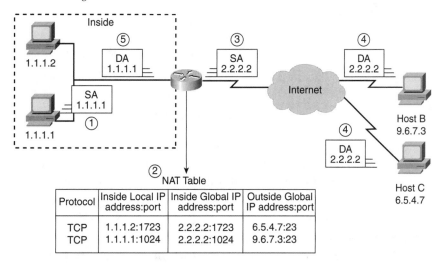

The TCP port numbers act as differentiators. Both Host B and Host C think they are talking to a single host at address 2.2.2.2. They are actually talking to different hosts; the port number is the differentiator. Many inside hosts could share the inside global IP address by using many port numbers.

The router performs the following process in overloading inside global addresses.

The following process describes inside source address translation, as shown in Figure 6-22:

1 The user at Host 1.1.1.1 opens a connection to Host B.

2 The first packet that the router receives from Host 1.1.1.1 causes the router to check its NAT table.

   If no translation entry exists, the router determines that address 1.1.1.1 must be translated and sets up a translation of inside local address 1.1.1.1 to a legal inside global address. If overloading is enabled and another translation is active, the router reuses the inside global address from that translation and saves enough information to translate back. This type of entry is called an *extended entry*.

3 The router replaces the inside local source address 1.1.1.1 with the selected inside global address and forwards the packet.

4 Host B receives the packet and responds to Host 1.1.1.1 by using the inside global IP address 2.2.2.2.

5 When the router receives the packet with the inside global IP address, it performs a NAT table lookup using the protocol, inside global address and port, and outside global address and port as a key, translates the address to inside local address 1.1.1.1, and forwards the packet to Host 1.1.1.1.

Host 1.1.1.1 receives the packet and continues the conversation. The router performs Steps 2 through 5 for each packet.

To accomplish overloading of inside global addresses, perform the following tasks:

Step 1   Define a standard access list permitting those addresses that are to be translated from the inside of the network:

```
Router(config)#access-list access-list-number permit source [source-
    wildcard]
```

Step 2   Establish dynamic source translation, specifying the access list defined in the prior step to identify which addresses will be translated, and specify which interface will be used as the address to be overloaded:

```
Router(config)#ip nat inside source list access-list-number interface
    interface overload
```

Step 3   In global configuration mode, choose the interface that will be on the inside of the network with the command **interface** to move to configuration mode for that interface:

```
Router(config)#interface type number
```

Step 4   In interface configuration mode, mark this interface as being connected
to the inside network for NAT with the command **ip nat inside**:

```
Router(config-if)#ip nat inside
```

Step 5   Exit to global configuration mode; then, specify the interface that will be
on the outside of the private network with the command **interface** to
move to configuration mode for that interface:

```
Router(config-if)#exit
Router(config)#interface type number
```

Step 6   In interface configuration mode, mark this interface as being connected
to the outside network for NAT with the command **ip nat outside**:

```
Router(config-if)#ip nat outside
```

Overload or PAT eliminates the management problems involved with static mappings and
the addressing limitations of dynamic mappings. It does this by translating all the specified
inside addresses to a single outside address using unique port numbers for each connection,
as shown in Figure 6-23.

Figure 6-23   *Overloading an Inside Global Address*

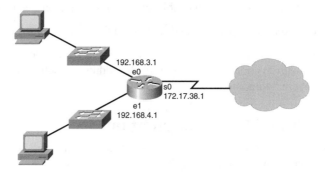

Example 6-12 shows the configuration for this translation. This example translates all
source addresses passing access list 1 (having a source address from the networks
192.168.3.0/24 and 192.168.4.0/24) to the address on interface Serial 0 using port address
translation.

Example 6-12   *Configuring NAT Overload*

```
Router(config)#access-list 1 permit 192.168.3.0 0.0.0.255
Router(config)#access-list 1 permit 192.168.4.0 0.0.0.255
Router(config)#ip nat inside source list 1 interface serial 0 overload
Router(config)#interface ethernet 0
Router(config-if)#ip address 192.168.3.1 255.255.255.0
Router(config-if)#ip nat inside
Router(config-if)#exit
```

continues

Example 6-12 *Configuring NAT Overload (Continued)*

```
Router(config)#interface ethernet 1
Router(config-if)#ip address 192.168.4.1 255.255.255.0
Router(config-if)#ip nat outside
Router(config-if)#exit
Router(config)#interface serial 0
Router(config-if)#description to ISP
Router(config-if)#ip address 192.168.38.1 255.255.255.0
Router(config-if)#ip nat outside
```

The NAT inside-to-outside process for this example works in the following sequence:

1 The incoming packet goes to the route table and the next hop is identified.

2 NAT statements are parsed to use the interface Serial 0 IP address in overload mode using PAT to create a source address to use.

3 The router encapsulates the packet and sends it out on interface Serial 0.

4 The NAT outside-to-inside address translation process works in sequence.

5 NAT statements are parsed. The router looks for an existing translation and identifies the appropriate destination address.

6 The packet goes to the route table and the next-hop interface is determined.

7 The packet is encapsulated and sent out to the local interface.

With this type of configuration, no internal addresses are visible to the outside networks; therefore, hosts do not have an external public address, which leads to improved security and ease of configuration.

Verifying the NAT and PAT Configuration

After you configure NAT, verify that it is operating as expected. You can do this using the **clear** and **show** commands.

By default, dynamic address translations time out from the NAT translation table at some point. Dynamic translations time out after a period of nonuse. When port translation is not configured, translation entries time out after 24 hours, unless you reconfigure them with the **ip nat translation** command. You can clear the entries before the timeout by using one of the commands in Table 6-4.

Table 6-4 *Commands to Clear NAT Translations*

Command	Description
clear ip nat translation *	Clears all dynamic address translation entries from the NAT translation table
clear ip nat translation inside *global-ip local-ip* **[outside** *local-ip global-ip*]	Clears a simple dynamic translation entry containing an inside translation, or both inside and outside translation

Table 6-4   *Commands to Clear NAT Translations (Continued)*

Command	Description
clear ip nat translation outside *local-ip global-ip*	Clears a simple dynamic translation entry containing an outside translation
clear ip nat translation protocol inside *global-ip global-port local-ip local-port* [outside *local-ip local-port global-ip global-port*]	Clears an extended dynamic translation entry

You can display translation information by performing one of the commands shown in Table 6-5 in EXEC mode.

Table 6-5   *Commands to Verify Network Address Translation*

Command	Description
show ip nat translations	Displays active translations
show ip nat statistics	Displays translation statistics

Alternatively, you can use the **show running-config** command and look for NAT, access list, interface, or pool commands with the required values.

In addition to using NAT to translate addresses when connecting to a global network, you can use NAT when merging two networks that use the same address space, as shown in Figure 6-24. In this figure, the network administrator is experiencing the following symptom: Host A (192.168.1.2) cannot ping Host B (192.168.2.2).

Figure 6-24   *Using NAT to Eliminate Overlapping Addresses*

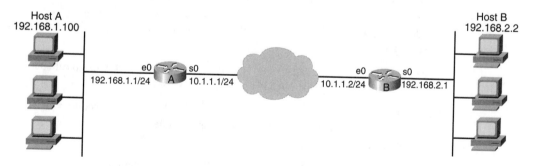

To fix the error, you need to change the Router A configuration as follows:

- Configure interface S0 to be the outside interface.
- Configure interface E0 to be the inside interface.

- Configure Router A with a loopback interface in the address space of the translated pool.

- Configure Router A to advertise network 172.16.0.0 because Router B does not know how to reach the 172.16.17.0/24 subnet.

- Configure the wildcard mask to match any host on the 192.168.1.0 network.

Example 6-13 shows the configuration for Router A.

Example 6-13 *Configuring NAT to Eliminate Overlapping*

```
Router(config)#access-list 1 permit 192.168.1.0 0.0.0.255
Router(config)#ip nat pool Becky 172.16.17.20 172.16.17.30
Router(config)#ip nat inside source list 1 pool Becky
Router(config)#interface loopback 0
Router(config-if)#ip address 172.16.17.1 255.255.255.0
Router(config-if)#exit
Router(config)#interface ethernet 0
Router(config-if)#ip address 192.168.1.1 255.255.255.0
Router(config-if)#ip inside
Router(config-if)#exit
Router(config)#interface serial 0
Router(config-if)#ip address 192.168.4.1 255.255.255.0
Router(config-if)#ip nat outside
Router(config-if)#exit
Router(config)#router rip
Router(config-router)#network 10.0.0.0
Router(config-router)#network 172.16.0.0
Router(config-if)#ip nat outside
```

Troubleshooting the NAT and PAT Configuration

When you have IP connectivity problems in a NAT environment, determining the cause of the problem is often difficult. Many times, NAT is mistakenly blamed when, in reality, there is an underlying problem. This section explains how to verify NAT operation using tools available on Cisco routers.

When trying to determine the cause of an IP connectivity problem, it helps to rule out NAT. Follow these steps to verify that NAT is operating as expected:

Step 1 Based on the configuration, clearly define what NAT is supposed to achieve. You might determine that there is a problem with the configuration.

Step 2 Verify that correct translations exist in the translation table.

Step 3 Verify the translation is occurring by using **show** and **debug** commands.

Step 4 Review in detail what is happening to the packet, and verify that routers have the correct routing information to move the packet along.

Use the **debug ip nat** command to verify the operation of the NAT feature by displaying information about every packet that the router translates. The **debug ip nat** *detailed* command generates a description of each packet considered for translation. This command also outputs information about certain errors or exception conditions, such as the failure to allocate a global address. Example 6-14 shows sample **debug ip nat** output.

Example 6-14 *debug ip nat output*

```
Router#debug ip nat
NAT:  s=192.168.1.95->172.31.233.209, d=172.31.2.132 [6825]
NAT:  s=172.31.2.132, d=172.31.233.209->192.168.1.95 [21852]
NAT:  s=192.168.1.95->172.31.233.209, d=172.31.1.161 [6826]
NAT*: s=172.31.1.161, d=172.31.233.209->192.168.1.95 [23311]
NAT*: s=192.168.1.95->172.31.233.209, d=172.31.1.161 [6827]
NAT*: s=192.168.1.95->172.31.233.209, d=172.31.1.161 [6828]
NAT*: s=172.31.1.161, d=172.31.233.209->192.168.1.95 [23313]
NAT*: s=172.31.1.161, d=172.31.233.209->192.168.1.95 [23325]
```

In this example, the first two lines show the debugging output that a Domain Name System (DNS) request and reply produced. The remaining lines show the debugging output from a Telnet connection from a host on the inside of the network to a host on the outside of the network.

The asterisk next to NAT indicates that the translation is occurring in the fast-switched path. The first packet in a conversation will always be process switched (sent to the router CPU). The remaining packets will go through the fast-switched path if a cache entry exists.

The final entry in each line, in brackets [ ], provides the packet's identification number. This information might be useful in the debugging process to correlate with other packet traces from protocol analyzers.

To determine if the appropriate translation is installed in the translation table, verify the following items:

- The configuration is correct.
- No inbound access lists are denying the packets from entering the NAT router.
- The access list referenced by the NAT command is permitting all necessary networks.
- There are enough addresses in the NAT pool.
- The router interfaces are appropriately defined as NAT inside or NAT outside.

Section 3 Quiz

1 Network Address Translation offers which of the following benefits? (Choose all that apply.)

A Eliminates the need to re-address a network

B Eliminates the need to have IP addresses for non-IP networks

C Conserves address space by multiplexing ports and addresses during translations

D Can only be configured on 3600 series routers

E Provides network security by hiding the internal network addresses

2 Network translation can be done in which of the following ways? (Choose all that apply.)

  A One-to-one static translations

  B One-to-many dynamic translations

  C Many-to-many dynamic translations

  D Many-to-one port translations

  E Many-to-one static translations

3 If you used a packet analyzer to capture a frame returning from the outside network to the sender, what would be the destination address in the IP frame?

  A The sending router's MAC address

  B The sending device's IP address

  C The translated IP address from the router

  D The receiving device's IP address

  E The loopback interface's IP address

  F The receiving device's MAC address

4 Which of the following commands would you use to set up a dynamic pool for NAT?

  A **ip nat inside source static** *local-ip global-ip*

  B **ip nat inside source list** *listnumber* **interface** *interface* overload

  C **access-list standard pool permit 192.168.255.0 0.0.0.255**

  D **ip nat inside source list** *listnumber* **pool** *poolname*

  E **ip nat pool** *name start-ip end-ip*

5 Which command could you use to view the active NAT translations?

  A **show ip nat translations**

  B **show nat translations**

  C **show active nat**

  D **debug ip nat**

  E **clear ip nat translation ***

  F **show nat statistics**

Access List Command Summary

Table 6-6 briefly describes the commands you learned in this chapter.

Table 6-6   *Access List and Network Address Translation Command Summary*

Command	Description
access-list *access-list-number (1-99, 1300-1399)* {**permit** | **deny**} *source-address* [*wildcard mask*]	Creates a standard IP access list
access-list *access-list-number (100-199, 2000-2699)* {**permit** | **deny**} *protocol source source-wildcard destination destination- wildcard* [*protocol-specific-option*] [**established**] [**log**]	Creates an extended access list
ip access-group *access-list-number* {**in** | **out**}	Enables an IP access list on an interface
line vty {# | vty-range}	Selects a virtual line or range of lines
access-class *access-list-number* {**in** | **out**}	Applies an access list as a filter on a virtual terminal line
ip access-list {**standard** | **extended**} *name*	Creates a named access list and places the router in standard or extended access list editing mode
show ip access-lists	Displays the IP access lists
show ip interface {*interface-type*} {*interface-number*}	Displays IP-specific information for an interface, including the access lists applied on that interface
ip nat inside source static *local-ip global-ip*	Establishes static translation between an inside local address and an inside global address
ip nat pool name *start-ip end-ip* {**netmask** *netmask* | **prefix-length** *prefix-length*}	Defines a pool of global addresses to be allocated, as needed
ip nat inside source list *access-list-number* **pool** *poolname*	Establishes dynamic source translation, specifying the access list and pool to be used
ip nat inside source list *access-list-number* **interface** *interface* **overload**	Establishes dynamic source translation, specifying the access list and interface to be used.
ip nat inside	Marks an interface as connected to the inside of the private network

continues

Table 6-6   *Access List and Network Address Translation Command Summary (Continued)*

Command	Description
ip nat outside	Marks an interface as connected to the outside of the private network
clear ip nat translation *	Clears all dynamic address translation entries from the NAT translation table
show ip nat translations	Displays all active translations
show ip nat statistics	Displays all translation statistics
debug ip nat	Displays translation output to the terminal

Summary

In this chapter, you learned how to apply IP access lists to interfaces as traffic filters. You read about how the standard access list checks against source addresses and how an extended access list checks source and destination addresses, and other options. You also learned how to determine which parts of these addresses are significant using wildcard masks. In addition, you saw how to apply a standard access list to a vty line to limit Telnet access to and from a router. Named access lists can also be configured to allow some flexibility in editing access lists. Finally, you learned about the guidelines for configuring these lists, placing them in your network and verifying their configuration and application.

Case Study

International Widgets Inc. is concerned about security between the VLANs and wants to insure that traffic can be passed only between the subnets for the four user VLANs and the two server VLANs:

1 What should Ann do to insure the security for these VLANS? Create a sample configuration using the addressing specified in the internetwork in Chapter 5.

2 Ann has also become responsible for connecting the network to the Internet using Serial interface 3/3 on the corporate 3640. The ISP has given Ann the address 171.69.68.13 with a 30-bit mask for the corporate router to attach to the Internet. What does Ann need to configure to allow users in the entire network to use the Internet?

Review Questions

1   Access lists applied as traffic filters help do what in a network?

2   Name one other use for an access list.

3   In which direction can an access list be applied to an interface?

4   During the outbound filtering process, what must exist in the route table before the packet is checked against the filter?

5   What is the number range for IP extended access lists?

6   How many IP access lists can be applied to an interface in a given direction?

7   Every access list acting as a packet filter must have at least one what?

8   What happens if a packet does not match any of the test conditions in an access list?

9   In a wildcard mask, what value indicates to match a bit value?

10 Instead of typing 0.0.0.0 255.255.255.255, what keyword can you use in an access list?

11 Which command verifies that a list was applied to an interface?

12 How do you remove an access list from an interface?

13 Which command allows you to view the access lists?

14 All access lists end with what?

15 Which form of NAT provides the most effective form of translations?

16 Which command would you use to clear all dynamic NAT mappings?

PART III

Interconnecting WANs

After completing this chapter, you will be able to perform the following tasks:

- Configure High-Level Data Link Control (HDLC) or Point-to-Point Protocol (PPP) at both ends of a dedicated point-to-point connection to allow exchange of data between remote sites.

- Configure Password Authentication Protocol (PAP) and Challenge Handshake Authentication Protocol (CHAP), when using PPP, to limit access to an internetwork to authorized users only.

- Verify proper configuration of HDLC or PPP, and troubleshoot an incorrect configuration of these protocols.

CHAPTER 7

Establishing Serial Point-to-Point Connections

This chapter introduces the concepts, terminology, and procedures for installing and connecting to WAN service providers. It also describes PPP and Cisco's proprietary implementation of HDLC.

WAN Overview

A WAN differs from a LAN in that a WAN makes data connections across a broad geographic area. A LAN, on the other hand, connects workstations, peripherals, terminals, and other devices in a single building or other small geographic area. Companies use a WAN to connect various company sites so that information can be exchanged between distant offices, as illustrated in Figure 7-1.

Figure 7-1 *WAN Services*

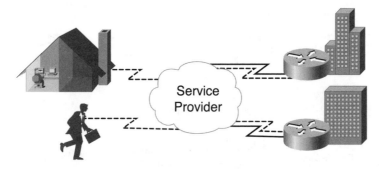

Because the cost of building out a global internetwork to connect remote sites can be astronomical, WAN services are generally leased from service providers. You must subscribe to an outside WAN provider to use internetwork resources that your organization does not own. Within the cloud (that is, the WAN connection that you lease), the service provider uses a portion of its internetwork that you leased to transport the information. Connection requirements vary depending on user requirements and costs.

The signaling and transport technologies that the service providers use are not accessible by the end user and may be proprietary in nature. Because understanding the nature of the service provider network is not required to use those services, these technologies are beyond the scope of this book.

NOTE   In some areas, a service provider might offer service to interconnect facilities within a metropolitan area using high-speed infrastructure such as ATM, SONET, FastEthernet, GigabitEthernet, or Wireless. These services provide connectivity across a large metropolitan area through an internetwork controlled by the service provider and are often referred to as a metropolitan-area network (MAN) or a Metro Ethernet. These services are currently very expensive because of the amount of bandwidth available; however, it is typically cheaper to purchase high-bandwidth connections using these services, where available, than purchasing dedicated leased lines utilizing the same amount of bandwidth. As service providers extend these high-speed infrastructures, metropolitan internetworks will replace many of the slower-speed WAN services.

WAN Connectivity Options

Many options are available for WAN connectivity; however, not all of these services are available in all areas. Figure 7-2 illustrates three of the connection types you might select. Each is described in the following list.

Figure 7-2   *WAN Connectivity Options*

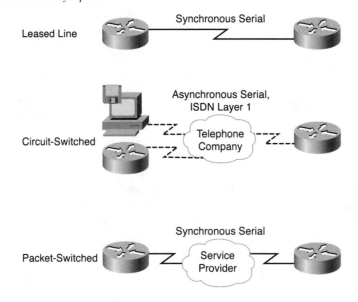

- **Leased lines**—A leased line, also known as a point-to-point or dedicated connection, provides a single pre-established WAN communications path from the customer premises through a service provider internetwork to a remote internetwork. This connection is reserved by the service provider for the client's private use. Leased lines eliminate issues such as privacy, security, and call set-up/tear-down that arise with a shared connection, but they are costly. Leased lines are typically employed over synchronous serial connections up to T3/E3 speeds, or 45 Mbps, with guaranteed bandwidth availability.

- **Circuit-switched**—A WAN switching method in which a dedicated circuit path must exist between sender and receiver for the duration of the call. Circuit switching is used by the service provider when providing basic telephone service or Integrated Services Digital Network (ISDN). The circuit establishes a pathway each time a call is made. These paths remain constant for that call's duration, but subsequent calls might or might not use the same path. Circuit-switched connections are commonly used in environments that require only sporadic WAN usage, such as backup links or bandwidth-on-demand connections. Basic telephone services can be used for circuit-switched networks by using an asynchronous serial connection on the router attached to a modem.

- **Packet-switched**—A WAN switching method in which network devices share a single point-to-point or point-to-multipoint link to transport packets from a source to a destination across a carrier internetwork. Packet-switched internetworks use permanent or switched virtual circuits (PVCs or SVCs) that provide end-to-end connectivity. Physical connections are provided by programmed switching devices. Packet headers generally identify the destination. Packet switching offers services similar to those of leased lines. There is a dedicated amount of bandwidth and service between the provider and the customer; however, after the frame is delivered to the provider, the available bandwidth on a packet-switched line inside the cloud is shared with other customers; therefore, the cost of the service is lower than for dedicated leased lines. Like leased lines, packet-switched internetworks are often employed over serial connections with speeds ranging from 56 Kbps to T3/E3 speeds.

- **Cell-switched**—Similar to packet switching, but instead of variable length packets, data is divided into fixed-length cells and then transported across virtual circuits. Cell-switched connections can range in speed from T1 (1.544 Mbps) to DS3 (45 Mbps) using copper cabling, and up to OC-192 (approximately 10 Gbps) using fiber cabling. Some of the advantages of cell switching are speed, better quality of service (QoS), and adaptation of multimedia such as voice and video. ATM is an example of public cell-switched services.

WAN Terminology

Many terms and concepts describe the services and equipment associated with WAN technologies. Although it is not within the scope of this book to discuss operation within the WAN cloud, you should understand some common terminology. Figure 7-3 illustrates a typical WAN setup and highlights the WAN terminology discussed in the following list.

Figure 7-3   *WAN Terminology*

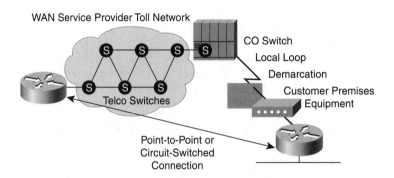

When your organization subscribes to an outside WAN provider for internetwork resources, the provider assigns your organization the parameters for making the WAN link. Here are some commonly used terms for the main physical parts:

- **Customer premises equipment (CPE)**—Devices physically located on the subscriber's (customer of the service provider) premises. The equipment includes both devices owned by the subscriber and devices leased to the subscriber by the service provider. The management of these devices can be restricted to the customer or can be shared by the customer and provider, depending on the service agreement.

- **Demarcation (or demarc)**—The juncture at which the CPE ends and the local loop portion of the service begins. The demarcation often occurs at a telecommunication closet on the subscriber's premises. This term can also refer to the boundary between the management authorities of the provider and the customer.

- **Local loop (or "last-mile")**—Cabling (usually copper wiring) that extends from the demarc into the WAN service provider's central office.

- **Central office (CO) switch**—A telco switching facility that provides the nearest point of presence (POP) for the provider's WAN service. Inside the long-distance toll network are several types of central offices.

- **Toll network**—The collective telco switches and facilities (called trunks) inside the WAN provider's cloud. The caller's traffic might cross a trunk to a primary center, go to a sectional center, and then go to a regional or international carrier center as the call travels the long distance to its destination. Switches operate in provider offices with toll charges based on tariffs or authorized rates.

WAN Serial Line Standards

To make a synchronous, serial leased line or packet-switched WAN connection such as a Frame Relay connection, Cisco devices support the following physical layer serial standards:

- EIA/TIA-232
- EIA/TIA-449
- V.35
- X.21
- EIA-530

Figure 7-4 illustrates the different physical connectors for the serial interfaces.

Figure 7-4   *Physical Layer Serial Standards*

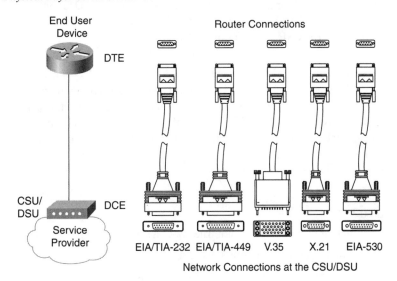

When you order the serial cable for a Cisco router, you receive a DB-60 shielded serial transition cable that has the appropriate connector for the standard you specify. The router end of the shielded serial transition cable has a DB-60 connector, which connects to the

DB-60 port on a serial WAN interface card. Because the DB-60 interface connector supports the five different media types specified in Figure 7-4, the interface is sometimes called a *5-in-1 serial port*. The other end of the serial transition cable is available with the connector appropriate for the standard you specify. This depends on the connection type of your data communications equipment (DCE) device. The documentation for the device to which you want to connect should indicate the standard used for that device.

NOTE   Although many Cisco routers use the DB-60 connector, some interfaces, such as the WAN interface card (WIC), include a SmartSerial interface. This allows higher densities in a smaller form factor. The serial end of the smart serial cable is a 26-pin connector and is much smaller than the DB-60 connector. These smart serial cables do, however, support the same five physical standard interfaces and are available in either a DTE or DCE configuration. For more information on these interface types, refer to the documentation at Cisco.com.

Your CPE that connects to a provider service is known as the data terminal equipment (DTE). The data communications equipment (DCE), such as a modem, or channel service unit/data service unit (CSU/DSU), is the device used to convert the user data from the DTE into a form acceptable to the WAN service provider. The synchronous serial port on a router is configured as DTE or DCE (except EIA/TIA-530, which is DTE only), depending on the attached cable. If the port is configured as DTE (the default setting), it requires external clocking from the CSU/DSU or other DCE device.

NOTE   DCE cables are not typically used to connect an enterprise router to provider service. They are most commonly found in back-to-back laboratory router connections. In this application, one router has a V.35 or EIA-232 DCE cable and connects to a DTE cable of the same physical standard on another router. The DCE router must be configured to provide clocking.

Section 1 Quiz

   1 Which of the following is not true about a service provider WAN?

   A WANs connect geographically disperse locations.

   B The WAN cloud belongs to the service provider.

   C A WAN connection is a one-time, fixed-cost connection.

   D WAN connection types vary depending on what the user needs.

2 Which two of these items could be considered CPE?

   A The CSU/DSU

   B Local circuit switch

   C Router

   D Telephone pole

3 True or False: A DB-60 connector allows a router to use only three different physical standards for connectivity to a provider internetwork?

4 In a cell-switched internetwork, which of the following statements are true?

   A Cell-switched internetworks use variable length cells.

   B Cell-switched internetworks can use copper or fiber media.

   C Cell-switched internetworks are only available in Europe.

   D Cell-switched internetworks build virtual circuits between locations.

   E Interfaces to cell-switched internetworks are not available on Cisco routers.

5 When connecting to a provider internetwork, which device typically derives the clocking from the provider network?

   A The router

   B The SmartJack

   C The PC

   D The CSU/DSU

   E An Atomic Clock

WAN Layer 2 Encapsulation

As you move up from the physical layer of the OSI model, serial devices must encapsulate data in a frame format at the data link layer (Layer 2). Different services can use different framing formats.

To ensure that the correct protocol is used, you need to configure the appropriate data link layer encapsulation type. The choice of protocol depends on the WAN technology and communicating equipment. Figure 7-5 shows the protocols that are associated with the three WAN connectivity options.

Figure 7-5   *Data Link Layer: WAN Encapsulation Types Based on Connection Type*

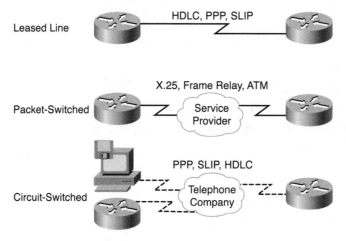

Typical WAN encapsulation types include the following:

- **Cisco High-Level Data Link Control (HDLC or cHDLC)**—cHDLC is the default encapsulation type for Cisco routers and is used on point-to-point dedicated links and circuit-switched connections. Cisco HDLC is a proprietary synchronous data link layer protocol typically used when communicating between two Cisco devices. HDLC is covered in more detail later in this chapter.

- **Point-to-Point Protocol (PPP)**—PPP is a standard protocol that provides router-to-router and host-to-network connections over many physical standards, including synchronous and asynchronous circuits. PPP was designed to work with several network layer protocols, such as IP. It also has built-in security mechanisms such as Password Authentication Protocol (PAP) and Challenge Handshake Authentication Protocol (CHAP). PPP is covered in more detail later in this chapter.

- **Serial Line Internet Protocol (SLIP)**—SLIP is a standard protocol for point-to-point serial connections using TCP/IP. SLIP has been largely displaced by PPP.

- **X.25/Link Access Procedure, Balanced (LAPB)**— LAPB is an International Telecommunications Union Telecommunications Standardization Sector (ITU-T) standard that defines how connections between DTE and DCE are established and maintained for remote terminal access and computer communications over unreliable links. The X.25 specification defines LAPB as its data link layer protocol.

- **Frame Relay**—Frame Relay is an industry-standard switched data link layer protocol based on ISDN framing technology that handles multiple virtual circuits. Frame Relay is viewed as a successor to X.25, streamlined to eliminate some of the time-consuming processes that were employed in X.25, such as error correction and flow control, that were employed to compensate for older, less-reliable communications links. Frame Relay is covered in more detail in Chapter 8, "Establishing a Frame Relay PVC Connection."

- **Asynchronous Transfer Mode (ATM)**—ATM is the international standard for cell relay in which multiple service types (such as voice, video, and data) are conveyed in fixed-length (53-byte) cells. Fixed-length cells allow processing to occur in hardware, reducing transit delays. ATM is designed to take advantage of high-speed transmission media such as T3, E3, and Synchronous Optical Network (SONET).

NOTE	SLIP, X.25, and ATM are not covered further in this book.

NOTE	This chapter discusses only how to employ HDLC and PPP protocols on a leased line. Later in this book, you will configure a Frame Relay packet-switched connection and PPP on an ISDN BRI connection. For more information on circuit switching and ISDN, see Chapter 9, "Completing an ISDN BRI Call." For information on packet switching and Frame Relay, see Chapter 8.

The next few sections discuss the serial data link layer framing formats of PPP and HDLC in greater detail.

Configuring HDLC Encapsulation

HDLC is often used as an encapsulation method for point-to-point leased line links between routers. HDLC is an ISO standard bit-oriented data-link protocol that encapsulates data on synchronous, serial data links. HDLC specifies a data encapsulation method on synchronous serial links using frame characters and checksums.

HDLC was originally designed to carry characters generated between dumb terminals to remote networks. HDLC does not inherently support multiple protocols on a single link because it does not have a standard way to indicate which protocol it is carrying. You might recall from Chapter 1, "Internetworking Concepts Review," that Ethernet frames that contain either the Type field or DSAP field indicate which network layer (Layer 3) protocol is used to transport the data. The lack of a Protocol field limits standard HDLC.

Cisco offers a proprietary version of HDLC, sometimes called cHDLC, which runs as the default encapsulation method on synchronous serial links. The Cisco HDLC frame uses a proprietary Type field that acts as a Protocol field, which makes it possible for multiple network-layer protocols to share the same serial link. This implementation can only be used between devices that can interpret the Cisco HDLC frame type. Figure 7-6 illustrates the frame formats for ISO standard HDLC and Cisco's proprietary version of HDLC.

Figure 7-6 *HDLC Frame Formats*

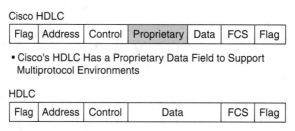

Cisco HDLC

| Flag | Address | Control | Proprietary | Data | FCS | Flag |

• Cisco's HDLC Has a Proprietary Data Field to Support
Multiprotocol Environments

HDLC

| Flag | Address | Control | Data | FCS | Flag |

• Standard HDLC Supports Only Single Protocol Environments

By default, synchronous serial lines use the Cisco HDLC serial encapsulation method (the term "HDLC" throughout this book refers to the Cisco-enhanced HDLC protocol). If the serial interface is configured with another encapsulation protocol, however, and you want to change the encapsulation back to HDLC, you must enter the interface configuration mode of the interface you want to change. Enter the following interface configuration command to specify HDLC encapsulation on the interface:

```
Router(config-if)#encapsulation hdlc
```

Cisco's HDLC is a point-to-point protocol that can be used on leased lines between two devices supporting Cisco proprietary HDLC encapsulation. If communicating with a non-Cisco device, the other manufacturer might not support Cisco's HDLC; then PPP encapsulation should be chosen as the encapsulation option.

PPP Encapsulation Overview

Unlike HDLC, the PPP encapsulation is not proprietary, and the PPP includes a protocol discriminator field within the frame. For this reason, it is often used to connect different vendor devices. Figure 7-7 illustrates how PPP provides end-to-end connectivity for multiple protocols.

Figure 7-7 *PPP Overview*

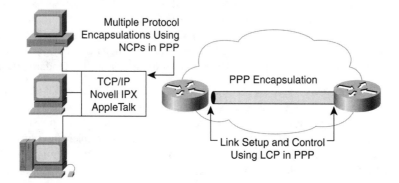

Multiple Protocol
Encapsulations Using
NCPs in PPP

TCP/IP
Novell IPX
AppleTalk

PPP Encapsulation

Link Setup and Control
Using LCP in PPP

Developers of the Internet designed PPP to make the connection for point-to-point links. PPP, described in RFCs 1661, 1962, and 1332, encapsulates network-layer protocol information over point-to-point links. RFC 1661 is an Internet Standard and has been updated by RFC 2153, *PPP Vendor Extensions*.

NOTE   You can find all RFCs online at http://www.isi.edu/in-notes/rfcxxxx.txt, where *xxxx* is the number of the RFC. If you do not know the number of the RFC, you can try searching by topic at http://www.rfc-editor.org/cgi-bin/rfcsearch.pl.

You can configure PPP on the following types of physical interfaces:

- Asynchronous serial
- ISDN
- Synchronous serial
- HSSI (High-Speed Serial Interface)

PPP Components: NCP and LCP

Functionally, PPP is primarily a data link protocol, but it also has the capability to negotiate network layer services. For this reason, PPP has two distinct sublayers. These sublayers enhance PPP's functionality. Figure 7-8 shows the breakout of these layers.

Figure 7-8   *PPP Sublayers*

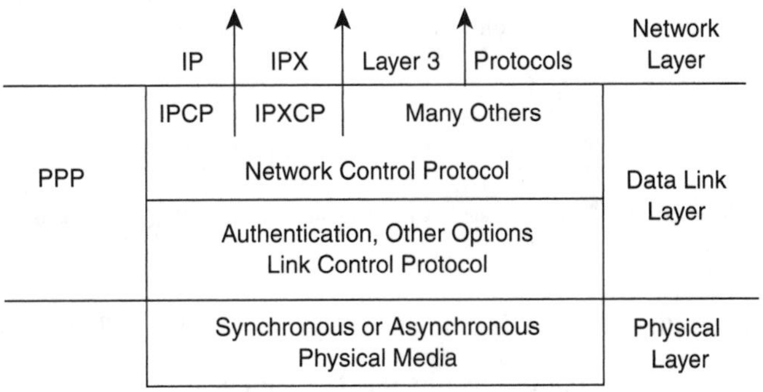

PPP uses its Network Control Program (NCP) component to encapsulate multiple protocols.

PPP uses another of its major components, the Link Control Protocol (LCP), to negotiate and set up control options on the WAN data link.

With its lower-level functions, PPP can use the following:

- Synchronous physical media

- Asynchronous physical media such as those that use basic telephone service for modem dialup connections

- ISDN

PPP offers a rich set of services that control setting up a data link. These services are options in LCP and are primarily used to negotiate and check frames to implement the point-to-point controls an administrator specifies for the connection. Many of these features, like authentication, are useful for dialup connections that use PPP as the encapsulation layer protocol.

With its higher-level functions, PPP carries packets from several network layer protocols in NCPs. These are functional fields containing standardized codes to indicate the network layer protocol type that PPP encapsulates.

One of the PPP protocol's major benefits is the functionality of the LCP options, as documented in Table 7-1.

Table 7-1   *LCP Options*

Feature	Protocol	How It Operates
Authentication	PAP	Requires a password
	CHAP	Performs Challenge Handshake
Compression	Stacker or Predictor	Compresses data at the source; decompress at the destination
Error Detection	Magic Number	Monitors data dropped on link
	Quality	Avoids frame looping
Multilink	Multilink Protocol (MP)	Loads balancing across multiple links

RFC 1548 describes PPP operation and LCP configuration options. RFC 1548 is updated by RFC 1570, *PPP LCP Extensions.*

Cisco routers that use PPP encapsulation might include the LCP options shown in Table 7-1:

- Authentication options require that the calling side of the link enter information to help ensure that the caller has the internetwork administrator's permission to make the call. Peer routers exchange authentication messages. Two alternatives are as follows:

    — Password Authentication Protocol (PAP)

    — Challenge Handshake Authentication Protocol (CHAP)

- Compression options increase the effective throughput on PPP connections by reducing the amount of data in the frame that must travel across the link by compressing the frame before sending it. The protocol then decompresses the frame at the other side of the link.

  Two compression protocols available in Cisco routers are Stacker and Predictor.

- Error-detection mechanisms with PPP allow a process to identify fault conditions. The Quality and Magic Number options help ensure link quality.

- Cisco IOS Software Release 11.1 and later supports the Multilink Protocol (MP), sometimes called multilink PPP. This option allows the use of multiple PPP interfaces going to the same destination to load-balance the traffic.

  Packet fragmentation and sequencing, as specified in RFC 1717, splits the load for PPP and sends fragments over parallel links. In some cases, this "bundle" of multilink PPP pipes functions as a single, logical link, improving throughput and reducing latency between peer routers. RFC 1990, *The PPP Multilink Protocol (MP),* makes RFC 1717 obsolete.

This book discusses only the PAP and CHAP authentication LCP options. To learn more about other LCP options, such as compression or multilink PPP, refer to Cisco.com.

Establishing a PPP Connection

For devices to communicate using PPP, the protocol must first open a session. Figure 7-9 illustrates this connection establishment.

Figure 7-9   *PPP Connection Establishment*

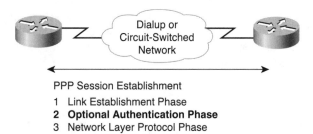

PPP Session Establishment
1 Link Establishment Phase
2 Optional Authentication Phase
3 Network Layer Protocol Phase

A PPP session establishment has three phases:

1 **Link establishment phase**—In this phase, each PPP device sends LCP packets to configure and test the data link. LCP packets contain a Configuration Option field that allows devices to negotiate the use of options such as the maximum reconstructed

receive unit (MRRU), compression of certain PPP fields, and the link authentication protocol. If a configuration option is not included in an LCP packet, the default value for that configuration option is assumed.

2 **Authentication phase (optional)**—After the link has been established and the authentication protocol chosen, the peer can be authenticated. Authentication, if used, takes place before entering the network layer negotiation phase.

   PPP **supports** two authentication protocols: PAP and CHAP. Both of these protocols were originally detailed in RFC 1334, *PPP Authentication Protocols*. However, RFC 1994, *PPP Challenge Handshake Authentication Protocol (CHAP)*, redefines the authentication methods and makes RFC 1334 obsolete.

3 **Network layer protocol phase**—In this phase, the PPP devices send NCP packets to choose and configure one or more network layer protocols, such as IP. As soon as each of the chosen network layer protocols has been configured, datagrams from each network layer protocol can be sent over the link.

Configuring PPP Encapsulation and PAP and CHAP Authentication

PPP authentication is an option that is typically used when you have no way of guaranteeing who will attempt to connect to the router, such as when using dialup connections. When configuring PPP authentication, you can select PAP or CHAP. CHAP is the preferred protocol because it uses a more secure authentication method. The sections that follow provide a brief description of both PAP and CHAP.

PAP Authentication

PAP provides a simple method for a remote node to establish its identity using a two-way handshake. PAP is done only upon initial link establishment and is considered the weaker of the two authentication choices. Figure 7-10 illustrates the transactions that take place during PAP authentication.

Figure 7-10 *PAP Authentication*

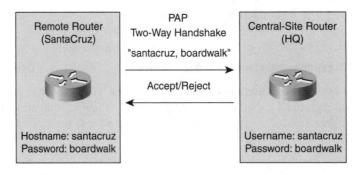

After the PPP link establishment phase is complete, the remote note repeatedly sends a username-and-password pair to the router until authentication is acknowledged or the connection is terminated.

PAP is not a strong authentication protocol. Passwords are sent across the link in clear text, and there is no protection from playback or repeated trial-and-error attacks. The remote node is in control of the frequency and timing of the login attempts. A clear-text password, however, might be sufficient in environments that use token-type passwords that change with each authentication.

CHAP Authentication

CHAP is a stronger authentication method than PAP. CHAP is used at the startup of a link, and periodically, to verify the identity of the remote node using a three-way handshake. CHAP is done upon initial link establishment and can be repeated any time after the link has been established. Figure 7-11 illustrates the transactions that take place during CHAP authentication.

Figure 7-11   *CHAP Authentication*

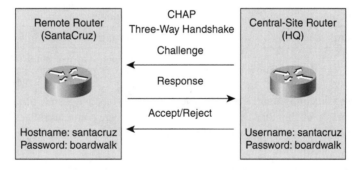

After the PPP link establishment phase is complete, the local router sends a "challenge" message to the remote node. The remote node responds with a value calculated using a one-way hash function (typically Message Digest 5, called MD5 for short). The MD5 hash is based on the commonly configured password and a challenge message. The local router checks the response against its own calculation of the expected hash value. If the values match, the authentication is acknowledged; otherwise, the connection is terminated immediately.

CHAP provides protection against playback attacks through the use of a variable challenge value that is unique and unpredictable. The use of repeated challenges is intended to limit the time of exposure to any single attack. The local router (or a third-party authentication server such as TACACS) controls the frequency and timing of the challenges.

Enabling PPP Encapsulation and PAP or CHAP Authentication

To enable PPP encapsulation and PAP or CHAP authentication on an interface, you need to configure the items listed in Table 7-2.

Table 7-2   *PPP Authentication Tasks*

Authenticating Router (The Router That Received the Call)	Router to Be Authenticated (The Router That Initiated the Call)
ppp encapsulation	ppp encapsulation
hostname	hostname
username	username
ppp authentication	ppp authentication
	ppp pap sent-username (PAP only)

Before you configure PPP authentication, the interface must be configured for PPP encapsulation. To enable PPP encapsulation, enter interface configuration mode. Enter the **encapsulation ppp** interface configuration command to specify PPP encapsulation on the interface as follows:

```
Router(config-if)#encapsulation ppp
```

You can then enable PAP or CHAP authentication by following these steps:

Step 1   Verify that each router has a host name assigned to it. The router will use its own host name to identify itself to its remote peer. The router uses the received host name to search its local database to find the password associated with the remote peers "username." To assign a host name, enter the **hostname** *name* command in global configuration mode:

```
Router(config)#hostname name
```

The *name* option must match a username that is configured on the peer router at the other end of the link.

Step 2   On each router, define the username and password to expect from the remote router with the **username** *name* **password** *password* global configuration command:

```
Router(config)#username name password password
```

The *name* argument is the remote router's host name. Note that it is case-sensitive.

The **password** option sets the password that will be used for the connection. On Cisco routers, the password must be the same for both routers. In Cisco IOS Software releases prior to 11.2, this password was displayed in the configuration as an encrypted, secret password. As of Cisco IOS Software Release 11.2, the password is displayed as a plain-text password and is not shown encrypted. To hide the passwords from view in the configuration on your IOS router, enter the **service password-encryption** command while in global configuration mode. (This command affects only how passwords are displayed in the router configuration. CHAP challenges are always exchanged as MD5 encrypted values.)

Add a username entry for each remote system that the local router communicates with and requires authentication from. The remote device must also have a username entry for the local router. Remember that the router will match these usernames with the remote router's host name for authentication.

Step 3   Configure PPP authentication with the **ppp authentication** interface configuration command. Here is its full syntax:

```
Router(config-if)#ppp authentication {chap ? chap pap ? pap chap ? pap}
```

NOTE   If both PAP and CHAP are enabled, the first method specified will be requested during link negotiation. If the peer suggests using the second method or simply refuses the first method, the second method will be tried.

Sample PAP/CHAP Configurations

In Figure 7-12, a three-way handshake occurs. The host name on one router must match the username that the other router has configured for it. The passwords must also match for both sides.

Figure 7-12 *Sample CHAP Configuration*

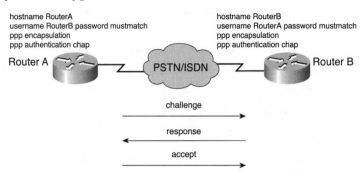

Example 7-1 demonstrates a point-to-point CHAP authentication configuration. Both routers must authenticate and be authenticated, so the CHAP authentication commands mirror each other. The router host name and password each router sends must match those specified on the other router's **username** *name* **password** *password* command. That is, the CHAP username for a router is the host name of the remote router. The password for the peer routers must match on both sides of the configuration.

Example 7-1 *CHAP Authentication Configuration*

```
hostname RouterA                          hostname RouterB
username RouterB password mustmatch       username RouterA password mustmatch
interface serial 0                        interface serial 0
ip address 10.0.1.1 255.255.255.0         ip address 10.0.1.2 255.255.255.0
encapsulation ppp                         encapsulation ppp
ppp authentication chap                    ppp authentication chap
```

Verifying PPP Encapsulation Configuration

When PPP is configured and a link is operational, you can check its LCP and NCP states using the **show interface** command. Use the **show interface** command to verify proper configuration. Example 7-2 provides some sample output from the **show interface** command.

Example 7-2 **show interface** *Verifies Proper PPP Configuration*

```
Router#show interface s0
Serial0 is up, line protocol is up
  Hardware is HD64570
  Internet address is 10.140.1.2/24
  MTU 1500 bytes, BW 1544 Kbit, DLY 20000 usec, rely 255/255, load 1/255
  Encapsulation PPP, loopback not set, keepalive set (10 sec)
  LCP Open
  Open: IPCP, CDPCP
  Last input 00:00:05, output 00:00:05, output hang never
  Last clearing of "show interface" counters never
```

Example 7-2 **show interface** *Verifies Proper PPP Configuration (Continued)*

```
Queueing strategy: fifo
Output queue 0/40, 0 drops; input queue 0/75, 0 drops
5 minute input rate 0 bits/sec, 0 packets/sec
5 minute output rate 0 bits/sec, 0 packets/sec
    38021 packets input, 5656110 bytes, 0 no buffer
    Received 23488 broadcasts, 0 runts, 0 giants, 0 throttles
    0 input errors, 0 CRC, 0 frame, 0 overrun, 0 ignored, 0 abort
    38097 packets output, 2135697 bytes, 0 underruns
    0 output errors, 0 collisions, 6045 interface resets
    0 output buffer failures, 0 output buffers swapped out
    482 carrier transitions
    DCD=up  DSR=up  DTR=up  RTS=up  CTS=up
```

Notice in Example 7-2 that the shaded output indicates the LCP is open. This means that the connection between the two PPP devices has been negotiated. This would include the authentication phase, if configured. The next line in the output indicates which NCP protocols have been opened; in this case, Cisco Discovery Protocol Control Protocol (CDPCP) and Internet Protocol Control Protocol (IPCP).

Example 7-3 shows the router output for the authenticating and authenticated router when **debug ppp authentication** is enabled. Use this command to display the exchange sequence as it occurs.

Example 7-3 *Output from* **debug ppp authentication** *Verifying PPP Authentication*

```
Router# debug ppp authentication
4d20h: %LINK-3-UPDOWN: Interface Serial0, changed state to up
4d20h: Se0 PPP: Treating connection as a dedicated line
4d20h: Se0 PPP: Phase is AUTHENTICATING, by both
4d20h: Se0 CHAP: O CHALLENGE id 2 len 28 from "RouterA"
4d20h: Se0 CHAP: I CHALLENGE id 3 len 28 from "RouterB"
4d20h: Se0 CHAP: O RESPONSE id 3 len 28 from "RouterA"
4d20h: Se0 CHAP: I RESPONSE id 2 len 28 from "RouterB"
4d20h: Se0 CHAP: O SUCCESS id 2 len 4
4d20h: Se0 CHAP: I SUCCESS id 3 len 4
4d20h: %LINEPROTO-5-UPDOWN: Line protocol on Interface Serial0, changed state to up
```

Example 7-4 highlights one router's **debug** output for a two-way PAP authentication.

Example 7-4 *Router Output for Two-Way PAP Authentication*

```
Se0 PPP: Phase is AUTHENTICATING, by both    (Two-way authentication)
Se0 PAP: O AUTH-REQ id 4 len 18 from "RouterA"  (Outgoing authentication request)
Se0 PAP: I AUTH-REQ id 1 len 18 from "RouterB" (Incoming authentication request)
Se0 PAP: Authenticating peer right             (Authenticating incoming)
Se0 PAP: O AUTH-ACK id 1 len 5                 (Outgoing acknowledgment)
Se0 PAP: I AUTH-ACK id 4 len 5                 (Incoming acknowledgment)
```

Serial Point-to-Point Connection Command Summary

Table 7-3 summarizes the commands relevant to point-to-point connections.

Table 7-3 *Serial Point-to-Point Connection-Related Commands*

Command	Description
encapsulation hdlc	Enables HDLC encapsulation on an interface
encapsulation ppp	Enables PPP on an interface
ppp authentication pap	Enables PAP authentication on an interface
ppp authentication chap	Enables CHAP authentication on an interface
username *name* **password** *password*	Establishes a username-based authentication system
show interface	Shows the status of an interface, including encapsulation method
debug ppp authentication	Debugs the PAP or CHAP authentication process

Section 2 Quiz

1 True or False: Cisco's HDLC uses the same Address and Control fields as the Standard HDLC?

2 PPP can be configured on which of the following interface types?

   A Asynchronous

   B HSSI

   C Synchronous

   D ISND

   E All of the above

   F A and D only

3 Which component of PPP negotiates the link options?

   A MP

   B NCP

   C LCP

   D CDPCP

4 True or False: Authentication is required for a PPP connection?

5 If PPP authentication has been enabled for a connection between two routers, which router must be configured with the username password settings?

A The host router only

B The calling router only

C The host router for PAP

D The host router for CHAP

E Both routers

Summary

In this chapter, you learned about the different Layers 1 and 2 standards involving point-to-point serial connections. You learned about Cisco's proprietary HDLC and the Internet standard PPP encapsulations. You also learned how to authenticate routers using PPP authentication such as PAP and CHAP. Finally, this chapter discussed the methods used to verify and test these configurations.

Case Study

Using what you have learned in this chapter, it is time to return to our case study company and help our Internetwork Administrator, Ann E. Won. Today, Ann has been tasked with connecting the corporate facility to two remote locations using a point-to-point, leased-line, serial connection to each location. Ann will be connecting Serial 3/0, 3/1, and 3/2 on the company's 3640 router to each location, respectively. Figure 7-13 shows a diagram of these connections.

Figure 7-13 *WAN Case Study Internetwork Diagram*

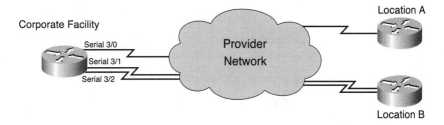

Remote location A will be using a non-Cisco router for connectivity back to the corporate facility across a T1 link. Remote location B will be using a Cisco router but will be connecting via two 56-Kbps circuits. The major concern with this connection is that it should be configured to provide maximum throughput between the locations.

Ann's first task is to choose the correct cable type to connect to the DCE. The telco has provisioned the circuits and is managing the DCE equipment, but has not specified to the IT staff at International Widgets Ltd. What type of cable is needed to connect to the CSU/DSU? On closer examination of the CSU/DSU, Ann sees the following types of connectors shown in Figure 7-14.

Figure 7-14   *CSU/DSU Connectors*

CSU/DSU to Location B

CSU/DSU to Location A

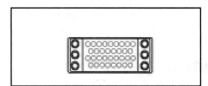

Based on the preceding information, answer the following questions about what Ann should do:

1   What cables does Ann need to connect to the router?

2   What Layer 2 encapsulation methods should she use for the connection to location A and why?

3   What encapsulation method should be used to connect to location B and why?

4   What LCP options should be configured for location B?

5   Is there an immediate need for authentication between these sites? Why or why not?

Final Review Questions

1   What are three connection types that you can use to connect routers over a WAN?

2   What is the default Layer 2 encapsulation type of Cisco serial interfaces?

3   Which encapsulation option discussed in this chapter would you select if you were connecting a Cisco router to a non-Cisco router?

4   How do you enable PPP encapsulation?

5   What are the two PPP authentication options?

6   Name one other PPP option.

7   How do you set the password for CHAP and PAP?

8 If both PAP and CHAP are configured, which method is tried first?

9 Which authentication option sends the password in clear text?

10 Which command is used to check the encapsulation?

After completing this chapter, you will be able to perform the following tasks:

- Identify the terminology and basic technical requirements needed to connect to a Frame Relay service provider.
- Configure a router for Frame Relay operation and verify permanent virtual circuit (PVC) connectivity.
- Configure Frame Relay subinterfaces.

CHAPTER 8

Establishing a Frame Relay PVC Connection

Frame Relay is an International Telecommunications Union, Telecommunications Standardization Sector (ITU-T) and American National Standards Institute (ANSI) standard that defines the process for sending data over a public data network (PDN). Frame Relay also has operational standards, such as traffic shaping, defined by an intervendor forum of Frame Relay vendors and users known as the Frame Relay Forum.

Frame Relay is a connection-oriented data link technology that is streamlined to provide high performance and efficiency. Connection-oriented means that a virtual circuit must be created and operational before the router can send data into the Frame Relay network. The Frame Relay network itself does not perform error correction on the user data; instead, it relies on the functions of upper-layer protocols such as Transmission Control Protocol (TCP) in the IP stack.

This chapter provides you with an overview of Frame Relay technology and provides the information needed to configure a router in a Frame Relay environment.

Frame Relay Overview

Frame Relay is a standards-based protocol that defines a communication method between a service provider network and a customer device, which provides communication over a WAN.

Devices in a Frame Relay network fall into two general categories:

- **Data terminal equipment (DTE)**—Generally terminates the Frame Relay connection at the customer site. Routers, bridges, and Frame Relay access devices (FRADs) are all examples of DTE.

- **Data circuit-terminating equipment (DCE)**—The carrier-owned internetworking devices. The DCE's purpose is to provide clocking and switching services in a network; they are the devices that actually transmit the data through the WAN and define the logical connections between the DTE. The DCE is typically a Frame Relay switch.

The purpose of Frame Relay is to define the interconnection process between your router and the service provider's local access switching equipment, as illustrated in Figure 8-1. It does not define how the data is transmitted within the service provider's Frame Relay cloud between the DCEs.

Figure 8-1   *Frame Relay Overview*

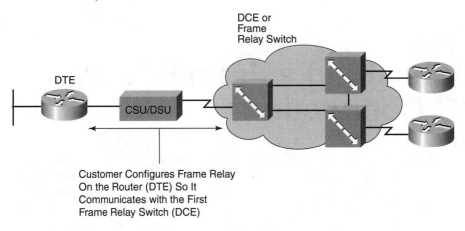

Frame Relay provides a means for statistically multiplexing many logical data conversations (referred to as virtual circuits or VCs) over a single physical transmission link by assigning a data-link connection identifier or (DLCI) to each pair of DTE.

The service provider's switching equipment constructs a table that maps DLCIs to its outbound ports. When a frame is received, the switching device analyzes the DLCI and delivers the frame to the associated outbound port. The complete path to the destination is established prior to the sending of the first frame.

The core aspects of Frame Relay function at the lower two layers of the OSI reference model, as shown in Figure 8-2.

Figure 8-2   *Frame Relay Operates at Physical Layer and Data Link Layer of the OSI Reference Model*

OSI Reference Model	Frame Relay
Application	
Presentation	
Session	
Transport	
Network	IP/IPX/AppleTalk, etc.
Data Link	Frame Relay
Physical	EIA/TIA-232, EIA/TIA-449, V.35, X.21, EIA/TIA-530

The same physical serial connections that support point-to-point environments also support the Frame Relay connection to the service provider. Cisco routers support the following serial connections:

- EIA/TIA-232
- EIA/TIA-449
- V.35
- X.21
- EIA/TIA-530

Working at the data link layer, Frame Relay encapsulates information from the upper layers of the OSI stack. For example, IP traffic is encapsulated into a frame format that can be transmitted over a Frame Relay link.

The Frame Relay frame contains the following fields:

- Opening flag (0x7E)
- Address
- Data
- Frame check sequence (FCS)
- Closing flags (0x7E)

The Address field, which is two bytes in length, is composed of 10 bits representing the actual circuit identifiers and 6 bits related to congestion and management functions.

The Data field contains the encapsulated packet from Layer 3 and above. The FCS provides a way of checking the frame for errors during transmission. Figure 8-3 shows the format of a Frame Relay frame.

Figure 8-3   *Frame Relay Frame*

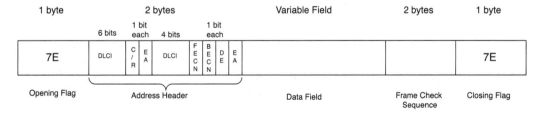

Frame Relay Components and Terminology

Frame Relay, like most WAN services, has some unique terminology associated with it. To understand the operation and configuration of Frame Relay, you need to be familiar with these terms. Figure 8-4 illustrates some Frame Relay components and terminology, which are described in detail in the text that follows.

Figure 8-4   *Frame Relay Components*

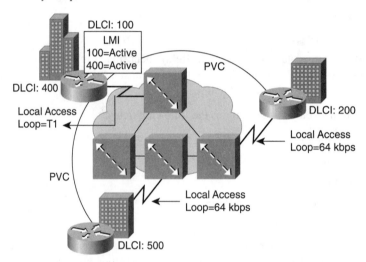

The following list defines some generic terms that are used frequently when discussing Frame Relay. They might be the same as, or slightly different than, the terms your Frame Relay service provider uses:

- **Local access rate**—The clock speed (port speed) of the connection (local loop) to the Frame Relay cloud. This is the maximum rate at which data travels into or out of the network, regardless of other settings.

- **Virtual circuit (VC)**—Logical circuit created to ensure bidirectional communication between two network (DTE) devices. The VC is uniquely identified by a data-link connection identifier (DLCI). A number of virtual circuits can be multiplexed into a single physical circuit for transmission across the Frame Relay network through any number of intermediate DCE devices (Frame Relay Switches). A VC can be either a permanent virtual circuit (PVC) or a switched virtual circuit (SVC).

- **PVC**—A virtual circuit that is permanently established. These circuits are useful for frequent and consistent data transfers between devices. Communication across a PVC does not require circuit establishment and tear down, which can save some overhead bandwidth. PVCs are useful in situations where virtual circuits need to exist all the time.

- **SVC**—A virtual circuit that is dynamically established on demand and is torn down when transmission is complete. SVCs are used in situations where data transmission is sporadic.

NOTE   With ANSI T1.617, ITU Q.933 (Layer 3), and Q.922 (Layer 2), Frame Relay now supports SVCs. Cisco IOS Software Release 11.2 and later support Frame Relay SVCs. Configuring Frame Relay SVCs is not covered in this book. You can find more information about SVCs online at Cisco.com.

- **Data-link connection identifier (DLCI)**—A 10-bit number in the Frame Relay frame's Address field that identifies the logical virtual circuit between the router and the Frame Relay switch. The Frame Relay switch maps the DLCIs between each pair of routers to create a PVC. DLCIs have local significance in that the identifier references the point between the local router and the Frame Relay switch to which it is connected. Devices at the opposite end of a connection can use different DLCI values to refer to the same virtual connection. Note in Figure 8-4 that the routers use different DLCI numbers on each end to point to the same PVC that interconnects them.

- **Committed information rate (CIR)**—(Not depicted in Figure 8-4) When subscribing to Frame Relay service, you will specify the local access rate, for example T1, that connects to the service provider network. You will also be asked to specify a CIR, up to the access rate, for each DLCI on the connection. The CIR value specifies the maximum average data rate that the network undertakes to deliver, when there is little or no congestion. If your traffic exceeds the CIR on a given DLCI, the network will flag some frames with a discard eligible (DE) bit. As long as these frames do not encounter any congestion in the network, they will be delivered; however, if they do encounter congestion, the frame relay switch will discard them. The lower the specified CIR, the less expensive the PVC cost. Many providers sell 0 CIR service to lower costs. In this environment, a user could access the network at full access rates, but every frame sent into the network would be discard eligible. As long as no congestion occurs in the provider network, the frames will be delivered.

- **Inverse Address Resolution Protocol (Inverse ARP)**—(Not depicted in Figure 8-4) A method of dynamically associating a remote network layer address with a local DLCI. It allows a router to discover the network address of the device at the other end of a VC.

- **Local Management Interface (LMI)**—A signaling standard between the router (DTE device) and the Frame Relay switch (DCE device) that is responsible for managing the connection and maintaining status between the devices.

- **Forward Explicit Congestion Notification (FECN)**—(Not depicted in Figure 8-4) The FECN is a bit in the Frame Relay frame header's Address field. The FECN mechanism is initiated when a DTE sends Frame Relay frames into the network, by setting the value to 0. As the frame travels through the network, if a Frame Relay switch (DCE) is congested, it sets the FECN bit in a Frame Relay packet to 1. As this frame travels forward to the destination device (DTE), the FECN bit informs that device that congestion has occurred as this frame traveled through the Frame cloud. The receiving DTE device can relay this information to a higher-layer protocol for processing. Depending on the implementation, the router might be able to tell the sender to reduce the rate at which it sends frames into the network to reduce congestion, or the receiver might ignore the DE bit.

- **Backward Explicit Congestion Notification (BECN)**—(Not depicted in Figure 8-4) The BECN is a bit in the Frame Relay frame header's Address field. A Frame Relay switch (DCE) sets the BECN value to 1 for frames traveling in the opposite directions of frames that have their FECN bit set when congestion occurs. As frames travel backward to the source router (DTE), the BECN informs the device that congestion exists on a particular VC. The DTE device can relay this information to a higher-layer protocol for processing. Depending on the implementation, the router can reduce the rate at which it is sending frames into the network to reduce congestion, or it can ignore the BECN.

NOTE   This book provides a generic introduction of Frame Relay services and terms. Your Frame Relay equipment might offer flow control and traffic-shaping features that are not covered in this book. Some other terms regarding Frame Relay flow control include committed burst, excess burst, and discard eligible. You can find additional Frame Relay information on the Frame Relay forum site at www.frforum.com.

Frame Relay Topologies

Frame Relay provides a connection to the provider network. One of the useful attributes of Frame Relay is the flexibility that is offered by a connection to the Frame Relay cloud. From that single connection, the provider can provision virtual circuits that allow you to interconnect the remote sites in a variety of topologies, such as those depicted in Figure 8-5. The list that follows describes the topologies in greater detail.

Figure 8-5   *Frame Relay Topologies*

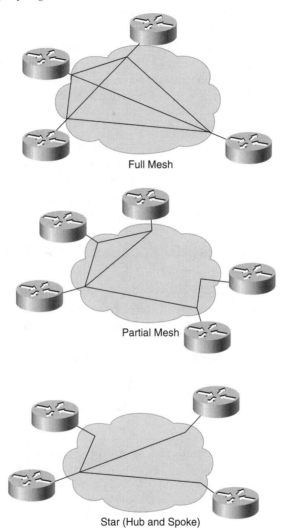

- **Full-mesh topology**—In this topology, all routers have virtual circuits to all other destinations. This topology, although costly, provides direct connections from each site to all other sites and allows for redundancy. When a VC goes down, a router can reroute traffic through another site. As the number of nodes (routers) in this topology increases, a full-mesh topology can become very expensive. To determine how many

VCs would be required to implement a full-mesh topology, use the formula $[n(n-1)]/2$ where n is the total number of nodes on the network. For example, to fully mesh a network of 7 devices (nodes), $[7(7-1)]/2 = 21$ VCs would be required.

- **Partial-mesh topology**—In this topology, not all sites have direct access to all other sites. This topology is a mix of a full-mesh and a star topology. Depending on the traffic patterns in your network, you might want to have additional PVCs connected to remote sites that have large data traffic requirements or where you need to guarantee a pathway between nodes.

- **Star topology**—Also known as a hub-and-spoke configuration, the star topology is the most popular Frame Relay network topology. In this topology, remote sites are connected to a central site that generally provides a service or application. This is the least-expensive topology because it requires the least number of PVCs. In this scenario, the central router provides a multipoint connection because it typically uses a single interface to interconnect multiple PVCs.

Frame Relay Nonbroadcast Multiaccess (NBMA) Reachability Problems

In any of the aforementioned Frame Relay topologies, when a single interface must be used to interconnect multiple sites, you might have reachability issues because of the nonbroadcast multiaccess (NBMA) nature of Frame Relay. Because a single interface connects to a cloud and can be mapped to many other sites, the cloud is said to be multi-access. Because the Frame Relay switch doesn't replicate a broadcast packet coming from a single DLCI to all DLCIs, it is said to be nonbroadcast. With Frame Relay running multiple PVCs over a single interface, the primary routing protocol issue is with split horizon. Figure 8-6 illustrates why the Frame Relay default of NBMA can be a problem.

NOTE   The routing protocol issue exists only when using routing protocols such as RIP that suffer from split horizon problems.

Figure 8-6   *Frame Relay Reachability*

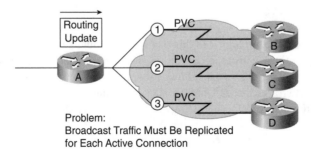

Problem:
Broadcast Traffic Must Be Replicated
for Each Active Connection

By default, a Frame Relay network provides NBMA connectivity between remote sites. In a routed network, this NBMA connectivity means that although all locations can be configured to reach each other through the cloud using a single subnet, routing update broadcasts received by one location might not be forwarded to all other locations on that same physical interface. This is because the routing protocol uses split horizon to reduce the potential for routing loops.

Split horizon reduces the potential for routing loops by not allowing a routing update received on one interface to be forwarded out the same interface. As a result, if a remote router sends an update to the headquarters router that is connecting multiple VCs over a single physical interface, the headquarters router cannot send that update through the same interface to other remote routers, even though they use separate VCs.

Broadcasts are not a problem if only a single VC is on a physical interface, because this would be a point-to-point connection type; however, they are a problem when more than one VC is on a physical interface.

When a router supports multipoint connections over a single interface, many DLCIs terminate in a single router, which must replicate broadcast packets (such as routing updates or management queries) on each VC to the remote routers. The updates can consume access-link bandwidth and cause significant latency variations in user traffic. The updates can also consume interface buffers and lead to higher packet rate loss for both user data and routing updates.

During the design phase of a Frame Relay network, you should evaluate the amount of broadcast traffic and the number of VCs terminating at each router. Overhead traffic, such as routing updates, can affect the delivery of critical user data, especially when the delivery path contains low-bandwidth (56-kbps) links. A static route might be better in this situation.

The simplest answer to resolving the reachability issues brought on by split horizon might seem to be to turn off split horizon. Two problems exist with this solution, however:

- Not all network layer protocols allow you to disable split horizon (however, most, such as IP, do allow this).
- Disabling split horizon increases the chances of routing loops in your network.

Disabling split horizon differs for each protocol. To disable split horizon, check the commands for the routing protocol you are using. Probably the best solution for this problem is to implement a routing protocol such as Open Shortest Path First (OSPF) or IS-IS which are not distance-vector protocols and do not implement split horizon.

Another method of solving the problem would be to use a single physical interface for each VC; however, this increases costs and defeats the purpose of a VC network topology.

The best way to solve the problem is to associate each VC with its own logical interface. Then each logical interface behaves like a physical interface, which enables the forwarding of broadcast routing updates in a Frame Relay network. On a router, you can configure multiple *subinterfaces* for a single physical interface. Subinterfaces are logical subdivisions of a single physical interface. In multipoint routing environments with subinterfaces, routing updates received on one subinterface can be sent out another subinterface. Each router interface is given an address on the same subnet.

In subinterface configuration, each VC can be configured as a point-to-point connection, which allows the subinterface to act similarly to a leased line. Using a Frame Relay point-to-point subinterface, each pair of the point-to-point routers is on its own subnet. Figure 8-7 illustrates how the subinterfaces logically map to each of the virtual circuits.

Figure 8-7   *Resolving Reachability Issues*

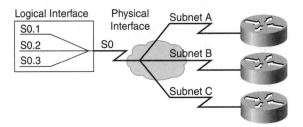

Address Mapping and LMI Signaling for Frame Relay Connections

Frame Relay VCs allow a single location to be connected to many remote locations. Each Frame Relay VC is uniquely identified by its local DLCI. The DLCI allows a router to distinguish among all the VCs terminated on an interface. Because the DLCI is a data-link address, upper-layer protocols such as IP need to resolve their logical addresses to DLCIs to route packets. Address resolution in Frame Relay involves mapping the IP address at the remote end of a VC to the local DLCI, as shown in Figure 8-8.

Figure 8-8   *Frame Relay Address Mapping*

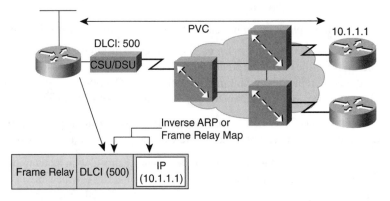

You can manually configure a static Frame Relay map in the map table on the router to describe the relationship between the VC and the remote end network layer address. In Figure 8-8, next-hop address 10.1.1.1 is mapped to a local DLCI 500. With this mapping statement, if the router needs to send traffic to the next-hop address 10.1.1.1, it would send it out the interface in a Frame Relay frame with DLCI 500.

On Cisco routers, the addresses can also be dynamically mapped with Inverse ARP, which associates a given DLCI to the next-hop protocol address for a specific connection. The router then updates its mapping table and uses the information in the table to route packets. RFC 1293 describes Inverse ARP in greater detail.

NOTE   You can find all RFCs online at http://www.isi.edu/in-notes/rfc*xxxx*.txt where *xxxx* is the number of the RFC. If you do not know the number of the RFC, you can try searching by topic at http://www.rfc-editor.org/cgi-bin/rfcsearch.pl.

The Local Management Interface (LMI) consists of several types of signaling standards between the router and the Frame Relay switch that are responsible for managing the connection and maintaining status between the devices. LMIs include support for a keepalive mechanism, a multicast mechanism, and a status mechanism. LMI exchange occurs over a predefined DLCI number, according to the LMI type being used. Figure 8-9 shows how LMI maintains the status of the PVC between the routers. The keepalives are exchanged between the switch and the router and give the PVC's status. Notice that the PVC for DLCI 500 is active, and the PVC for DLCI 400 is inactive. This shows how LMI can provide management for the VC connection from end to end.

Figure 8-9   *Frame Relay Signaling*

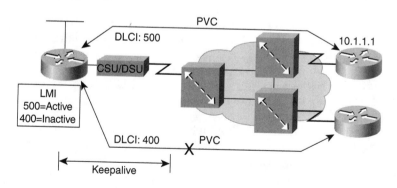

Although the LMI type is configurable, beginning with Cisco IOS Software Release 11.2, the Cisco router tries to autosense which LMI type the Frame Relay switch is using by sending one or more full-status requests to the Frame Relay switch. The Frame Relay switch responds with one or more LMI types. The router configures itself with the last LMI type received. This capability to autodetect the correct LMI is important because Cisco LMI uses DLCI 1023 for communication with the switch and the other two types use DLCI 0.

Three types of LMIs are supported:

- **cisco**—LMI type defined jointly by Cisco, StrataCom, Northern Telecom, and Digital Equipment Corporation, nicknamed "the gang of four"
- **ansi**—Annex D, defined by the ANSI standard T1.617
- **q933a**—ITU-T Q.933 Annex A

An administrator setting up a connection to a Frame Relay network can choose and manually configure the appropriate LMI type from the three supported types to ensure proper Frame Relay operation.

When the router receives LMI information, it updates its VC status to one of three states:

- **Active state**—Indicates that the connection is active and that routers can exchange data
- **Inactive state**—Indicates that the local connection to the Frame Relay switch is working, but the remote router's connection to the Frame Relay switch is not working
- **Deleted state**—Indicates that no LMI is being received from the Frame Relay switch, or that no service exists between the router and the Frame Relay switch

NOTE   Although the router's autosensing feature is useful, it should be noted that autosensing doesn't always work. When it doesn't, it is best to contact your provider to determine which type is supported, and then manually set the LMI type on your router; however, if your provider changes its equipment or reconfigures a link, your configuration might suddenly stop working. So, you need to document when you are setting the LMI type on a Frame Relay interface.

When the router interface initializes, it begins a process of communication with the switch in which it initializes the link and attempts to map the remote IP address through Inverse ARP. The next few pages show how an interface initializes. Figure 8-10 shows the beginning of this process. The following list describes the numbered steps shown in the figure.

Figure 8-10 *Link Initialization*

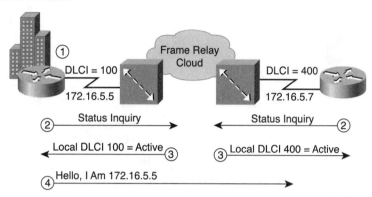

1   Each router, through a CSU/DSU, connects to the Frame Relay switch.

2   When Frame Relay is configured on an interface, the router sends a status inquiry message to the Frame Relay switch. The message notifies the switch of the router's status and asks the switch for the connection status of the router's VCs.

3   When the Frame Relay switch receives the request, it responds with a status message that includes the local DLCIs of the PVCs to the remote routers to which the local router can send data.

4   For each active DLCI, each router sends an Inverse ARP packet containing the IP address configured on its end of the VC.

Figure 8-11 continues the process by showing how an address is mapped to a DLCI through Inverse ARP. The following list describes the numbered steps illustrated in the figure (with the exception of Step 4, which is described in the preceding list).

Figure 8-11 *Inverse ARP*

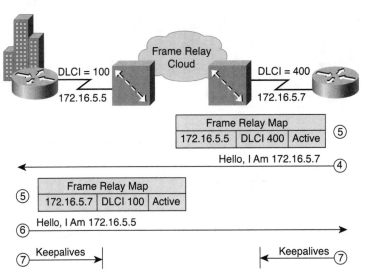

5   When a router receives an Inverse ARP message, it creates a map entry in its Frame Relay map table that includes the local DLCI and the remote router's network layer address. Note that the DLCI is the router's local DLCI, not the DLCI that the remote router is using. Three possible connection states appear in the Frame Relay map table: active, inactive, and deleted (as described previously).

If Inverse ARP is not working, or if the remote router does not support Inverse ARP, static maps (DLCIs and IP addresses) must be configured.

6   Every 60 seconds, routers send Inverse ARP messages on all active DLCIs.

7   Every 10 seconds, the router exchanges LMI information with the switch (keepalives).

The router changes the status of each DLCI (active, inactive, or deleted) based on the LMI response from the Frame Relay switch. For example, if one router on a Frame Relay PVC were turned off, the functioning router on the other side would see the VC as deleted. After the router on the far side goes through the initialization process, the link is advertised as active by the LMI function.

Frame Relay Inside the Service Provider Network

Over the years, there has been much confusion about how Frame Relay interacts within the cloud of the service provider network. Among the most confusing points is the DLCI's significance. Many people believe that the DLCI has significance throughout the provider network; however, this is not true. It is not possible when you consider that you have only 10 bits to define a DLCI number and well over 1024 VCs exist in a provider network.

Within the service provider network, an address maps a local switch.slot.port relationship to a corresponding relationship on the remote switch. The Frame Relay switch uses a table to map each slot.port relationship on a switch to the corresponding DLCIs. Each switch is configured with a DLCI to the customer's network.

Some service providers attempt to use a numbering plan that is somewhat logical for each user. One possible plan is one that inverts the DLCI number at one end to obtain the corresponding DLCI number for the remote end; for example, 112 becomes 211 and 114 becomes 411 on the other end. Each device is only aware of what DLCI they use to connect to the remote site. Again, the DLCI in Figure 8-12 shows the relationship of a service provider view of the DLCIs and the port mappings for each VC within the network and that of the user network.

Figure 8-12   *Service Providers View of the Frame Relay Network*

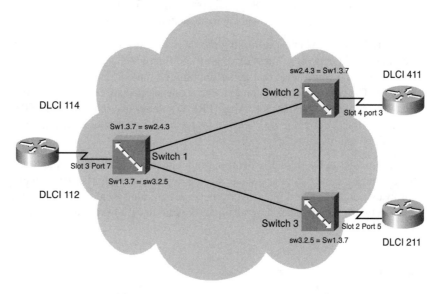

In Figure 8-12, the service provider sees the Frame Relay network DLCI associated with a switch.slot.port value making each DLCI unique within the provider network. The customer sees the local DLCI number only as the way to reach the remote site.

When a frame comes into a Frame Relay switch, the switch performs the following actions:

1   The switch checks the frame's inbound DLCI number.

2   The switch looks into the table to determine to which outbound DLCI the frame should be sent.

3   The switch forwards the frame to the appropriate switch.slot.port, including the two DLCI values.

NOTE	While this numbering scheme is common, it applies only to certain vendors' products and is used here to illustrate the relationship of the DLCI to the internal mappings in a Frame Relay network.

When the remote switch receives a frame, the frame contains values about which slot.port and DLCI it is going to, based on the mapping, so that the switch can send it out the appropriate VC.

Many different methods can be used to carry traffic between the Frame Relay switches. The capability of Asynchronous Transfer Mode (ATM) to operate at very high speeds and to carry a wide range of traffic types has given it an important role as a backbone switch within provider networks. ATM technology supports many of today's Frame Relay services as the preferred transport mechanism between the switches.

Frame Relay-to-ATM internetworking provides a means to seamlessly integrate Frame Relay and ATM networks. The ATM Forum and Frame Relay Forum have endorsed several implementation agreements that make combining Frame Relay and ATM networks possible. The two implementation agreements developed specifically for current Frame Relay users are Network Interworking (FRF.5) and Service Interworking (FRF.8). Both solutions protect current investments in Frame Relay while providing a migration path to ATM.

FRF.5 provides network internetworking functionality that allows Frame Relay end users to communicate over an intermediate ATM network that supports FRF.5. Multiprotocol encapsulation and other higher-layer procedures are transported transparently over the ATM network. Figure 8-13 shows a typical Frame-to-ATM service provider network.

Figure 8-13   *Frame-to-ATM Service Provider Network*

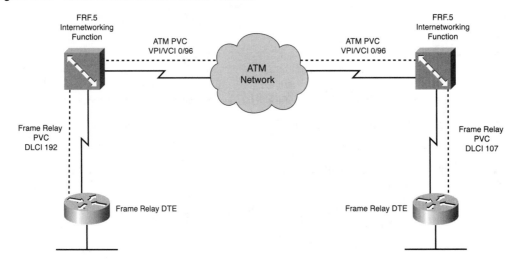

Section 1 Quiz

1 Frame Relay is standardized by what standards organizations? Choose all that apply.

    A ANSI

    B EIA/TIA

    C IETF

    D IEEE

    E ITU-T

    F Frame Relay Forum

2 Frame Relay encapsulates which of the following layers of the OSI model? Choose the best answers.

    A Layer 7

    B Layer 6

    C Layer 5

    D Layer 4

    E Layer 3

    F Layer 2

    G Layer 1

    H All of the above

3 Which of the following are NOT fields in the Frame Relay frame? Choose all that apply.

    A BECN

    B FECN

    C CIR

    D DLCI

    E PVC

    F DE

4 How many VCs would be required for a fully meshed Frame Relay network consisting of 12 routers?

A 12

B 6

C 24

D 66

E 120

5 If you connect a router to a Frame Relay network and the device on the other side of the PVC is powered down, what would you expect the state of the PVC to be?

A Active

B Down

C Unavailable

D Inactive

E Deleted

Configuring Frame Relay

To configure a router for operation in a Frame Relay environment, you must first enable the serial interface for Frame Relay encapsulation. Beyond that, you might or might not have to configure several items. In its simplest form, configuring Frame Relay is merely the process of specifying the encapsulation on a serial interface and connecting that interface to a CSU/DSU that connects to a provider network, but it might be necessary to configure many options. The next few pages detail how to configure a Cisco interface for operation in a Frame Relay environment using PVCs.

Example 8-1 and Example 8-2 are basic Frame Relay configurations for the routers shown in Figure 8-14.

Figure 8-14 *Basic Frame Relay Network for Configuration*

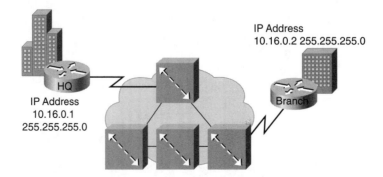

Example 8-1 *Basic Frame Relay Configuration*

```
HQ(config)#interface Serial1
HQ(config-if)#ip address 10.16.0.1 255.255.255.0
HQ(config-if)#encapsulation frame-relay
HQ(config-if)#bandwidth 256
```

Example 8-2 *Setting the LMI Type*

```
Branch(config)#interface Serial1
Branch(config-if)#ip address 10.16.0.2 255.255.255.0
Branch(config-if)#encapsulation frame-relay
Branch(config-if)#bandwidth 256
Branch(config-if)#frame-relay lmi-type ansi
```

A basic Frame Relay configuration assumes that you want to configure Frame Relay on one or more physical interfaces, and that LMI and Inverse ARP are supported by the remote routers. In this type of environment, the LMI notifies the router of the available DLCIs. Use the following steps to configure basic Frame Relay:

Step 1 Select the serial interface and move to interface configuration mode.

Step 2 Configure a network layer address, such as an IP address.

Step 3 Select the Frame Relay encapsulation type used to encapsulate data traffic end-to-end. The command to accomplish this is as follows:

```
router(config-if)#encapsulation frame-relay [cisco | ietf ]
```

The default encapsulation type is **cisco**. Use the **cisco** option if you're connecting through the cloud to another Cisco router. Use the **ietf** option if you're connecting to a router on the other side of the Frame Relay cloud that does not support the Cisco frame type.

If you're using Cisco IOS Software Release 11.1 or earlier, specify the LMI type used by the Frame Relay switch, using the following command:

```
router(config-if)#frame-relay lmi-type {ansi | cisco | q933a}
```

The default LMI type is **cisco**. With Cisco IOS Software Release 11.2 and later, the LMI type is autosensed by default, so no configuration is needed.

Step 4 Configure the bandwidth for the link using the following command:

```
router(config-if)#bandwidth kbps
```

The **bandwidth** command affects routing operation by protocols such as IGRP. Bandwidth is a critical metric for many routing features and should be determined carefully. Without a **bandwidth** statement, the default for E1/T1 serial lines and below is 1.544 kbps.

Step 5   If Inverse ARP was disabled on the router, re-enable it. Inverse ARP is on by default. To re-enable Inverse ARP, use the following command:

```
router(config-if)#frame-relay inverse-arp [protocol] [dlci]
```

Supported protocols indicated by the *protocol* option include **ip**, **ipx**, **appletalk**, **decnet**, **vines**, **dlsw**, **llc2**, **rsrb**, and **xns**.

The *dlci* option indicates the DLCI number on the local interface that you want to use to exchange Inverse ARP messages. Acceptable numbers are integers in the range 16 through 1007.

Configuring Static Mapping for a Router

When the router does not support Inverse ARP, or when you want to control broadcast and multicast traffic over the PVC, you must define the remote address-to-DLCI table entry statically. These static entries are referred to as *static maps*. Figure 8-15 illustrates a Frame Relay network candidate for static Frame Relay maps.

Figure 8-15   *Configuring a Static Frame Relay Map*

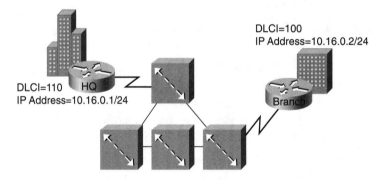

To configure a static mapping for the HQ router in Figure 8-15, you would enter the configuration shown in Example 8-3.

Example 8-3   *Configuring a Static Mapping for the HQ Router*

```
HQ(config)#interface Serial1
HQ(config-if)#ip address 10.16.0.1 255.255.255.0
HQ(config-if)#encapsulation frame-relay
HQ(config-if)#bandwidth 64
HQ(config-if)#frame-relay map ip 10.16.0.2 110 broadcast
```

The **frame-relay map** command can be used, when necessary, to statically map the far end's network layer address to the local DLCI number. The syntax for this command is as follows:

```
router(config-if)#frame-relay map protocol protocol-address dlci [broadcast]
   [ietf | cisco] [payload-compress packet-by-packet]
```

Where:

- *protocol* defines the supported protocol, bridging, or logical link control.

- *protocol-address* defines the destination router interface's network layer address.

- *dlci* defines the local DLCI used to connect to the remote protocol address.

- **broadcast** is an optional parameter that forwards broadcasts and multicasts over the VC. This permits the use of dynamic routing protocols over the VC.

- **ietf | cisco** enables IETF or Cisco encapsulations.

- **payload-compress packet-by-packet** is an optional parameter that enables packet-by-packet payload compression using the Stacker method. This is a Cisco proprietary compression method.

Configuring Frame Relay Subinterfaces

When you connect the physical interface to the CSU/DSU, the service provider can provision multiple PVCs to a single connection. To take advantage of the multiple connections and to prevent problems such as split horizon, configuring subinterfaces to act as logical interfaces connecting to the PVCs might be necessary.

A subinterface can be configured as a **point-to-point** interface or a **multipoint** interface. Each interface type is unique in how it provides connectivity to the PVCs. The characteristics and uses of the subinterface types are as follows:

- **Point-to-point**—Each point-to-point subinterface establishes a single PVC connection through the Frame cloud to another physical interface or subinterface on the remote router. In this case, each pair of point-to-point routers is on its own subnet, and each point-to-point subinterface is associated with a single DLCI. Point-to-point interfaces are typically used in a hub and spoke. In a point-to-point environment, because each subinterface is acting like a physical point-to-point interface, the routing update traffic is not subject to the split-horizon rule.

- **Multipoint**—A multipoint subinterface establishes multiple PVC connections through the Frame cloud to multiple physical interfaces or subinterfaces on remote routers. In the case of a multipoint subinterface, all the participating interfaces are in the same subnet. Multipoint interfaces are typically used in a partially meshed or fully meshed environment to conserve address space and to make routing convergence more efficient. In this environment, because the interface is acting like a regular NBMA Frame Relay interface, routing update traffic is subject to the split-horizon rule.

TIP   Although a subinterface is not required for an interface that has only one PVC, the often recommended practice is to set up the connection as a point-to-point subinterface. This configuration allows for the addition of future subinterfaces without having to reconfigure the physical interface, which will cause a loss of connectivity.

To configure subinterfaces on a physical interface, do the following:

Step 1   Select the interface on which you want to create subinterfaces, and enter interface configuration mode.

Step 2   It is recommended that you remove any network layer address assigned to the physical interface and assign the network layer address to the subinterface.

Step 3   Configure Frame Relay encapsulation on the physical interface, as discussed in Step 3 of the six-step procedure in the "Configuring Frame Relay" section.

Step 4   Select the subinterface you want to configure, using the following command:

```
router(config)#interface serial number.subinterface-number
  {multipoint | point-to-point}
```

Where:

— *number.subinterface-number* is the subinterface number. The interface number that precedes the period (.) must match the physical interface number to which this subinterface belongs. The *subinterface-number* after the period can be arbitrarily chosen from a range of 1 to 4,294,967,293.

— **multipoint** should be selected if you're routing IP and you want all routers in the same subnet.

— **point-to-point** should be selected if you want each pair of point-to-point routers to have its own subnet.

You are required to select either the **multipoint** or **point-to-point** parameter; there is no default.

Step 5   If you configured the subinterface as point-to-point, you must configure
the local DLCI for the subinterface to distinguish it from the physical
interface. This is also required for multipoint subinterfaces for which
Inverse ARP is enabled. This is not required for multipoint subinterfaces
configured with static DLCI maps. The command to configure the local
DLCI on the subinterface is as follows:

```
router(config-if)#frame-relay interface-dlci dlci-number
```

The *dlci-number* parameter defines the local DLCI number being linked
to the subinterface. This is the only way to link an LMI-derived PVC to
a subinterface because LMI does not know about subinterfaces defined
on the router.

NOTE   If you defined a subinterface for point-to-point communication, you cannot reassign the
same subinterface number to be used for multipoint communication without first rebooting
the router. Instead, you can leave the point-to-point subinterface intact but disabled and
create a new multipoint subinterface with a different subinterface number. Because you
arbitrarily choose the subinterface numbers, the actual number or the order of subinterfaces
is meaningless.

Point-to-Point Subinterface Configuration Example

Example 8-4 provides point-to-point subinterface configuration for the Frame Relay setup
illustrated in Figure 8-16.

Figure 8-16   *Point-to-Point Subinterface Configuration*

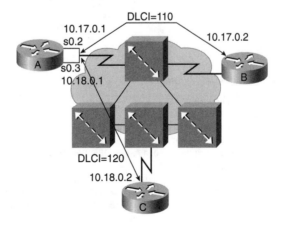

Example 8-4   *Point-to-Point Subinterface Configuration*

```
RouterA(config)#interface Serial0
RouterA(config-if)# no ip address
RouterA(config-if)# encapsulation frame-relay
RouterA(config-if)#interface Serial0.2 point-to-point
RouterA(config-subif)# ip address 10.17.0.1 255.255.255.0
RouterA(config-subif)#bandwidth 64
RouterA(config-subif)#frame-relay interface-dlci 110
RouterA(config-subif)#interface Serial0.3 point-to-point
RouterA(config-subif)# ip address 10.18.0.1 255.255.255.0
RouterA(config-subif)#bandwidth 64
RouterA(config-subif)# frame-relay interface-dlci 120
```

Example 8-4 shows you how to configure point-to-point subinterfaces. With this type of configuration, each subinterface is treated as a separate physical interface and is not subject to split horizon.

Multipoint Subinterface Configuration Example

Example 8-5 provides multipoint subinterface configuration for RTR1, shown in Figure 8-17.

Figure 8-17   *Multipoint Subinterface Configuration*

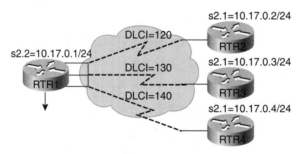

Example 8-5   *Multipoint Subinterface Configuration*

```
RTR1(config)#interface Serial2
RTR1(config-if)# no ip address
RTR1(config-if)# encapsulation frame-relay
RTR1(config-if)#interface Serial2.2 multipoint
RTR1(config-subif)#ip address 10.17.0.1 255.255.255.0
RTR1(config-subif)#bandwidth 64
RTR1(config-subif)#frame-relay map ip 10.17.0.2 120 broadcast
RTR1(config-subif)#frame-relay map ip 10.17.0.3 130 broadcast
RTR1(config-subif)#frame-relay map ip 10.17.0.4 140 broadcast
```

Example 8-5 shows you how to configure multipoint subinterfaces. With this type of config-uration, the subinterface takes on the same Frame Relay characteristics as a physical interface; that is, it is NBMA and is subject to split-horizon operation. The advantage over a point-to-point interface is that you need only a single network layer address.

While a multipoint subinterface is similar to a physical interface, there are a few differences. A physical interface has split horizon disabled by default, and a multipoint subinterface does not. With the subinterface configuration, you may have to disable split horizon to prevent routing problems. The other difference is flexibility. With a physical interface supporting multiple PVCs, you would have all the PVCs going to the same interface and subnet, but with a multipoint subinterface, you could create multiple interfaces supporting different PVCs and create more than one multipoint network.

Displaying Frame Relay Connection Status and Information

After you configure Frame Relay, you can verify that the connections are active using the available **show** commands. The **show interface** command displays information regarding the encapsulation and Layer 1 and Layer 2 status. It also displays information about the DLCIs used on the Frame Relay-configured serial interface and the LMI DLCI used for the local management interface. Example 8-6 shows some sample output from the **show interface** command.

Example 8-6   **show interface** *Displays Frame Relay Connection Status and Information*

```
Router#show interface s1
Serial0 is up, line protocol is up
  Hardware is HD64570
  Internet address is 10.16.0.1/24
  MTU 1500 bytes, BW 64 Kbit, DLY 20000 usec, rely 255/255, load 1/255
  Encapsulation FRAME-RELAY, loopback not set, keepalive set (10 sec)
  LMI enq sent   19, LMI stat recvd 20, LMI upd recvd 0, DTE LMI up
  LMI enq recvd 0, LMI stat sent  0, LMI upd sent  0
  LMI DLCI 1023  LMI type is CISCO  frame relay DTE
  FR SVC disabled, LAPF state down
  Broadcast queue 0/64, broadcasts sent/dropped 8/0, interface broadcasts 5
  Last input 00:00:02, output 00:00:02, output hang never
  Last clearing of "show interface" counters never
  Queuing strategy: fifo
  Output queue 0/40, 0 drops; input queue 0/75, 0 drops
  <Output omitted>
```

The highlighted line shows the LMI type for interface Serial 1.

Displaying LMI Traffic Statistics

The **show frame-relay lmi** command displays LMI traffic statistics. For example, as highlighted in Example 8-7, **show frame-relay lmi** shows the number of status messages exchanged between the local router and the Frame Relay switch. This is useful when determining if your router is receiving and sending LMI to the provider switch. If you are not sending or receiving LMI, it could indicate that the LMI type is misconfigured.

Example 8-7   show frame-relay lmi *Displays LMI Traffic Statistics*

```
Router#show frame-relay lmi

LMI Statistics for interface Serial0 (Frame Relay DTE) LMI TYPE = CISCO
 Invalid Unnumbered info 0 Invalid Prot Disc 0
 Invalid dummy Call Ref 0 Invalid Msg Type 0
 Invalid Status Message 0 Invalid Lock Shift 0
 Invalid Information ID 0 Invalid Report IE Len 0
 Invalid Report Request 0 Invalid Keep IE Len 0
 Num Status Enq. Sent 113100 Num Status msgs Rcvd 113100
 Num Update Status Rcvd 0 Num Status Timeouts 0
```

Displaying Frame Relay Connection and Traffic Statistics

The **show frame-relay pvc** command displays the status of each configured connection as well as traffic statistics. This command is also useful for viewing the number of BECN and FECN packets received by the router. The **PVC STATUS** can be **active**, **inactive**, or **deleted**. Example 8-8 shows some sample output from the **show frame-relay pvc** command.

Example 8-8   show frame-relay pvc *Displays Frame Relay Connection and Traffic Statistics*

```
Router#show frame-relay pvc 100

PVC Statistics for interface Serial0 (Frame Relay DTE)

DLCI = 100, DLCI USAGE = LOCAL, PVC STATUS = ACTIVE, INTERFACE = Serial0

    input pkts 28          output pkts 10         in bytes 8398
    out bytes 1198         dropped pkts 0         in FECN pkts 0
    in BECN pkts 0         out FECN pkts 0        out BECN pkts 0
    in DE pkts 0           out DE pkts 0
    out bcast pkts 10       out bcast bytes 1198
    pvc create time 00:03:46, last time pvc status changed 00:03:47
```

If you enter **show frame-relay pvc**, you will see the status of all the PVCs configured on the router. If you enter a specific PVC, you will see the status of only that PVC. In Example 8-8, **show frame-relay pvc 100** displays the status of PVC 100 only.

Displaying Frame Relay Connection Map Entry Information

To display the current map entries and information about the connections, use the **show frame-relay map** command. This command can be useful to see the static map entries configured, as well as what Inverse ARP entries the router has learned. Example 8-9 shows some sample output from the **show frame-relay map** command.

Example 8-9   **show frame-relay map** *Displays Frame Relay Connection Map Entry Information*

```
Router#show frame-relay map
Serial0 (up): ip 10.140.1.1 dlci 100(0x64,0x1840), dynamic,
              broadcast, status defined, active
```

The following list explains the Frame Relay DLCI numbering that appears in Example 8-9:

- 100 is the decimal DLCI number.

- 0x64 is the hex conversion of this number (0x64 = 100 decimal).

Clearing Dynamically Created Frame Relay Maps

To clear dynamically created Frame Relay maps, which are created using Inverse ARP, use the **clear frame-relay-inarp** privileged EXEC command. Example 8-10 shows some sample output from the **clear frame-relay-inarp** privileged EXEC command. The **show frame-relay map** command verifies that the mappings have been cleared. If inverse ARP has mapped a remote address that has changed, clearing the mapping to reach the remote device might be necessary.

Example 8-10   **clear frame-relay-inarp** *Clears Dynamically Created Frame Relay Maps*

```
Router#clear frame-relay-inarp
Router#show frame map
Router#
```

Verifying and Troubleshooting Frame Relay Connections

The **debug frame-relay lmi** command allows you to verify and troubleshoot the Frame Relay connection. Use this command to determine whether the router and the Frame Relay switch are sending and receiving LMI packets properly. Example 8-11 shows some sample output from the **debug frame-relay lmi** command.

Example 8-11   **debug frame-relay lmi** *Verifies and Troubleshoots Frame Relay Connections*

```
Router#debug frame-relay lmi
Frame Relay LMI debugging is on
Displaying all Frame Relay LMI data
Router#
1w2d: Serial0(out): StEnq, myseq 140, yourseen 139, DTE up
1w2d: datagramstart = 0xE008EC, datagramsize = 13
1w2d: FR encap = 0xFCF10309
1w2d: 00 75 01 01 01 03 02 8C 8B
1w2d:
1w2d: Serial0(in): Status, myseq 140
1w2d: RT IE 1, length 1, type 1
```

continues

Example 8-11 debug frame-relay lmi *Verifies and Troubleshoots Frame Relay Connections (Continued)*

```
1w2d: KA IE 3, length 2, yourseq 140, myseq 140
1w2d: Serial0(out): StEnq, myseq 141, yourseen 140, DTE up
1w2d: datagramstart = 0xE008EC, datagramsize = 13
1w2d: FR encap = 0xFCF10309
1w2d: 00 75 01 01 01 03 02 8D 8C
1w2d:
1w2d: Serial0(in): Status, myseq 142
1w2d: RT IE 1, length 1, type 0
1w2d: KA IE 3, length 2, yourseq 142, myseq 142
1w2d: PVC IE 0x7 , length 0x6 , dlci 100, status 0x2 , bw 0
```

(out) is an LMI status message sent by the router. **(in)** is a message received from the Frame Relay switch.

type 0 is a full LMI status message. **type 1** is an LMI exchange.

dlci 100, status 0x2 says that the status of DLCI 100 is active. Here are the Status field's possible values:

- **0x0**—Added/inactive. Means that the switch has this DLCI programmed, but for some reason (such as the other end of this PVC is down), it is not usable.

- **0x2**—Added/active. Means that the Frame Relay switch has the DLCI, and everything is operational. You can start sending it traffic with this DLCI in the header.

- **0x4**—Deleted. Means that the Frame Relay switch does not have this DLCI programmed for the router, but it was programmed at some point in the past. This could also be caused by the DLCIs being reversed on the router, or by the PVC being deleted by the service provider in the Frame Relay cloud.

Troubleshooting Frame Relay

Configuring Frame Relay involves many components and options, which also means that many components and functions can cause problems. Troubleshooting Frame Relay connections requires an understanding of the operation of the protocol and the steps involved in configuration.

Two main areas of problems exist when configuring Frame Relay:

- Compromised connectivity between the two routers connected by the Frame cloud

- The inability to access or ping across the Frame Relay network

Troubleshooting Connectivity Between the Two Routers Connected via the Frame Cloud

The output of the **show interfaces serial** command may show that the interface and line protocol are down, or that the serial is up and the line protocol is down. If both the line protocol and interface are in a down status, the most common problem is a cabling, hardware, or carrier problem; otherwise, there is most likely some issue with the communication between the devices concerning the configuration or status of the Frame Relay circuit. Use Table 8-1 as a guideline for troubleshooting connectivity issues.

Table 8-1   *Connectivity Troubleshooting Guidelines*

Symptom	Possible Problem	Solution
The interface and line protocol are both down.	A cabling, hardware, or carrier problem has occurred.	Check the cable to make sure that it is a DTE1 serial cable.
		If the cable is correct, try moving it to a different port. If that port works, the first port is defective. Replace either the card or the router.
		If the cable does not work on the second port, try replacing the cable. If it still doesn't work, a problem might exist with the DCE2. Contact your carrier about the problem.
The interface is up and the line protocol is down.	An LMI-type mismatch has occurred.	Use the **show frame-relay lmi** command to see which LMI type is configured on the Frame Relay interface.
		Make sure that the LMI type is the same for all devices in the path from source to destination. Use the **frame-relay lmi-type {ansi	cisco	q933a}** interface configuration command to change the LMI type on the router.
	Keepalives are not being sent.	Enter the **show interfaces** command to find out whether keepalives are configured. If you see a line that says "keepalives not set," keepalives are not configured.
		Use the **keepalive** *seconds* **interface** configuration command to configure keepalives. The default value for this command is 10 seconds. Keepalives must match on both ends of the link.

continues

Table 8-1   *Connectivity Troubleshooting Guidelines*

Symptom	Possible Problem	Solution
	Encapsulation mismatch has occurred.	When connecting Cisco devices with non-Cisco devices, you must use IETF4 encapsulation on both devices. Check the type on the Cisco device with the **show frame-relay map** command.
		If the Cisco device is not using IETF encapsulation, use the **encapsulation frame-relay ietf** command to configure IETF encapsulation on the Cisco Frame Relay interface.
	The DLCI is inactive or has been deleted.	Use the **show frame-relay pvc** command to view the status of the interface's PVC.
		If the output shows that the PVC6 is inactive or deleted, a problem exists along the path to the remote router. Check the remote router or contact your carrier to check the status of the PVC.
	The DLCI is assigned to the wrong subinterface.	Use the **show frame-relay pvc** command to check the assigned DLCIs. Make sure that the correct DLCIs are assigned to the correct subinterface. If the DLCI is incorrect, use the **no frame-relay map interface-dlci** command to delete the incorrect DLCI number entry under the interface.
		Use the **frame-relay map interface-dlci** command to define the mapping between an address and the correct DLCI used to connect to the address.

Troubleshooting Reachability Problems

The other problem area with Frame Relay is the inability to access or ping across the Frame Relay network. Use Table 8-2 as a guideline for troubleshooting reachability problems.

Table 8-2   *Reachability Troubleshooting Guidelines*

Symptom	Possible Problem	Solution
Cannot ping the device on the remote side of the Frame Relay cloud.	Encapsulation mismatch has occurred.	When connecting Cisco devices with non-Cisco devices, you must use IETF encapsulation on both devices. Check the encapsulation type on the Cisco device with the **show frame-relay map** command. If the Cisco device is not using IETF encapsulation, use the **encapsulation frame-relay ietf** command to configure IETF encapsulation on the Cisco Frame Relay interface.
	DLCI is inactive or has been deleted.	Use the **show frame-relay pvc** command to view the status of the interface's PVC. If the output shows that the PVC is inactive or deleted, a problem exists along the path to the remote router. Check the remote router, or contact your carrier to check the status of the PVC.
	DLCI is assigned to the wrong subinterface.	Use the **show frame-relay pvc** command to check the assigned DLCIs. Make sure that the correct DLCIs are assigned to the correct subinterfaces. If the DLCIs appear to be correct, shut down the main interface using the **shutdown** command, and then bring the interface back up using the **no shutdown** command.
	The **frame-relay map** command is missing.	Use the **show frame-relay map** command to see whether an address map is configured for the DLCI. If you do not see an address map for the DLCI, enter the **clear frame-relay-inarp** privileged EXEC command, and then use the **show frame-relay map** command again to see whether a map to the DLCI now exists. If there is no map to the DLCI, add a static address map. Use the **frame-relay map** command.

Section 2 Quiz

1 Assuming you are connecting two Cisco routers running IOS version 12.2 to a major provider network, what commands are you required to enter to establish IP connectivity? Choose all that apply.

A encapsulation frame-relay

B frame-relay lmi-type {ansi I cisco I q933a}

C bandwidth *value*

D ip address *address netmask*

E frame-relay map *protocol protocol-address dlci* [**broadcast**] [**ietf** I **cisco**] [**payload-compress packet-by-packet**]

F frame-relay inverse-arp [*protocol*] [*dlci*]

G no shutdown

2 If you are connecting across a Frame Relay network to a non-Cisco device, which of the following options must be configured?

A LMI type of ANSI

B LMI type of q933a

C Encapsulation of IETF

D Inverse ARP for IP

E Packet-by-packet payload compression

3 Say you have entered the following line on a Frame Relay interface on a Cisco router:

```
frame-relay map ip 10.18.0.1 120
```

Which of the following statements are true? Choose all that apply.

A The far side device's IP address is 10.18.0.1.

B The far side DLCI is 120.

C The local DLCI is 120.

D OSPF updates will be sent across this link.

E Static routes may be required to reach the far-side networks.

4 When configuring a point-to-point Frame Relay interface for IP, which of the following commands is required on the subinterface? Choose all that apply.

A encapsulation frame-relay

B ip address *address mask*

   C   **bandwidth 64**

   D   **frame-relay interface-dlci** *dlci-number*

   E   **frame-relay map** *protocol protocol-address dlci* [**broadcast**] [**ietf** | **cisco**] [**payload-compress packet-by-packet**]

5 Which command can you use to determine the LMI type of an interface running Frame Relay? Choose all that apply.

   A   **show interface**

   B   **show frame-relay pvc**

   C   **show frame-relay map**

   D   **show frame-relay lmi**

   E   **debug frame-relay lmi**

Frame Relay Command Summary

Table 8-3 summarizes the commands you learned in this chapter.

Table 8-3   *Frame Relay Command Summary*

Command	Description
encapsulation frame-relay [**cisco**	**ietf**]	Sets the interface to use Frame Relay encapsulation.
frame-relay lmi-type {**ansi**	**cisco**	**q933a**}	Sets the LMI type to be used. (Don't use this command for LMI type autosensing.)
frame-relay inverse-arp [*protocol*] [*dlci*]	Used to re-enable Inverse ARP for a protocol.
frame-relay map *protocol protocol-address dlci* [**broadcast**] [**ietf**	**cisco**] [**payload-compress packet-by-packet**]	Defines a static mapping from DLCI to protocol address.
show frame-relay lmi	Displays LMI information.
show frame-relay pvc	Displays PVC traffic statistics.
show frame-relay map	Displays Frame Relay DLCI-to-IP address mappings.
debug frame-relay lmi	Displays LMI debug information.
interface serial *number.subinterface-number* {**multipoint**	**point-to-point**}	Creates a serial subinterface.

Case Study

Using what you have learned in this chapter, it is time to return to the case study company and help the network administrator, Ann E. Won. Ann must now upgrade the connections from the corporate facility to remote location B to a Frame Relay circuit and add a new connection to remote location C. Previously, remote facility B connected back to the corporate location using Serial 3/1 and 3/2 on the company's 3640 with two 56-kbps circuits. Serial 3/1 will now be used to connect to the Frame Relay network, and Serial 3/2 will be disabled. At the corporate facility, Ann needs to provision a circuit capable of sending traffic to four sites at a maximum rate of 256 kbps each. Also, the two remote sites need to be able to send traffic back to the host site with a maximum rate of 256 kbps, but they expect only about 128 kbps on average. No site will need to communicate directly with any other site, so a Star topology is acceptable. Figure 8-18 shows a diagram of the proposed solution.

Figure 8-18 *Frame Relay Case Study Network Diagram*

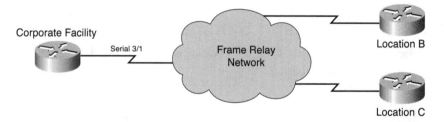

Remote location B needs to upgrade its local loop connection back to the service provider to support a fractional T1 connection of 256 kbps. The router at location B is running IOS Release 11.0. Remote location C is a recent acquisition and the remote router is not a Cisco device. Ann must plan for connectivity to remote location A in the future. The existing networking staff will set up the remote router at location C. Ann should work with them to establish connectivity.

Based on the preceding information, answer the following questions about what Ann should do:

1 Does Ann need to be concerned about the cables and CSU/DSU connecting to the service provider network?

2 What speed circuit does Ann need at the corporate and remote sites?

3 What type of interfaces will Ann want to configure on the routers at the corporate site and remote location B?

4 Do you see any potential problems with the remote connections. If so, what should be done to eliminate these issues?

5 What information does Ann need from the service provider?

Summary

This chapter discussed the Frame Relay technology and how you implement it on a serial interface on your Cisco router. You learned about the technology and terms associated with Frame Relay and the different topologies that can connect your Frame Relay network devices. In addition, you learned how to set Frame Relay encapsulation and LMI types. Also, you now know how IP addresses can be mapped to DLCI numbers automatically with Inverse ARP and how to manually map these components on subinterfaces. Finally, you saw how to show vital configuration information to aid in configuration and trouble-shooting of Frame Relay circuits.

Review Questions

1 Frame Relay operates at which OSI layer?

2 Name at least one physical layer standard that can be used for Frame Relay connection.

3 Which component identifies the local logical connection between the router and the switch?

4 Which method used by Frame Relay allows for the dynamic mapping of IP address to DLCI number?

5 Name the three LMI standards that Cisco routers support.

6 By default, how often do routers exchange LMI information with the switch?

7 What is the default encapsulation type for Frame Relay on a Cisco router?

8 Which command is used to verify the LMI type?

9 What routing issue occurs with a Frame Relay network running multiple PVCs over a single interface?

10 What is the default subinterface type, point-to-point or multipoint?

After completing this chapter, you will be able to perform the following tasks:

- Identify the physical components and determine how the connection operates, given a requirement to enable an ISDN BRI and/or an ISDN PRI connection.

- Configure ISDN BRI and ISDN PRI, given a function router and physical ISDN connection.

- Configure standard DDR on a BRI interface and complete the call, given a physical ISDN BRI connection.

- Verify proper operation with **show** and **debug** commands, given a dial-on-demand ISDN connection.

CHAPTER 9

Completing an ISDN BRI Call

This chapter describes the Integrated Services Digital Network (ISDN) Basic Rate Interface (BRI), ISDN Primary Rate Interface (PRI), and standard dial-on-demand routing (DDR). This chapter provides a high-level overview of ISDN and shows you how to enable ISDN services using Cisco's DDR capabilities. This chapter also explains how to troubleshoot DDR and ISDN services on a Cisco router.

You read in Chapter 7, "Establishing Serial Point-to-Point Connections," that ISDN is a circuit-switched solution that allows for data transfer between data devices. ISDN is very valuable in today's networking strategy because it allows administrators to provide reliable high-speed links to remote offices without the high cost of dedicated circuits.

In most areas, a customer is charged for the amount of time an ISDN call takes; therefore, ISDN is ideal for the telecommuter or the remote office that needs only sporadic access to the central site using bandwidth-on-demand, or as a backup if a dedicated circuit fails. To use these services with your Cisco router, you must first understand the ISDN technology and then learn how to configure it on your router. The next few pages provide an overview of ISDN BRI technology.

ISDN BRI Overview

ISDN refers to a collection of standards that define a digital architecture that provides an integrated voice/data capability to the customer premises facility, utilizing the Public Switched Telephone Network (PSTN). The ISDN standards define the hardware and call setup schemes for end-to-end digital connectivity. Prior to ISDN, many telephone companies used digital networks within their clouds but used analog lines for the local access loop between the cloud and the actual customer site. Bringing digital connectivity through ISDN to the local site has many benefits:

- The capability to carry a variety of user-traffic feeds. ISDN provides access to all digital facilities for video, voice, packet-switched data, and enriched telephone network services.

- Much faster call setup using out-of-band (Delta [D] channel) signaling than modem connections. For example, ISDN calls can often be set up and completed in less than one second.

- Much faster data transfer rate using Bearer (B) channel services at 64 kbps per channel, compared to common modem alternatives of 28.8 to 56 kbps. With multiple B channels, ISDN offers users more bandwidth on WANs (for example, two B channels equal 128 kbps) than they receive with a leased line at 56 kbps in North America, or 64 kbps in much of the rest of the world.

- Service providers also use ISDN PRI to aggregate residential modem lines rather than build racks and racks of modems.

Figure 9-1 illustrates the different uses for ISDN technology.

Figure 9-1   *What Is ISDN?*

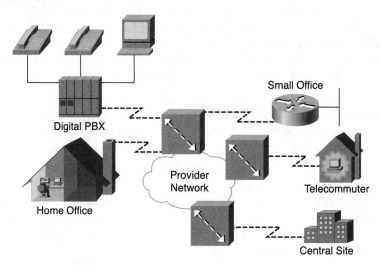

ISDN is a popular transport choice for applications using remote connectivity, for access to the Internet, and for the World Wide Web. Even with the addition of DSL and cable modems for telecommuters and home users, ISDN still continues to grow and provides services in places where DSL and cable services still do not reach.

Work on standards for ISDN began in the late 1960s. A comprehensive set of ISDN recommendations was published in 1984 and is continuously updated by the Consultative Committee for International Telegraph and Telephone (CCITT)—an organization that has since become the International Telecommunication Union Telecommunication Standardization Sector (ITU-T). ITU-T groups and organizes ISDN protocols according to the general topic areas, as outlined in Table 9-1.

Table 9-1   *ISDN Protocols Grouped by Topic Area*

Issue	Protocol	Key Examples
Telephone network and ISDN	E-Series	E.163-International telephone numbering plan E.164-International ISDN addressing
ISDN concepts, aspects, and interfaces	I-Series	I.100 series-Concepts, structures, and terminology I.400-User-Network Interfaces (UNIs)
Switching and signaling	Q-Series	Q.921-LAPD (Link Access Procedures on the D-channel encapsulation) Q.931-ISDN network layer between terminal and switch

The following list elaborates on the ISDN protocol series documented in Table 9-1:

- Protocols that begin with **E** recommend telephone network standards for ISDN. For example, the E.164 protocol describes international addressing for ISDN.

NOTE   E.164 also describes standard voice and cellular voice line numbering.

- Protocols that begin with **I** deal with concepts, terminology, and general methods. The I.100 series includes general ISDN concepts and the structure of other I-series recommendations. I.200 deals with service aspects of ISDN. I.300 describes network aspects. I.400 describes how the User-Network Interface (UNI) is provided.
- Protocols that begin with **Q** cover how switching and signaling should operate. The term *signaling* in this context means the process of call setup used. Q.921 describes the ISDN data-link processes of LAPD, which function like Layer 2 processes in the ISO/OSI reference model. Q.931 specifies ISO/OSI reference model Layer 3 functions.

  Q.931 recommends a network layer between the terminal endpoint and the local ISDN switch. The various ISDN providers and switch types use various implementations of Q.931. Other switches were developed before the standards groups finalized this standard.

Because switch types are not standardized, when configuring the router, you need to specify the type of ISDN switch to which you are connecting. In addition, Cisco routers have **debug** commands to monitor Q.931 and Q.921 processes when an ISDN call is initiated or terminated.

ISDN Components

ISDN services are composed of many components, which are important to learn to configure and troubleshoot ISDN services. The items described in this section define the end-to-end physical and data link layer organization of ISDN.

ISDN specifies two standard access methods, as illustrated in Figure 9-2 and documented in the following list.

Figure 9-2   *ISDN Access Methods*

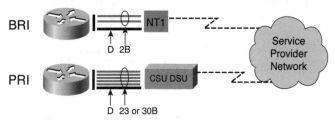

Basic Rate Interface (BRI)—Consists of two 64-kbps Bearer (B) channels plus one 16-kbps D channel service. A standard BRI is available on many Cisco routers. Any router with a serial interface can be connected to a BRI with an external terminal adapter (discussed later in this chapter):

- — BRI is sometimes written as 2B + D. A BRI provides two B channels at 64 kbps and an additional 16-kbps D signaling channel.

- — You can use the B channels for digitized speech transmission or for relatively high-speed data transport. Narrowband ISDN is circuit-switching–oriented. The B channel is the elemental circuit-switching unit.

- — The D channel carries signaling information (for example, call setup) to control calls on B channels at the User-Network Interface (UNI). In addition to carrying signaling information, the D channel can carry subscriber low-rate packet data, such as alarm information or credit card numbers. This service is known as 0B+D service. Although this is a supported feature of many ISDN vendors, implementation and results vary. Traffic over the D channel employs the LAPD data link layer protocol. LAPD is based on High-Level Data Link Control (HDLC).

- **Primary Rate Interface (PRI)**—In the United States, Canada, and Japan, PRI offers twenty-three 64-kbps B channels and one 64-kbps D channel (a T1/DS1 facility):

  - — In Europe and much of the rest of the world, PRI offers 30 B channels and a single D channel (an E1 facility).

  - — PRI uses a data service unit/channel service unit (DSU/CSU) for a T1/E1 connection.

BRI Call Processing

Figure 9-3 shows the sequence of events that occurs during the establishment of a BRI call.

Figure 9-3   *RI Call Processing*

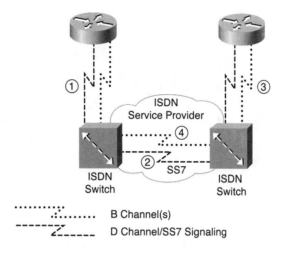

The following list describes the event sequence in greater detail:

11   The D channel between the router and the ISDN switch is always up. When the call is initiated, the called number is sent to the local ISDN switch. The D channel is used for call setup, signaling, and call termination (the call control functions).

12   The local switch uses the SS7 (Signaling System 7—used by telco switches to set up calls) signaling protocols to set up a path and pass the called number to the terminating ISDN switch.

13   The far-end ISDN switch signals the destination over the D channel.

14   The B channel is then connected end-to-end. A B channel carries the conversation or data. Both B channels can be used simultaneously.

NOTE   For data transmission, the connected devices must still negotiate a common data link protocol such as PPP, X.25, or Frame Relay.

ISDN is the protocol that is used between the endpoints and the local service provider ISDN switch. Within the service provider network, the ISDN call is treated as a 56- or 64-kbps stream of data and is handled the same as any other stream of data or voice.

ISDN CPE Equipment and Reference Points

Like many WAN protocols, ISDN has many special terms that deal with connectivity to the network services. Figure 9-4 and Table 9-2 detail the types of ISDN equipment and network reference points you might encounter.

Figure 9-4 *ISDN Equipment Types and Reference Points*

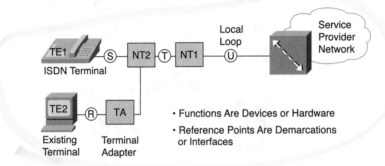

To access the ISDN network, you must use customer premises equipment (CPE) that performs specific functions to properly connect to the ISDN switch. The ISDN standards define device- and hardware-specific functions. These functions represent transitions between the reference points. Hardware can be created to support one or more of these functions. To select the correct CPE, you must be aware of what functions are available and how the functions relate to each other. Table 9-2 defines the customer premises ISDN device types and their functions.

Table 9-2 *ISDN Device Types/Functionality*

Device Type	Device Function
TE1 (Terminal Endpoint 1)	Designates a router or ISDN telephone as a device having a native ISDN interface
NT-2 (Network Termination 2)	The point at which all ISDN lines at a customer site are aggregated and switched using a customer-switching device (seen with an ISDN private branch exchange [PBX])
NT-1 (Network Termination 1)	Converts four-wire BRI signals from an S/T interface into two-wire signals of a U interface used by the ISDN digital line
TE2 (Terminal Endpoint 2)	Designates a device such as an older router or a PC requiring a TA for its BRI signals
TA (Terminal Adapter)	Converts EIA/TIA-232, V.35, and other signals into BRI signals

In Europe, the NT1 is CPE that is owned by the Post, Telephone, and Telegraph (PTT). You must buy a device that supports the appropriate connectivity.

To connect devices that perform specific functions, as defined in Table 9-2, the devices must support specific reference points. Because CPE can include one or more functions, the reference points they use to connect to other devices that support other functions can vary. As a result, the standards do not define interfaces in terms of hardware but refer to them as *reference points*. A reference point defines a connection type between two functions. In other words, reference points are a series of specifications that define the connection between specific devices, depending on their function in the end-to-end connection.

Knowing about these interface types is important because a CPE device, such as a router, can support different reference points, which could result in the need for additional equipment. Figure 9-4 shows the location of each reference point. The reference points that affect the customer side of the ISDN connection are as follows:

- **R**—References the point (connection) that is between a non-ISDN–compatible device and a terminal adapter.

- **S**—References the points that connect into the NT2, or customer-switching device. It is the interface that enables calls between the various CPE.

- **T**—Electrically identical to the S interface, it references the outbound connection from the NT2 to the ISDN network.

    The electrical similarities between the S and T references are why some interfaces are labeled S/T interface. Although they perform different functions, the port is electrically the same and can be used for either function.

- **U**—References the connection between the NT1 and the ISDN network owned by the telephone company.

Not all Cisco routers include a native ISDN terminal, and they do not all include interfaces for the same reference point, so you must evaluate each router carefully. Figure 9-5 shows the different types of ISDN equipment and their associated reference points.

The type of connection you need to access the ISDN network depends on what reference point it provides. In the United States and Canada, the service provider provides a U reference point, which means the user is required to provide NT-1 connectivity. In Europe and various other countries, the service provider owns and provides an S/T interface to the customer; the customer does NOT need the NT-1 functionality. When ordering your equipment, be sure to order the interfaces and modules accordingly.

Figure 9-5 *ISDN BRI Interfaces*

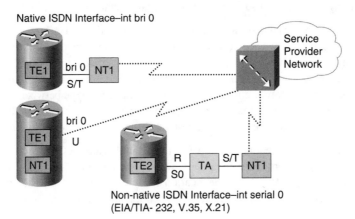

To select a Cisco router, do the following:

Step 1 Determine whether the router supports ISDN BRI. Look on the back of your router for one of the following:

— If you see a connector labeled "BRI," you have an ISDN interface. With a native ISDN interface built in, your router is a TE1. Your router contains the ISDN TA function. (Your router might also have a built-in NT1; if the interface is labeled with a U under the RJ-45 connector, the router has a built-in NT1.)

— If you do not see a connector labeled "BRI," your router can use a serial interface. With non-native interfaces such as serial interfaces, you need to obtain an external TA device and attach it to the serial interface to provide an ISDN connection. If you have a modular router, upgrading to a native ISDN interface might be possible if you have an available slot.

Step 2 Determine whether you or the service provider provides the NT1. An NT1 terminates the local loop of wires to the central office (CO) of your ISDN service provider. In the United States, for example, the customer is responsible for the NT1. In Europe, the service provider typically provides the NT1.

If you must supply the NT1, make sure your router has a U interface, or you must purchase an external NT1.

CAUTION	Never connect a router with a U interface into an NT1. Doing so will most likely damage the interface.

As mentioned previously, ISDN supports both BRI and PRI connectivity. PRI technology is somewhat simpler than BRI, which is considered multipoint, meaning it has the capability to have multiple ISDN devices connected to the same B Channel. As a result, in multipoint networks there is arbitration at Layer 1 and Layer 2, allowing multiple devices to access the network without collisions or interruptions between devices that need to share the ISDN network.

For a PRI interface, the wiring is not multipoint and does not require arbitration or multiple reference points. Instead, there is only a straight connection between the CSU/DSU and the PRI, or just a straight connection to the service provider if the device has an integrated CSU/DSU. Figure 9-6 shows the PRI connection.

Figure 9-6   *ISDN PRI Interface*

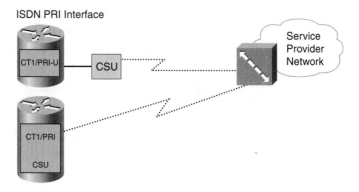

ISDN Switch Types and SPIDs

ISDN service providers use a variety of switch types for their ISDN services. Services offered by the national PTT or other carriers vary considerably from nation to nation or region to region. Just like modem standards, each switch type operates slightly differently and has a specific set of call setup requirements. Before you can connect your router to an ISDN service, you must be aware of the switch types used at the CO. You must specify this information during router configuration so that the router can place ISDN network-level calls and send data.

Table 9-3 is a sample of countries and ISDN switch types you are likely to encounter in your provider's ISDN cloud.

Table 9-3   *ISDN Switch Types by Locale*

Country	Switch Type
United States and Canada	AT&T 5ESS and 4ESS; Northern Telecom DMS-100
France	VN2, VN3
Japan	NTT
United Kingdom	Net3 and Net5
Europe	Net3

Some service providers program their switches to emulate another switch type. Therefore, you might need to configure a router to match the emulated switch type for proper operation.

In addition to learning about which switch type your service provider is using, you might also need to know what service profile identifiers (SPIDs) are assigned to your connection. In many cases, such as when configuring the router to connect to a DMS-100 switch, you need to input the SPIDs.

SPIDs are a series of characters (which can look like phone numbers) that identify your ISDN device to the switch at the central office. When identified, the switch links the services you ordered to the connection. Remember, ISDN is typically used for dialup connectivity. The SPIDs are processed during each call setup operation.

Enabling ISDN BRI

To enable ISDN BRI, you must perform two tasks:

1 Configure ISDN-specific commands

2 Configure an encapsulation to use over ISDN

The rest of this section concentrates on Task 1 for enabling ISDN BRI, configuring ISDN-specific commands only. The section "Step 3: Configuring the Dialer Information" covers Task 2, configuring an encapsulation to use over ISDN.

Before using ISDN BRI, you must define the **isdn switch-type** global or interface command to specify the ISDN switch to which the router connects. The global and interface versions of the **isdn switch-type** command, respectively, are as follows:

```
Router(config)#isdn switch-type switch-type
Router(config-if)#isdn switch-type switch-type
```

Commonly, when connecting a site to a provider, any ISDN connections from the router use the same switch type, and the global command covers all ISDN interfaces. If, however, the router has two ISDN interfaces that connect to different switch types, it is necessary to set the switch type on an interface-by-interface configuration.

For ISDN BRI service, Table 9-4 documents sample *switch-type* values.

Table 9-4   *Switch Types for ISDN BRI Service*

switch-type Value	Description
basic-5ess	AT&T basic-rate switches (USA)
basic-dms100	NT (Nortel or Northern Telecom) DMS-100 (North America)
basic-ni1	National ISDN-1 (North America)
basic-ts013	Australian TS013 switches
basic-net3	Switch type for Net3 in the United Kingdom and Europe
ntt	NTT ISDN switch (Japan)
none	No specific switch specified

When your ISDN service is installed, the service provider gives you information about your connection. Depending on the switch type your provider uses, you might be given two numbers, called SPIDS, to use, in which case, you need to add them to your configuration. For example, the National ISDN-1 and DMS-100 ISDN switches require SPIDs to be configured, but the AT&T 5ESS switch does not.

The SPID format can vary, depending on the ISDN switch type and specific provider requirements.

Use the **isdn spid1** and **isdn spid2** commands to specify the SPID required to access the ISDN network when your router makes its call to the local ISDN exchange. The syntax for these commands is as follows:

```
Router(config-if)#isdn spid1 spid-number [ldn]
Router(config-if)#isdn spid2 spid-number [ldn]
```

Where:

- *spid-number* identifies the service to which you subscribed. The ISDN service provider assigns this value.

- *ldn* (optional) is the local dial number. This number must match the called-party information coming from the ISDN switch to use both B channels on most switches.

NOTE   SPID numbers and switch type information are available from your service provider and should be given to you after the service is set up.

Enabling ISDN PRI

The ISDN PRI is a T1 connection to the service provider. You can have two possible connection types on the router:

- A CT1/PRI-U interface that requires a connection to an external CSU/DSU
- A CT1/PRI CSU that has an integrated CSU/DSU

When connecting a PRI interface to the provider network, you need to set up the control for communications to the provider network, specify which channels will be used, and configure the D channel switch type. To enable ISDN PRI, you must perform these tasks:

1 Configure the controller clock source, framing, and line code characteristics.

2 Configure specifically the range of channels or time slots of the T1 or E1 to be used by the PRI.

3 Specify the ISDN switch type for the D channel.

Before using ISDN PRI, you must define how the T1 or E1 PRI controller (CT1) will communicate with the provider network. The first step is to access the controller by entering the **controller** command at the global configuration mode. A controller is either T1 or E1 depending on the type installed, and it is analogous to an interface. The following command shows how to access the controller configuration mode:

```
Router(config)#controller {t1 | e1} slot/port
```

After you access the controller, you must configure the frame type that the provider will use to communicate on this line. The provider should give you the frame type, which can be one of the following for a T1 controller: super frame (SF) or extended super frame (ESF); or one of these for an E1 controller: cyclic redundancy check 4 (CRC4) or no cyclic redundancy check (no-CRC4). In addition, you can add the **australia** option to specify the E1 frame type used in Australia. The following command shows how to configure the framing for the controller:

```
Router(config-controller)framing {sf | esf | crc4 | no-crc4} [australia]
```

The next controller setting that you might need to configure is the clock source for the T1 or E1 signaling. By default, the clock source is the line (or the provider line). This is generally what you want to have configured; however, it could be changed to use internal clocking or it could be loop-timed. The following command shows how to configure the clock source for the controller:

```
Router(config-controller)clocking {line | internal | loop-timed}
```

You also have to set the line code signaling for the T1 or E1 link. For T1, the valid settings are alternate mark inversion (AMI), or binary 8-zero substitution (B8ZS), and the valid settings for an E1 are AMI and high density bipolar 3 (HDB3). For T1, the default is AMI, and the default is HDB3 for E1. In North America, ESF is the most common T1 framing and B8ZS is the common provider signaling. The following command shows how to set the linecode for the controller:

```
Router(config-controller)linecode {ami | b8zs | hdb3}
```

Finally, on the controller, you need to establish that the controller is functioning as a PRI. To do so, create a PRI-group and add the appropriate range of timeslots for the PRI interface. For a T1, the timeslots are 1-24, and for an E1, the timeslots are 1-31. The following command shows how to create the range of timeslots for the PRI group:

```
Router(config-controller)pri-group timeslots {1-24 | 1-31}
```

After you have created the timeslots, the router automatically creates the D channel interface. For a T1 controller, the D channel is the **serial** slot/port:**23** interface, and for the E1 controller, the D channel is the **serial** slot/port:**15**.

You then need to configure the **isdn switch-type** global command on the D channel interface to specify the ISDN switch to which the router connects. The global and interface versions of the **isdn switch-type** command, respectively, are as follows:

```
Router(config)#isdn switch-type switch-type
Router(config-if)isdn switch-type switch-type
```

Commonly, when connecting a site to a provider, any ISDN connections from the router will use the same switch type, and the global command covers all ISDN interfaces. If, however, the router has two ISDN interfaces that connect to different switch types, you need to set the switch type on an interface-by-interface configuration.

For ISDN PRI service, Table 9-5 documents sample *switch-type* values.

Table 9-5   *Switch Types for ISDN PRI Service*

switch-type Value	Description
primary-5ess	AT&T switches (USA)
primary-dms100	NT (Nortel or Northern Telecom) DMS-100 (North America)
primary-ni1	National ISDN-1 (North America)
primary-net5	Switch type for Net3 in the United Kingdom, Europe, and Australia
Primary-ntt	NTT ISDN switch (Japan)

Section 1 Quiz

1   ISDN services provide which of the following? (Choose all that apply.)

   A   Digital network connectivity for voice, video, and data traffic

   B   Only a single channel for user traffic

   C   A single channel for call setup and tear down

   D   Voice-only services

   E   Dial service for connections

   F   Faster call setup and tear down than an asynchronous modem connection

2 An ISDN BRI uses which reference point to connect to a service provider network where the NT1 has already been provided?

    A U

    B NT-2

    C TE-1

    D S/T

    E R

    F TA

3 An ISDN with a BRI 0 interface is what type of ISDN equipment?

    A T1

    B TE2

    C TA

    D NT1

    E TE1

4 Which ISDN PRI switch types are common in the United Kingdom? (Choose all that apply.)

    A 5ESS

    B VN2

    C Net3

    D NTT

    E Net5

    F DMS-100

5 Select the required configuration steps to set up a PRI interface on a router.

    A Configure the T1 or E1 framing.

    B Specify the encapsulation on the controller.

    C Set an IP address on the controller.

    D Specify the linecode on the controller.

    E Set the ISDN switching type on the router or interface.

    F Specify the timeslots used by the PRI group.

    G Disable CDP on the interface.

Dial-on-Demand Routing Overview

You can use ISDN services for a variety of networking services. A useful application for ISDN is dial-on-demand routing (DDR). Now that you learned how to configure an ISDN interface, you find out how to configure DDR to bring this interface up when you need to transfer traffic.

DDR refers to a collection of Cisco features that allows two or more Cisco routers to establish a dynamic connection over simple dialup facilities to route packets and exchange routing updates on an as-needed basis. DDR is used for low-volume, periodic network connections over the plain old telephone service (POTS) or an ISDN network. Figure 9-7 illustrates a typical DDR setup.

Figure 9-7   *Dial-on-Demand Routing*

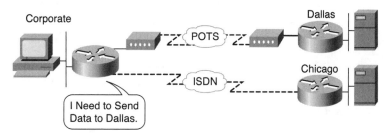

Traditionally, networks have been interconnected by dedicated WAN lines. DDR addresses the need for periodic network connections over a circuit-switched WAN service. By using WAN connections only on an as-needed basis, DDR can reduce WAN usage costs.

NOTE   More advanced features of DDR are beyond the scope of this book. You can find information on these options at Cisco.com. These advanced features include the following:

- **Dialer profiles**—The capability to configure DDR such that the physical interface configurations are separate from the logical configurations required for making a DDR call.

- **Dial backup**—The capability to enable a secondary link when the primary link fails.

- **Multilink PPP**—The capability to aggregate traffic over multiple ISDN channels simultaneously.

DDR is the process of having the router connect to a public telephone network (or ISDN network) when there is traffic to send and disconnect when the data transfer is complete.

Not all WAN connectivity will be DDR connections. For example, you might also have DDR connections in the following situations:

- Telecommuters need to connect to the company network periodically during the day.
- As a customer, you want to order products through the automated order system that your vendor has in place.
- You have satellite offices that need to send sales transactions or order entry requests to the main computer at the central office.
- Your customers prefer that you send them reports (for example) by e-mail.

Figure 9-8 illustrates the first two uses for DDR connections cited in the preceding list.

Figure 9-8 *DDR Connections Used for Periodic Connections and Small Amounts of Data from a Vendor*

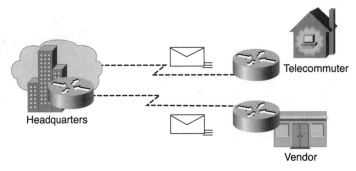

DDR is a straightforward process in which traffic that is defined as "interesting" causes the router to bring up a link to a remote site, as shown in Figure 9-9.

Figure 9-9 *DDR Operation*

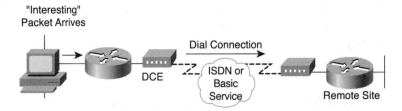

A basic description of how DDR is implemented in Cisco routers can be listed in five steps:

1 The router receives traffic and does a route table lookup to determine if a route exists to the destination. If one exists, the outbound interface is identified. If the outbound interface is configured for DDR, the router does a lookup to determine if the traffic is "interesting."

You, the administrator, define interesting traffic as any traffic that should trigger a call so that the traffic can be transferred.

2 The router identifies the next-hop router and locates the dialing instructions in the dialer map.

3 The router checks to see if the dialer map is in use—that is, if the interface is currently connected to the remote destination:

  — If the interface is currently connected to the desired remote destination, the traffic is sent without dialing, and the idle timer is reset based on the packet's being interesting.

  — If the interface is not currently connected to the remote destination, the router, which is attached to a DCE such as an ISDN BRI, ISDN TA, or modem that supports V.25bis dialing, sends call setup information to the DCE device on the specified serial line or ISDN D channel.

4 After the link is enabled, the router transmits both interesting and uninteresting traffic. Uninteresting traffic can include data and routing updates. However, uninteresting traffic does not reset the idle timer.

5 When the link connects, an idle timer starts. When no more interesting traffic is transmitted over the link, the idle timer begins to run down. The call is disconnected after no interesting traffic is seen for the duration of the idle timeout period.

Configuring Standard DDR

There are two types of DDR routing. This book discusses the type known as standard DDR (sometimes referred to as Legacy DDR in other documentation). In this section, you learn to configure standard DDR. Figure 9-9 showed the general operation of DDR routing. The task in configuring this technology is to tell the router how to get to the remote network, what traffic brings up the link, and what number to dial to reach that network. The following steps detail this information and show you how to configure it on the router.

To configure standard DDR, follow these steps:

Step 1 **Define static routes**—What route do I take to get to the destination?

Step 2 **Specify interesting traffic**—What traffic type should enable the link?

Step 3 **Configure the dialer information**—What number do I call to get to the next-hop router, and what service parameters do I use for the call?

Step 1: Defining Static Routes

Configuring standard DDR consists of telling the router how to get to the remote network. Figure 9-10 shows a sample network in which you can use DDR to reach the remote site.

Figure 9-10 *Defining Static Routes (Step 1)*

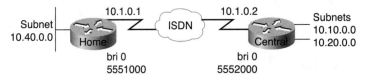

To forward traffic, routers need to know what route to use for a given destination. You don't want dynamic routing protocols running across the link because they would cause the DDR interface to dial the remote sites for every periodic routing update. Instead, you can manually configure the necessary DDR routes using static routes. The static route command for IP, for example, is as follows:

```
Router(config)#ip route prefix mask {address ? interface} [distance] [permanent]
```

As discussed in Chapter 4, "Determining IP Routes," when you're configuring static routes, keep in mind the following considerations:

- When using static routes, all participating routers must have static routes defined so that they can reach the remote networks. This requirement is necessary because static routes replace dynamic routing updates.

- To reduce the number of static route entries, you can define a default static route.

Step 2: Specifying Interesting Traffic

Configuring standard DDR involves identifying the protocol packets designated as interesting that will trigger a DDR call. You identify the interesting packets; they can be identified on the basis of a variety of criteria, such as protocol type or addresses for source or destination hosts. Use the **dialer-list** global command to identify interesting traffic:

```
Router(config)#dialer-list dialer-group protocol protocol-name
   {permit ? deny ? list access-list-number}
```

Where:

- *dialer-group* is the number that identifies the dialer list. (**dialer-list** will be applied to an interface in steps described later in this section.)

- *protocol-name* specifies the protocol used by interesting packets. Choices include IP, IPX, AppleTalk, DECnet, and VINES.

- **permit | deny**, if used, specifically permits or denies a protocol for DDR consideration.

- **list**, if used, assigns an access list to the dialer group. The access list contains test conditions that identify the interesting traffic. Use an access list to create the interesting traffic definition if you want finer granularity of protocol choices.

Using the **dialer-list** command in conjunction with access lists gives you far greater control over what traffic you define as interesting. For example, if you wanted only Telnet or Simple Mail Transfer Protocol (SMTP) to bring up the link, use the configuration shown in Example 9-1.

Example 9-1   *Defining Telnet and SMTP Traffic as Interesting*

```
Router(config)#dialer-list 1 protocol ip list 101
Router(config)#access-list 101 permit tcp any any eq telnet
Router(config)#access-list 101 permit tcp any any eq smtp
```

CAUTION   If you use the **dialer-list 1 protocol ip permit** command without any further qualification, you will allow all IP traffic destined out the dial-on-demand interface to trigger a call. This might keep a DDR link up indefinitely, costing your organization a lot of money in unnecessary line charges.

Step 3: Configuring the Dialer Information

Configuring standard DDR involves configuring the physical interface to perform the dialing function, as detailed in the following list:

Step 1   Select the physical interface that you use as the dialup line.

Step 2   Configure the network address for the interface. For example:

```
Router(config-if)#ip address ip-address mask
```

Step 3   Configure the encapsulation type. For example, if configuring PPP, do the following:

```
Router(config-if)#encapsulation ppp
```

Also, you might choose to configure PPP authentication. In this case, the **ppp authentication chap** command is used to specify CHAP authentication for this interface:

```
Router(config-if)#ppp authentication chap
```

Step 4   Bind the traffic definition to an interface by linking the interesting traffic definition you created in Step 1 to the interface:

```
Router(config-if)# dialer-group group-number
```

The *group-number* parameter specifies the number of the dialer group to which the interface belongs. The group number can be an integer from 1 to 10. This number must match the **dialer-list** *group-number*.

Each interface can have only one dialer group, but the same dialer list (using the **dialer-group** command) can be assigned to multiple interfaces.

Step 5   A crucial configuration parameter for the DDR interface is how to connect to the remote site. Figure 9-11 shows the remote network and its telephone number. The **dialer map** statement in Example 9-2 configures the router to dial.

Figure 9-11   *Mapping a Remote Network to a Telephone Number*

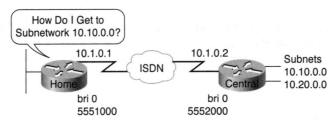

You can define one or more dial-on-demand numbers to reach one or more destinations for a particular interface with the **dialer map** command, the syntax for which is as follows:

```
Router(config-if)#dialer map protocol next-hop-address [name hostname]
[speed 56 ? 64] [broadcast] dialer-string
```

Where:

— *protocol* can be IP, IPX, AppleTalk, DECnet, VINES, and others.

— *next-hop-address* is the network address of the next-hop router.

— **name** *hostname* is the remote device's host name. This name is used for PPP authentication (CHAP or PAP) or ISDN calls supporting caller ID.

— **speed 56 | 64** is used for ISDN and indicates the link speed in kbps to use. The default is 64.

— **broadcast** indicates that broadcasts and multicasts are allowed to be forwarded to this destination (only when the link is enabled by interesting traffic). DDR is nonbroadcast by default, so no update traffic will cross the link unless this is set. This permits the use of dynamic routing protocols over the connection.

— *dialer-string* is the telephone number sent to the DCE device when packets with the specified next-hop address are received.

You must use the **dialer map** command with the **dialer-group** command and its associated access list to initiate dialing on an interface.

Example: Configuring a Router for DDR Over an ISDN BRI Line

Example 9-2 is an example of the previous steps used to configure a router for DDR operation over an ISDN BRI line.

Example 9-2   *Defining Telnet and SMTP Traffic as Interesting*

```
hostname Home
username Central password cisco
!
isdn switch-type basic-5ess
!
interface BRI0
 ip address 10.1.0.1 255.255.255.0
 encapsulation ppp
 dialer idle-timeout 180
 dialer map ip 10.1.0.2 name Central 5552000
 dialer-group 1
 no fair-queue
 ppp authentication chap
!
router rip
network 10.0.0.0
!
no ip classless
ip route 10.10.0.0 255.255.0.0 10.1.0.2
ip route 10.20.0.0 255.255.0.0 10.1.0.2
!
dialer-list 1 protocol ip list 101
!
access-list 101 permit tcp any any eq telnet
access-list 101 permit tcp any any eq smtp
```

The tasks to configure DDR (as shown collectively in Example 9-2) are as follows:

Step 1   **Define static routes**—What route do I take to get to the destination? The commands necessary to accomplish this step are as follows:

```
ip route 10.10.0.0 255.255.0.0 10.1.0.2
ip route 10.20.0.0 255.255.0.0 10.1.0.2
```

Step 2   **Specify interesting traffic**—What traffic type should enable the link? The commands necessary to accomplish this step are as follows:

```
dialer-list 1 protocol ip list 101
!
access-list 101 permit tcp any any eq telnet
access-list 101 permit tcp any any eq smtp
```

Step 3 **Configure the dialer information**—What number do I call to get to the next-hop router, and what service parameters do I use for the call? The commands necessary to accomplish this step are as follows:

```
interface BRI0
 ip address 10.1.0.1 255.255.255.0
 encapsulation ppp
 dialer idle-timeout 180
 dialer map ip 10.1.0.2 name Central 5552000
 dialer-group 1
 no fair-queue
 ppp authentication chap
username Central password cisco
```

You can use the optional **dialer idle-timeout** *seconds* command with standard DDR to specify the number of idle seconds before a call is disconnected. The *seconds* option specifies the number of seconds until a call is disconnected after the last interesting traffic is sent. (The default is 120.)

Configuring ISDN PRI and Dialer Profiles

Both the BRI and PRI have multiple B channels used to carry user traffic. In the case of a BRI, it is 2 channels, but in the case of a PRI, it is either 23 or 30 (for T1 or E1). These B channels could be used to make separate calls, but if the dialer information is configured on a single physical interface, all of the B channels have the same dialer characteristics. To configure the BRI and PRI to use the B channels as separate logical network connections, Cisco routers can be configured with *dialer profiles*.

A dialer profile is a logical configuration that is separate from a physical connection. This configuration identifies how to make or receive calls using any physical interface that is placed in a pool associated with the profile. Each profile can define a separate network, encapsulation, access control list, number of calls, and features independently of all other profiles.

The profile then allows a single physical interface, such as a PRI or BRI, to take on these features as the profile (the logical configuration) is bound to the interface (the physical port) on a per-call basis. This enables the interface to take on different characteristics based on the incoming or outgoing call requirements.

Dialer profiles help users design and deploy complex and scalable circuit-switched internetworks by implementing a new DDR model in Cisco routers and access servers. Using dialer profiles, you can perform the following tasks:

- Configure an ISDN interface's B channels with different IP subnets.
- Use different encapsulations of an ISDN interface's B channels.
- Set different DDR dial parameters for an ISDN interface's B channels.
- Eliminate the waste of ISDN B channels by letting the ISDN interfaces belong to multiple dialer pools.

Figure 9-12 shows how dialer profiles allow multiple connections from separate routers and subnets to connect to a single ISDN physical interface using profiles to map logical connections to each B channel.

Figure 9-12   *Dialer Profiles Overview*

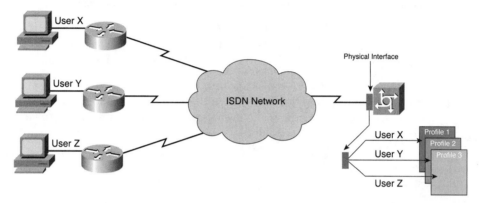

ISDN PRI interfaces are typically set up in this manner because doing so allows a user to connect to a service provider using a PRI at the central site that provides multiple (23 or 30) B channels over a single connection. As calls are received, the appropriate profile is mapped to a B channel and a separate connection is formed over that link.

Dialer profiles consist of three main components, each of which defines a portion of the connectivity. Collectively, these components provide the dialer services. The components are as follows:

- **Dialer interface**—This is the logical entity that is configured to define the profile. It is configured with the dial characteristics, such as addressing and dial maps.

- **Dialer pool**—Each dialer interface references a particular dialer pool as part of the configuration. The dialer pool is a group of one or more physical interfaces associated with the dialer profile. The dialer interface can use any physical interface in a given pool.

- **Physical interface**—These are the physical components on the router that are used by the dialer interfaces. A physical interface must be configured only with encapsulation type, PPP authentication, and multilink options that will be used. The physical interface is placed in a pool, and any dialer interface that is associated with that pool can use the physical interface to complete a call.

You can access the dialer interface (or profile) by entering the interface configuration mode using the following command:

```
Router(config)#interface dialer number
```

The *number* specifies a logical interface number, which is unique from any other dialer interface.

This interface is configured with the dial parameters, as discussed in Legacy DDR ("Step 3. Configuring the Dialer Information"). The only difference is that instead of using the map command, the dial information is specified by the following command:

```
Router(config-if)#dialer string dialnumber class map class-name
```

The *dialnumber* is the number used to call the destination device. The **class map** option can be used to specify physical parameters that should be associated with the interface for a given set of calls.

The logical interface must then be associated with a pool so that it can choose a physical interface to complete the call. The following command associates the logical interface to the pool:

```
Router(config-if)#dialer pool-member number [priority priority] [min-link minimum]
[max-link maximum]
```

Where:

- *number* specifies the dialer pooling number from 1 to 255.

- **priority** *priority* sets the priority value of the physical interfaces within the pool. This value from 1 to 255 determines which physical interface will be chosen first out of the pool. The interface with the highest priority is used first.

- **min-link** *minimum* sets the minimum number of ISDN B channels on an interface reserved for a given pool. The value is 1 to 255.

- **max-link** *maximum* sets the maximum number of ISDN B channels on an interface reserved for a given pool. The value is 1 to 255.

The dialer pool is central to the entire configuration process. The dialer interface specifies which pool of physical interfaces it can use to make the connection. You add the physical interface to a pool by using the **dialer pool-member** *number* command at the interface configuration mode. The *number* parameter specifies a particular pool to which the interface belongs. Only dialer profiles associated with that pool can use the interface.

Figure 9-13 shows the relationship between the dialer interface, physical interface, and dialer pool.

Figure 9-13   *Dialer Pool Association*

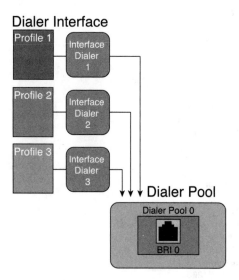

Example: Configuring a Router for Dialer Pools

Example 9-3 is an example of how dialer profiles can connect a central site with a PRI
interface to three different remote sites using dialer profiles.

Example 9-3   *ISDN PRI Dialer Profiles Configuration*

```
isdn switch-type primary-5ess
!
controller T1 1/0
 framing esf
 linecode b8zs
 pri-group timeslots 1-24
!
interface Serial1/0:23
 no ip address
 no ip directed-broadcast
 encapsulation ppp
 ppp authentication chap
 dialer pool-member 1
 no shutdown
!
interface dialer1
 ip address 10.1.1.1 255.255.255.0
 encapsulation ppp
 dialer idle-timeout 180
 dialer remote-name SiteA
 dialer string 5551201
 dialer-group 1
```

Example 9-3 *ISDN PRI Dialer Profiles Configuration (Continued)*

```
 dialer pool 1
 no fair-queue
 ppp authentication chap
!
interface dialer2
 ip address 10.1.2.1 255.255.255.0
 encapsulation ppp
 dialer idle-timeout 180
 dialer remote-name SiteB
 dialer string 5551202
 dialer-group 2
 dialer pool 1
 no fair-queue
 ppp authentication chap
!
interface dialer3
 ip address 10.1.3.1 255.255.255.0
 encapsulation ppp
 dialer idle-timeout 180
 dialer remote-name SiteC
 dialer string 5551203
 dialer-group 3
 dialer pool 1
 no fair-queue
 ppp authentication chap
!
dialer-list 1 protocol ip list 101
dialer-list 2 protocol ip list 102
dialer-list 3 protocol ip list 103
!
access-list 101 permit tcp any 10.1.1.0 0.0.0.255 eq telnet
access-list 101 permit tcp any 10.1.1.0 0.0.0.255 eq smtp
access-list 102 permit tcp any 10.1.2.0 0.0.0.255 eq telnet
access-list 102 permit tcp any 10.1.2.0 0.0.0.255 eq smtp
access-list 103 permit tcp any 10.1.3.0 0.0.0.255 eq telnet
access-list 103 permit tcp any 10.1.3.0 0.0.0.255 eq smtp
```

The tasks to configure DDR (as shown collectively in Example 9-3) are as follows:

Step 1 **Configure dialer profiles**—Configure the dialer interface with the remote site's call characteristics. Use the dialer string to specify the remote location's phone number. Repeat this for each logical connection that will be made:

```
interface dialer1
 ip address 10.1.1.1 255.255.255.0
 encapsulation ppp
 dialer idle-timeout 180
 dialer remote-name SiteA
```

```
dialer string 5551201
dialer-group 1
no fair-queue
ppp authentication chap
```

Step 2   **Specify a dialer pool**—While still in the dialer interface, specify which dialer pool this logical interface can select a physical interface for use. The command necessary to accomplish this step is as follows:

```
dialer pool 1
```

Step 3   **Configure the physical interface and add to dialer pool**—You must configure the physical interface with the encapsulation and authentication method used by the dialer interfaces. It must also be added to the dialer pool for use by the dialer interfaces. The commands necessary to accomplish this step are as follows:

```
encapsulation ppp
ppp authentication chap
dialer pool-member 1
```

Verifying DDR Over ISDN Configuration and Operation

To verify the configuration of ISDN and DDR configuration and operation, you can use the commands listed in Table 9-6.

Table 9-6   *Commands to Verify DDR over ISDN Configuration and Operation*

Command	Description
ping/telnet	When you ping or Telnet a remote site via DDR (assuming these are not filtered), or when other interesting traffic triggers a DDR link, the router sends a change in link status message to the console.
show dialer	Lists general diagnostic information about an interface configured for DDR, such as the number of times the dialer string has been successfully reached. Current call-specific information is also provided, such as the length of the call and the number and name of the device to which the interface is currently connected.
show isdn active	Shows that a call is in progress and lists the number called.
show isdn status	Shows the ISDN connection's statistics.
show ip route	Displays the routes known to the router, including static and dynamically learned routes.

Troubleshooting DDR Operation

ISDN troubleshooting can be an intense process. Essentially, two separate processes are taking place that have to be examined during an ISDN call:

- Communication between the ISDN switch and the router. Each component of this configuration and communications must work properly to complete the call.

- The dialer process.

Table 9-7 includes some other useful commands that can aid in troubleshooting the operation of DDR.

Table 9-7 *Commands to Troubleshoot DDR Operation*

Command	Description
debug isdn q921	Verifies that you have a connection to the ISDN switch
debug isdn q931	Displays call setup and teardown messages
debug dialer [**events** | **packets**]	Shows information such as what number the interface is dialing
shutdown	Administrative shutdown of the interface; disconnects any call in progress

If a problem occurs in communication with the ISDN switch, you can use the q921 information to check that connection. Example 9-4 shows the output from the **debug isdn q921** command for an outgoing call.

Example 9-4 **debug isdn q921** *Command Output*

```
Jun 26 14:52:24.475: ISDN BR0: TX -> INFOc sapi = 0  tei = 64  ns = 5  nr = 2
                     i = 0x080107050402889018018370068036631383835
Jun  26 14:52:24.503: ISDN BR0: RX <- RRr sapi = 0  tei = 64  nr = 6
Jun  26 14:52:24.527: ISDN BR0: RX <-  INFOc sapi = 0  tei = 64  ns = 2  nr = 6
                     i = 0x08018702180189
Jun  26 14:52:24.535: ISDN BR0: TX -> RRr sapi = 0  tei = 64  nr = 3
Jun  26 14:52:24.643: ISDN BR0: RX <-  INFOc sapi = 0  tei = 64  ns = 3  nr = 6
                     i = 0x08018707
Jun  26 14:52:24.655: ISDN BR0: TX -> RRr sapi = 0  tei = 64  nr = 4
%LINK-3-UPDOWN: Interface BRI0:1, changed state to up
Jun  26 14:52:24.683: ISDN BR0: TX -> INFOc sapi = 0  tei = 64  ns = 6  nr = 4
                     i = 0x0801070F
Jun  26 14:52:24.699: ISDN BR0: RX <- RRr sapi = 0  tei = 64  nr = 7
%LINEPROTO-5-UPDOWN: Line protocol on Interface BRI0:1, changed state to up
%ISDN-6-CONNECT: Interface BRI0:1 is now connected to 61885 goodie
Jun  26 14:52:34.415: ISDN BR0: RX <- RRp sapi = 0  tei = 64 nr = 7
Jun  26 14:52:34.419: ISDN BR0: TX -> RRf sapi = 0  tei = 64  nr = 4
```

In the shaded lines, the seventh and eighth most significant hexadecimal numbers indicate the type of message. 0x05 indicates a call setup message, 0x02 indicates a call proceeding message, 0x07 indicates a call connect message, and 0x0F indicates a connect ack (acknowledgment) message.

If a problem occurs with the call setup, you can use the 931 information to determine how the call is proceeding. Example 9-5 shows output from the **debug isdn q931** command of a call setup procedure for an outgoing call.

Example 9-5   **debug isdn q931** *for an Outgoing Call*

```
Router#debug isdn q931

TX -> SETUP pd = 8 callref = 0x04
 Bearer Capability i = 0x8890
 Channel ID i = 0x83
 Called Party Number i = 0x80, `415555121202'
RX <- CALL_PROC pd = 8 callref = 0x84
 Channel ID i = 0x89
RX <- CONNECT pd = 8 callref = 0x84
TX -> CONNECT_ACK pd = 8 callref = 0x04....
```

Example 9-6 shows output from the **debug isdn q931** command of a call setup procedure for an incoming call.

Example 9-6   **debug isdn q931** *for an Incoming Call*

```
Router#debug isdn q931

RX <- SETUP pd = 8 callref = 0x06
 Bearer Capability i = 0x8890
 Channel ID i = 0x89
 Calling Party Number i = 0x0083, `81012345678902'
TX -> CONNECT pd = 8 callref = 0x86
RX <- CONNECT_ACK pd = 8 callref = 0x06
```

For the call to proceed, DDR must initiate the call. If this does not occur, the call cannot be placed. When DDR is enabled on the interface, information concerning the cause of any call (called the *dialing cause*) is displayed using the **debug dialer events** command. The following line of output for an IP packet lists the name of the DDR interface and the source and destination addresses of the packet:

```
Dialing cause: Serial0: ip (s=172.16.1.111 d=172.16.2.22)
```

In the next sample output from the **debug dialer packets** command, the message shows the interface type, the type of packet (protocol) being sent, the source and destination addresses, the size of the packet, and the default action for the packet (in this example, PERMIT).

```
BRI0: ip (s=10.1.1.8, d=10.1.1.1), 100 bytes, interesting (ip PERMIT)
```

Each of the commands shown here is useful, but a process should be followed to trouble-shoot a dial ISDN connection.

Troubleshooting Inbound Calls

When troubleshooting an inbound call, you should start at the physical layer and work up the protocol stack. The general flow of reasoning looks for answers to the following questions. A "yes" answer to a question takes you to the next question. The **show** or **debug** command used to determine the answer to the question is shown to the right of each question. Be sure to use only one **debug** command at a time during low usage times to avoid overloading the router.

Step 1 Is there a physical connection to the ISDN switch?

Use the **show isdn status** command to verify Layer 1 connectivity to the switch.

Step 2 Did you see the call arrive?

Use the **debug isdn q931** command to verify that the call is being received, as shown in Example 9-6. The SETUP message indicates that the remote end is initiating a connection. The call reference numbers are maintained as a pair. In this case, the call reference number for the incoming side of the connection is 0x06, while the call reference number for the outbound side of the connection is 0x86. The bearer capability (often referred to as the bearercap) tells the router what kind of call is coming in. In this case, the connection is type 0x8890. That value indicates "ISDN speed 64 kbps."

Step 3 Does the receiving end answer the call?

Look at the **debug isdn q931** output to determine if the call was answered.

Step 4 Does the call complete?

Using the **debug isdn q931** output, determine if the call was answered.

Step 5 Is data passing across the link?

Using the **show interfaces bri** command, verify that traffic is passing.

Step 6 Is the session established?

Using the(**debug ppp [authentication | negotiation]**) command, verify that the session is established.

Troubleshooting Outbound Connections

When troubleshooting an outbound connection, you start at the top of the protocol stack. To troubleshoot an outbound connection, answer the following questions. A "yes" answer to a question takes you to the next question. The **show** and **debug** command used to determine the answer to the question is shown to the right of each question. Be sure to use only one **debug** command at a time during low usage times to avoid overloading the router.

Step 1   Does dial-on-demand routing initiate a call?

Use the **debug dialer events** command to verify that the router is initiating a call based on interesting traffic. The following line of **debug dialer events** output for an IP packet lists the name of the DDR interface and the source and destination addresses of the packet:

```
BRI0: Dialing cause ip (s=172.16.1.111 d=172.16.2.22)
```

Step 2   Does the call make it out to the ISDN network?

Use the **debug isdn q931** command to verify that the call is being processed out, as shown in Example 9-5.

Step 3   Does the remote end answer the call?

Using the **debug isdn q931** command, verify that the call was answered by the other side of the link.

Step 4   Does the call complete?

Using the **debug isdn q931** command, verify that the call was completed.

Step 5   Is data passing over the link?

Use the **show interfaces** command to verify that traffic is passing over the link.

Step 6   Is the session established?

Use the (**debug ppp [authentication | negotiation]**) commands to verify link establishment.

The most common reason for outbound call problems is improper configuration. The following table describes possible causes of outbound call problems and suggested solutions. Use Table 9-8 as a guideline for troubleshooting connectivity issues.

Table 9-8 *Connectivity Troubleshooting Guidelines*

Symptom	Possible Problem	Solution
No call is initiated by the router.	Missing or incorrect interesting traffic definitions	Using the **show running-configuration** command, ensure that the interface is configured with a dialer group and that there is a global-level dialer list configured with a matching number.
		Ensure that the **dialer-list** command is configured to permit either an entire protocol or to permit traffic matching an access list.
		Verify that the access list declares packets going across the link to be interesting. One useful test is to use the privileged EXEC command **debug ip packet [list number]** using the number of the pertinent access list, and then attempt to ping or otherwise send traffic across the link. If the interesting traffic filters have been properly defined, you see the packets in the debug output. If no debug output results from this test, the access list is not matching the packets.
	Incorrect interface state	Using the **show interfaces [interface name]** command, ensure that the interface is in the state "up/up (spoofing)."
	Misconfigured dialer map	Use the **show running-configuration** command to ensure that the dialing interface is configured with at least one dialer map statement that points to the remote site's protocol address and called number.
	Misconfigured dialer profile	Use the **show running-configuration** command to ensure that the dialer interface is configured with a **dialer pool X** command, and that a dialer interface on the router is configured with a matching dialer pool, member X. If dialer profiles are not properly configured, you might see a debug message such as "Dialer1: Can't place call, no dialer pool set."
		Make sure that a dialer string is configured.

Section 2 Quiz

1 DDR routing is commonly useful for which of the following cases? (Choose all that apply.)

   A Home users checking e-mail periodically

   B Satellite offices that need to transmit large amounts of data all day long

C Periodic updates or reports to a remote site

D Contacting a site at the end of the day to get sales information

E Backup link in the event of a primary link failure

F Continuous connection between sites

2 Which of the following is the first step in initiating a DDR connection?

A Dialer information is looked up.

B Traffic is transmitted.

C Interesting traffic is identified.

D Route across the dial link is determined.

E The call is terminated.

3 After a DDR connection has been established, which of the following statements are true?

A Only interesting traffic can be transmitted across the link.

B Any traffic can be transmitted across the link.

C All traffic that has been configured can cross that link.

D The link will go down only after all transmissions have ended.

E The link will go down after no interesting traffic has been transmitted for a timeout period.

4 Dialer profiles are associated with which of the following to use a physical interface?

A Dialer pool

B Route

C Dialer map

D Class map

E Subnet

5 Which command should you use to check the call setup for an incoming ISDN call?

A **show interface**

B **debug ISDN dialer**

C **debug ISDN q931**

D **debug dialer**

E **debug all**

ISDN BRI Command Summary

Table 9-9 summarizes the commands you learned in this chapter.

Table 9-9   *DDR over ISDN Command Summary*

Command	Description
isdn switch-type basic-*switch-type*	Specifies a BRI switch type.
isdn spid1 *spid-number*	Configures the service provider ID of B channel 1.
isdn spid2 *spid-number*	Configures the service provider ID of B channel 2.
dialer-list *dialer-group* **protocol** *protocol-name* {**permit** | **deny** | **list** *access-list-number* | *access group*}	Specifies interesting traffic and associates it with a dialer group.
dialer-group *group-number*	Assigns a dialer group to an interface.
dialer map ip *next-hop-address* **name** *destination-router-name phone-number*	Specifies how to call a destination.
dialer idle-timeout *seconds*	Specifies the idle time before the line is disconnected.
show dialer	Lists general diagnostic information about an interface configured for DDR, such as the number of times the dialer string has been successfully reached, and the idle timer and fast idle timer values for each B channel. Current call-specific information is also provided, such as the length of the call and the number and name of the device to which the interface is currently connected.
show isdn active	Use this command when using ISDN. It shows that a call is in progress and lists the number called.
show isdn status	Shows the ISDN connection's statistics.
show ip route	Displays the routes known to the router, including static and dynamically learned routes.
debug isdn q921	Verifies that you have a connection to the ISDN switch.
debug isdn q931	Displays call setup and teardown messages.
debug dialer	Shows information such as what number the interface is dialing.
shutdown	Administrative shutdown of the interface. Disconnects any call in progress.
no shutdown	Enables an interface.

Case Study

Using what you learned in this chapter, it is time to return to the case study company. This week, Ann has been asked to help set up a new connection to two new vendors. Vendor A and Vendor B have provided an application that periodically send updates about production to a server in their facility. Ann needs to set up the BRI 0/1 interface on the 3640 router to dial each vendor when the appropriate traffic is being sent by the user application. Figure 9-14 shows a diagram of the connectivity between the organization and the vendors.

Figure 9-14 *ISDN Case Study*

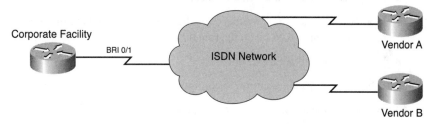

Based on the preceding information, answer the following questions about what Ann should do:

1 What information will Ann need from each vendor to set up this configuration?

2 What information does Ann need from the service provider to set up this configuration?

3 Which Dial solution should Ann use to provide DDR connectivity?

4 What measures can Ann take to insure that the BRI only connects to the Vendors and that no unauthorized users call the interface?

5 Is there any way for Ann to specify what time of day or day of the week a call can be generated to each vendor?

Summary

In this chapter, you learned how to identify the physical components of an ISDN interface. In addition, you learned how to determine the type of device you need and the reference points to connect this device to an ISDN service. Also, you should now know how to configure an ISDN BRI and PRI and how to configure an interface to act as a DDR circuit. Finally, you now know how to verify proper operation with **show** and **debug** commands, given a dial-on-demand ISDN connection.

Review Questions

1 What does ISDN stand for?

2 ISDN carries what type of user-traffic feeds?

3 The ISDN Q series protocol standards cover what issues?

4 The ISDN BRI consists of what services?

5 TE2 refers to what type of ISDN equipment?

6 A U interface references what connection?

7 In a location where the provider furnishes the NT1, what type of native ISDN reference point should be on the router?

8 Where do you obtain SPID numbers?

9 What three steps are required to configure DDR?

10 Which command specifies interesting traffic?

11 How is the correct command from question 10 linked to a dialer interface?

12 Which command could you use to display an ISDN interface's current status?

PART IV

Appendixes

After completing this appendix, you will be able to perform the following tasks:

- Perform router password recovery.
- Perform switch password recovery.

Password Recovery

Password recovery allows you to regain administrative control of your device if you have lost or forgotten the password. The basic premise is simple. You need to get access to your device without the password taking effect. Then, you need to restore the configuration and reset the password to a known value.

The Password Recovery Process

Three password discovery processes are discussed in this book. The first two deal with the different router platforms, and the third process deals with the 2950 and 3550 switches. The three password recovery procedures all involve the following basic steps:

Step 1   Reboot the system without reading the configuration memory (NVRAM).

Step 2   Access enable mode (which can be done without a password if you have not read a configuration from NVRAM).

Step 3   View or change the password, or erase the configuration.

Step 4   Reconfigure the router or switch to boot up and read the configuration in NVRAM as it normally does.

Step 5   Reboot the system.

NOTE   Some password recovery requires that a console terminal issue a Break signal, so you must be familiar with how your terminal or PC terminal emulator issues this signal. For example, ProComm uses the default keys **Alt-b** to generate the Break signal. Windows HyperTerminal requires that you press **Ctrl-Break**. You can find possible break-key sequences for other terminal emulators at http://www.cisco.com/en/US/products/hw/routers/ps133/products_tech_note09186a0080174a34.shtml.

Password Recovery Procedure 1

Use the first password recovery method to recover lost passwords on the following Cisco routers:

- Cisco 2000 series.
- Cisco 2500 series.
- Cisco 3000 series.
- Cisco 4000 series with 680x0 Motorola CPU.
- Cisco 7000 series running Cisco IOS Release 10.0 or later in ROMs installed on the RP card. The router can be booting Cisco IOS Release 10.0 Software in Flash memory, but it needs the actual ROMs on the processor card, too.
- IGS series running Cisco IOS Release 9.1 or later in ROMs.

To recover an enable password using Procedure 1, follow these steps:

Step 1   Attach a terminal or PC with terminal emulation software to the router's console port, log into the router, and issue the command **show version**.

The configuration register value is on the last line of the display. Note whether the configuration register is set to enable Break or disable Break.

The factory-default configuration register value is 0x2102. Notice that the third digit from the right in this value is odd, which disables Break after the boot process has completed. If the third digit is not odd, Break is enabled and can be issued at any time when the router is operational.

Step 2   Turn off the router, and then turn it on again.

Step 3   Press the **Break** key on the terminal within the first 45 to 60 seconds of turning on the router.

The > prompt with no router name appears. If the prompt does not appear, the terminal is not sending the correct Break signal. In that case, check the terminal or terminal emulation setup. To view the current configuration register, type in the value **e/s 2000002**.

NOTE   The number that references the location of the configuration register can change from platform to platform. Check your specific product documentation for the exact number to be used.

Step 4   Enter **o/r 0x2142** at the > prompt to boot from Flash memory or **o/r 0x2141** to boot from the boot ROMs. Changing to this config-register value tells the router where to locate its operating system when it boots and *not* to load the configuration file in NVRAM. (This is where the unknown passwords are located.)

| NOTE | The first character is the letter o, not the numeral zero. If you have Flash memory and it is intact, 0x2142 is the best setting. Use 0x2141 only if Flash memory is erased or not installed. |

Step 5 At the > prompt, enter the **initialize** command to initialize the router.

This causes the router to reboot but ignore its saved configuration, which contains the unknown passwords. The system configuration display appears.

| NOTE | If you normally use the **boot network** command, or if you have multiple images in Flash memory and you boot a nondefault image, the image in Flash might be different. |

Step 6 Enter **no** in response to the System Configuration dialog prompts until the following message appears:

```
Press RETURN to get started!
```

Step 7 Press **Return**.

The Router> prompt appears.

Step 8 Enter the **enable** command.

The Router# prompt appears.

Step 9 Choose one of the following options:

To view the password, if it is not encrypted, enter the **show startup- config** command.

To change the password (if it is encrypted, for example), enter the following commands:

```
Router # copy startup-config running-config
Router # configure terminal
Router(config)# enable secret 1234abcd
```

Step 10 Because ignoring the NVRAM and choosing to abort setup would leave all interfaces in the shutdown state, you need to enable all interfaces with the **no shutdown** command, as demonstrated here:

```
Router(config)# interface ethernet 0
Router(config-if)# no shutdown
```

Step 11 Save your new password with the following commands:

```
Router(config-if)# ctrl-z
Router # copy running-config startup-config
```

Step 12 Enter the **configure terminal** command at the EXEC prompt to enter
configuration mode.

Step 13 Enter the **config-register** command and the original value you recorded in
Step 1.

Step 14 Press **Ctrl-z** to quit the configuration editor.

Step 15 Enter the **reload** command at the privileged EXEC prompt.

Password Recovery Procedure 2

Use the second password recovery method to recover lost passwords on the following Cisco
routers:

- Cisco 1003
- Cisco 1600 series
- Cisco 2600 series
- Cisco 3600 series
- Cisco 4500 series
- Cisco 7200 series
- Cisco 7500 series
- AS5200 and AS5300 platforms

To recover a password using Procedure 2, follow these steps:

Step 1 Attach a terminal or PC with terminal emulation software to the router's
console port.

The configuration register value is on the last line of the display. Note
whether the configuration register is set to enable Break or disable Break.

The factory-default configuration register value is 0x2102. Notice that the
third digit from the left in this value is odd, which disables Break after the
boot process. If the third digit is not odd, Break is enabled at all times and
issuing a break causes the device to stop functioning.

Step 2 Turn off the router, and then turn it back on.

Step 3 Press the **Break** key on the terminal within 60 seconds of turning on the router.

The rommon> prompt appears. If it does not appear, the terminal is not sending the correct Break signal. In that case, check the terminal or terminal emulation setup.

Step 4 Enter the **confreg** command at the rommon> prompt. Record the current value of the virtual configuration register as it is output from this command.

The following prompt appears:

```
Do you wish to change configuration[y/n]?
```

Step 5 Enter **yes** and press **Return**.

Step 6 Accept the defaults for subsequent questions until the following prompt appears:

```
ignore system config info[y/n]?
```

Step 7 Enter **yes**.

Step 8 Enter **no** to subsequent questions until the following prompt appears:

```
change boot characteristics[y/n]?
```

Step 9 Enter **yes**.

The following prompt appears:

```
enter to boot:
```

Step 10 At this prompt, enter **2** and press **Return** if booting from Flash memory. Or if Flash memory is erased, enter **1**.

A configuration summary is displayed, and the following prompt appears:

```
Do you wish to change configuration[y/n]?
```

Step 11 Answer **no** and press **Return**.

The following prompt appears:

```
rommon>
```

Step 12 Enter the **reset** command at the privileged rommon> prompt, or power cycle the router.

Step 13 As the router boots, enter **no** to all the setup questions until the following prompt appears:

```
Router>
```

Step 14 Enter the **enable** command to enter enable mode.

The Router# prompt appears.

Step 15 Choose one of the following options:

To view the password, if it is not encrypted, enter the **show startup- config** command.

To change the password (if it is encrypted, for example), enter the following commands:

```
Router # copy startup-config running-config
Router # configure terminal
Router(config)# enable secret 1234abcd
```

Step 16 Because ignoring the NVRAM and choosing to abort setup leaves all interfaces in the shutdown state, you need to enable all interfaces with the **no shutdown** command, as demonstrated here:

```
Router(config)# interface ethernet 0
Router(config-if)# no shutdown
```

Step 17 Save your new password with the following commands:

```
Router(config-if)# ctrl-z
Router # copy running-config startup-config
```

The **enable secret** command provides increased security by storing the enable secret password using a nonreversible cryptographic function; however, you cannot recover a lost password that has been encrypted.

Step 18 Enter the **configure terminal** command at the prompt.

Step 19 Enter the **config-register** command and the original value you recorded in Step 1.

Step 20 Press **Ctrl-Z** to quit the configuration editor.

Step 21 Enter the **reload** command at the prompt.

Password Recovery Procedure 3

Password recovery procedure 3 covers the 2950 and 3550. Use this recovery process if you have lost or forgotten your passwords to gain access to the device, or if you want to bypass the configuration file.

To recover from a lost IOS password, you need to stop the boot process and then direct the IOS switch to not use the configuration file. After the switch loads without a file, you have no passwords and can enter into privileged mode. From there, you can copy the configuration file into active memory and then change and save the passwords. To complete the recovery process, follow these steps:

Step 1 Attach a device to the switch's console, make sure you have connectivity, and then unplug the power cord from the switch.

Step 2 Press and hold the mode button and plug the switch back in. Release the mode button after the LED above port 1x has been off for at least 2 seconds.

Step 3 You receive some information indicating that the Flash initialization has been interrupted. After you receive this information, at the prompt, type the command **flash_init**:

```
The system has been interrupted prior to initializing the flash file system.
The following commands will initialize the flash file system, and finish
  loading the operating system software:
Switch: flash_init
```

Step 4 Type the command **load_helper**:

```
Switch: load_helper
```

Step 5 Get a listing of the Flash with the command **dir flash:**. (The : is required.)

```
Switch: dir flash:
 Directory of flash:
2 -rwx 843947 Mar 01 1993 00:02:18 C2900XL-ms-12.2.8.bin
4 drwx   3776 Mar 01 1993 01:23:24 html
66 -rwx    130 Jan 01 1970 00:01:19 env_vars
68 -rwx 1296   Mar 01 1993 06:55:51 config.text
1728000 bytes total (456704 bytes free)
```

Step 6 Rename the file config.text with the command **rename flash:config.text flash:config.old**:

```
Switch:  rename flash:config.text flash:config.old
```

Step 7 Continue the boot process with the command **boot**:

```
Switch:boot
```

Step 8 Answer **n** to the question about entering setup mode:

```
Continue with the configuration dialog? [yes/no] : N
```

Step 9 Press **Enter** to access the user mode, and enter into privileged mode with the command **enable**:

```
Switch>enable
Switch#
```

Step 10 Rename the configuration file back to config.text with the command **rename flash:config.old flash:config.text**:

```
Switch# rename flash:config.old flash:config.text
```

Step 11 Copy the configuration file into active memory with the command **copy flash:config.text system:running-config**:

```
Switch# copy flash:config.text system:running-config
```

Step 12 Enter configuration mode with the command **configure terminal**:

```
Switch# configure terminal
```

Step 13 Change the line and secret passwords:

```
Switch(config)# enable secret newpassword
Switch(config)# line vty 0 4
Switch(config-line)# password newpassword
Switch(config)# line con 0
Switch(config-line)# password newpassword
Switch#(config-line)# end
```

Step 14 Save the configuration:

```
Switch# copy running-config startup-config
```

Step 15 Reboot the device and verify that it works:

```
Switch# reload
```

After completing this appendix, you will be able to perform the following task:

- Recover a switch with no IOS image.

Recovering a Lost Switch Image Using Xmodem

The Catalyst 2950 and 3550 series switches use a Flash file system to store image files. During the management of this file system, you could delete or corrupt the image so that the switch will not boot. In the event that this happens, a useable image must be loaded into the switch through the console port using an asynchronous transfer protocol known as Xmodem. This appendix describes the process for restoring an image using Xmodem and HyperTerminal.

Catalyst IOS Image

The Flash file systems for the 2950 and 3550 contain the IOS file image. This image is required for the Ethernet ports on the switch to be active. You can view the Flash file system by issuing the command **show flash**, as shown in Example B-1.

Example B-1 *Use* **show flash** *to Display IOS Image*

```
Switch# show flash

Directory of flash:/

    2  -rwx     2664051   Mar 01 1993 00:03:16  c2950-i6q4l2-mz.121-11.EA1.bin
    3  -rwx         273   Jan 01 1970 00:01:30  env_vars
    4  -rwx           5   Mar 01 1993 04:23:23  private-config.text
    5  -rwx        1278   Mar 01 1993 04:23:23  config.text
    7  drwx         704   Mar 01 1993 00:03:51  html
   19  -rwx         109   Mar 01 1993 00:03:52  info
   20  -rwx         109   Mar 01 1993 00:03:52  info.ver
   21  -rwx        2162   Mar 03 1993 11:04:12  config.tmp

7741440 bytes total (3777024 bytes free)
```

The highlighted line shows the IOS image for this switch. During the boot process, this image is uncompressed and loaded into RAM. If the image is erased from Flash or becomes corrupted, the switch cannot boot. The result is a **Switch:** prompt, as shown in Example B-2.

Example B-2 *Switch Prompt After Failed Boot*

```
Error loading "flash:c2950-i6q4l2-mz.121-11.EA1.bin"
Interrupt within 5 seconds to abort boot process.
Boot process failed...
Switch:
```

To recover from a failed boot, use the following steps:

Step 1 Obtain a valid image for the switch from a functioning switch or from the Cisco website.

Step 2 Load this image onto the hard drive of the device that connects to the switch's console port.

Step 3 If the switch is in a continual boot loop (that is, it continues to try and boot over and over), you must break the boot sequence (**ctrl-break** for HyperTerminal) after you see the following message:

```
*** The system will autoboot in 15 seconds ***
Send break character to prevent autobooting.
```

Note   Other possible break key sequences for terminal emulators other than HyperTerminal can be found at http://www.cisco.com/en/ US/products/hw/routers/ps133/products_tech_note09186a 0080174a34.shtml.

After you properly issue the break sequence, you receive the following output:

```
The system has been interrupted prior to initializing the
flash filesystem. The following commands will initialize
the flash filesystem, and finish loading the operating
system software:
  flash_init
  load_helper
  boot
switch:
```

Step 4 Issue the **flash_init** and **load_helper** commands:

```
switch:flash_init
```

If the Flash has already been initialized, you receive the following output from the switch:

```
Initializing Flash...
...The flash is already initialized.
switch:
```

Otherwise, you receive the following output:

```
Initializing Flash...
flashfs[0]: 21 files, 2 directories
```

```
flashfs[0]: 0 orphaned files, 0 orphaned directories
flashfs[0]: Total bytes: 7741440
flashfs[0]: Bytes used: 4499456
flashfs[0]: Bytes available: 3241984
flashfs[0]: flashfs fsck took 7 seconds.
...done initializing flash.
Boot Sector Filesystem (bs:) installed, fsid: 3
Parameter Block Filesystem (pb:) installed, fsid: 4
switch:
```

The **load_helper** returns the following output:

```
switch:load_helper
switch:
```

Step 5 You can now examine the contents of the Flash file system using the command **dir flash**:

```
switch:dir flash
Directory of flash:/
      3  -rwx        273   Jan 01 1970 00:01:30  env_vars
      4  -rwx          5   Mar 01 1993 04:23:23  private-config.text
      5  -rwx       1278   Mar 01 1993 04:23:23  config.text
      7  drwx        704   Mar 01 1993 00:03:51  html
     19  -rwx        109   Mar 01 1993 00:03:52  info
     20  -rwx        109   Mar 01 1993 00:03:52  info.ver
     21  -rwx       2162   Mar 03 1993 11:04:12  config.tmp

 5077389 bytes total (6441075 bytes free)
```

In this output, no IOS file exists in Flash. You need to recover the Flash file system using Xmodem.

Step 6 At the switch prompt, issue the command **copy xmodem: flash:***filename*. Use the filename of the IOS that is located on the hard drive of the console-connected PC:

```
switch: copy xmodem: flash:c2955-i6q4l2-mz.121-11.EA1.bin
Begin the Xmodem or Xmodem-1K transfer now...
CCC
```

Step 7 In the HyperTerminal application, click **transfer** on the menu; then, click **send file** in the drop-down box, as shown in Figure B-1.

Use the Browse button to locate the image on the device's hard drive and choose Xmodem, as shown in Figure B-2. Placing the image into the root directory on the hard drive might be easiest because this is the default location that HyperTerminal uses.

Figure B-1 *HyperTerminal File Transfer*

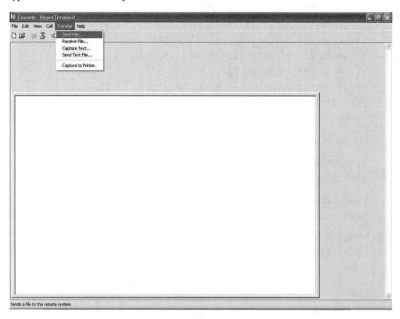

Figure B-2 *File and Protocol Select*

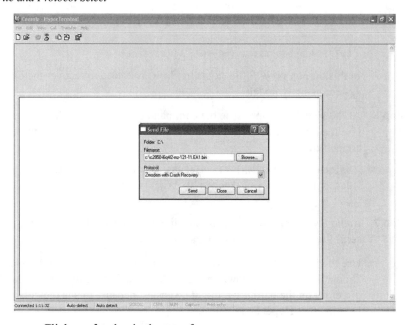

Click **send** to begin the transfer.

Step 8   After the transfer is complete, verify that the file has been copied using the
command **dir flash**:

```
switch:dir flash
Directory of flash:/
    2  -rwx    2664051  Mar 01 1993 00:03:16  c2950-i6q4l2-mz.121-11.EA1.bin
    3  -rwx         273  Jan 01 1970 00:01:30  env_vars
    4  -rwx           5  Mar 01 1993 04:23:23  private-config.text
    5  -rwx        1278  Mar 01 1993 04:23:23  config.text
    7  drwx         704  Mar 01 1993 00:03:51  html
   19  -rwx         109  Mar 01 1993 00:03:52  info
   20  -rwx         109  Mar 01 1993 00:03:52  info.ver
   21  -rwx        2162  Mar 03 1993 11:04:12  config.tmp

7741440 bytes total (3777024 bytes free)
```

Step 9   Boot the image using the **boot** command at the switch: prompt and specify
the image filename in Flash:

```
switch: boot flash:c2955-i6q4l2-mz.121-13.EA1.bin
#####################################################################
######
<output omitted>
Press RETURN to get started!
Switch>
```

Step 10   The image has been restored and loaded onto the system. Verify the operating
system with the commands **show version** and **show flash**.

NOTE   If the image is not missing but is instead corrupted, at Step 5, delete the corrupted image using
the **delete** command before proceeding to Step 6:

```
delete flash:c2955-i6q4l2-mz.121-13.EA1.bin
```

Upon completion of this appendix, you will be able to perform the following tasks:

- Identify the default configuration for a 1900 series switch.
- Configure a 1900 Series switch for basic operation.

Configuring the Catalyst 1900 Series Switch

The Catalyst 1900 series switch is a unique Cisco IOS switch in that it does not have many of the standard commands used in all the other IOS switches. Catalyst 1900s are no longer sold by Cisco Systems, but they have been part of the ICND materials for several years. For this purpose, this appendix on the Catalyst 1900 series switch appears here so that you can compare and contrast the differences in the current IOS switches and the 1900 series platform.

Default Configuration Settings for the Catalyst 1900 Switch

The Catalyst 1900 switch comes with factory default settings. For many parameters, the default configuration will suit your needs. However, you might want to change some of the default values to meet your specific network topology. The default values vary depending on the features of the switch. The following list provides some of the default settings for the Catalyst 1900 switch. Not all the defaults are listed:

- IP address: 0.0.0.0
- CDP: Enabled
- Switching mode: Fragment-free
- 100BASE-T port: Autonegotiate duplex mode
- 10BASE-T port: Half duplex
- Spanning Tree: Enabled
- Console password: None

Default Port Configurations for the Catalyst 1900 Switch

The 1912 and 1924 are two of the switches in the Catalyst 1900 switch family. Table C-1 documents the ports found on the 1912 and 1924 switches.

Table C-1   *Catalyst 1912 and 1924 Ports*

	Catalyst 1912	**Catalyst 1924**
10BASE-T Ports	12 total (e0/1 to e0/12)	24 total (e0/1 to e0/24)
AUI Port	e0/25	e0/25
100BASE-T Uplink Ports	fa0/26 (port A)	fa0/26 (port A)
	fa0/27 (port B)	fa0/27 (port B)

Ports on the Catalyst 1900 are referenced as either port or interface.

For example, for e0/1, the following points are true:

- The **show running-config** output (see Example C-1) refers to e0/1 as interface Ethernet 0/1.
- The **show spantree** output (see Example C-2) refers to e0/1 as Port Ethernet 0/1.
- The **show vlan-membership** output (see Example C-3) refers to e0/1 as just Port 1.

Example C-1   **show running-config** Output Refers to Port e0/1 as Interface Ethernet 0/1

```
wg_sw_d#show running-config

Building configuration...
Current configuration:
!
!
interface Ethernet 0/1
!
interface Ethernet 0/2
```

Example C-2   **show spantree** *Output Refers to Port e0/1 as Designated Port Ethernet 0/1*

```
wg_sw_d#show spantree

Port Ethernet 0/1 of VLAN1 is Forwarding
   Port path cost 100, Port priority 128
   Designated root has priority 32768, address 0090.8673.3340
   Designated bridge has priority 32768, address 0090.8673.3340
   Designated port is Ethernet 0/1, path cost 0
   Timers: message age 20, forward delay 15, hold 1
```

Example C-3 **show vlan-membership** Output Refers to Port e0/1 as Port 1

```
wg_sw_a#show vlan-membership

  Port  VLAN   Membership Type    Port  VLAN   Membership Type
  ----------------------------------------------------------------
  1     5           Static        13    1           Static
  2     1           Static        14    1           Static
  3     1           Static        15    1           Static
```

Configuring the Catalyst 1900 Switch

Similar to the router IOS, the Catalyst 1900 switch has various configuration modes. To configure global switch parameters such as the switch host name or IP address, use the global configuration mode; the prompts for which are as follows:

```
wg_sw_a# conf term
wg_sw_a(config)#
```

To configure a particular port (interface), use the interface configuration mode; the prompts for which are as follows:

```
wg_sw_a(config)# interface e0/1
wg_sw_a(config-if)#
```

Configuring the IP Address, Subnet Mask, and Default Gateway on the Catalyst 1900 Switch

To configure an IP address and subnet mask on the switch, use the **ip address** global configuration command, which takes the following form:

```
wg_sw_a(config)# ip address address mask
```

For example, to configure a switch with IP address 10.5.5.11 and subnet mask 255.255.255.0, you would enter the following command:

```
wg_sw_a(config)# ip address 10.5.5.11 255.255.255.0
```

An IP address is required on the switch for management purposes. For example, using the VPN Service Model (VSM) requires the switch to have an IP address configured and IP connectivity to communicate with a web browser such as Netscape or Microsoft Internet Explorer. An IP address must also be assigned if you plan to connect to the switch through Telnet, or if you plan to use Simple Network Management Protocol (SNMP) to manage the switch. This address is assigned to the entire switch and is the management connection. Use the **no ip address** global configuration command to reset the IP address to the factory default of 0.0.0.0.

Use the **ip default-gateway** global configuration command to configure the default gateway. The **ip default-gateway** command takes the following form:

```
wg_sw_a(config)# ip default-gateway ip-address
```

For example, to configure the default gateway with IP address 10.5.5.3 for a switch, you would enter the following command:

```
wg_sw_a(config)# ip default-gateway 10.5.5.3
```

The switch is assigned an IP address for management purposes. If the switch needs to send traffic to a different IP network than the one it is on, the switch sends the traffic to the default gateway, which is typically the router. A router is used to route traffic between different networks. Use the **no ip default-gateway** command to delete a configured default gateway, and set the gateway address to the default value of 0.0.0.0.

To verify the IP address, subnet mask, and default gateway settings, use the **show ip** command from the privileged EXEC mode, as demonstrated in Example C-4.

Example C-4 *Command Verifies the IP Address, Subnet Mask, and Default Gateway Settings for a Catalyst 1900 Switch*

```
wg_sw_a#show ip
IP address: 10.5.5.11
Subnet mask: 255.255.255.0
Default gateway: 10.5.5.3
Management VLAN:  1
Domain name:
Name server 1: 0.0.0.0
Name server 2: 0.0.0.0
HTTP server: Enabled
HTTP port:  80
RIP: Enabled
wg_sw_a#
```

Configuring the Duplex Mode for a Catalyst 1900 Switch Interface

Use the **duplex** interface configuration command to change the duplex mode for an interface. The syntax for this command (on interface e0/1, for example) is as follows:

```
wg_sw_a(config)# interface e0/1
wg_sw_a(config-if)# duplex {auto | full | full-flow-control | half}
```

The options for the **duplex** interface configuration command include the following:

- **auto**—Sets the autonegotiation of duplex mode; **auto** is the default option for 100 Mbps TX ports.
- **full**—Sets full-duplex mode.
- **full-flow-control**—Sets full-duplex mode with flow control.
- **half**—Sets half-duplex mode; **half** is the default option for 10 Mbps TX ports.

For example, if you were to set half-duplex mode for interface e0/1 on Switch A, you would enter the following:

```
wg_sw_a(config)# interface e0/1
wg_sw_a(config-if)# duplex half
```

To verify the duplex settings on a given interface, use the **show interface** command. To display statistics for and the status of all or specified interfaces, use the **show interfaces** privileged EXEC command, as demonstrated in Example C-5.

Example C-5 **show interfaces** *Output Displays Statistics and Status of All or Specified Switch Interfaces*

```
wg_sw_a#show interfaces

Ethernet 0/1 is Enabled
Hardware is Built-in 10Base-T
Address is 0090.8673.3341
MTU 1500 bytes, BW 10000 Kbits
802.1d STP State:  Forwarding      Forward Transitions:  1
Port monitoring: Disabled
Unknown unicast flooding: Enabled
Unregistered multicast flooding:  Enabled
Description:
Duplex setting: Half duplex
Back pressure: Disabled

     Receive Statistics                    Transmit Statistics
- - - - - - - - - - - - - - - - - - - -   - - - - - - - - - - - - - - - - - - - -
Total good frames            44841    Total frames                 404502
Total octets               4944550    Total octets               29591574
Broadcast/multicast frames   31011    Broadcast/multicast frames   390913
Broadcast/multicast octets 3865029    Broadcast/multicast octets 28478154
Good frames forwarded        44832    Deferrals                         0
Frames filtered                  9    Single collisions                 0
Runt frames                      0    Multiple collisions               0
No buffer discards               0    Excessive collisions              0
                                      Queue full discards               0
Errors:                               Errors:
  FCS errors                     0      Late collisions                 0
  Alinment errors                0      Excessive deferrals             0
  Giant frames                   0      Jabber errors                   0
  Address violations             0      Other transmit errors           0
```

As can be seen in the highlighted line in Example C-5, the duplex setting for any given interface can be determined by the **show interface** command.

Autonegotiation can, at times, produce unpredictable results. If an attached device does not support autonegotiation and is operating in full duplex, by default the Catalyst switch sets the corresponding switch port to half-duplex mode. This configuration—half duplex on one end and full duplex on the other—causes late collision errors at the full-duplex end. To avoid this situation, manually set the switch's duplex parameters to match the attached device.

If the switch port is in full-duplex mode, and the attached device is in half-duplex mode, check for frame check sequence (FCS) errors and late collisions on the switch full-duplex port.

Use the **show interfaces** command to check for FCS or late collision errors. A high number of late collisions often indicates a mismatch in duplex configuration. A mismatch results in slow network response for the client. You can see late collision counters in the second highlighted line in Example C-5.

MAC Addresses and Catalyst 1900 Switch Port Interfaces

Switches use the MAC address table to forward traffic between ports. The MAC table includes dynamic, permanent, and static addresses. Entering the **show mac-address-table** command displays the MAC address table and helps you determine how many dynamic, permanent, and static addresses are present and which type is used for each interface. (See Example C-6.)

Example C-6   **show mac-address-table** *Output Displays the MAC Address Table for the Port Interfaces on a Specified Switch*

```
wg_sw_a#show mac-address-table
Number of permanent addresses : 0
Number of restricted static addresses : 0
Number of dynamic addresses : 6

Address            Dest Interface     Type          Source Interface List
-------------------------------------------------------------------------
00E0.1E5D.AE2F     Ethernet 0/2       Dynamic       All
00D0.588F.B604     FastEthernet 0/26  Dynamic       All
00E0.1E5D.AE2B     FastEthernet 0/26  Dynamic       All
0090.273B.87A4     FastEthernet 0/26  Dynamic       All
00D0.588F.B600     FastEthernet 0/26  Dynamic       All
00D0.5892.38C4     FastEthernet 0/27  Dynamic       All
```

Dynamic MAC Addresses

Dynamic addresses are source Media Access Control (MAC) addresses that are learned by the switch and then dropped when they are not in use. The switch provides dynamic address learning by noting the source address of each packet it receives on each port and adding the address and its associated port number to the address table. As stations are added to or removed from the network, the switch updates the address table, adding new entries and removing those that are currently not in use.

Permanent MAC Addresses

An administrator can specifically assign permanent addresses to certain ports using the **mac-address-table permanent** command, the syntax for which is as follows:

    wg_sw_a(config)# **mac-address-table permanent** *mac-address type module/port*

Table C-2 provides descriptions for the **mac-address-table permanent** command arguments.

Table C-2   **mac-address-table permanent** *Command Arguments*

Command Argument	Meaning
mac-address	A MAC unicast address
type	The interface type: ethernet, fastethernet, fddi, atm, or port-channel
module/port	Module number: 0 for a Catalyst 1900 series
	Port number: 1-25 Ethernet
	26 and 27 Fast Ethernet
	28 Port-channel

Unlike dynamic addresses, permanent addresses are not aged out.

The Catalyst 1900 can store a maximum of 1024 MAC addresses in its MAC address table. When the MAC address table is full, it floods all new addresses until one of the existing entries gets aged out.

In order to ensure that an address will always be in the MAC table, you can use the **mac-address-table permanent** global configuration command to associate a permanent MAC address with a particular switched port interface (specified by type and module/port). Use the **no mac-address-table permanent** command to delete a permanent MAC address.

A permanent address in the MAC address table does not age out, and all interfaces can send traffic to this port, even if the device is moved.

For example, entering the following command:

```
wg_sw_a(config)# mac-address-table permanent 2222.2222.2222 ethernet 0/3
```

specifies that frames with the destination MAC address of 2222.2222.2222 should be forwarded out on the interface ethernet 0/3, and all interfaces can send traffic to 2222.2222.2222.

To verify that assigning the permanent MAC address was successful, enter the **show mac-address-table** command as demonstrated in Example C-7.

Example C-7 **show mac-address-table** *Output Verifies Permanent MAC Addresses*

```
wg_sw_a#show mac-address-table
Number of permanent addresses : 1
Number of restricted static addresses : 0
Number of dynamic addresses : 4

Address            Dest Interface      Type        Source Interface List
------------------------------------------------------------------------
00E0.1E5D.AE2F     Ethernet 0/2        Dynamic     All
2222.2222.2222     Ethernet 0/3        Permanent   All
00D0.588F.B604     FastEthernet 0/26   Dynamic     All
00E0.1E5D.AE2B     FastEthernet 0/26   Dynamic     All
00D0.5892.38C4     FastEthernet 0/27   Dynamic     All
```

Static MAC Addresses

A static address allows you to restrict traffic to a particular MAC address from a specific source interface.

Use the **mac-address-table restricted static** global configuration command to associate a restricted static address with a particular switched port interface. The syntax for this command is as follows:

```
wg_sw_a(config)# mac-address-table restricted static mac-address
type module/port src-if-list
```

Table C-3 describes the **mac-address-table restricted static** command arguments.

Table C-3 *mac-address-table restricted static Command Arguments*

Command Argument	Meaning
mac-address	A MAC unicast address
type	The interface type: ethernet, fastethernet, fddi, atm, or port-channel
module/port	Module number: 0 for a Catalyst 1900 series
	Port number: 1-25 Ethernet
	26 and 27 Fast Ethernet
	28 Port-channel
src-if-list	List of acceptable interfaces separated by spaces

Use the **no mac-address-table restricted static** command to delete a restricted static address.

By entering the following command:

```
wg_sw_a(config)# mac-address-table restricted static 1111.1111.1111 e0/4 e0/1
```

the switch allows traffic to the restricted static address 1111.1111.1111 on e0/4 only from interface e0/1. To verify that assigning the restricted static MAC address was successful, enter the **show mac-address-table** command as demonstrated in Example C-8.

Example C-8 show mac-address-table *Output Verifies Restricted Static MAC Addresses*

```
wg_sw_a#show mac-address-table
Number of permanent addresses : 1
Number of restricted static addresses : 1
Number of dynamic addresses : 4

Address            Dest Interface       Type        Source Interface List
- - - - - - - - - - - - - - - - - - - - - - - - - - - - - - - - - - - - - - - -
1111.1111.1111     Ethernet 0/4         Static      Et0/1
00E0.1E5D.AE2F     Ethernet 0/2         Dynamic     All
2222.2222.2222     Ethernet 0/3         Permanent   All
00D0.588F.B604     FastEthernet 0/26    Dynamic     All
00E0.1E5D.AE2B     FastEthernet 0/26    Dynamic     All
00D0.5892.38C4     FastEthernet 0/27    Dynamic     All
```

Configuring Port Security on a Catalyst 1900 Switch

Another MAC-based restriction available as an option on the switch is port security. Port security has the following advantages:

- It configures an interface to be a secured port so that only certain devices are permitted to connect to a given switch port.

- It defines the maximum number of MAC addresses allowed in the address table for this port (ranging from 1 to 132, where 132 is the default).

Use the **port secure** interface configuration command to enable addressing security. The syntax for this command is as follows:

```
wg_sw_a(config-if)#port secure [max-mac-count count]
```

The *count* value entered for **max-mac-count** stipulates the maximum number of addresses allowed on the port. For example, to set to 1 the maximum number of addresses allowed to connect to interface e0/4, you enter the following command:

```
wg_sw_a(config)#interface e0/4
wg_sw_a(config-if)#port secure max-mac-count 1
```

Use the **no port secure** command to disable addressing security, or set the maximum number of addresses allowed on the interface to the default value (132).

Secured ports restrict the use of a port to a user-defined group of stations. The number of devices on a secured port can range from 1 to 132. The MAC addresses for the devices on a secure port are statically assigned by an administrator or are *sticky-learned*. Sticky learning takes place when the address table for a secured port does not contain a full complement of static addresses. The port sticky-learns the source address of incoming frames and automatically assigns them as permanent addresses.

Use the **show mac-address-table security** privileged EXEC command to display and verify the port security configurations. Example C-9 shows some sample output from the **show mac-address-table security** command.

Example C-9 **show mac-address-table security** *Output Verifies Port Security Configurations*

```
wg_sw_a#show mac-address-table security
Action upon address violation : Suspend

Interface        Addressing Security     Address Table Size
- - - - - - - - - - - - - - - - - - - - - - - - - - - - - - - - - - - - - -
Ethernet 0/1     Disabled                     N/A
Ethernet 0/2     Disabled                     N/A
Ethernet 0/3     Disabled                     N/A
Ethernet 0/4     Enabled                      1
Ethernet 0/5     Disabled                     N/A
Ethernet 0/6     Disabled                     N/A
Ethernet 0/7     Disabled                     N/A
Ethernet 0/8     Disabled                     N/A
Ethernet 0/9     Disabled                     N/A
Ethernet 0/10    Disabled                     N/A
Ethernet 0/11    Disabled                     N/A
Ethernet 0/12    Disabled                     N/A
```

An address violation occurs when a secured port receives a source address that has been assigned to another secured port or when a port tries to learn an address that exceeds its address table size limit. When a security violation occurs, the options for action to be taken on a port include suspending, ignoring, or disabling the port. When a port is suspended, it is re-enabled when a packet containing a valid address is received. When a port is disabled, it must be manually re-enabled. If the action is ignored, the switch ignores the security violation and keeps the port enabled.

Use the **address-violation** global configuration command to specify the action for a port address violation. The syntax for this command is as follows:

```
wg_sw_a(config)# address-violation {suspend | disable | ignore}
```

Use the **no address-violation** command to set the switch to its default value (**suspend**).

Configuring VLAN Trunking Protoc0l (VTP) and Virtual LANs (VLANs)

Use the **vtp** global configuration command to specify the operating mode, domain name, password, generation of traps, and pruning capabilities of VTP. The syntax for this command is as follows:

```
switch(config)# vtp {[server | transparent | client] [domain domain-name]
  [trap (enable | disable)] [password password] [pruning {enable | disable}]}
```

To verify a recent configuration change, or to just view the VTP configuration information, use the **show vtp** privileged EXEC command, as demonstrated in Example C-10. Also displayed is the IP address of the device that last modified the configuration and a time stamp showing when the modification was made. VTP has two versions. VTP version 1 only supports Ethernet. VTP version 2 supports Ethernet and Token Ring.

Example C-10 show vtp *Output*

```
switch# show vtp
VTP version: 1
Configuration revision: 4
Maximum VLANs supported locally: 1005
Number of existing VLANs: 6
VTP domain name:switchdomain
VTP password:
VTP operating mode: Transparent
VTP pruning mode: Enabled
VTP traps generation: Enabled
Configuration last modified by: 10.1.1.40 at 00-00-0000 00:00:00
```

To reset the configuration revision number on the Catalyst 1900, use the **delete vtp** privileged EXEC command. Example C-11 demonstrates the **delete vtp** privileged EXEC command. The **show vtp** command is executed before and after the **delete vtp** command to show the changes made by **delete vtp**.

Example C-11 delete vtp *Command Resets the Switch Configuration Revision Number*

```
Switch#show vtp
    VTP version: 1
    Configuration revision: 53
    Maximum VLANs supported locally: 1005
    Number of existing VLANs: 5
    VTP domain name       : Wildcats
    VTP password          :
```

Example C-11 delete vtp *Command Resets the Switch Configuration Revision Number (Continued)*

```
        VTP operating mode      : Server
        VTP pruning mode        : Disabled
        VTP traps generation    : Enabled
        Configuration last modified by: 172.16.100.8 at 00-00-0000 00:00:00
Switch#delete vtp
This command resets the switch with VTP parameters set to factory defaults.
All other parameters will be unchanged.

Reset system with VTP parameters set to factory defaults, [Y]es or [N]o?  Yes

Switch#show vtp
        VTP version: 1
        Configuration revision: 0
        Maximum VLANs supported locally: 1005
        Number of existing VLANs: 5
        VTP domain name         :
        VTP password            :
        VTP operating mode      : Server
        VTP pruning mode        : Disabled
        VTP traps generation    : Enabled
        Configuration last modified by: 0.0.0.0 at 00-00-0000 00:00:00
Switch#
```

After you answer **yes** to reset the VTP parameters, the switch returns you to the console menu.

Trunk Line Configuration

Use the **trunk** interface configuration command to set a FastEthernet port to trunk mode. On the Catalyst 1900, the two FastEthernet ports are interfaces fa0/26 and fa0/27. The Catalyst 1900 supports the Dynamic Inter-Switch Link (DISL) protocol. DISL manages automatic ISL trunk negotiation. The syntax for the **trunk** interface configuration command is as follows:

```
switch(config)# trunk [on | off | desirable | auto | nonnegotiate]
```

The options for the **trunk** command are as follows:

- **on**—Configures the port to permanent ISL trunk mode and negotiates with the connected device to convert the link to trunk mode.

- **off**—Disables port trunk mode and negotiates with the connected device to convert the link to nontrunk.

- **desirable**—Triggers the port to negotiate the link from nontrunk to trunk mode. The port negotiates to a trunk port if the connected device is in the **on**, **desirable**, or **auto** state. Otherwise, the port becomes a nontrunk port.

- **auto**—Enables the port to become a trunk only if the connected device has the state set to **on** or **desirable**.

- **nonnegotiate**—Configures the port to permanent ISL trunk mode. No negotiation takes place with the partner.

Verifying Trunk Line Configuration

To verify a trunk configuration, use the **show trunk** privileged EXEC command to display the trunk parameters, as demonstrated in Example C-12. The syntax for the **show trunk** privileged EXEC command is as follows:

```
switch(config)# show trunk [a | b]
```

The parameters **a** and **b** represent the Fast Ethernet ports:

- Port a represents Fast Ethernet 0/26.

- Port b represents Fast Ethernet 0/27.

Example C-12 show trunk *Output*

```
switch# show trunk a
DISL state: On, Trunking: On, Encapsulation type: ISL
```

Adding a VLAN

Use the **vlan** global configuration command to configure a VLAN. The syntax for the **vlan** global configuration command is as follows:

```
vlan vlan# [name vlan_name]
```

Each VLAN has a unique four-digit ID that can be a number from 0001 to 1005. To add a VLAN to the VLAN database, assign a number and name to the VLAN. VLAN1, VLAN1002, VLAN1003, VLAN1004, and VLAN1005 are the factory default VLANs. These VLANs exist on all Catalyst switches and are used as default VLANs for other topologies, such as Token Ring and FDDI. No default VLAN can be modified or deleted.

To add an Ethernet VLAN, you must specify at least a VLAN number. If no VLAN name is entered for the VLAN, the default is to append the VLAN number to the word VLAN. For example, VLAN0004 could be a default name for VLAN4 if no name is assigned.

Remember, to add, change, or delete VLANs, the switch must be in VTP server or transparent mode.

Verifying a VLAN or Modifying VLAN Parameters

When the VLAN is configured, the parameters for that VLAN should be confirmed to ensure validity. To verify the parameters of a VLAN, use the **show vlan** *vlan#* privileged EXEC command to display information about a particular VLAN. Use **show vlan** to show all configured VLANs.

The **show vlan** command output in Example C-13 also shows which switch ports are assigned to the VLAN.

Example C-13 show vlan *Output*

```
switch# show vlan 9

VLAN Name              Status    Ports
-------------------------------------------------
9   switchlab2         Enabled
-------------------------------------------------


VLAN Type          SAID   MTU    Parent RingNo BridgeNo Stp  Trans1 Trans2
---------------------------------------------------------------------------
9   Ethernet       100009 1500      0     1      1      Unkn   0      0
---------------------------------------------------------------------------
```

Other VLAN parameters shown in Example C-13 include the type (default is Ethernet), SAID (used for FDDI trunk), MTU (default is 1500 for Ethernet VLAN), Spanning Tree Protocol (the 1900 supports only the 802.1D Spanning Tree Protocol standard), and other parameters used for Token Ring or FDDI VLANs.

To modify an existing VLAN parameter (such as the VLAN name), use the same command syntax used to add a VLAN.

In Example C-14, the VLAN name for VLAN9 is changed to switchlab90.

Example C-14 *Change VLAN Name*

```
switch# conf terminal
Enter configuration commands, one per line.  End with CNTL/Z
switch(config)# vlan 9 name switchlab90
```

Use the **show vlan 9** command as demonstrated in Example C-15 to verify the change.

Example C-15 *Verify VLAN Change*

```
wg_sw_a# show vlan 9

VLAN Name              Status    Ports
-------------------------------------------------
9   switchlab90        Enabled
-------------------------------------------------
```

Assigning Ports to a VLAN

After creating a VLAN, you can statically assign a port or a number of ports to that VLAN. A port can belong to only one VLAN at a time.

Configure the VLAN port assignment from the interface configuration mode using the **vlan-membership** command. Here is the syntax:

```
vlan-membership {static {vlan#} | dynamic}
```

dynamic means that the Catalyst 1900 queries a VMPS for VLAN information based on a MAC address.

By default, all ports are members of the default VLAN—VLAN1.

Use the **show vlan-membership** privileged EXEC command to display the VLAN assignment and membership type for all switch ports as demonstrated in Example C-16, where Port 1 refers to Ethernet 0/1, Port 2 refers to Ethernet 0/2, and so on.

Example C-16 *Displaying VLAN Assignments and Membership for All Switch Ports*

```
Switch#show vlan-membership

   Port  VLAN   Membership Type      Port   VLAN   Membership Type
   ----------------------------------------------------------------
   1      5         Static           13      1         Static
   2      1         Static           14      1         Static
   3      1         Static           15      1         Static
   4      1         Static           16      1         Static
   5      1         Static           17      1         Static
   6      1         Static           18      1         Static
   7      1         Static           19      1         Static
   8      9         Static           20      1         Static
```

Displaying Spanning-Tree Protocol Configuration Status

Use the **show spantree** privileged EXEC command to display the Spanning Tree Protocol configuration status of the switch, as demonstrated in Example C-17. The basic syntax for the **show spantree** privileged EXEC command is as follows:

```
switch# show spantree [vlannumber]
```

Example C-17 show spantree *Output*

```
switch# show spantree 1
VLAN1 is executing the IEEE compatible Spanning Tree Protocol
   Bridge Identifier has priority 32768, address 0050.F037.DA00
   Configured hello time 2, max age 20, forward delay 15
   Current root has priority 0, address 00D0.588F.B600
   Root port is FastEthernet 0/26, cost of root path is 10
   Topology change flag not set, detected flag not set
   Topology changes 53, last topology change occured 0d00h17m14s ago
   Times:  hold 1, topology change 8960
           hello 2, max age 20, forward delay 15
   Timers: hello 2, topology change 35, notification 2
Port Ethernet 0/1 of VLAN1 is Forwarding
   Port path cost 100, Port priority 128
   Designated root has priority 0, address 00D0.588F.B600
   Designated bridge has priority 32768, address 0050.F037.DA00
   Designated port is Ethernet 0/1, path cost 10
   Timers: message age 20, forward delay 15, hold 1
```

Example C-17 displays various Spanning Tree information for VLAN1, including the following:

- Port e0/1 is in the forwarding state for VLAN1.
- The root bridge for VLAN1 has a bridge priority of 0 with a MAC address of 00D0.588F.B600.
- The switch is running the IEEE 802.1d Spanning Tree Protocol.

Displaying Switch IOS Information

The IOS is the functional software that runs the switch's major operations and provides the management interface for configuration.

Use the **show version** user EXEC command to display basic information about hardware and the Cisco IOS Software version, as demonstrated in Example C-18.

Example C-18 **show version** *Output Displays Switch Hardware and IOS Information*

```
wg_sw_a#show version

Cisco Catalyst 1900/2820 Enterprise Edition Software
Version V8.01.01
Copyright  Cisco Systems, Inc.   1993-1998
ROM:  System Bootstrap, Version 3.03
wg_sw_d uptime is 8day(s) 17hour(s) 53minute(s) 25second(s)
cisco Catalyst 1900 (486sx1) processor with 2048K/1024K bytes of memory
Hardware board revision is 1
Upgrade Status:  No upgrade currently in progress
Config File Status:  File wgswd.cfg downloaded from 10.1.1.1
27 Fixed Ethernet/IEEE 802.3 interface(s)
Base Ethernet Address:  00-90-86-73-33-40
wg_sw_a#
```

As shown in Example C-18, the **show version** command contains valuable information about the operation of the switch software, including version number, memory information, and uptime.

Managing Switch Configuration Files

It is also important for you to manage the configuration files on the switch. It is useful to copy these files to and from a TFTP server.

Use the **copy nvram tftp** privileged EXEC command to upload the running configuration to a TFTP server. The syntax for this command is as follows:

```
wg_sw_a#copy nvram tftp://host/dst_file
```

For example, to upload the running configuration file for Switch A to a targeted TFTP server with IP address 10.1.1.1, where the destination file is named wgswd.cfg, enter the following command:

```
wg_sw_a#copy nvram tftp://10.1.1.1/wgswd.cfg
Configuration upload is successfully completed
```

Use the **copy tftp nvram** privileged EXEC command to download a configuration file from the TFTP server. The syntax for this command is as follows:

```
wg_sw_a#copy tftp://host/src_file nvram
```

For example, to download a configuration file from a TFTP server with IP address 10.1.1.1 to Switch A's NVRAM, enter the following command:

```
wg_sw_a#copy tftp://10.1.1.1/wgswd.cfg nvram
TFTP successfully downloaded configuration file
```

On the Catalyst 1900, the running configuration is automatically saved to NVRAM whenever a change is made to the running configuration.

If for some reason the device needs to be reset to the factory settings, you need to erase the switch's configuration by using the **delete nvram** privileged EXEC command. For example, to reset Switch D's configuration to the factory defaults, enter the following:

```
wg_sw_d#delete nvram
```

Catalyst 1900 Switch Command Summary

Table C-4 lists some useful commands discussed in this chapter.

Table C-4   *Commands for Catalyst 1900 Switch Configuration*

Command	Description
ip address *address mask*	Sets the IP address for in-band management of the switch.
ip default-gateway	Sets the default gateway so that the management interface can be reached from a remote network.
show ip	Displays IP address configuration.
show interfaces	Displays interface information.
mac-address-table permanent *mac-address type module/port*	Sets a permanent MAC address.
mac-address-table restricted static *mac-address type module/port src-if-list*	Sets a restricted static MAC address.
port secure [max-mac-count *count*]	Sets port security.

Table C-4   *Commands for Catalyst 1900 Switch Configuration (Continued)*

Command	Description
show mac-address-table {security}	Displays the MAC address table. The **security** option displays information about the restricted or static settings.
address violation	Sets the action to be taken by the switch if there is a security address violation.
delete vtp	Resets the VTP revision number and resets all VTP parameters to factory defaults.
vtp domain *name* **transparent**	Assigns a VTP domain name and sets transparent mode.
show vtp	Displays VTP status.
interface *interfacenumber* trunk on	Configures a trunk interface.
show trunk	Displays trunk status.
vlan *vlan# name vlanname*	Defines a VLAN and VLAN name.
show vlan	Displays VLAN information.
interface *interfacenumber* **vlan-membership static** *vlan#*	Assigns a port to a VLAN.
show vlan-membership	Displays VLAN membership.
show spantree *vlan#*	Displays Spanning Tree information for a VLAN.
show version	Displays version information.
copy tftp://10.1.1.1/config.cfg nvram	Copies a configuration file from the TFTP server at IP address 10.1.1.1.
copy nvram tftp://10.1.1.1/config.cfg	Saves a configuration file to the TFTP server at IP address 10.1.1.1.
delete nvram	Removes all configuration parameters and returns the switch to factory default settings.

Summary

This appendix discussed the default configuration for a Catalyst 1900 series switch and how to use the IOS CLI to configure the Catalyst 1900 switch.

Answers to Section Quizzes and Final Review Questions

Chapter 1

Final Review Questions

1 Which three functions does the Cisco hierarchical model define?

Answer: Core, distribution, and access

2 What is one advantage of the OSI reference model?

Answer: Any of the following:

— It allows you to break down the complex operation of networking into simpler elements.

— It lets engineers specialize design and development efforts on modular functions.

— It provides the capability to define standard interfaces for "plug-and-play" compatibility and multivendor integration.

3 Describe the data encapsulation process.

Answer: Data is passed down a protocol stack. At each layer, a header is added, and the data with the header is passed down as data to the next-lower layer until it reaches the physical layer. At this point, it is converted into bits and transmitted across the media.

4 Define a collision domain and give an example of a device that combines all devices into a single collision domain.

Answer: A collision domain is a group of devices residing on the same physical media. It can send signals onto the media, and these signals can collide. A hub interconnects all devices into a single collision domain.

5 Define a broadcast domain and give an example of a device that separates each segment into different broadcast domains and provides connectivity between the segments.

Answer: A broadcast domain is a group of devices that reside in a network and all receive each other's broadcasts. A router separates each connected segment into distinct broadcast domains and provides connectivity between the segments.

6 At which layer of the OSI model does a bridge or switch operate?

Answer: Layer 2

7 How many broadcast domains are associated with a bridge or switch (assuming no VLANs)?

Answer: One. All segments connected to a switch or bridge are in the same broadcast domain.

8 Which OSI layer defines an address that consists of a network portion and a node portion?

Answer: Layer 3 addresses have a logical network portion as well as a node identifier.

9 Which OSI layer defines a flat address space?

Answer: Layer 2 addresses are flat in nature.

10 Which process establishes a connection between two end stations using a reliable TCP/IP transport layer protocol?

Answer: The three-way handshake

Chapter 2

Section 1 Quiz

1 A Layer 2 switch normally uses which of the following Ethernet Frame fields to decide where to forward a frame?

   a. Source Address

   b. Destination Address

   c. Length field

   d. Type field

   e. FCS

   Answer: Destination Address

2 The process of sending out a frame to all ports except the one on which it was received is known as what?

   a. Filtering

   b. Learning

   c. Designated port

   d. Forwarding

   e. Flooding

   Answer: Flooding

3 Which of the following frame types are flooded?

   a. Multicast frames

   b. Unicast frames

   c. Broadcast frames

   d. Unknown unicast frames

   Answer: Multicast frames, broadcast frames, and unknown unicast frames

4 What default priority do Catalyst switches use in the Bridge ID? (Choose all that apply.)

   a. The switch MAC Address

   b. The switch serial number

   c. 0

   d. 8000

   e. 32,768

   f. 0x8000

   g. Answer: 32,768 and 0x8000

5 Which of the following are true concerning STP and RSTP?

   a. RSTP chooses a root bridge differently than STP.

   b. RSTP port states are slightly different than STP port states.

   c. For STP, backup and alternate paths are not known until a failure occurs.

   d. RSTP and STP use the same calculations for choosing the best path.

   e. RSTP converges faster than STP on a shared segment.

   Answer: B, C, and D

Section 2 Quiz

1 Which of the following is not a default on a Catalyst Switch running IOS? (Choose all that apply.)

   a. IP address is 0.0.0.0.

   b. All ports are set to full duplex.

   c. The system password is cisco.

   d. CDP is enabled.

   e. Spanning Tree is enabled.

   Answer: B and C

2 If 10/100Mbps port 0/1 is configured to run at 10 Mbps, which of the following port names will be used to identify the port in the **show spanning-tree** command?

   a. Interface Ethernet 0/1

   b. Interface FastEthernet 0/1

   c. Fa0/1

   d. Interface Fa0/1

   e. E0/1

   f. Interface E0/1

   Answer: Interface Fa0/1

3 Which of the following command sequences will set the IP address for the switch in VLAN 1 to 10.1.1.1 with a mask of 255.255.255.0 and activate the port?

```
a. Switch(config)# ip address 10.1.1.1 255.255.255.0
   Switch(config)# management-vlan 1

b. Switch(config)# interface vlan 1
   Switch(config-if)# ip address 10.1.1.1 255.255.255.0

c. Switch(config)# interface vlan 1
   Switch(config-if)# ip address 10.1.1.1/24
   Switch(config-if)# no shutdown

d. Switch(config)# interface vlan 1
   Switch(config-if)# ip address 10.1.1.1 255.255.255.0
   Switch(config-if)# no shutdown
```

   Answer:

```
d. Switch(config)# interface vlan 1
   Switch(config-if)# ip address 10.1.1.1 255.255.255.0
   Switch(config-if)# no shutdown
```

4 Which commands display the duplex settings for a port? (Choose all that apply.)

   a. **show interface**

   b. **show port**

   c. **show interface summary**

   d. **show duplex**

   e. **show interface status**

   f. **show interface duplex**

   Answer: show interface and show interface status

5 What is the maximum number of MAC address that can be learned by a Catalyst 2950?

   a. 1024

   b. 16,384

   c. 32,768

   d. 2048

   e. 8192

   f. There is no limit

   Answer: 8192

Final Review Questions

1 What function does the Spanning Tree Protocol provide?

   Answer: Spanning Tree prunes the bridge or switch topology to a loop-free environment by placing ports in blocking state so that only one path exists from a network to the root of Spanning Tree.

2 Which version of Spanning Tree Protocol do the Catalyst switches support?

   Answer: The Catalyst switch supports the IEEE 802.1D Spanning Tree Protocol and 802.1w RSTP.

3 What are the different Spanning Tree port states for IEEE 802.1D?

   Answer: Listening, learning, forwarding, blocking

4 Describe the difference between full-duplex and half-duplex operations.

Answer: Half-duplex Ethernet operation is a communications process that allows only one device to transmit at a time. This is the normal mode for Ethernet. Full-duplex Ethernet can be configured in a point-to-point Ethernet network (switch to server, switch to switch, and so on) in which there are only two devices. Full duplex allows for simultaneous communications between the devices, which doubles the effective bandwidth.

5 What is the default duplex setting on the Catalyst switch ports?

Answer: Autonegotiate

6 What is the switching mode used by the 2950?

Answer: Store-and-forward

7 What are the commands to assign the IP address to the default VLAN 192.168.1.5 with a mask of 255.255.255.0 and activate that interface?

Answer: interface vlan 1, then **ip address** 192.168.1.5 255.255.255.0, and then **no shutdown**

8 What is the IP address used for on the Catalyst switch?

Answer: Management. An IP address allows you to Telnet to the CLI, use the web-based management function, or use SNMP to configure and manage the switch.

9 Which type of MAC address entry does not age out of the MAC address table?

Answer: Static. It must be removed manually.

10 What is the command to display the dynamic contents of the MAC address table?

Answer: show mac-address-table dynamic

Chapter 3

Section 1 Quiz

1 Which of the following are valid Layer 2 (switchport) types?

   a. Static Access Port

   b. Trunk Port

   c. Common Spanning Tree Port

d. Root Port

e. Dynamic Access Port

Answer: Static Access Port, Trunk Port, and Dynamic Access Port

2 True or False: A Catalyst 2950 cannot act as a VMPS server and it cannot have ports with dynamically assigned VLANs.

Answer: False. The 2950 cannot act as a VMPS server, but it can have ports with dynamically assigned VLANs.

3 VLANs provide which of the following? (Choose all that apply.)

a. Security

b. Redundancy

c. Segmentation

d. Loop prevention

e. Collision domains

f. Flexibility

g. All of the above

Answer: Security, segmentation, and flexibility

4 How many bytes of overhead are added to a frame for 802.1Q frame tagging and ISL frame tagging?

a. 4 bytes ISL & 30 bytes 802.1Q

b. 8 bytes ISL & 26 bytes 802.1Q

c. 26 bytes ISL & 4 bytes 802.1Q

d. 30 bytes ISL & 8 bytes 802.1Q

e. 30 bytes ISL & 4 bytes 802.1Q

f. None. The frame tagging is performed in Hardware ASICs.

Answer: 30 bytes ISL and 4 bytes 802.1Q

5 Which of the following is true for VTP? (Choose the best answers.)

a. VTP is required for proper VLAN operation.

b. VTP eases VLAN creation for a switched network.

c. Changes need to be made to only one VTP server in a domain.

  d. A switch in VTP transparent mode will increment its configuration revision number but will not synchronize with other switches.

  e. VTP will run only across trunk links.

  f. VTP requires a domain name to operate.

  g. The default VTP domain name for all Catalyst switches is Cisco.

  h. VTP is completely safe and will never cause problems in your network.

 Answer: A, B, D, and E

Section 2 Quiz

1 A VLAN can be created or modified on a switch in which of the following VTP modes? (Choose all that apply.)

  a. Server

  b. Access

  c. Client

  d. Transparent

  e. Root

 Answer: A and D

2 Regarding VTP configuration revision numbers, which of the following statements are true? (Choose all that apply.)

  a. A transparent switch will always have a higher configuration revision number than any other switch on the network.

  b. VTP configuration revision numbers are changed on a switch when a VLAN is created, deleted, or modified.

  c. If a switch with a higher configuration revision number is added to an existing network with the same VTP domain name, it will have no effect on the VLANs on all the functioning switches.

  d. VTP configuration revision numbers can be reset to 0 by changing the VTP to transparent mode and then back to server or client.

  e. You can view a switch's current VTP configuration revision number by issuing the command **show vtp status**.

 Answer: B, D, E

3 Choose the commands that force an IOS switch to perform trunking on a FastEthernet interface 0/12. (Choose the best answer.)

   a. **set trunk on**

   b. **interface Fa0/12 trunk on**

   c. **switchport mode trunk**

   d. **interface Fa0/12 mode trunk**

   e. **interface Fa0/12 then switchport mode trunk**

   Answer: interface Fa0/12 then switchport mode trunk

4 Which of the following is the default mode for a Layer 2 port on an IOS switch?

   a. **switchport mode access**

   b. **switchport mode dynamic auto**

   c. **switchport mode nonegotiate**

   d. **switchport mode dynamic desirable**

   e. **switchport mode trunk**

   Answer: switchport mode dynamic desirable

5 Which of the following commands can you use to see which VLAN a port is assigned to? (Choose all that apply.)

   a. **show interface trunk**

   b. **show interface** *type slot/port*

   c. **show vtp status**

   d. **show interface status**

   e. **show vlan brief**

   f. **show interface** *type slot/port* **switchport**

   Answer: D, E, and F

Final Review Questions

1 VLANs allow for the creation of what in switched networks?

   Answer: VLANs allow for the creation of multiple broadcast domains in a switched network.

2 What are the two types of VLAN port assignments?

Answer: Static VLANs, configured and assigned by the user, and dynamic VLANs, which are assigned by the end-device MAC address.

3 What type of port is capable of carrying all VLAN traffic?

Answer: A trunk port carries all VLAN traffic and interconnects network devices to carry and communicate all VLAN packets.

4 What mechanism is used by switches to provide inter-switch communication between devices about which VLAN a packet originated from?

Answer: Trunking with ISL or IEEE 802.1Q frames between switches

5 What is the purpose of VTP?

Answer: VTP allows consistent VLAN configuration across all the switches in the network.

6 What is the default VTP mode for a Catalyst Switch?

Answer: Server mode

7 Assume that a Catalyst switch is being added to your network. The switch needs to learn VLANs from the other switches in the network. You are not sure of the current VTP configuration and are fearful that it might overwrite your current VLAN information. How could you prevent the switch from accidentally overwriting the VLANs in your VTP domain?

Answer: Place the device in transparent mode; then switch it to client or server before attaching it to the network, or change the VTP domain name and change it back.

8 What is unique about the Native VLAN on an IEEE 802.1Q trunk link?

Answer: Frames on the Native VLAN are not tagged on an 802.1Q trunk link.

9 List all the steps required to configure a VLAN on a Catalyst switch port.

Answer: Configure VTP to transparent mode or set a VTP domain name, create the VLAN, and assign the port to a VLAN.

10 Which command would you use to view the Spanning Tree configuration for VLAN9 on a Catalyst switch?

Answer: show spanning-tree vlan 9

Chapter 4

Section 1 Quiz

1 By default, which of the following networks are known by a router that has configured interfaces?

    a. All routes in the network

    b. Only the statically configured routes

    c. The default route

    d. Connected Networks

    e. All of the above

    Answer: Connected Networks

2 In the routing table displayed with the **show ip route** command, which of the following symbols indicates a route to be used for networks not found in the routing table?

    a. S

    b. C

    c. D

    d. E

    e. O

    f. *

    Answer: *

3 True or False: A static route dynamically adjusts to changes in the routing topology without any user intervention?

    Answer: False. The main problem with a static route is that it cannot adjust to changes in the routing topology and requires intervention by an administrator.

4 A router connected only to a trunk link on a switch is called which of the following?

    a. A bad design

    b. A router on a stick

    c. A jalapeño on a stick

    d. Impossible

    e. InterVLAN router

f. Trunk router

Answer: A router on a stick

NOTE   For more information about a jalapeño on a stick, please refer to
http://www.onastick.com/website/main.html.

---

5 For the 802.1Q native VLAN, which of the following methods satisfy the requirement of not tagging the native VLAN frames?

a. Configure the major interface with an IP address.

b. Use ISL as the encapsulation type.

c. Configure Frame Relay for the subinterface.

d. Configure the subinterface of the Native VLAN with the encapsulation option **native**.

e. Use the global command **dot1q native vlan 1**.

Answer: A and D

Section 2 Quiz

1 Which of the following describe classes of Cisco routing protocols?

a. Distance vector

b. Classless

c. Classful

d. Open systems

e. SPF

f. Link-state

g. Hybrid

Answer: Distance vector, link-state, and hybrid

2 Classful routing protocols provide which of the following features?

a. Use of variable length subnet masks

b. Auto summarization across networks

c. Fixed-length subnet masks

d. Manual summarization

e. Link-state databases

Answer: Auto summarization across networks and fixed-length subnet masks

3 True or False: The Bellman-Ford-Moore algorithm is used for distance vector routing protocols?

Answer: True

4 OSPF uses a hierarchy that consists of which of the following elements?

   a. Topology database

   b. Areas

   c. Core

   d. Access

   e. Hybrid

   f. Autonomous system

Answer: Areas and autonomous system

5 EIGRP is considered which of the following types of routing protocols?

   a. Link-state

   b. Distance vector

   c. Classful

   d. Classless

   e. Hybrid

   f. Proprietary

   g. Interior Gateway Protocol

   h. Exterior Gateway Protocol

   i. Advanced distance vector

Answer: D, E, F, G, and I

Final Review Questions

1 Which four things does a router need to route?

Answer: Identify sources of routing information, discover routes, select routes, and maintain routes.

2 What are the three types of routes?

Answer: Connected, static, and dynamic

3 Which type of route do administrators enter based on their knowledge of the network environment?

Answer: A static route

4 When does a router use a default route?

Answer: A default route is used for any packet destined for a network that is not in the router's routing table.

5 Give two examples of an Interior Gateway Protocol.

Answer: Any two: RIP, IGRP, OSPF, EIGRP, IS-IS

6 When faced with two routes from different protocols for the same network, what does a Cisco router employ to determine which route to use?

Answer: Administrative distance

7 Which metric is used by RIP? IGRP? OSPF?

Answer: RIP uses hop counts. IGRP uses a composite metric of bandwidth, delay, load, reliability, and MTU. OSPF uses cost calculated by bandwidth.

8 Name one method used to eliminate routing loops.

Answer: Any one: split horizon, poison reverse, defining a maximum, triggered updates, holddown timers

9 What happens to traffic destined for a network that is currently in a holddown state?

Answer: The router assumes that the network status is unchanged and forwards the packet.

10 What command displays the routing table?

Answer: show ip route.

Chapter 5

Section 1 Quiz

1 Which of the following are true of RIPv1. (Choose all that apply.)

   a. It is a distance vector protocol.

    b. It uses bandwidth for a metric.

    c. It stores information about all routes in the network in a database.

    d. It sends broadcast updates.

    e. It sends updates every 30 seconds.

    Answer: A, D, and E

2 True or False: When a router has a route to a network in holddown state, it will not attempt to forward packets to that network.

    Answer: False. When a route is in holddown state, the router continues to forward frames for that network until the timer expires and the route is removed.

3 RIP will advertise for which networks?

    a. All connected networks

    b. All connected networks identified with a network statement

    c. Networks learned via the RIP protocol

    d. All networks identified with a network statement

    Answer: B and C

4 Which of the following is the administrative distance for RIP?

    a. 110

    b. 100

    c. 155

    d. 90

    e. 120

    Answer: 120

5 Which **show** command will display the local networks being advertised by the RIP process?

    a. show ip route

    b. **show ip protocol**

    c. **show rip networks**

    d. **show rip protocol**

    e. **show ip route rip**

    Answer: show ip protocol

Section 2 Quiz

1 Which of the following are true of IGRP. (Choose all that apply.)

   a. It is a distance vector protocol.

   b. It uses bandwidth when computing the metric.

   c. It stores information about all routes in the network in a database.

   d. It sends broadcast updates.

   e. It sends updates every 45 seconds.

Answer: A, B, and D

2 True or False: IGRP can be configured to route packets using routes with unequal paths?

Answer: True

3 If a router had three interfaces with the addresses 172.16.1.1/24, 172.16.2.1/24, and 172.61.3.1/24, which of the following **network** statements would need to be added to advertise all these networks?

   a. network 172.16.0.0

   b. **network 172.16.1.0**

   c. **network 172.16.2.0**

   d. **network 172.16.3.0**

   e. **network 172.61.3.0**

   f. **network 172.61.0.0**

Answer: network 172.16.0.0 and network 172.61.0.0

4 Which of the following is the administrative distance for IGRP?

   a. 110

   b. 100

   c. 155

   d. 90

   e. 120

Answer: 100

5 Which **debug** command displays a summary of the IGRP routing updates being sent?

   a. debug ip route

   b. **debug ip igrp events**

   c. **debug igrp events**

   d. **debug igrp transactions**

   e. **debug igrp summary**

   Answer: debug ip igrp events

Section 3 Quiz

1 What is the name of the routing algorithm used by EIGRP?

   a. Link-State

   b. Bellman-Ford

   c. Dijkstra

   d. DUAL

   e. Hybrid

   Answer: DUAL

2 True or False: EIGRP maintains a topology table of available routes in the network.

   Answer: True

3 EIGRP can route for which of the following protocols?

   a. IP

   b. IPX

   c. VINES

   d. AppleTalk

   e. NetBEUI

   Answer: A, B, and D

4 Which of the following does EIGRP choose as the route to be displayed in the routing table?

   a. Default route

   b. Static route

   c. Feasible successor

   d. Defacto

   e. Successor

Answer: Successor

5   Which of the following is a shortcoming of EIGRP?

   a. Slow convergence

   b. Multiprotocol support

   c. Advanced distance vector protocol

   d. Proprietary

Answer: Proprietary

Section 4 Quiz

1   Which of the following are true of OSPF? (Choose all that apply.)

   a. It is a distance vector protocol.

   b. It is a hierarchical protocol.

   c. It uses multicast updates.

   d. It only sends advertisements when a link change occurs.

   e. It sends broadcast updates.

   f. It is a classful routing protocol.

   Answer: B, C, and D

2   True or False: OSPF process IDs must match on every router in the network.

   Answer: False. For OSPF, the process ID is an internal number that the local router uses to maintain OSPF information.

3   What **network** statement would you use to run OSPF only on an interface with the address 192.168.255.1/27 and place it in Area 0?

   a. network 192.168.255.0 0.0.0.0 area 0

   b. **network 192.168.255.1 0.0.0.255 area 1**

   c. **network 192.168.255.1 255.255.255.224 area 0**

   d. **network 192.168.255.1 0.0.0.0 area 0**

   Answer: network 192.168.255.1 0.0.0.0 area 0

4 Which of the following is the administrative distance for OSPF?

   a. 110

   b. 100

   c. 155

   d. 90

   e. 155

   f. 120

Answer: 110

5 Which command can you use to troubleshoot problems with OSPF adjacencies?

   a. show ip ospf adjacencies

   b. **debug ip ospf events**

   c. **debug ospf adjacencies**

   d. **debug ospf events**

Answer: debug ip ospf events

Section 5 Quiz

1 VLSM helps with which of the following problems in network design?

   a. IP addressing waste

   b. Illegal IP addresses

   c. Route summarization

   d. Network Address Translation

Answer: IP addressing waste and route summarization

2 True or False: VLSMs allow you to further divide a subnetted network.

Answer: True

3 What would be the best summary address for the following networks: 172.16.16.0, 172.16.17.0, 172.16.18.0, 172.16.19.0, and 172.16.24.0?

   a. 172.16.0.0 255.255.0.0

   b. 172.16.16.0 0.0.15.255

   c. 172.0.0.0 255.0.0.0

    d. 172.16.16.0 255.255.240.0

    e. 172.16.16.0 255.255.248.0

  Answer: 172.16.16.0 255.255.240.0

4 Which of the following routing protocols support VLSMs?

    a. IGRP

    b. OSPF

    c. RIPv1

    d. EIGRP

    e. RTMP

  Answer: OSPF and EIGRP

5 True or False: RIP-1 provides route summarization.

  Answer: True

Final Review Questions

1 Why are dynamic routing protocols important?

  Answer: Dynamic routing protocols allow the router to dynamically advertise and learn routes without the intervention of the administrator after the protocols have been configured.

2 RIP uses what as a metric?

  Answer: Hop count

3 What are the five composite metrics used by IGRP and EIGRP?

  Answer: Bandwidth, load, delay, reliability, MTU

4 What command do you use to choose a routing protocol?

  Answer: Router *protocol*

5 Which command do you use to show the routing protocols and the networks they are advertising?

  Answer: show ip protocol

6 What does DUAL stand for?

Answer: Diffusing Update Algorithm

7 All OSPF networks must have which area?

Answer: Area 0

8 What are the advantages of a hierarchical routing protocol?

Answer: Reduced frequency of SPF calculations, smaller routing tables, and reduced link-state overhead

9 What type of routing protocol supports VLSMs?

Answer: Classless

10 What command do you use to stop all debugging?

Answer: undebug all or **no debug all**

Chapter 6

Section 1 Quiz

1 True or False: Access lists are used only for security purposes to deny traffic through a device.

Answer: False. Access lists identify traffic for security, quality of service, policy routing, dial-on-demand, and address translation.

2 Which of the following are valid types of access lists? (Choose all that apply.)

   a. Standard access lists

   b. Global access lists

   c. Extended access lists

   d. Named access lists

   e. Interface access lists

   f. Routing access lists

Answer: A, C, and D

3 Choose the valid number ranges for IP extended access lists. (Choose all that apply.)

   a. 1 to 99

   b. 199 to 2699

   c. 100 to 199

   d. 1300 to 1399

   e. 2000 to 2699

   f. 2000 to 2999

Answer: C and E

4 Which of the following are true statements? (Choose all that apply.)

   a. If a packet does not match any explicit condition in the list, an implicit **permit** allows the packet to be forwarded.

   b. After a packet matches an entry, it is acted upon by that statement and no other entries are checked.

   c. When an interface receives a packet, all entries in the access list are checked before any decision is made.

   d. A condition can test only against source and destination addresses.

   e. If no entry is matched, the packet is denied by an implicit **deny all**.

   f. All access lists acting as packet filters should have at least one **permit** statement.

Answer: B, E, and F

5 Given the address 192.168.255.3 and the wildcard mask 0.0.0.252, which of the following addresses would be a match? (Choose all that apply.)

   a. 192.168.255.3

   b. **192.166.255.7**

   c. **192.168.255.19**

   d. **192.168.255.255**

   e. **192.168.252.51**

Answer: While a mask of 0.0.0.252 is not common, it illustrates the nature of a wildcard mask. For this address and mask combination, the matches would need 192.168.255 in the first three octets. In the last octet, the first six bits can be any value, but the last two bits must be 1s, so answers a, c, and d all meet these conditions.

Section 2 Quiz

1   Which command creates a standard access list? (Choose all that apply.)

   a. **access-list 101**

   b. **access-list 1 standard**

   c. **access-list 1**

   d. **access-list standard mylist**

   e. **standard-access-list 1**

   Answer: C and D

2   Which of the following commands would you use to allow traffic from the 192.168.255.0 subnet to be allowed in on interface Ethernet 0? (Choose all that apply.)

   a. **access-list 1 permit 192.168.255.0**

   b. **ip access-group 1 in**

   c. **access-group 101 permit 192.168.255.0 0.0.0.255**

   d. **interface Ethernet 0**

   e. **access-list standard OK-Traffic permit 192.168.255.0 0.0.0.255**

   Answer: D and E

3   Which of the following statements are true? (Choose all that apply.)

   a. Access lists can be applied only to an interface.

   b. An interface can only have one access list, per protocol, per direction.

   c. If you delete an access list, the mapping will be automatically deleted.

   d. All access lists have an implicit deny any at the bottom.

   e. Standard access lists should be placed close to the source.

   f. Extended access lists should be placed close to the source.

   g. Access list placement does not matter.

   Answer: B, C, and E

4   Which of the following commands would you use to check the mapping of an access list on Ethernet 0? (Choose all that apply.)

   a. **show interface Ethernet 0**

   b. **show ip interface Ethernet 0**

   c. **show access-lists**

    d. show running-config

    e. show security

    f. show ip interface brief

  Answer: B and D

5 True or False: You can delete an individual entry in a numbered access list by using the command **no access-list** *number*.

  Answer: False. When you delete an access list by number, it removes the entire list.

Section 3 Quiz

1 Network Address Translation offers which of the following benefits? (Choose all that apply.)

  a. Eliminates the need to re-address a network

  b. Eliminates the need to have IP addresses for non-IP networks

  c. Conserves address space by multiplexing ports and addresses during translations

  d. Can only be configured on 3600 series routers

  e. Provides network security by hiding the internal network addresses

  Answer: A, C, and E

2 Network translation can be done in which of the following ways? (Choose all that apply.)

  a. One-to-one static translations

  b. One-to-many dynamic translations

  c. Many-to-many dynamic translations

  d. Many-to-one port translations

  e. Many-to-one static translations

  Answer: A, C, and D

3 If you used a packet analyzer to capture a frame returning from the outside network to the sender, what would be the destination address in the IP frame?

  a. The sending router's MAC address

  b. The sending device's IP address

  c. The translated IP address from the router

  d. The receiving device's IP address

    e. The loopback interface's IP address

    f. The receiving device's MAC address

Answer: D

4 Which of the following commands would you use to set up a dynamic pool for NAT?

    a. **ip nat inside source static** *local-ip global-ip*

    b. **ip nat inside source list** *listnumber* **interface** *interface* **overload**

    c. **access-list standard pool permit 192.168.255.0 0.0.0.255**

    d. **ip nat inside source list** *listnumber* **pool** *poolname*

    e. **ip nat pool** *name start-ip end-ip*

Answer: E

5 Which command could you use to view the active NAT translations?

    a. **show ip nat translations**

    b. **show nat translations**

    c. **show active nat**

    d. **debug ip nat**

    e. **clear ip nat translation ***

    f. **show nat statistics**

Answer: A

Final Review Questions

1 Access lists applied as traffic filters help do what in a network?

Answer: Control network traffic

2 Name one other use for an access list.

Answer: Any one: dial-on-demand routing, queuing, route filters, network address translations, policy routing

3 In which direction can an access list be applied to an interface?

Answer: In or out

4 During the outbound filtering process, what must exist in the route table before the packet is checked against the filter?

Answer: A route to the destination

5 What is the number range for IP extended access lists?

Answer: 100 to 199 and 2600 to 2699

6 How many IP access lists can be applied to an interface in a given direction?

Answer: One access list, per protocol, per interface, per direction

7 Every access list acting as a packet filter must have at least one what?

Answer: One **permit** statement

8 What happens if a packet does not match any of the test conditions in an access list?

Answer: It is denied by the implicit **deny any** statement at the end of the access list.

9 In a wildcard mask, what value indicates to match a bit value?

Answer: 0

10 Instead of typing 0.0.0.0 255.255.255.255, what keyword can you use in an access list?

Answer: any

11 Which command verifies that a list was applied to an interface?

Answer: show ip interface

12 How do you remove an access list from an interface?

Answer: At the interface, type the command **no ip access-group** *access-list-number* {**in** ı **out**}.

13 Which command allows you to view the access lists?

Answer: show ip access-lists or **show access-lists**

14 All access lists end with what?

Answer: An implicit deny any statement

15 Which form of NAT provides the most effective form of translations?

Answer: PAT or Overload requires only one address and requires no pool configuration or mapping configuration.

16 Which command would you use to clear all dynamic NAT mappings?

Answer: clear ip nat translation *.

Chapter 7

Section 1 Quiz

1 Which of the following is not true about a service provider WAN?

    a. WANs connect geographically disperse locations.

    b. The WAN cloud belongs to the service provider.

    c. A WAN connection is a one-time, fixed-cost connection.

    d. WAN connection types vary depending on what the user needs.

Answer: C

2 Which two of these items could be considered CPE?

    a. The CSU/DSU

    b. Local circuit switch

    c. Router

    d. Telephone pole

Answer: A and C

3 True or False: A DB-60 connector allows a router to use only three different physical standards for connectivity to a provider internetwork?

Answer: False. The DB-60 connector allows for five different physical standards.

4 In a cell-switched internetwork, which of the following statements are true?

    a. Cell-switched internetworks use variable length cells.

    b. Cell-switched internetworks can use copper or fiber media.

    c. Cell-switched internetworks are only available in Europe.

 d. Cell-switched internetworks build virtual circuits between locations.

 e. Interfaces to cell-switched internetworks are not available on Cisco routers.

 Answer: B and D

5 When connecting to a provider internetwork, which device typically derives the clocking from the provider network?

 a. The router

 b. The SmartJack

 c. The PC

 d. The CSU/DSU

 e. An Atomic Clock

 Answer: The CSU/DSU

Section 2 Quiz

1 True or False: Cisco's HDLC uses the same Address and Control fields as the Standard HDLC?

 True: The only difference in the HDLC protocols is the addition of a Proprietary field that supports multiple protocol environments.

2 PPP can be configured on which of the following interface types?

 a. Asynchronous

 b. HSSI

 c. Synchronous

 d. ISND

 e. All of the above

 f. A and D only

 Answer: All of the above

3 Which component of PPP negotiates the link options?

 a. MP

 b. NCP

 c. LCP

 d. CDPCP

 Answer: LCP

4 True or False: Authentication is required for a PPP connection?

False: Authentication is an optional part of establishing a PPP connection.

5 If PPP authentication has been enabled for a connection between two routers, which router must be configured with the username password settings?

   a. The host router only

   b. The calling router only

   c. The host router for PAP

   d. The host router for CHAP

   e. Both routers

Answer: Both routers

Final Review Questions

1 What are three connection types that you can use to connect routers over a WAN?

Answer: Leased lines, circuit-switched, and packet-switched

2 What is the default Layer 2 encapsulation type of Cisco serial interfaces?

Answer: Cisco HDLC

3 Which encapsulation option discussed in this chapter would you select if you were connecting a Cisco router to a non-Cisco router?

Answer: PPP

4 How do you enable PPP encapsulation?

Answer: With the **encapsulation ppp** interface configuration command

5 What are the two PPP authentication options?

Answer: PAP and CHAP

6 Name one other PPP option.

Answer: Multilink, error correction, or compression

7 How do you set the password for CHAP and PAP?

Answer: Use the **username** *name* **password** *password* command.

   8 If both PAP and CHAP are configured, which method is tried first?

   Answer: The one that is listed first in the **ppp authentication** interface configuration command

   9 Which authentication option sends the password in clear text?

   Answer: PAP

   10 Which command is used to check the encapsulation?

   Answer: show interface

Chapter 8

Section 1 Quiz

   1 Frame Relay is standardized by what standards organization(s)? (Choose all that apply.)

   a. ANSI

   b. EIA/TIA

   c. IETF

   d. IEEE

   e. ITU-T

   f. Frame Relay Forum

   Answer: A, E, and F

   2 Frame Relay encapsulates which of the following layers of the OSI model? (Choose the best answers.)

   a. Layer 7

   b. Layer 6

   c. Layer 5

   d. Layer 4

   e. Layer 3

   f. Layer 2

   g. Layer 1

   h. All of the above

   Answer: A, b, C, D and E

3 Which of the following are NOT fields in the Frame Relay frame? (Choose all that apply.)

    a. BECN

    b. FECN

    c. CIR

    d. DLCI

    e. PVC

    f. DE

Answer: C and E

4 How many VCs would be required for a fully meshed Frame Relay network consisting of 12 routers?

    a. 12

    b. 6

    c. 24

    d. 66

    e. 120

Answer: 66

5 If you connect a router to a Frame Relay network and the device on the other side of the PVC is powered down, what would you expect the state of the PVC to be?

    a. Active

    b. Down

    c. Unavailable

    d. Inactive

    e. Deleted

Answer: Deleted

Section 2 Quiz

1 Assuming you are connecting two Cisco routers running IOS version 12.2 to a major provider network, what commands are you required to enter to establish IP connectivity? Choose all that apply.)

    a. **encapsulation frame-relay**

    b. **frame-relay lmi-type {ansi ı cisco ı q933a}**

    c. **bandwidth** *value*

    d. **ip address** *address netmask*

    e. **frame-relay map** *protocol protocol-address dlci* **[broadcast] [ietf ı cisco] [pay-load-compress packet-by-packet]**

    f. **frame-relay inverse-arp** *[protocol] [dlci]*

    g. **no shutdown**

    Answer: A, D, and G

2 If you are connecting across a Frame Relay network to a non-Cisco device, which of the following options must be configured?

    a. LMI type of ANSI

    b. LMI type of q933a

    c. Encapsulation of IETF

    d. Inverse ARP for IP

    e. Packet-by-packet payload compression

    Answer: C

3 Say you have entered the following line on a Frame Relay interface on a Cisco router:

```
frame-relay map ip 10.18.0.1 120
```

Which of the following statements are true? (Choose all that apply.)

    a. The far side device's IP address is 10.18.0.1.

    b. The far side DLCI is 120.

    c. The local DLCI is 120.

    d. OSPF updates will be sent across this link.

    e. Static routes may be required to reach the far-side networks.

    Answer: A, C, and E

4 When configuring a point-to-point Frame Relay interface for IP, which of the following commands is required on the subinterface? (Choose all that apply.)

   a. **encapsulation frame-relay**

   b. **ip address** *address mask*

   c. **bandwidth 64**

   d. **frame-relay interface-dlci** *dlci-number*

   e. **frame-relay map** *protocol protocol-address dlci* **[broadcast] [ietf ı cisco] [pay-load-compress packet-by-packet]**

   Answer: B and D

5 Which command can you use to determine the LMI type of an interface running Frame Relay? (Choose all that apply.)

   a. **show interface**

   b. **show frame-relay pvc**

   c. **show frame-relay map**

   d. **show frame-relay lmi**

   e. **debug frame-relay lmi**

   Answer: A, and DG

Final Review Questions

1 Frame Relay operates at which OSI layer?

   Answer: Layer 2

2 Name at least one physical layer standard that can be used for Frame Relay connection.

   Answer: Any of the following: EIA/TIA-232, EIA/TIA-449, V.35, X.21, EIA/TIA-530

3 Which component identifies the local logical connection between the router and the switch?

   Answer: DLCI (Data-Link Connection Identifier)

4 Which method used by Frame Relay allows for the dynamic mapping of IP address to DLCI number?

   Answer: Inverse ARP

5 Name the three LMI standards that Cisco routers support.

Answer: cisco, ansi (Annex D), and q933a (Annex A)

6 By default, how often do routers exchange LMI information with the switch?

Answer: Every 10 seconds

7 What is the default encapsulation type for Frame Relay on a Cisco router?

Answer: cisco

8 Which command is used to verify the LMI type?

Answer: show interface or show frame-relay lmi

9 What routing issue occurs with a Frame Relay network running multiple PVCs over a single interface?

Answer: Split horizon

10 What is the default subinterface type, point-to-point or multipoint?

Answer: There is no default. You must select a type when creating a subinterface.

Chapter 9

Section 1 Quiz

1 ISDN services provide which of the following? (Choose all that apply.)

a. Digital network connectivity for voice, video, and data traffic

b. Only a single channel for user traffic

c. A single channel for call setup and tear down

d. Voice-only services

e. Dial service for connections

f. Faster call setup and tear down than an asynchronous modem connection

Answer: A, C, E, and F

2 An ISDN BRI uses which reference point to connect to a service provider network where the NT1 has already been provided?

    a. U

    b. NT-2

    c. TE-1

    d. S/T

    e. R

    f. TA

Answer: D

3 An ISDN with a BRI 0 interface is what type of ISDN equipment?

    a. T1

    b. TE2

    c. TA

    d. NT1

    e. TE1

Answer: E

4 Which ISDN PRI switch types are common in the United Kingdom? (Choose all that apply.)

    a. 5ESS

    b. VN2

    c. Net3

    d. NTT

    e. Net5

    f. DMS-100

Answer: E

5 Select the required configuration steps to set up a PRI interface on a router.

    a. Configure the T1 or E1 framing.

    b. Specify the encapsulation on the controller.

    c. Set an IP address on the controller.

    d. Specify the linecode on the controller.

   e. Set the ISDN switching type on the router or interface.

   f. Specify the timeslots used by the PRI group.

   g. Disable CDP on the interface.

   Answer: A, D, E and F

Section 2 Quiz

1 DDR routing is commonly useful for which of the following cases? (Choose all that apply.)

   a. Home users checking e-mail periodically

   b. Satellite offices that need to transmit large amounts of data all day long

   c. Periodic updates or reports to a remote site

   d. Contacting a site at the end of the day to get sales information

   e. Backup link in the event of a primary link failure

   f. Continuous connection between sites

   Answer: A, C, D, and E

2 Which of the following is the first step in initiating a DDR connection?

   a. Dialer information is looked up.

   b. Traffic is transmitted.

   c. Interesting traffic is identified.

   d. Route across the dial link is determined.

   e. The call is terminated.

   Answer: D

3 After a DDR connection has been established, which of the following statements are true?

   a. Only interesting traffic can be transmitted across the link.

   b. Any traffic can be transmitted across the link.

   c. All traffic that has been configured can cross that link.

   d. The link will go down only after all transmissions have ended.

   e. The link will go down after no interesting traffic has been transmitted for a timeout period.

   Answer: C and E

4 Dialer profiles are associated with which of the following to use a physical interface?

   a. Dialer pool

   b. Route

   c. Dialer map

   d. Class map

   e. Subnet

Answer: Dialer pool

5 Which command should you use to check the call setup for an incoming ISDN call?

   a. show interface

   b. debug ISDN dialer

   c. debug ISDN q931

   d. debug dialer

   e. debug all

Answer: C

Final Review Questions

1 What does ISDN stand for?

Answer: Integrated Services Digital Network

2 ISDN carries what type of user-traffic feeds?

Answer: Video, telex, data, and voice

3 The ISDN Q series protocol standards cover what issues?

Answer: Signaling and switching

4 The ISDN BRI consists of what services?

Answer: Two Bearer channels plus one Delta channel

5 TE2 refers to what type of ISDN equipment?

Answer: Terminal Endpoint 2 (TE2) designates a router as a device requiring a terminal adapter for its BRI signals. This is a non-native ISDN device, such as a router, with a synchronous or asynchronous serial connection.

6 A U interface references what connection?

Answer: The connection between the NT1 and the ISDN network

7 In a location where the provider furnishes the NT1, what type of native ISDN reference point should be on the router?

Answer: An S/T BRI interface

8 Where do you obtain SPID numbers?

Answer: From the service provider

9 What three steps are required to configure DDR?

Answer: Define static routes, specify interesting traffic, and configure dialer information.

10 Which command specifies interesting traffic?

Answer: dialer-list *group-number* **protocol** *protocol-name*

11 How is the correct command from question 10 linked to a dialer interface?

Answer: With the command **dialer-group** *group-number* on the interface

12 Which command could you use to display an ISDN interface's current status?

Answer: show isdn status

Case Study Review

Chapter 2

Ann E. Won has been hired by International Widgets, Ltd. to help upgrade and maintain the company's network. International Widgets, Ltd. has multiple offices in various locations, and each office is currently using shared networks (hubs) operating at 10 Mbps to connect to all the PCs and servers in the organization. Because of the number of users on each segment, the company is experiencing delay and sluggishness in the network.

The corporate location has 90 users on 2 floors, and 2 wiring closets on each floor, each with a 24-port hub. These 4 closet hubs connect to a hub in the computer room that connects to 4 servers and a router, which is used to connect to branch offices and the Internet. Figure 2-25 shows the layout of the current network.

Figure 2-25   *International Widgets, Ltd. Network Diagram*

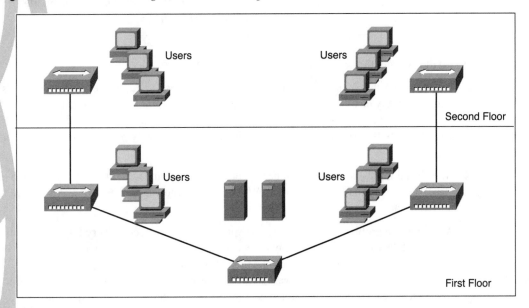

Ann's first task is to devise a plan for installing switches in the network to replace the hubs. The PCs will remain at 10 Mbps. Ann must first answer the following questions:

1 How should the links between the switches be configured to insure maximum throughput?

Answer: Ann should replace the five hubs with switches. In this case, assume 2950-24s in each location. The four switches on the floors will act as access switches for the users, and the switch in the computer room will act as a distribution/core switch. Because all the users can now access the switch at the same time, the links between the access switches and the distribution/core switch need to be at a higher throughput than the ports connected to the PCs. At this point in the network's design, it has been decided that the PCs will remain at 10 Mbps, so the links between the switches should be configured as 100 Mbps full duplex; because all the switches are of the same type, autonegotiate might work, but if Ann wants to be sure, she can set the speed and duplex for each port connected between the switches.

2 Are any special cables needed to interconnect the switches?

Answer: Because the switches use the same pins for sending and receiving, Ann will probably want to use a crossover cable to interconnect the switches.

NOTE For some Cisco switches, if the duplex and speed are in auto mode, the switch can determine the cable type needed to communicate with the other side of the link. This is not supported across all platforms, so using a crossover cable insures consistency.

3 Do the NICs in the servers need to be upgraded and, if so, why?

Answer: Ann should upgrade all the servers to 100 Mbps full duplex because the 90 users will most likely be trying to access the server most of the time. If all 90 users were to send 10 Mbps of data, the result would be 900 Mbps of throughput required. If the switch is configured as 100 Mbps full duplex, it will be more adequately prepared to handle these requests.

4 After installing the switches, Ann has encountered problems with PCs not getting their DHCP address when they are booted. What could be causing this problem, and how can it be corrected?

Answer: The problem is most likely the Spanning Tree Protocol. Every Layer 2 switch port runs STP to prevent loops. Any time a port is initialized (such as when a computer is powered on or rebooted), the port must run the STP algorithm. This means that for a period of two times (2x) the forward delay (15-second default), the port will not be able to pass a DHCP request. The device is probably timing out before the request is ever transmitted. If Ann enables spanning-tree portfast on the user ports, she will most likely eliminate the problem.

5 One application server that is connected to the network rarely sends out frames; because of this, when devices send data to the device, the switches flood the traffic everywhere in the network. How can Ann configure the switch so that this flooding will not occur?

Answer: Because the application server is not regularly sending frames that contain its source address, the switch's entry for this address times out. The switches then have to flood traffic destined for this address the next time a station tries to get to that server because the MAC address is not in their forwarding tables. Ann can correct this problem by configuring a static MAC address table entry pointing to the destination device.

6 There have been some problems with people plugging into the network using the conference room port. Only the training laptops are supposed to be able to access the port. What option can Ann configure to prevent anyone from using this port?

Answer: To prevent this unauthorized use, Ann can enable port security on the port connected to the conference room and enter the MAC addresses of the laptops allowed to use the port, which will prevent any other devices from using the port.

Chapter 3

Now that Ann has used switches to segment the network using switches, the network performance has noticeably improved. However, some of the servers are having some CPU utilization issues. After some research by the vendor who installed the servers, it has been determined that the problem is the amount of broadcast traffic. It seems that one of the servers runs an application that uses broadcasts to locate and poll all of its clients on the network. These broadcasts are affecting both servers and clients throughout the network, but it is more noticeable on the servers. Because of this, Ann has decided to implement VLANs. Based on the following requirements, what steps should Ann take in creating her VLANs? Figure 3-16 shows the layout of the switched network and location of the servers.

Figure 3-16 *International Widgets Ltd. Switched Network Diagram*

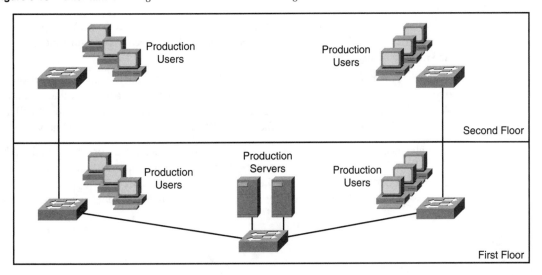

Ann has five servers. One server for production uses an all network broadcast to communicate with its clients. Those clients are located on both floors of the building, as shown in Figure 3-16. Of the other four servers, all use TCP/IP to communicate with various departments all over the company. It has been decided that for clients not using the production server, PCs and servers will be placed in a VLAN base at the location:

1   How many VLANs will Ann need and where will they need to be located in relation to the switches?

   Answer: Ann will need six total VLANs: one VLAN for the production devices and then a separate VLAN for each of the four switches connected to the other end devices and a VLAN for the servers connected to the core switch.

2   Do any of the switches have multiple VLANs on them? If so, what will Ann need to configure to ensure that multiple VLANs can pass between the switches?

   Answer: Yes, all of the switches have at least two VLANs, so Ann will need to make sure that the links between the switches are configured as trunk links.

3   In the future, Ann might need to create VLANs that will need to be used on some or all of the switches. To ensure that all VLANs exist on all trunked switches, what should Ann do?

   Answer: Ann is not required to do anything to create these VLANs in the future; however, if she is going to be trunking VLANs between switches, she must make sure that a given VLAN is created on all the switches in the trunk path. Because this could easily be overlooked, Ann might want to consider setting up a VTP domain name on one of the switches and then creating all the VLANs from that switch. The VLANs will be propagated out the trunk links to the other switches in the network, and any future VLANs will also be propagated.

Chapter 5

1   Now that Ann has subdivided the networks using VLANs, she needs to enable packets to be routed between the five TCP/IP VLANs. What will Ann need to configure and how will she need to configure this?

   Answer: Ann needs to configure InterVLAN routing on the 3640 connected via Fa0/0 to the 2950 switch. To do this, she needs to use dot1q encapsulation and verify that the native VLAN is identified during the process. At this point, a dynamic routing protocol will not be needed because all the subinterfaces on Fa0/0 will be directly connected networks.

2   Ann also needs to plan the networks needed for communication across the routed WAN links. For each VLAN that supports users, Ann will have an IP address range that supports 255 device addresses. For the WAN links, the address space needs to support only 2 addresses, and for the remote offices, the address space needs to support between 50 and

100 users. Ann needs to choose a routing protocol that will work across multiple vendor platforms and support summarization between the sites. What is Ann's best choice and why?

Answer: OSPF is the best choice. OSPF supports VLSMs and route summarization. It is also the best choice for Ann because she will be required to communicate with other routers that will not run EIGRP.

Chapter 6

International Widgets Inc. has become concerned about security between the VLANs and wants to insure that traffic can be passed only between the subnets for the four user VLANs and the two server VLANs:

1 What should Ann do to insure the security for these VLANS? Create a sample configuration using the addressing specified in the internetwork in Chapter 5.

   Answer: Ann should create an access control list that allows traffic between a given subnet for a VLAN and the two router subnets. These lists should then be applied inbound to the subinterfaces for each VLAN.

   Example list:

   ```
   access-list 101 permit 192.168.1.0 0.0.0.255 192.168.5.0 0.0.0.255
   access-list 101 permit 192.168.1.0 0.0.0.255 192.168.6.0 0.0.0.255
   interafce Fa0/1.1
   ip access-group 101 in
   ```

2 Ann is also responsible for connecting the network to the Internet using Serial interface 3/3 on the corporate 3640. The ISP has given Ann the address 171.69.68.13 with a 30-bit mask for the corporate router to attach to the Internet. What does Ann need to configure to allow users in the entire network to use the Internet?

   Answer: Ann needs to configure NAT overload using the Serial 3/3 interface as the outside interface, and using all the VLAN subinterfaces and serial interfaces as the inside interfaces. She also needs to create an access list to permit (or match) all traffic that begins with 192.168.0.0. Finally, Ann needs to create a static default route on the core router pointing to the Serial 3/3 interface and advertise that route to all the other routers in the network.

Chapter 7

Using what you have learned in this chapter, it is time to return to our case study company and help our Internetwork Administrator, Ann E. Won. Today, Ann has been tasked with connecting the corporate facility to two remote locations using a point-to-point, leased-line, serial connection to each location. Ann will be connecting Serial 3/0, 3/1, and 3/2 on the company's 3640 router to each location, respectively. Figure 7-13 shows a diagram of these connections.

Figure 7-13 *WAN Case Study Internetwork Diagram*

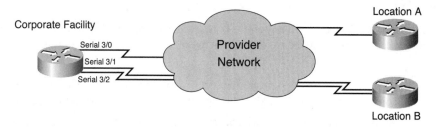

Remote location A will be using a non-Cisco router for connectivity back to the corporate facility across a T1 link. Remote location B will be using a Cisco router but will be connecting via two 56-Kbps circuits. The major concern with this connection is that it should be configured to provide maximum throughput between the locations.

Ann's first task is to choose the correct cable type to connect to the DCE. The telco has provisioned the circuits and is managing the DCE equipment but has not specified to the IT staff at International Widgets Ltd. What type of cable is needed to connect to the CSU/DSU? On closer examination of the CSU/DSU, Ann sees the following types of connectors shown in Figure 7-14.

Figure 7-14 *CSU/DSU Connectors*

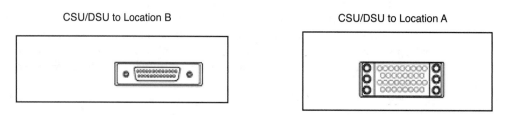

Based on the preceding information, answer the following questions about what Ann should do:

1 What cables does Ann need to connect to the router?

Answer: The CSU/DSU connection for the T-1 link is a V.35 cable, and the two connections for the 56-kbps links are EIA/TIA-232 cables.

2 What Layer 2 encapsulation methods should she use for the connection to location A and why?

Answer: The router on the other side of the serial point-to-point link is not a Cisco router, so it will probably not support the Cisco HDLC encapsulation protocol. Ann should choose PPP as the encapsulation method to accommodate the non-Cisco device.

3 What encapsulation method should be used to connect to location B and why?

Answer: While the router at location B is a Cisco router, the Cisco HDLC encapsulation method does not provide any options that will help deal with the bandwidth issues that Ann is confronted with. Again, Ann should choose PPP as the encapsulation method so that options can be enabled to help with the bandwidth problems.

4 What LCP options should be configured for location B?

Answer: There are two configuration options that could help deal with the bandwidth issues. The first option would be compression. The second option would be to use Multilink PPP across the parallel links to balance the load across both connections.

5 Is there an immediate need for authentication between these sites? Why or why not?

Answer: Most likely not. A leased line is a dedicated circuit between two points. It is highly unlikely that anyone could plug a device into this line on either side without direct access to each location. If this had been a dialup connection that could have originated anywhere, authentication would have made more sense.

Chapter 8

Using what you have learned in this chapter, it is time to return to the case study company and help the network administrator, Ann E. Won. Ann must now upgrade the connections from the corporate facility to remote location B to a Frame Relay circuit and add a new connection to remote location C. Previously, remote facility B connected back to the corporate location using Serial 3/1 and 3/2 on the company's 3640 with two 56-kbps circuits. Serial 3/1 will now be used to connect to the Frame Relay network, and Serial 3/2 will be disabled. At the corporate facility, Ann needs to provision a circuit capable of sending traffic to four sites at a maximum rate of 256 kbps each. Also, the two remote sites need to be able to send traffic back to the host site with a maximum rate of 256 kbps, but they expect only about 128 kbps on average. No site will need to communicate directly with any other site, so a Star topology is acceptable. Figure 8-18 shows a diagram of the proposed solution.

Figure 8-18 *Frame Relay Case Study Network Diagram*

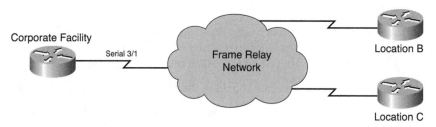

Remote location B needs to upgrade its local loop connection back to the service provider to support a fractional T1 connection of 256 kbps. The router at location B is running IOS Release 11.0. Remote location C is a recent acquisition and the remote router is not a Cisco device. Ann must plan for connectivity to remote location A in the future. The existing networking staff will set up the remote router at location C. Ann should work with them to establish connectivity.

Based on the preceding information, answer the following questions about what Ann should do:

1 Does Ann need to be concerned about the cables and CSU/DSU connecting to the service provider network?

Answer: The CSU/DSU connection for Serial 3/1 to the 56K link and on the remote side are EIA/TIA-232 cable, as is the CSU/DSU. The maximum support BW of an EIA/TIA-232 cable is 115.2 K; therefore, Ann needs to upgrade the CSU/DSU and change the cables out (most likely to V.35 depending on the new CSU/DSU).

2 What speed circuit does Ann need at the corporate and remote sites?

Answer: Ann needs a T-1 link at the corporate site to handle 1MB of traffic from the four potential remote sites. Ann probably also needs a CIR of T1 speed to guarantee the bandwidth if all sites are operating at full 256 kbps. At the remote sites, the local loop could be anything from a fractional T1 operating at 256 kbps up to T1 speeds, but the CIR would most likely be 128 kbps.

3 What type of interfaces will Ann want to configure on the routers at the corporate site and remote location B?

Answer: The corporate router needs to be configured with a point-to-point subinterface for each remote location. As for location B, Frame Relay could be configured on the primary interface, but it would probably be better to configure a point-to-point subinterface in the event that Ann needs to add more PVCs to that interface at a later date.

4 Do you see any potential problems with the remote connections. If so, what should be done to eliminate these issues?

Answer: Yes. If the device at location C is not a Cisco router, it will not support a Cisco Frame Relay frame. This means that the Serial 3/1 major interface needs to be configured for IETF encapsulation. Because this is a primary interface command, it affects all the subinterfaces, which means that the router at location B must also be configured to use IETF encapsulation, as must all future routers. Also, if the router at location C does not support inverse arp, a Mapping statement will be required for each protocol going from the central router to remote location B.

5 What information does Ann need from the service provider?

Answer: Ann needs two pieces of information from the service provider. First is the DLCI numbers at each location. Because a subinterface cannot use LMI to derive the DLCI, the number must be configured as part of the subinterface configuration. Also, for remote device B, Ann needs to know the LMI type. Routers using versions 11.2 or earlier cannot autodetect the LMI type. If the service provider will not tell her the type or says that it doesn't matter, Ann must choose a type and verify that the link is in an UP and UP status for more that 60 seconds. If not, she should change the LMI type until this occurs.

Chapter 9

Using what you have learned in this chapter, it is time to return to the case study company. This week, Ann has been asked to help set up a new connection to two new vendors. Vendor A and Vendor B have provided an application that will periodically send updates about production to a server in their facility. Ann needs to set up the BRI 0/1 interface on the 3640 router to dial each vendor when the appropriate traffic is being sent by the user application. Figure 9-14 shows a diagram of the connectivity between the organization and the vendors.

Figure 9-14 *ISDN Case Study*

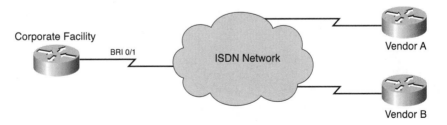

Based on the preceding information, answer the following questions about what Ann should do:

1 What information does Ann need from each vendor to set up this configuration?

Answer: Initially, Ann needs to know what the remote network address is that traffic will be sent to, and she needs to enter a static route in the router for that network. Ann needs to know what network addressing will be used between the links. Ann also needs to know what number to dial to access the remote devices.

2 What information does Ann need from the service provider to set up this configuration?

Answer: Ann needs to know the switch type. Depending on the switch type, she also needs to know the Service Provider IDs (SPIDs) for the link.

3 Which Dial solution should Ann use to provide DDR connectivity?

Answer: Because there is only one BRI interface connected to the ISDN network, but two separate locations will be called, Ann needs to use dialer profiles for connectivity to the vendor sites.

4 What measures can Ann take to insure that the BRI connects only to the vendors and that no unauthorized users call the interface?

Answer: Ann should probably consider setting the link up for PPP authentication using CHAP. To do this, Ann needs to talk to both vendors and insure that CHAP is set up on the remote side. This would also mean that Ann needs to know the remote router's name and passwords for CHAP purposes.

5 Is there any way for Ann to specify what time of day or day of the week a call can be generated to each vendor?

Answer: Yes. Because the dialer keys off of interesting traffic, it would be possible to build a timed access control list to specify a time along with the traffic type to be permitted. Using the timed ACL, the call could be initiated only on certain days and certain times of the day.

GLOSSARY

A

algorithm   A well-defined rule or process for arriving at a solution to a problem. In networking, algorithms commonly are used to determine the best route for traffic from a particular source to a particular destination.

ANSI   American National Standards Institute. A voluntary organization composed of corporate, government, and other members that coordinates standards-related activities, approves U.S. standards, and develops positions for the United States in international standards organizations. ANSI helps develop international and U.S. standards relating to, among other things, communications and networking. ANSI is a member of the IEC and the ISO.

ARP   Address Resolution Protocol. An Internet protocol used to map an IP address to a MAC address. Defined in RFC 826.

ARPA   Advanced Research Projects Agency. Research and development organization that is part of the U.S. Department of Defense (DoD). ARPA is responsible for numerous technological advances in communications and networking. ARPA evolved into DARPA and then back into ARPA again (in 1994).

ASIC   application-specific integrated circuit. An integrated circuit that has been programmed to perform a specific application at a high rate of speed. These circuits are used heavily in Layer 2 and Layer 3 switches.

asynchronous transmission   A term describing digital signals that are transmitted without precise clocking. Such signals generally have different frequencies and phase relationships. Asynchronous transmissions usually encapsulate individual characters in control bits (called start and stop bits) that designate the beginning and the end of each character.

ATM   Asynchronous Transfer Mode. The international standard for cell relay in which multiple service types (such as voice, video, or data) are conveyed in fixed-length (53-byte) cells. Fixed-length cells allow cell processing to occur in hardware, thereby reducing transit delays. ATM is designed to take advantage of high-speed transmission media, such as E3, SONET, and T3.

AUI attachment unit interface. IEEE 802.3 interface between a media access unit (MAU) and a network interface card (NIC). The term AUI also can refer to the rear panel port to which an AUI cable might attach. Also called *transceiver cable* .

authentication In security, the verification of the identity of a person or a process.

autonomous system A collection of networks under a common administration sharing a common routing strategy. Autonomous systems are subdivided by areas. An autonomous system must be assigned a unique 16-bit number by the IANA. Sometimes abbreviated as *AS*.

B

Bellman-Ford-Moore algorithm The algorithm used by the Routing Information Protocol (RIP) to calculate the best routing.

BIA burned-in MAC address. An identifier hardcoded into a network device by the manufacturer.

binary A numbering system characterized by ones and zeros (1 = on, 0 = off).

BPDU bridge protocol data unit. A Spanning Tree Protocol hello packet that is sent out at configurable intervals to exchange information among bridges in the network.

bridge A device that connects and passes packets between two network segments that use the same communications protocol. Bridges operate at the data link layer (Layer 2) of the OSI reference model. In general, a bridge filters, forwards, or floods an incoming frame based on the MAC address of that frame.

broadcast A data packet that is sent to all nodes on a network. Broadcasts are identified by a broadcast address.

broadcast domain A set of all devices that receive broadcast frames originating from any device within the set. Broadcast domains typically are bounded by routers because routers do not forward broadcast frames.

buffer A storage area used for handling data in transit. Buffers are used in internetworking to compensate for differences in processing speed between network devices. Bursts of data can be stored in buffers until they can be handled by slower processing devices. Also called a *packet buffer* .

C

canonical   Addresses that are sent on the wire with the least significant bit first. Ethernet addresses are canonical. For each byte of the Ethernet address, the last bit of the byte is sent first.

CCITT   Consultative Committee for International Telegraph and Telephone. An international organization responsible for the development of communications standards. Now called the ITU-T.

CDP   Cisco Discovery Protocol. A media- and protocol-independent device-discovery protocol that runs on all Cisco-manufactured equipment, including routers, access servers, bridges, and switches. Using Cisco Discovery Protocol, a device can advertise its existence to other devices and receive information about other devices on the same LAN or on the remote side of a WAN. Runs on all media that support SNA systems, including LANs, Frame Relay, and ATM media.

cell   The basic data unit for ATM switching and multiplexing. Cells contain identifiers that specify the data stream to which they belong. Each cell consists of a 5-byte header and 48 bytes of payload.

Cisco IOS Software   Cisco operating system software that provides common functionality, scalability, and security for all Cisco products. Cisco IOS Software allows centralized, integrated, and automated installation and management of internetworks while ensuring support for a wide variety of protocols, media, services, and platforms.

coaxial cable   A cable consisting of a hollow outer cylindrical conductor that surrounds a single inner wire conductor. Two types of coaxial cable currently are used in LANs: 50-ohm cable, which is used for digital signaling, and 75-ohm cable, which is used for analog signaling and high-speed digital signaling.

collision domain   In Ethernet, the network area within which frames that have collided are propagated. Repeaters and hubs propagate collisions; LAN switches, bridges, and routers do not.

compression   The running of a data set through an algorithm that reduces the space required to store or the bandwidth required to transmit the data set.

convergence   The speed and capability of a group of internetworking devices running a specific routing protocol to agree on the topology of an internetwork after a change in that topology.

CoS   class of service. An indication of how an upper-layer protocol requires a lower-layer protocol to treat its messages. In Systems Network Architecture (SNA) subarea routing, CoS definitions are used by subarea nodes to determine the optimal route to establish a given session. A CoS definition comprises a virtual route number and a transmission priority field. Also called *ToS*.

CRC   cyclic redundancy check. An error-checking technique in which the frame recipient calculates a remainder by dividing frame contents by a prime binary divisor and compares the calculated remainder to a value stored in the frame by the sending node.

D

daemon   A program that is not invoked explicitly but lies dormant waiting for some condition(s) to occur.

DDR   dial-on-demand routing. Technique whereby a router can automatically initiate and close a circuit-switched session as transmitting stations demand. The router spoofs keepalives so that end stations treat the session as active. DDR permits routing over ISDN or telephone lines using an external ISDN terminal adaptor or modem.

debug   An application used by Cisco IOS devices that displays output for operations being performed by the device. The debug application is extremely processor-intensive and can disrupt network service if not used carefully.

DECnet   A group of communications products (including a protocol suite) developed and supported by Digital Equipment Corporation. DECnet/OSI (also called DECnet Phase V) is the most recent iteration and supports both OSI protocols and proprietary digital protocols. Phase IV Prime supports inherent MAC addresses that allow DECnet nodes to coexist with systems running other protocols that have MAC address restrictions.

delay   The time between the initiation of a transaction by a sender and the first response received by the sender. Also, the time required to move a packet from source to destination over a given path.

Dijkstra's algorithm   An algorithm developed by Dr. Edsger Dijkstra that is sometimes used to calculate routes given a link- and a nodal-state topology database. This algorithm is also known as the Shortest Path First (SPF) algorithm.

dot1Q   A Cisco abbreviation for the IEEE standard 802.1Q that specifies standards for bridged virtual LANs (VLANs).

E-F

EIA/TIA   Electronic Industries Alliance/ Telecommunications Industry Alliance. A group that specifies electrical transmission standards. The EIA and the TIA have developed numerous well-known communications standards, including EIA/TIA-232 and EIA/TIA-449.

encapsulation   The wrapping of data in a particular protocol header. For example, Ethernet data is wrapped in a specific Ethernet header before network transit. Also, when bridging dissimilar networks, the entire frame from one network is simply placed in the header used by the data link layer protocol of the other network.

encrypt   The process of applying a specific algorithm to data to alter the appearance of the data, making it incomprehensible to those who are not authorized to see the information.

Ethernet   A baseband LAN specification invented by Xerox Corporation and developed jointly by Xerox, Intel, and Digital Equipment Corporation. Ethernet networks use CSMA/CD and run over a variety of cable types at 10 Mbps. Ethernet is similar to the IEEE 802.3 series of standards.

FCS   frame check sequence. Extra characters added to a frame for error control purposes. Used in HDLC, Frame Relay, and other data link layer protocols.

FDDI   Fiber Distributed Data Interface. (LAN Access) A LAN standard, defined by ANSI X3T9.5, specifying a 100-Mbps token-passing network using fiber-optic cable, with transmission distances of up to 2 km. FDDI uses a dual-ring architecture to provide redundancy.

Flash   A special type of EEPROM that can be erased and reprogrammed in blocks instead of one byte at a time. Many modern PCs have their BIOS stored on a Flash memory chip so that it can be updated easily if necessary. Such a BIOS is sometimes called a *Flash BIOS*. Flash memory is also popular in modems because it enables the modem manufacturer to support new protocols as they become standardized.

flooding   A traffic-passing technique used by switches and bridges in which traffic received on an interface is sent out through all the interfaces of that device except the interface on which the information was received originally.

flush   A process used by switches to remove aged out entries from the MAC address table.

FRAD   Frame Relay access device. Any network device that provides a connection between a LAN and a Frame Relay WAN.

frame   A logical grouping of information sent as a data link layer unit over a transmission medium. Often refers to the header and the trailer, used for synchronization and error control, which surround the user data contained in the unit. The terms *cell*, *datagram*, *message*, *packet*, and *segment* also are used to describe logical information groupings at various layers of the OSI reference model and in various technology circles.

Frame Relay   An industry-standard, switched data link layer protocol that handles multiple virtual circuits using HDLC encapsulation between connected devices. Frame Relay is more efficient than X.25, the protocol for which it generally is considered a replacement.

G-I

global configuration mode   The main configuration mode for a Cisco IOS device that is used to configure parameters common to the device or to move to other configuration modes.

hexadecimal   A numbering system used in computers and networking that consists of 16 characters, 10 digits, and 5 letters. This numbering system is used in specifying Layer 2 Media Access Control addresses.

holddown   A state into which a route is placed so that routers neither advertise the route nor accept advertisements about the route for a specific length of time (the holddown period). Holddown is used to flush bad information about a route from all routers in the network. A route typically is placed in holddown when a link in that route fails.

IANA   Internet Assigned Numbers Authority. An organization operated under the auspices of the ISOC as a part of the IAB. The IANA delegates authority for IP address–space allocation and domain-name assignment to the InterNIC and other organizations. IANA also maintains a database of assigned protocol identifiers used in the TCP/IP stack, including autonomous system numbers.

IEEE   Institute of Electrical and Electronics Engineers. A professional organization that develops communications and network standards, among other activities.

infrastructures   The foundational building blocks of internetworking systems. Infrastructures include wiring and networking devices that are interconnected to form a computer internetwork.

interface configuration mode   A subconfiguration mode of Cisco IOS Software that is used to configure attributes of physical or virtual interfaces on a given device.

Internetwork   A collection of physical networks that are interconnected via internetworking devices such as routers and switches.

IPX   Internetwork Packet Exchange. A Novell NetWare network-layer (Layer 3) protocol used for transferring data from servers to workstations. IPX is similar to IP and XNS.

ISDN   Integrated Services Digital Network. A communication protocol offered by telephone companies that permits telephone networks to carry data, voice, and other source traffic.

ISL   Inter-Switch Link. A Cisco proprietary protocol that maintains VLAN information as traffic flows between switches and routers.

ITU-T   International Telecommunication Union Telecommunication Standardization Sector. An international body that develops worldwide standards for telecommunications technologies. The ITU-T carries out the functions of the former CCITT.

L

LAN   local-area network. A high-speed, low-error data network covering a relatively small geographic area (up to a few thousand meters). LANs connect workstations, peripherals, terminals, and other devices in a single building or in another geographically limited area. LAN standards specify cabling and signaling at the physical and data link layers of the OSI model. Ethernet, FDDI, and Token Ring are widely used LAN technologies.

latency   The delay between the time a device receives a frame and the time that frame is forwarded out the destination port.

Layer 2 switch   An internetworking device that uses specialized hardware to provide high-speed connectivity using Layer 2 Media Access Control (MAC) addressing for forwarding frames between segments.

Layer 3 switch   An internetworking device that uses specialized hardware to provide high-speed connectivity using Layer 3 network addressing for forwarding packets between networks.

Layer 4 switch   An internetworking device that uses specialized hardware to provide high-speed connectivity using Layer 4 protocol and port information along with either Layer 2 Media Access Control (MAC) or Layer 3 network addressing for forwarding frames between segments.

Linux A public domain version operating system that runs on RISC and Intel-based processors based on the UNIX operating system.

LLC Logical Link Control. The higher of the two data link layer sublayers defined by the IEEE. The LLC sublayer handles error control, flow control, framing, and MAC-sublayer addressing. The most prevalent LLC protocol is IEEE 802.2, which includes both connectionless and connection-oriented variants.

loop A route where packets never reach their destination but simply cycle repeatedly through a constant series of network nodes.

M

MAC Media Access Control. The lower of the two sublayers of the data link layer defined by the IEEE. The MAC sublayer handles access to shared media, such as whether token passing or contention will be used.

MAN metropolitan-area network. A network that spans a metropolitan area. Generally, a MAN spans a larger geographic area than a local-area network (LAN) but a smaller geographic area than a wide-area network (WAN).

mapping A process in networking that is used to link a Layer 2 address to a Layer 3 address.

MD5 Message Digest 5. A one-way hashing algorithm that produces a 128-bit hash. Both MD5 and Secure Hash Algorithm (SHA) are variations on MD4 and are designed to strengthen the security of the MD4 hashing algorithm. Cisco uses hashes for authentication within the IPSec framework. Also used for message authentication in Simple Network Management Protocol (SNMP) v.2. MD5 verifies the integrity of the communication, authenticates the origin, and checks for timeliness.

media Plural of medium. Various physical environments through which transmission signals pass. Common network media include twisted-pair, coaxial, and fiber-optic cable, and the atmosphere (through which microwave, laser, and infrared transmission occurs). Sometimes called *physical media* .

media contention In Ethernet or other shared media networks, this is what occurs when devices are forced to wait for other devices to finish transmitting before transmitting their own data. Media contention causes latency in shared media networks.

MTU maximum transmission unit. The maximum packet size, in bytes, that a particular interface can handle.

N

NBMA   nonbroadcast multiaccess. A term describing a multiaccess network that either does not support broadcasting (such as X.25) or in which broadcasting is not feasible (for example, a Switched Multimegabit Data Service [SMDS] broadcast group or an extended Ethernet that is too large).

neighbor (router)   In Open Shortest Path First (OSPF), two routers that have interfaces to a common network. On multiaccess networks, neighbors are discovered dynamically by the OSPF Hello protocol.

next hop   The next Layer 3-addressed interface for an internetwork path.

NIC   **1.** network interface card. A board that provides network communication capabilities to and from a computer system. Also called an *adapter*. **2.** Network Information Center. An organization whose functions have been assumed by the IANA.

noncanonical   Addresses that are sent on the wire with the most significant bit first. Token Ring addresses are noncanonical. For each byte of the Token Ring address, the first bit of the byte is sent first.

NVRAM   nonvolatile RAM. A type of random-access memory (RAM) that retains its contents when a unit is powered off.

O-P

octet   A term meaning 8 bits. In networking, the term *octet* often is used (rather than byte) because some machine architectures employ bytes that are not 8 bits long.

OSI   Open System Interconnection. An international standardization program created by ISO and ITU-T to develop data networking standards that facilitate multivendor equipment interoperability.

PDU   protocol data unit. An OSI term used to describe a unit of data from a particular layer of the OSI model.

POP   point of presence. In OSS, a physical location where an interexchange carrier has equipment installed to interconnect with a *local exchange carrier (LEC)*.

POTS   plain old telephone service. A general term referring to the variety of telephone networks and services in place worldwide. Sometimes called *Public Switched Telephone Network (PSTN)*.

privileged EXEC mode   A mode used to view the operational and configurational parameters for a Cisco IOS device. This mode is also used to access global configuration mode.

proprietary   Refers to information (or other property) that is owned by an individual or an organization and for which the use is restricted by that entity.

protocol   A formal description of a set of rules and conventions that govern how devices on a network exchange information.

PSTN   Public Switched Telephone Network. A general term referring to the variety of telephone networks and services in place worldwide. Sometimes called *POTS*.

PTT   Post, Telephone, and Telegraph. A government agency that provides telephone services. PTTs exist in most areas outside of North America and provide both local and long-distance telephone services.

public domain   Computer software that has been written to be shared for free with everyone. These programs and operating systems are free for anyone to use and altered but cannot be resold or copyrighted by anyone.

Q-R

QoS   quality of service. A measure of performance for a transmission system that reflects its transmission quality and service availability.

queue   **1.** An ordered list of elements waiting to be processed. **2.** A backlog of packets waiting to be forwarded over a router interface.

RADIUS   Remote Authentication Dial-In User Service. A database for authenticating modem and Integrated Services Digital Network (ISDN) connections and for tracking connection time.

RAM   random-access memory. A type of volatile memory that can be read and written by a microprocessor.

RFC   Request For Comments. A document series used as the primary means for communicating information about the Internet. Some RFCs are designated by the Internet Architecture Board (IAB) as Internet standards. Most RFCs document protocol specifications, such as Telnet and File Transfer Protocol (FTP), but some are humorous or historical. RFCs are available online from numerous sources.

ROM   read-only memory. A type of nonvolatile memory that can be read, but not written, by the microprocessor.

Rommon   Read Only Memory monitor. This is a command-line interface used to allow direct interaction with the processor involved in system startup.

router   A network layer device that uses one or more metrics to determine the optimal path along which network traffic should be forwarded. Routers forward packets from one network to another based on network layer information.

S

SAID   Security Association ID. A valued used in IEEE 802.10 FDDI frames for security purposes.

segment   **1.** A section of a network that is bounded by bridges, routers, or switches. **2.** In a LAN using a bus topology, a segment is a continuous electrical circuit that often is connected to other such segments with repeaters. **3.** A term used in the TCP specification to describe a single transport layer unit of information.

segmenting   In networking, this is the process of dividing large networks or groups of users into smaller more manageable groups.

service provider   A company or corporation the provides and sells internetwork services and connections between geographically dispersed locations.

signaling   **1.** A process of sending a transmission signal over a physical medium for the purposes of communication. **2.** The sending of call information across a telephone connection. This information can be transmitted by many techniques, such as opening and closing a loop to stop and start the flow of DC loop current (used to indicate on-hook and off-hook state and to transmit dial-pulsing of digits), sending of ringing voltage to alert the other side of an incoming call, sending digit information in the form of dual-tone multifrequency (DTMF) or multifrequency (MF) tones, or sending call state information on a digital service 0 (DS0) timeslot by using robbed bits.

SNAP   Subnetwork Access Protocol. An Internet protocol that operates between a network entity in the subnetwork and a network entity in the end system. SNAP specifies a standard method of encapsulating IP datagrams and Address Resolution Protocol (ARP) messages on IEEE networks. The SNAP entity in the end system makes use of the services of the subnetwork and performs three key functions: data transfer, connection management, and quality of service (QoS) selection.

SONET   Synchronous Optical Network. A standard format for transporting a wide range of digital telecommunications services over optical fiber. SONET is characterized by standard line rates, optical interfaces, and signal formats. SONET is a high-speed (up to 2.5 Gbps) synchronous network specification developed by Bellcore and designed to run on optical fiber. STS-1 is the basic building block of SONET. Approved as an international standard in 1988.

SPF   Shortest Path First is an algorithm developed by Dr. Edsger Dijkstra used by link-state protocols such as Open Shortest Path First (OSPF) and Intermediate System-to-Intermediate System (IS-IS) to determine the best route through a network system.

subnet   **1.** In IP networks, a network sharing a particular subnet address. Subnetworks are networks arbitrarily segmented by a network administrator in order to provide a multilevel, hierarchical routing structure while shielding the subnetwork from the addressing complexity of attached networks. Sometimes called a *subnet*. **2.** In Open System Interconnections (OSI) networks, a collection of end systems and intermediate systems under the control of a single administrative domain and using a single network access protocol.

supernet   An aggregation of IP network addresses advertised as a single classless network address. For example, given four Class C IP networks, 192.0.8.0, 192.0.9.0, 192.0.10.0, and 192.0.11.0, with each having the intrinsic network mask of 255.255.255.0, you can advertise the address 192.0.8.0 with a subnet mask of 255.255.252.0.

switch   **1.** A network device that filters, forwards, and floods frames based on the destination address of each frame. The switch operates at the data link layer of the Open System Interconnections (OSI) reference model. **2.** A general term applied to an electronic or mechanical device that allows a connection to be established as necessary and terminated when there is no longer a session to support. **3.** In telephony, a general term for any device, such as a private branch exchange (PBX), that connects individual phones to phone lines.

switch fabric   The internal connections between the ports of a switch used to transmit data between end devices connected to these ports.

synchronous transmission   A term describing digital signals that are transmitted with precise clocking. Such signals have the same frequency, with individual characters encapsulated in control bits (called start bits and stop bits) that designate the beginning and the end of each character.

T

TACACS   Terminal Access Controller Access Control System. An authentication protocol, developed by the Defense Data Network (DDN) community, which provides remote access authentication and related services, such as event logging. User passwords are administered in a central database rather than in individual routers, providing an easily scalable network security solution.

tag   Identification information, including a number plus other information.

TCP/IP   Transmission Control Protocol/Internet Protocol. A common name for the suite of protocols developed by the U.S. Department of Defense in the 1970s to support the construction of worldwide internetworks. TCP and IP are the two best-known protocols in the suite.

Telnet   The standard terminal emulation protocol in the TCP/IP protocol stack. Telnet is used for remote terminal connection, enabling users to log in to remote systems and use resources as if they were connected to a local system. Telnet is defined in RFC 854.

TFTP   Trivial File Transfer Protocol. A simplified version of File Transfer Protocol (FTP) that allows files to be transferred from one computer to another over a network, usually without the use of client authentication (for example, username and password).

Token Ring   A token-passing LAN developed and supported by IBM. Token Ring runs at 4 or 16 megabits per second (Mbps) over a ring topology.

topology   A physical arrangement of network nodes and media within an enterprise networking structure.

trunk   **1.** A physical and logical connection between two switches across which network traffic travels. A backbone is composed of a number of trunks. **2.** A phone line between two central offices (COs) or between a CO and a private branch exchange (PBX).

trunking   The Cisco term used to describe marking Layer 2 virtual LAN (VLAN) identifiers on Inter-Switch Link (ISL) or IEEE 802.1Q links between network devices.

tunneling   An architecture that is designed to provide the services necessary to implement any standard point-to-point encapsulation scheme.

U-Z

UNIX   An operating system developed in 1969 at Bell Laboratories. UNIX has gone through several iterations since its inception, which include UNIX 4.3 BSD (Berkeley Standard Distribution), developed at the University of California at Berkeley, and UNIX System V, Release 4.0, developed by AT&T.

WAN   wide-area network. A data communications network that serves users across a broad geographic area and often uses transmission devices provided by common carriers. Frame Relay, SMDS, and X.25 are examples of WANs.

x-modem   An asynchronous transfer protocol that can be used to recover lost operating systems for Cisco devices.

K-L

S

T

U

V

W

X